Lecture Notes in Computer Science

Lecture Notes in Computer Science

Edited by G. Goos and J. Hartmanis

135

R.L. Constable
S.D. Johnson
C.D. Eichenlaub

An Introduction
to the PL/CV2
Programming Logic

Springer-Verlag
Berlin Heidelberg New York 1982

Authors

R.L. Constable
S.D. Johnson
C.D. Eichenlaub
Cornell University, Dept. of Computer Science
405 Upson Hall, Ithaca, NY 14853, USA

ISBN 978-3-540-11492-5 Springer-Verlag Berlin Heidelberg New York
ISBN 978-0-387-11492-7 Springer-Verlag New York Heidelberg Berlin

2145/3140-543210

This book is based on the reference manual for the PL/CV Programming Logic and on lecture notes used to teach the logic to first year college students. The Programming Logic consists of a formal system for reasoning about integers, arrays, and programming language commands (in the PL/I dialect called PL/CS). The arguments can be checked by the PL/CV Proof Checker (available in PL/I and in C, see [-14-]). The programs can be executed by PL/CS compilers (see [-10-]), including the Cornell **Program** Synthesizer ([-19-]) and the Cornell Program Environment.

The notes are written from the point of view that computer programming is **formal algorithmic problem solving**. The subject is formal because problem solutions must be written so that a computer can execute them. In **some** cases this formality can be extended to the entire argument **which** led to the solution, and the computer can be used to verify the **argument**.

In cases when the entire argument can be formalized, there are obvious advantages to doing so. For one thing, one's confidence in the solution is appreciably increased. This observation has been the basis for research in the subject called **program verification** (see the discussion in [5,6]). Another advantage of formalization is pedagogical - one is able to see the complete structure of the argument and explain it to someone who is learning to reason algorithmically. This is the same advantage that rigorous argument offers to any subject, and is a justification for teaching formal logic in the college curriculum.

Various computer systems to check proofs have been employed in the teaching of formal logic ([-13,17-]). We feel that such systems can play an especially interesting role in computer science courses. In the first place, programming courses by necessity teach a great deal of formalism and logic. For example, the treatment of boolean expressions in modern programming languages is an introduction to the propositional calculus, and the definition of a program state and its effect on assertions in programs is the same as the concept of an **interpretation** in the predicate calculus.

In the second place, the concepts of program verification, especially the notions of asserted program, weakest pre-condition, loop invariant, procedure call rules, etc. have an increasing place in the computer science curriculum. A rigorous treatment of these concepts is close to a formal treatment in a very high level logic such as PL/CV. A formal treatment allows computer assistance in teaching the subject. In particular, the student can experiment with forms of argument in private and at his own pace.

In the third place, the Proof Checker, like the language translator, is an interesting piece of computer software. Exposing students to it will enhance their appreciation of the potential of computer automation.

For these reasons we feel it is appropriate to teach a programming logic in the computer science curriculum. These notes can be used for that purpose. They introduce a completely formal programming logic, PL/CV2. The logic and its Proof Checker were designed by R. L. Constable, S. D. Johnson, and M. J. O'Donnell. The logic has been reported in the book A Programming Logic [-6-] and in various articles [-5,7,14-], and the Proof Checker is described in [-7-] and in the book A Computer System for Checking Proofs [-14-]. The underlying programming language PL/CS is described in the textbook [-11-]. The system is a merging of the predicate calculus and the Floyd-Hoare style of reasoning about programs [-16-]. It was designed to be simple, conventional, high level and efficient so that it could be used in college courses, and so that it could be used to explore elementary program verification.

The odd-numbered chapters introduce topics informally at a very elementary level, and the even-numbered chapters provide a succinct and precise summary of the logic (which may be skipped on a first reading). Numerous examples are provided, and all of the complete proofs have been checked by the Proof Checker (PL/I version). The exposition in the odd-numbered sections is oriented toward the reader with almost no programming experience. A more advanced account of the logic appears in A Programming Logic.

Experience with the system

We have used PL/CV2 at Cornell to teach logic and basic program verification in a sophomore discrete mathematics course. Our experiences here have been very positive. We also used PL/CV2 to teach introductory programming. We found that students were overwhelmed by the amount of formalism to be grasped at first encounter. We surmise that the system could be successfully used in a second course on programming to help teach the basics of programming methodology.

The interactive synthesizer version improves useability of PL/CV by a factor of 2 or 3 over the batch oriented system. We have not yet used that system in a course however.

The PL/CV programming logic has been considerably extended to include a rich constructive theory of types. In this language, called PL/CV3 it appears possible to formalize the kind of non-elementary algorithmic problem solving exhibited in such textbooks as The Design and Analysis of Computer Algorithms by Aho, Hopcroft and Ullman. The language was designed to allow a feasible formalization of any argument solving a sequential algorithmic problem

The reader interested in the concept of a constructive formal logic as a programming tool should follow the work of the Cornell Automated Logic group. The project on Program Refinement Logics, PRL, is building a programming system which extracts executable code fom formal constructive proofs (see [-1-]).

ACKNOWLEDGEMENTS

We gratefully acknowledge the support of the National Science Foundation; the project started under MCS-76-14293 and continued under MCS-78-00953. Finally the grant SED-79-18966 allowed us to experiment with PL/CV in the classroom and provided the impetus for the expository chapters of the monongraph.

The PL/CV1 logic was designed with Michael J. O'Donnell whose active interest and keen insights have shaped the project at every stage. Our initial effort relied on the stability of the PL/C system and the support of its director, Richard Conway.

Our faculty colleagues at Cornell provided both constructive criticism and encouragement. In particular we thank Corky Cartwright, Alan Demers, Jim Donahue, and David Gries. Work on the interactive system, AVID, owes a great deal to Tim Teitelbaum and the Cornell Program Synthesizer Project.

Many former students were active participants in discussions of the logic and implementation. Carl Hauser was co-author of the first manual. Gary Levin and Barry Bakalor were especially helpful.

Special thanks are due the contributing authors, all of whom have also worked on the implementation, including Tat-hung Chan, Dean B. Krafft, Ryan Stansifer and Daniel Zlatin.

Michelle Fish prepared large parts of the manuscript using the UNIX text editing facilities. We are grateful for her very careful work.

Finally we thank our department and its chairman, Juris Hartmanis, who have provided such a stimulating and tolerant atmosphere for our work.

R. L. Constable
S. D. Johnson
C. D. Eichenlaub

Ithaca, N.Y.
August 1981

TABLE OF CONTENTS

X

I THE LANGUAGE

Values

The notion of a "value" is a basic to computer science. For the time
being, we will only be considering two kinds of values: integer values,
such as 3, 12, or -9, and boolean values. There are only two boolean
values: '1'B and '0'B. The PL/CV names for these types of values are
"FIXED" and "BIT" respectively.

You can not write down a value; the closest you can come is to write down a
"constant." (The difference between a value and a constant is precisely
the difference between a number and a numeral.) A FIXED constant is just a
string of digits, such as 17, 0, or 292. There are two BIT constants: '1'B
(pronounced "true") and '0'B (pronounced "false").

Expressions

An expression is an instruction for computing a value. The simplest
expressions are constants. But there are ways of forming more complex
expressions. For example, we can take two expressions and place a binary
(meaning "two-way") operator between them. Or, we can place a unary (meaning "one-way") operator in front of an expression to get a new expression.

Here is a list of PL/CV operators:

    binary operators: + - * / ** = < <= > >= & | => <=>
    unary operators: - ~

Every expression has a value. We know what the value of each constant is.
For example, the value of 17 is seventeen. The way to get the value of an
expression formed from one or two smaller expressions and an operator is to
get the value of each smaller expression(s) and combine the values as follows (where I, J, P and Q stand for the values of the smaller expressions):

	expression	value
Arithmetic	I+J	I plus J
Operators	I-J	I minus J
	I*J	I times J
	I/J	I divided by J and truncated toward zero
	I**J	I raised to the J'th power
Relational	I=J	'1'B iff I is equal to J
Operators	I<J	'1'B iff I is less than J
	I<=J	'1'B iff I is less than or equal to J
	I>J	'1'B iff I is greater than J
	I>=J	'1'B iff I is greater than or equal to J
Logical	P&Q	'1'B iff both P and Q are '1'B
Operators	P|Q	'1'B iff either P, Q, or both are '1'B
	P=>Q	'1'B iff P is '0'B or Q is '1'B
	P<=>Q	'1'B iff P and Q are both '1'B, or both '0'B
	~P	'1'B iff P is '0'B

The expression I+J*K could mean "add I to J, and multiply the result by K," or it could mean "add I to the product of J and K." Each of these meanings can be indicated explicitly by the use of parentheses: (I+J)*K and I+(J*K). In absence of parentheses, always apply the operator with the higher precedence first. In this case, * has a higher precedence than +, so that I+J*K means I+(J*K). Here is a list of the operators in order of their precedence, from highest to lowest. Operators on the same line have the same precedence.

- ~	unary operators
**	right associative
* /	left associative
+ -	left associative
= < <= > >=	cascading
& |	combining
=>	right associative
<=>	cascading

Notice that the - operator has two different precedences; one for its use as a binary operator, and one for its use as a unary operator. The expression -I**J means the same as (-I)**J, whereas 0-I**J means 0-(I**J).

When an expression contains binary operators with the same precedence, special rules are used to decide the order of evaluation. As indicated in the above chart, the operators * and / are "left associative". This means that the expression I*J/K, for example, is evaluated as (I*J)/K. On the other hand, the operator => is "right associative," so that P=>Q=>R is evaluated as P=>(Q=>R).

The operator | is an example of a "combining" operator. It is a property of | that (P|Q)|R always has the same value as P|(Q|R). Therefore, it doesn't matter which meaning we choose for P|Q|R. We just think of this expression as the "or" operator applied to three operands.

The operator < is an example of a "cascading" operator. It would not make sense to have I<J<K mean either (I<J) < K or I < (J<K); you can't compare a bit with an integer. Instead, I<J<K is taken to be an abbreviation for I<J & J<K. Any number of operators at the same precedence level can be cascaded. For example, H<=I<J=K means H<=I & I<J & J=K. Since <=> is at a different precedence level than <, these two operators cannot be cascaded together. The expression H<I<=>J<K means (H<I) <=> (J<K).

Functions
Another way of building complex expressions from simpler ones is with functions. The following functions are available in PL/CV:

function	value
MIN(I, J)	I or J, whichever is smaller
MAX(I, J)	I or J, whichever is larger
ABS(I)	I or -I, whichever is positive
SIGN(I)	-1, 0, or 1 as I is <0, =0, or >0
MOD(I, J)	the remainder when I is divided by J
EXP(I,J)	I to the J'th power where I~=0 and J>=0

Since whenever you reference a function you use parentheses, there are no precedences associated with functions.

Variables

Expressions that are built up from constants have a precisely defined and unchanging value, regardless of their complexity. In our proofs however, we are rarely interested in any such particular expressions. It is much more interesting and useful to be able to talk about large classes of values. We are able to do this by allowing an expression to have variables in place of constants. The result represents all the expressions that can be obtained by replacing each variable in the expression by a constant. Thus J < 5 < J+3 stands for both 4 < 5 < 7 (which has value '1'B) and 8 < 5 < 11 (which has value '0'B), as well as for an infinite number of similar expressions.

Note in this example that the same variable (J) occurring more than once must be replaced by the same constant. It is also necessary that a variable be replaced by a constant of the proper type. '1'B < 5 < '0'B is not an instance of the above expression, and is in fact not even a legal expression. We will see later how to tell the type of any variable in an expression we have written. Informally speaking, it is the only type that makes sense to substitute for the variable.

A variable is written as a letter, optionally followed up to 30 letters, digits, and underscores. The following is a list of exception words that cannot be used as variables:

ALL	CHECK	ENTRY	INIT	PROCEDURE	STATIC
ALLOCATE	CHOOSE	EXIT	INITIAL	PROOF	STOP
ARB	CLOSE	EXT	LEAVE	PUT	THEN
ARBITRARY	DATA	EXTERNAL	LIST	QED	TO
ASSERT	DATAEND	FIXED	MAIN	READ	UNTIL
ASSUME	DCL	FLOAT	NO	READONLY	VAR
ATTAIN	DECLARE	FLOW	NOCHECK	RETURN	VARYING
BEGIN	DEFINE	FOR	NOFLOW	RETURNS	WHEN
BIT	DELETE	FORMAT	ON	REVERT	WHERE
BY	DO	FREE	OPEN	REWRITE	WHILE
CALL	EDIT	GET	OPTIONS	SELECT	WRITE
CASE	ELSE	GO	OTHER	SIGNAL	
CHAR	END	GOTO	OTHERWISE	SKIP	
CHARACTER	ENDFILE	IF	PROC	SOME	

Don't worry about the length of this list. If you forget and use a reserved word as a variable, it won't matter at all for now, and won't matter very much later.

Quantifiers and Assertions

How can we "talk about" the class of values represented by an expression with variables? Well, for that matter, how can we use PL/CV to talk about anything at all? By introducing the concept of an assertion. Assertions are analogous to declarative sentences (where we think of expressions as analogous to nouns). You are already familiar with the simplest assertions (called atomic) because they are just another way of looking at BIT valued expressions.

Remember that we defined BIT-valued operators like "$>$" and "$\&$". These symbols have commonly accepted mathematical meanings, and our definitions for them assign a value '1'B when the meaning of the expression containing them is true, and '0'B when the meaning is false. So we can look at these "boolean expressions" in two ways: as expressions with values that can be computed, or as assertions that are either true or false.

More complicated assertions are built from atomic assertions using the logical operators ($\&$, $|$, $\sim$, $=>$ and $<=>$) and two new operators. The new operators are called quantifiers. They are written "SOME" and "ALL". Even though they look like variables, they are not; they are on the list of exception words that cannot be used as variables.

An example of a quantified assertion is:

    SOME J FIXED. 2<J<5

A quantifier has the following parts, written one after the other: a keyword (SOME or ALL), a variable, a type name (FIXED or BIT), and a dot. A quantified assertion is a quantifier followed by an assertion.

An assertion quantified by SOME means that there is some value of the indicated type that the quantified variable could be replaced by that would make the assertion true. In the above example, the quantified assertion is true because if J is replaced by 3, then 2<J<5 is true (since the expression 2<3<5 has value '1'B).

An assertion quantified by ALL means that all values of the indicated type make the assertion true when they are put in place of the quantified variable. If SOME in the above quantified assertion were replaced by ALL, it would be false because there are many FIXED values which are not between 2 and 5 (and all we need is one such value to know that an ALL quantification is false).

The meaning of quantified assertions is more clear if you read "ALL" as "for all" and "SOME" as "for some".

What is the value of just the boolean expression 2<J<5? Of course there is none; it depends on what value we substitute for J. In this case, where the meaning of the assertion depends on J, J is said to be a "free" variable. On the other hand, the meaning of the assertion SOME J FIXED. 2<J<5 is constant. We do not think of substituting for J in this assertion, since we do not mean for it to represent a class of assertions. (Note that SOME K FIXED. 2<K<5 means exactly the same thing.) In this case, J is said to be a "bound" variable. The free occurrence of J in 2<J<5 has been bound by the quantifier.

For the purpose of building assertions, quantifiers act just like any unary operator. For example,

    (SOME X FIXED. I<=X<=J) => I<=J

is an assertion that will be true, no matter what values we substitute for
the free variables I and J.

Quantifiers have a precedence that is higher than & and lower than =. For
example, the assertion ALL X FIXED. X>=0 | X<0 means the same as
(ALL X FIXED. X>=0) | X<0, and is probably not what its author intended.
ALL X FIXED. (X>=0 | X<0) is a true assertion, while in
(ALL X FIXED. X>=0) | X<0 the last occurrence of X is a free variable.

Proofs
We would like to be able to tell when an assertion is true. We know that
we can do this for assertions that don't use quantifiers and variables by
simply evaluating them as expressions. But if you consider the quantifiers
and the definition of their meaning, you will see that there is no process
of "evaluation" which is guaranteed to tell us when a quantified assertion
is true. We can't substitute all the integers into an assertion to see if
they all work, or to see if we can find one that does.

(This difference accounts for the following convention: assertions whose
only logical operators are &, |, and ~ are also called "boolean expres-
sions". The reason that the operators => and <=> are not allowed in
boolean expressions, even though they too have the property of being
decideable in a finite amount of time, has to do with the programming
language we will be using. Note that P => Q will always have the same
value as ~P|Q, and that P <=> Q the same as (P&Q) | (~P&~Q), so that we
can implicitly use these operators inside boolean expressions.)

So far we have been able to look at any of the assertions with quantifiers
that we have written and tell whether or not it was true. However, it is
easy to write assertions for which we can not do this. For example, the
following assertion is one of the most famous outstanding problems in
mathematics:

    ALL I FIXED. ALL J FIXED. ALL K FIXED. ALL H FIXED.
      ((I>0 & J>0 & K>0 & H>2) => ~(I**H + J**H = K**H))

As with other quantified assertions, there is no way to evaluate the truth
of this statement. The reason that it is still open is that nobody has yet
provided a proof or disproof of it.

A proof is what we use to convince somebody (perhaps ourselves) that an
assertion is true. (A disproof of an assertion P is just a proof of the
assertion ~P.) The style of the proof and the level of detail which is made
explicit in it will depend on who it is written for. For ourselves or for
a friend we can perhaps assume some background knowledge about what is
being proven, and only include the important steps. For the mechanical
proof checker used here (the PL/CV checker), we must adhere to a specific
format, and the level of detail is a constant part of that format. The
PL/CV checker regrettably does not get any smarter by having seen lots of
proofs! The language accepted by the PL/CV checker is called PL/CV.

A PL/CV proof consists of a sequence of lines. Each line will look like one
of the following:

```
Assertion;
Assertion BY justification;
```

The assertion that begins each line is called the "conclusion". As we will see, "justification" varies depending on the kind of proof line.

The PL/CV logic consists of a collection of "proof rules". Each rule tells us a set of circumstances under which a new line can be added to the proof. Whenever we discuss a rule, we will talk about the assertions that are its "hypotheses" and conclusion. Whenever we write a new line in a proof, the hypothesis assertions for that line must have appeared as conclusions in previous lines. For example, in the line

```
I <= J+1 BY ARITH, I <= J;
```

I <= J+1 is the conclusion, and I <= J is the hypothesis. If this line appears in a proof, then a line with I <= J as a conclusion, such as

```
I <= J BY ARITH, J >= I;
```

must come before it in the proof.

The idea behind each proof rule is that, if the hypothesis assertions are true, then the conclusion will be true as well. Therefore if we start with only assertions known to be true, we know that every line we write in the proof will be a true assertion.

Note that while we do not prove assertions with free variables in them, the proofs of assertions with bound variables will often contain lines whose conclusion assertion contains free variables. For instance, the above two lines might be part of a proof of the assertion

```
ALL I FIXED. ALL J FIXED.(J >= I  => I <= J+1)
```

When we get to the rules for lines with quantifiers, we will see exactly how we get these free variables into our proof, and how the rules insure that the only things we can prove are assertions that are either true or false. (It will turn out, in fact, that in a more general sense, all of the variables that appear in any of our proofs are bound.) In the meantime, don't be concerned if our descriptions of the various proof rules seem to include assertions with free variables.

In the next section we will summarize the facts described informally in this section. We begin with the notion of an informal proof or argument.

II LOGICAL SYNTAX

2.1 Introduction

Proofs are distinguished from ordinary discourse by their logical
structure. An abstract description of arguments involves only this
structure. The simplest language adequate for the expression of the
abstract logical reasoning found in most mathematical arguments is the
predicate calculus. The PL/CV logic is based on this predicate calculus.

This section of the manual describes the syntax of the PL/CV version of the predicate calculus. The language of the calculus allows the
programmer to express properties of the PL/I integer and boolean data
types, as well as arrays of these. However, in the predicate calculus
only the purely logical facts about these data types can be deduced,
e.g. that x>0 & y>0 => x>0 but not that x>1 => x>0. (Reasoning about
the properties of integers and of built-in functions will be covered in
section IV. In terms of the syntax presented here, it will mean the
introduction of new forms of justification. See the ARITH and FUNCTION
proof rules.) Moreover, only arguments written specifically in terms of
these data types are allowed. So for example, one cannot use the
language of set theory since sets are not PL/I data types.

2.2 Overview

The programmer can regard the predicate calculus as an extension of
the set of PL/I boolean expressions (relations) obtained by adding the
connectives => (arrow for implication) and <=> (double arrow for
equivalence) to &, |, ~ and by adding logical operators on boolean
expressions called quantifiers. The existential quantifier begins with
the keyword SOME (logicians usually begin it with $\exists$). The universal
quantifier begins with the key word ALL (logicians usually begin it with
$\forall$).

2.3 Conventions

The syntax of the predicate calculus presents in order the grammat-
ical categories: expressions, assertions and arguments.

In the BNF syntax, square brackets, [], are used to indicate an
optional phrase. Braces, { }, indicate a group of words or phrases to be
repeated the number of times given by a superscript; $\{a_1,\ldots,a_n\}^+$
denotes the set of all finite nonempty strings of a_1 to a_n; $\{a_1,\ldots,a_n\}^*$
is similar but includes the empty string as well; $\{a_1,\ldots,a_n\}$ abbreviates $\{a_1,\ldots,a_n\}^1$, that is, one of the elements a_i is chosen. In the
BNF equations, when symbols such as commas, braces, asterisks, etc., are
part of the language being defined (e.g. terminal characters of the

grammar), they are underlined as in $\underline{*}$, $\underline{\lambda}$, $\underline{]}$, etc. (except for underscore itself, _, and except when no confusion is likely).

2.4 Expressions

Informally, an expression is either a constant, a variable, or a function application (including arrays as functions) either of type integer or boolean. The functions are denoted by the ordinary infix operators +, -, *, ** and identifiers.

$$\text{expression} \rightarrow \text{integer\_exp}$$
$$\rightarrow \text{boolean\_exp}$$

(i) integer expressions

$$\text{integer\_exp} \rightarrow \text{addend } \{\{+,-\}\text{addend}\}^*$$

$$\text{addend} \rightarrow \text{multiplicand } \{* \text{ multiplicand}\}^*$$

$$\text{multiplicand} \rightarrow \text{base } [** \text{ multiplicand}]$$

$$\text{base} \rightarrow \{+,-\}^*_* \text{ integer constant}$$
$$\rightarrow \{+,-\}^*_* \text{ identifier}$$
$$\rightarrow \{+,-\}^*_* \text{ function\_application}$$
$$\rightarrow \{+,-\}^* \text{ (integer\_exp)}$$

$$\text{integer\_constant} \rightarrow \{\text{digit}\}^+$$

identifier → letter {letter,digit,_}*   (except for the reserved words listed in section 1)

$$\text{function\_application} \rightarrow \text{identifier (expression } \{\underline{\lambda} \text{ expression}\}^*)$$

$$\text{expression\_list} \rightarrow \text{expression } \{\underline{\lambda} \text{ expression}\}^*$$

Examples of integer expressions
+x*+y--z**+2, 2**z+3, (ABS(x)+y)*2+z, A(I)+A(J), 1+2, +1--2, x**y**-z, 1+++2.

(ii) boolean expressions

Boolean expressions evaluate to true ('1'B) or false ('0'B). They are built up using the operators & (and), | (or), ~ (not) from constants, variables, boolean function evaluations and simple relations, such as x<y.

$$\text{boolean\_exp} \rightarrow \text{boolean\_disjunct } \{| \text{ boolean\_disjunct}\}^*$$

$$\text{boolean\_disjunct} \rightarrow \text{atomic\_boolean } \{\& \text{ atomic\_boolean}\}^*$$

$$atomic\_boolean \rightarrow \{\sim\}^{*}\ '0'B$$
$$\rightarrow \{\sim\}^{*}\ '1'B$$
$$\rightarrow \{\sim\}^{*}\ identifier$$
$$\rightarrow \{\sim\}^{*}\ function\_application$$
$$\rightarrow \{\sim\}^{*}\ (boolean\_exp)$$
$$\rightarrow integer\_exp\ relator\ integer\_exp$$
$$\rightarrow atomic\_boolean\ \{=,\sim=\}\ atomic\_boolean$$

$$relator \rightarrow =$$
$$\rightarrow \sim=$$
$$\rightarrow <=$$
$$\rightarrow <$$
$$\rightarrow \sim<$$
$$\rightarrow >$$
$$\rightarrow \sim>$$
$$\rightarrow >=$$

Examples: X|Y, A(I)&B(I), ~A(I)|X&Y,
'0'B&X, X+Y<Z | X+Y>W,
X=Y & F('0'B),

Note, $exp_1\sim=exp_2$ is treated as $\sim(exp_1=exp_2)$. This will be clear from the proof rules.

2.5 Assertions

Assertions are the formal equivalent of declarative sentences. They are built with &, |, ~, =>, <=>, and quantifiers starting from atomic relations. A quantified assertion begins with a quantifier, either existential, SOME, or universal ALL.

(i) propositional structure

assertion → equivalent {<=> equivalent}*
(Note, A<=>B<=>C means A<=>B & B<=>C.)

equivalent → implicant => equivalent
            → implicant

implicant → disjunct {| disjunct}*

disjunct → conjunct {& conjunct}*

```
conjunct → atomic_boolean
         → atomic_relation
         → {~}*  function_application
         → {~}*  (assertion)
         → {~}   quantifier . conjunct
```
(Note, the assertion following the period after a quantifier is called the
scope of the quantifier.)

```
atomic_relation → integer_exp {relator integer_exp}+
               → atomic_boolean { {=, ~=} atomic_boolean}+
```
(Note, the identifiers in integer expressions are allowed
to be definitions.)

(ii) quantifier

```
quantifier → {SOME,ALL} variable_list type
            {. variable_list type}*
            [WHERE assertion]
```

```
variable_list → variable
             → (variable {. variable}*)
```

variable → identifier[(*{.*}*)]

```
type → FIXED
     → BIT
```


Examples of atomic relations

```
X~=Y, X~<Y
1<2, 2<=X<=4, X+1<=3<=F(X),
1<2<3<4
```


Examples of quantifiers

```
SOME X FIXED
SOME Y BIT WHERE Y <=> Z
ALL(X,Y) FIXED WHERE X~=1
```


Examples of assertions

```
ALL X FIXED . X=0 => 1=0
SOME X FIXED . SOME Y FIXED . X<Y
ALL A(*) BIT . ALL I FIXED . A(I) = '0'B | A(I) = '1'B
ALL A(*) BIT . ALL I FIXED . (A(I) & A(I+1) => A(I))
```


2.6 Arguments

An argument is a sequence of assertions with certain internal

logical structure made manifest in justifications for these assertions.
An argument may also contain definitions of predicates (define statements) and of variables (choose statements). A basic building unit for
an argument is a proof-group which encapsulates an argument into a single unit which may be used to justify assertions. The details of this
section will be clarified in section IV on proof rules.

(i) proof group

          proof_group → introduction_proof_group
                      → cases_proof_group

          introduction_proof_group → PROOF; [qualifier] argument QED

          cases_proof_group → PROOF; {CASE[label:] assertion;

                                  argument}* QED
          (Note, the scope of the qualifier to a proof group is the set
          of assertions and statements between PROOF and its matching QED.)

(ii) qualifiers

          qualifier → {ARB,ARBITRARY} variable_list type {▲
                          variable_list type}* [WHERE assertion_list];
                    → ASSUME assertion_list;

          assertion_list → [label:] assertion {▲ [label:] assertion}*

(iii) statements

          statement → define_statement
                    → choose_statement
                    → proof_statement

          parameter_list → identifier {▲ identifier}*

          define_statement → [FOR variable_list type {▲ variable_list type}*]
                                  DEFINE identifier[(identifier{▲ identifier}*)]
                                  = {assertion,expression};

          choose_statement → CHOOSE variable_list type {▲ variable_list type}*
                                  WHERE assertion_list;

          proof_statement → [label:] assertion [justification];

(iv) justifications

```
justification → BY INTRO[▲ introduction_proof_group];
               BY INTRO▲ expression_list;
               BY CASES[▲ disjunct, cases_proof_group];
               BY CONTRA[▲ introduction_proof_group];
               BY ALLEL▲ {assertion, label}▲ expression_list;
```

(v) arguments

```
argument → {statement}*
```

Examples of proof groups and justified assertions.

```
PROOF;
 ASSUME L: ALL X FIXED. X = 0;
 1 = 0 BY ALLEL, L, 1;
QED;

PROOF;
 ARBITRARY (A(*),X,Y) FIXED WHERE X = Y;
 A(X) = A(Y);
QED;
```

2.7 Files (for IBM 370/168 version of PL/CV)

The PL/CV verifier takes input from a file with filetype PL/CV. The first line of the file must be "*PLCV" and must start in column 1. Following this may be any number of repetitions of the following:

```
*THEOREM     (starting in column 1)
     .                                        .
     . Any number of define or choose statements  .
     .                                        .
A proof_statement
```

where no lines other than *THEOREM's begin in column 1. Note that the recursive definition of proof will result in several proof_statements occurring at various levels of nesting in a file. A "*THEOREM" line is needed only for those at the top level, since they are the assertions actually being proved.

Assertions which have been proven may be used in the proofs of theorems further on in the file. To avoid frequent re-checking of assertions that have been verified once and which are used in many files, the contents of a verified file may be saved. This is done by including "save" as an option on the PLCV command line. The result of this command will be to replace the "*PLCV" line in the file with a "*CHECKED" line, and to add a "*ENDCHECKED" line at the end of the file. This checked file may then be inserted in any other which is to be verified, and all of its top-level proof, define, and choose statements will be accessible from the point where it was inserted.

In the case of verified procedures (introduced in section V) the block must begin with *PROCESS instead of *THEOREM. The first line of the procedure heading must follow immediately (i.e. any define or choose statements must be made within the procedure body). Procedures have access to theorems and other procedures which precede them in the same file, and may be saved just as theorems are.

In order that verified programs may be compiled by a PL/CS (PL/C or PL/I) compiler, the PL/CV lines inside a file to be verified must be shielded by special comment delimiters "/*/" and "*/". Since "*THEOREM" blocks have no program text, they must be completely shielded.

Here is an example of an input file. This is indeed a valid argument according to the rules of section IV. For now it is merely a piece of correct syntax.

```
*PLCV
*THEOREM
  /*/ ALL (G, ITH, NYC) BIT WHERE (G => (ITH|NYC)) & ~NYC.
        (~ITH => ~G) BY INTRO,
      PROOF;
        ARBITRARY (G, ITH, NYC) BIT WHERE (G => (ITH|NYC)) & ~NYC;
          ~ITH => ~G BY INTRO,
          PROOF;
            ASSUME ~ITH;
             ~G BY INTRO,
              PROOF;
                ASSUME G;
                'O'B BY CASES, ITH|NYC,
                  PROOF;
                  CASE ITH;
                        ~ITH;
                  CASE NYC;
                        ~NYC;
                  QED;
                QED;
              QED;
          QED;           */
```

(In the above argument, let G be the assertion "Mr. Jones is Governor of New York," ITH be the assertion "Mr. Jones is from Ithaca," and NYC be the assertion "Mr. Jones is from New York City." We have justified the reasoning that, if the Governor of New York is from Ithaca or New York City, and Mr. Jones is not from New York City, then if he is not from Ithaca he is not Governor.)

2.8 Type Restrictions

The words FIXED and BIT are PL/CV simple type symbols. They describe the intended range of expressions of their type. To insure that each expression has associated with it a unique type, we require that every syntactic object generated by the BNF productions given above also satisfy certain syntactic type restrictions stated here.

To describe the type of any expression, we must first assign to each constant, function symbol, predicate symbol, infix operator and infix relator a type symbol. Some of these are compound type symbols. Then in an assertion, we must assign to each variable a type description. Given these initial type descriptions, the type of any type correct expression can be determined. (Note, some forms of type correctness can only be checked inside assertions.) To describe these assignments, we let array denote any of the function types

$$\begin{array}{ll}
\text{FIXED } \{\times \text{ FIXED}\}\ast \to \text{FIXED} & \text{FIXED array} \\
\text{FIXED } \{\times \text{ FIXED}\}\ast \to \text{BIT} & \text{BIT array}
\end{array}$$

(i) The initial assignments are:

symbol	type description
constants	
0, 1, 2,...	FIXED
'0'B, '1'B	BIT
infix operators	
+, -, *, **	FIXED × FIXED → FIXED
&, |, =>, <=>	BIT × BIT → BIT
~	BIT → BIT
basic functions	
LBOUND, HBOUND	array × FIXED → FIXED
relators	
=, ~=	FIXED × FIXED → BIT
	BIT × BIT → BIT
<, <=, >, >=, ~<, ~>	FIXED × FIXED → BIT

(ii)   In order to extend the type descriptions to expressions, we need the notion of free and bound variables. The type of the binding occurrences of a bound variable in an assertion gives its type.

Definition: An occurrence of a variable x of the form SOME x or ALL x is a binding occurrence (also included are all the variants of this, such as SOME x(*), SOME(...x...), etc.). An occurrence of x within an assertion R of the form ALL(...x...) type symbol.P or SOME(...x...) type symbol.P (or any of the variants such as ALL (x(*,*)) type symbol WHERE assertion. P) is called a bound occurrence of x. Any other occurence is free.

Recalling that the scope of a quantifier is the assertion following it (delimited by the period), we say that a bound variable occurring in a subassertion Q is **bound by** the binding occurrence of that variable in the quantifier of smallest scope containing Q. We say that the variable has this scope, i.e. the scope of a bound variable is the scope of its binding operator. We also say that the quantifier containing the binding occurrence **binds** the variable.

The **type of a binding occurrence** of a variable is the type following the variable_list in which it occurs. The **type of a bound variable** is the type of the binding occurrence which binds it. The type of a variable free in an assertion is not explicitly determined by the assertion itself.

We now examine the similar notions of free and bound variables in arguments.

Definition: An occurrence of a variable x of the form ARBITRARY...x... or CHOOSE...x... or FOR...x... or DEFINE x or x: (i.e. x as a label) is called a binding occurrence of x. (As before, we include also the variants of this such as ARB x, ARB...x(*), etc.). An occurrence of x within a subargument qualified by a qualifier containing a binding occurrence of x or containing a choose statement or define statement or label which binds x is called **bound**. All variables in an argument which are neither bound in this way nor bound in assertions are called **free** in that argument.

A bound variable is bound by the qualifier or choose statement or define statement or label in the argument of the smallest scope containing it. Except in the case of variables bound by labels, this scope is called the scope of the variable and of the binding occurrence of the variable. For label names, the scope is the segment of the innermost argument from the occurrence of the label to the end of the argument. The type of a bound variable is determined by the type of its binding occurrence except in the case of a label (whose type is always BIT).

(iii) Type descriptions are extended to expressions in the obvious way. For instance, if f is of type $atype_1 \times ... \times atype_n \to btype$ (where the $atype_i$ are simple types or array types, and btype is a simple type), and exp_i are of type $atype_i$ respectively, then $f(exp_1, ..., exp_n)$ is of type btype. If p is a predicate of type $atype_1 \times ... \times atype_n$, then $p(exp_1, ..., exp_n)$ is of type BIT. If $\square$ is an infix operator of type $atype_1 \times atype_2 \to btype$, then $exp_1 \square exp_2$ is of type btype. If $\perp$ is a relator of type $atype_1 \times atype_2$, then $exp_1 \perp exp_2$ is of type BIT.

(iv) An expression is _type correct_ if and only if it (and consequently every subexpression) is assigned a unique type by these rules. An _argument_ is _type correct_ if and only if each expression in it has a unique type.

Examples

(2+3)**7 < 5 is of type BIT, each side of the relation is of type FIXED.

(2&3)+1 < '1'B is not type correct because 2&3 cannot be assigned a type.

2+1 < '1'B is not type correct because no relator compares FIXED and BIT, thus no type can be assigned.

X+Y < Z is neither type correct nor type incorrect until we know the types of X, Y, Z.

Notice X&Y = Z can only be type correct if X, Y, Z are all BIT, but X = Y is correct if all are BIT or all are FIXED.

A(X+Y,1) = 5 is neither correct nor incorrect. It depends on A,X and Y. But A(X&Y,1) is type incorrect if A is an array.

In SOME(X,Y,Z) BIT. (X|Y&Z = X) the expressions Y&Z and X|Y&Z and X are all of type BIT. In the sample argument about the governor of New York, all variables are of type BIT.

The ARITH Rule

A proof rule specifies the relation between the hypotheses and conclusion
of a proof line. The first rule we will be looking at is ARITH. Actually,
ARITH is one name for a collection of different rules. Figure 1 shows templates for the various ARITH rules.

The Commutative Rules
I+J = J+I BY ARITH;
I*J = J*I BY ARITH;

The Associative Rules
(I+J)+K = I+(J+K) BY ARITH;
(I*J)*K = I*(J*K) BY ARITH;

The Distributive Rule
I*(J+K) = (I*J)+(I*K) BY ARITH;

The Rules of Identity
I+0 = I BY ARITH;
I*1 = I BY ARITH;

The Inverse Rule
I+(-I) = 0 BY ARITH;

The Subtraction Rule
I-J = I+(-J) BY ARITH;

The Annihilation Rule
I*0 = 0 BY ARITH;

The Comparison Rules
I<=J BY ARITH, J>=I;
J>=I BY ARITH, I<=J;
I<J BY ARITH, J>I;
J>I BY ARITH, I<J;
I<J BY ARITH, I<=J-1;
I<=J-1 BY ARITH, I<J;
~(I<J) BY ARITH, I>=J;
I>=J BY ARITH, ~(I<J);
~(I<=J) BY ARITH, I>J;
I>J BY ARITH, ~(I<=J);

The Shifting Rules
I<J BY ARITH, I+1 < J+1;
I<J BY ARITH, I-1 < J-1;

The Weakening Rules
I<=J+1 BY ARITH, I<=J;
I<=J BY ARITH, I=J;

The Splitting Rules
I<J | I=J BY ARITH, I<=J;
I<=J | I>J BY ARITH;
I=J | ~(I=J) BY ARITH;

The Transitivity Rule
I<=K BY ARITH, I<=J, J<=K;

The Intersection Rule
I=J BY ARITH, I<=J, J<=I;

The Relation Addition Rule
I+J <= K+L BY ARITH, I<=K, +, J<=L;

The Relation Subtraction Rule
I-J <= K-L BY ARITH, I<=K, -, J>=L;

The Relation Multiplication Rules
I*K <= J*K BY ARITH, I<=J, *, K>=0;
I*K >= J*K BY ARITH, I<=J, *, K<=0;

The Cancellation Rules
I <= J BY ARITH, I*K <= J*K, /, K>0;
I >= J BY ARITH, I*K <= J*K, /, K<0;

The Rule of Negation
-I = (-1)*I BY ARITH

Figure 1   Templates for ARITH Rules

In order to get a proof line, first select one of the templates. Then substitute a FIXED expression for each of the variables in the template. For
example, the proof line

(K+2)*(H+1) = (H+1)*(K+2) BY ARITH;

is obtained by selecting the second Commutative Rule template and substituting K+2 for I, and H+1 for J. Note that you must substitute the same
expression for _every_ occurrence of the variable. It is sometimes necessary
(as in this example) to put parentheses around the expression you are substituting for a variable.

There is one more ARITH rule, the Rule of Computation. This rule has two
templates:

        I ρ J BY ARITH;
        ~(I ρ J) BY ARITH;

To get a proof line from one of these templates, substitute any FIXED
expressions that contain no variables, quantifiers, or functions for I and
J, and any one of <, <=, >, >=, or = for ρ. The other provision is that
the assertion obtained by this process must be true. An example of the
Rule of Computation is:

        2+3*2 = 8 BY ARITH;

Equality Rules
The hypothesis of the ARITH rules are whatever assertions are written after
the BY. (Note that some of the rules have no hypotheses.) When using
ARITH, each hypothesis assertion is written at least twice: once on the
proof line, and once as the conclusion of some previous proof line. The
following rules have the advantage that their hypotheses are not written on
the proof line, so that the hypotheses need only be written once. However,
the templates for these rules need a bit of explanation.

        Transitive Rule of Equality   Symmetric Rule of Equality
        I = J ...   I = J ...
        J = K ...   .
        .   .
        .   .
        .   J = I;
        I = K;

As with ARITH, any FIXED expression is substituted for each of the variables in the template. The proof line, which in this case is only a conclusion, is the last line of the template. The assertions above the vertical dots are the hypotheses to the rule. The vertical dots are an indication that the hypotheses must precede the proof line, although they may be
in any order, and need not be next to each other. The horizontal dots
after the hypotheses are an indication that there may be some justification
after the assertion, and it doesn't matter what it is.

Substitution Rules of Equality
```
P ...          P...
I = J ...      J = I ...
.              .
.              .
.              .
P{I/J};        P{I/J};
```

This template introduces a bit of new notation. First of all, an assertion (not a FIXED expression) should be substituted for P. You should read P{I/J} as "substitute I into P for some occurrences of J." For example, suppose you substitute H+1 for I, K+1 for J, and (H+1) * (K+1) > (K+1) for P. Then, to get P{I/J}, you start with (H+1) * (K+1) > (K+1), and for any occurrences of (K+1) you like, substitute (H+1). For example, two possible results are (H+1) * (K+1) > (H+1) and (H+1) * (H+1) > (H+1).

If the assertion P contains quantifiers, then some restrictions must be placed on the use of this rule. No variable in P which is bound may be replaced by a substitution, nor may a variable in I become bound after the substitution. Examples:

If P is ALL X FIXED. X<X+1, and we have shown X+1=Y, we may not conclude ALL X FIXED. X<Y because of the first restriction (since X is bound in P).

If P is SOME Y FIXED. X<Y<2*X and we have the equality 2*X = Y-1, then SOME Y FIXED. X<Y<Y-1 is wrong for the second reason (since the Y in Y-1 becomes bound in the result).

Finally, we finish off with a simple rule that has no hypotheses or justification:

Reflexive Rule of Equality
```
I = I;
```

An Example
As a simple example of a formal proof, let us prove the assertion H+I+J = J+I+H. Remember that + is left associative, so that the assertion is actually (H+I)+J = (J+I)+H. The annotation enclosed in /# and #/ is not part of the proof; it is only there to help you follow what is going on. The verifier considers any part of the proof between /# and #/ to be a comment, and ignores it.

```
(H+I)+J = H+(I+J) BY ARITH;    /# associativity of + #/
I+J = J+I BY ARITH;            /# commutativity of + #/
(H+I)+J = H+(J+I);             /# substitution      #/
H+(J+I) = (J+I)+H BY ARITH;    /# commutativity of + #/
(H+I)+J = (J+I)+H;             /# substitution      #/
```

Function Rules

If you examine the templates given for the ARITH rule, you will notice that
they do not allow you to conclude anything about division, exponentiation,
or any of the special functions. In order to prove anything about these
operators and functions, you need to use the FUNCTION rule. Templates for
the function rule are shown in figure 2. When a rule has a hypothesis, it

```
J >= 0 => ABS(J) = J BY FUNCTION, ABS(J);
J <= 0 => ABS(J) = -J BY FUNCTION, ABS(J);
J  = 0 => ABS(J) = 0 BY FUNCTION, ABS(J);


~(J = 0) ...
.
.
.
SOME Q FIXED . I = J * Q + MOD(I, J) BY FUNCTION, MOD(I, J);
0 <= MOD(I, J) < ABS(J) BY FUNCTION, MOD(I, J);
ALL (Q, R) FIXED. ((I=J*Q+R & 0<=R<ABS(J)) => R=MOD(I, J))
      BY FUNCTION, MOD(I, J);

J < 0 <=> SIGN(J) = -1 BY FUNCTION, SIGN(J);
J = 0 <=> SIGN(J) = 0  BY FUNCTION, SIGN(J);
J > 0 <=> SIGN(J) = 1  BY FUNCTION, SIGN(J);

MAX(I, J) >= I BY FUNCTION, MAX(I, J);
MAX(I, J) >= J BY FUNCTION, MAX(I, J);
MAX(I, J) = I | MAX(I, J) = J BY FUNCTION, MAX(I, J);

MIN(I, J) <= I BY FUNCTION, MIN(I, J);
MIN(I, J) <= J BY FUNCTION, MIN(I, J);
MIN(I, J) = I | MIN(I, J) = J BY FUNCTION, MIN(I, J);


~(J = 0) & I >= 0 ...
.
.
.
I  = 0 => J ** I = 1 BY FUNCTION, EXP(J, I);
I >= 1 => J ** I = J * (J ** (I - 1)) BY FUNCTION, EXP(J, I);
I >= 1 => (J ** I) / J = J ** (I - 1) BY FUNCTION, EXP(J, I);


~(J = 0) ...
.
.
.
I >= 0 => I = J * (I / J) + MOD(I, J) BY FUNCTION, DIVISION(I, J);
I <= 0 => I = J * (I / J) - MOD(I, J) BY FUNCTION, DIVISION(I, J);
ALL (Q, R) FIXED . (
  (I >= 0 => ((I = J*Q+R & 0 <= R < ABS(J)) => (Q = I/J & R = MOD(I, J))))
& (I <= 0 => ((I = J*Q-R & 0 <= R < ABS(J)) => (Q = I/J & R = MOD(I, J))))
                  ) BY FUNCTION, DIVISION(I, J);
```

Figure 2 FUNCTION templates

is indicated by horizontal and vertical dots as with the equality templates. The only difference is that when a group of templates has the same hypothesis, as in the MOD templates, the hypothesis appears in the template only once. It should be understood that whenever you use any of the three MOD templates, that the hypothesis ~(J = 0) should be the conclusion of a previous proof line. (Note: although the given rules completely characterize the division function, there are many additional useful conclusions which may be asserted without laboriously deriving them from these rules. See section 4.12 for the full division template.)

Logical Connectives

The operators &, |, =>, <=>, ~, and the quantifiers are called the "logical connectives." For each logical connective, there is an "introduction rule" and an "elimination rule." The introduction rule for a connective will have an assertion using that connective as a conclusion. Conversely, the elimination rule for a connective will have an assertion using that connective as a hypothesis.

Here are the templates for some of the simpler introduction and elimination rules.

```
& intro     & elim        & elim        | intro      | intro      => elim
P ...       P & Q ...      P & Q ...      P ...        Q ...       P ...
Q ...       .             .             .            .           P => Q ...
.           .             .             .            .           .
.           .             .             .            .           .
.           P;            Q;            P | Q;       P | Q;       .
P & Q;                                                            Q;


<=> intro       <=> elim        <=> elim
P => Q ...       P <=> Q ...      P <=> Q ...
Q => P ...       .               .
.               .               .
.               .               .
.               P => Q;          Q => P;
P <=> Q;
```

The templates given above are for the two-place & and |, but there are also templates for operators with three or more operands. Recall that & and | are combining operators, meaning, for example that P & Q & R means neither (P & Q) & R nor P & (Q & R). The elimination rule allows you to "pull away" any number of combined & operators in one step. Thus, if you have established P & Q & R, you may conclude either P, Q, or R by & elimination. Given (P & Q) & R, you would need two steps to conclude P; you would first have to prove P & Q. The introduction rules work in a similar fashion. If you establish P, you can then prove P | Q | R in one introduction, but to prove (P | Q) | R, you would first have to prove P | Q.

<=> RULES

The special rules we had for the "=" operator reflected the fact that, as an assertion, X=Y meant that the FIXED or BIT expressions X and Y had the same value, and could therefore be substituted for each other in an assertion P, subject to certain restrictions about bound variables which insured that the result of the substitution had the same meaning as P.

We have analogous rules for the "<=>" operator. These rules reflect the fact that the assertion P<=>Q says that the sub-assertions P and Q mean the same thing, and can therefore be substituted for each other in an assertion R as long as the meaning of R is not thereby changed. The templates for these rules are:

```
        SUBSTITUTION RULES OF EQUIVALENCE
        R ...            R ...
        P <=> Q ...      Q <=> P ...
        .                .
        .                .
        .                .
        R{P/Q};          R{P/Q};
```
(as long as no bound variable of R is replaced by the substitution, nor any free variable of P bound in the result)

and two that need no hypotheses:

```
        REFLEXIVE RULE OF EQUIVALENCE    RE-NAMING OF BOUND VARIABLES
                P <=> P;                 ALL I type.P <=> ALL J type.P{J//I}
                                         SOME I type.P <=> SOME J type.P{J//I}
```

(Note that, as with the "=" operator, the transitive and symmetric rules for "<=>" are derivable from the reflexive and substitution rules.)

There is a new notation in the template for the re-naming rule. Read the notation P{J//I} as "substitute J for every I free in P." There is a difference between this notation and the P{J/I} used in the other templates for the equality rules. When only one / is used, for each I in P you have your choice of substituting a J or leaving the I alone. Therefore, P{J/I} can have several meanings. The notation P{J//I} has only one meaning. You must substitute a J for every free I; you have no choice in the matter.

In the re-naming template, any variable can be used in place of I and J, and any assertion in place of P subject to the following restriction: if an occurrence of I in P is free, then the occurrence of J there that results from the substitution must also be free. For instance:

```
        ALL X FIXED. SOME Y FIXED. X < Y   <=>
                        ALL Y FIXED. SOME Y FIXED. Y < Y
```

is not a legitimate use of this template since P (SOME Y FIXED. X < Y) has a free occurrence of X that becomes bound when X is changed to Y. The assertion:

```
        ALL X FIXED. SOME Y FIXED. X < Y   <=>
                        ALL Z FIXED. SOME Y FIXED. Z < Y
```

is a legitimate renaming of bound variables.

=> Introduction

Imagine that you are in a Space Sciences class, and your professor tries to convince you that the statment, "If there is life on Mars, it must be very primitive" is true. He might make a statement like, "Suppose there is life on Mars," and go on to talk about the environment it would have to endure, its possible effects on the planet, and so forth. For the next few minutes he would go on talking as if a recent space probe <u>had</u> discovered life, and convince you that the life must be very primitive. But when the class was over, you wouldn't rush over to your friends and ask them if they had heard that life was discovered on Mars. You accepted the assumption for the sake of discussion, and when the discussion was over, the assumption was dropped.

Here is the template for the => introduction rule:

```
P => Q BY INTRO,
PROOF;
    [ASSUME P;]
    .
    .
    .
    Q ...
QED;
```

Brackets ([]) in a template indicate an optional part. When you are using the => introduction template, you don't have to write out the ASSUME P part if you don't want to. As before, the vertical dots indicate where proof lines go, and the horizontal dots stand for any kind of justification.

The hypothesis to the => introduction rule is a little different from others we have seen. Instead of certain assertions, it requires a whole proof. This proof has a special part called the assumption. Any proof lines you write between the PROOF and the QED can use P as a hypothesis. If, by assuming P, you can write out a proof of Q, then P => Q must also be true. Each line in the proof can get its hypotheses from any previous proof line, or from the ASSUME line (even if you decided not to write it). The proof can't use P => Q as a hypothesis though; that hasn't been proved yet. Here is an example of the use of the => introduction rule:

```
I<=J => I+1<=J+1 BY INTRO,
PROOF;
    ASSUME I<=J;
    1<=1 BY ARITH;
    I+1 <= J+1 BY ARITH, I<=J, +, 1<=1;
QED;
```

Proof lines written after the QED can get their hypotheses from any lines written before the PROOF (including the P => Q line) or after the QED. However, a line that comes after the QED <u>cannot</u> reach inside, between the PROOF and QED for a hypothesis. That would be like after Space Science class telling your friends there is life on Mars.

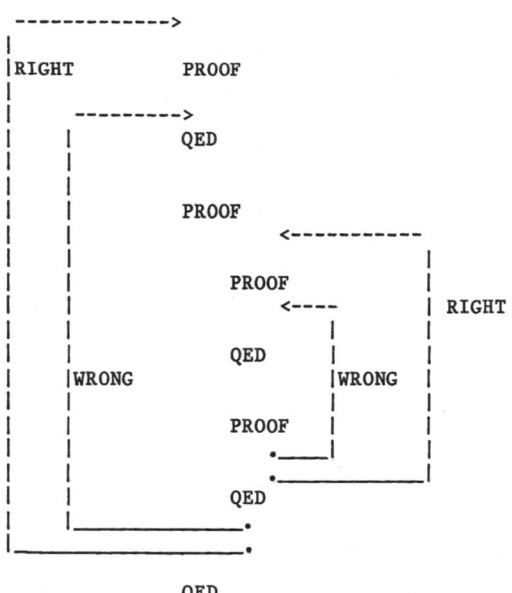

Figure 3   Hypotheses and Proof Blocks

The reason we write the hypothesis-proof for the => introduction rule <u>after</u> the line we are trying to prove is for ease in reading. Once we see that the prover wishes to show an implication, we can read the following lines keeping in mind the assumption being made (P) and the conclusion we are trying to reach (Q).

Any kind of proof whatsoever can be written where the vertical dots are in the template, even a proof that uses the => introduction rule. Here is an example of such a use.

```
        I<=J => (J<=I => I=J) BY INTRO,
        PROOF;
            ASSUME I<=J;
            J<=I => I=J BY INTRO,
            PROOF;
                ASSUME J<=I;
                I=J BY ARITH, I<=J, J<=I;
            QED;
        QED;
```

The part of the proof between a PROOF and its corresponding QED is called a "proof" block. The above proof blocks are said to be "nested," because one is inside the other. The rule for reaching back and getting hypotheses in the presence of nested proof blocks is that you can always reach around a proof block, but you can never reach into one. Figure 3 shows examples of

right and wrong ways of reaching back for hypotheses. If a proof line is
allowed to reach back to a previous proof line for a hypothesis, the assertion on the previous line is said to be "accessible" to the later line.
Later we will see more restrictions on which assertions are accessible to
proof lines.

The notion of assumptions and proof blocks alters our idea of the meaning
of assertions in the proofs we write. For assertions at "top level" (i.e.
not within any proof block) the meaning is unchanged from that described in
section I. But in general we must say of an assertion in our proofs that
if all the assumptions accessible to it are true, then its meaning as
described in section I is true. (Of course, top level assertions have no
assumptions.) The meaning of an assertion with free variables is that any
assignment of values to those free variables that makes all accessible
assumptions true will also make the assertion itself true.

The Cases Rule
The | elimination rule is also called the CASES rule. Here is the idea
behind the CASES rule. Suppose you know that Q or R is true, though you
don't know which one, and you want to show that P follows. If you first
assume Q, and show that P follows, and then assume R, and show that P follows, then P must be true. Here is the template for the CASES rule.

```
P BY CASES, Q|R,
PROOF;
CASE Q;
    .
    .
    .
    P ...
CASE R;
    .
    .
    .
    P ...
QED;
```

The assertion Q|R is a hypothesis of this rule that has to be written out,
just like the hypotheses of the ARITH rule. Each CASE line introduces an
assumption, just like the ASSUME line of the => introduction rule. The
part of the proof between CASE Q and CASE R is a proof block, and so is the
part of the proof between CASE R and QED. The same accessibility rules
that apply to the => introduction proof blocks apply for these proof blocks
as well: it is all right to reach around a proof block for a hypothesis,
but you are not allowed to reach into a proof block.

The above template is for a hypothesis with a two-place |. There are simi-
lar templates for an | operator with three or more places. You simply
include a CASE line and a proof block for each operand. If you applied the
| elimination rule to P | Q | R, you would have three cases: P, Q, and R.
However, if you applied the rule to the hypothesis (P | Q) | R, you would
have only two cases: P | Q and R. The cases must be split in the same
manner as they appear in the hypothesis.

```
ABS(I)>J => I>J | -I>J BY INTRO,
PROOF;
    ASSUME ABS(I) > J;
    C: I<=0 | I>0 BY ARITH; /# SPLITTING #/
    I>J | -I>J BY CASES, C,
    PROOF;
    CASE I <= 0;
        I<=0 => ABS(I) = -I BY FUNCTION, ABS(I);
        ABS(I) = -I; /# => ELIMINATION #/
        -I > J;      /# SUBSTITUTE INTO ABS(I) > J #/
        I>J | -I>J;  /# | INTRODUCTION #/
    CASE I>0;
        0 < I BY ARITH, I > 0;              /# COMPARISON   #/
        0 <= I-1 BY ARITH, 0 < I;           /# COMPARISON   #/
        0 <= I-1+1 BY ARITH, 0 <= I-1;      /# WEAKENING     #/
        I-1 = I+(-1) BY ARITH;              /# SUBTRACTION   #/
        I-1+1 = I+(-1)+1;                   /# SUBSTITUTION  #/
        I+(-1)+1 = I+((-1)+1) BY ARITH;     /# ASSOCIATIVITY #/
        I-1+1 = I+((-1)+1);                 /# SUBSTITUTION  #/
        -1+1 = 0 BY ARITH;                  /# COMPUTATION   #/
        I-1+1 = I+0;                        /# SUBSTITUTION  #/
        I+0 = I BY ARITH;                   /# IDENTITY      #/
        I-1+1 = I;                          /# SUBSTITUTION  #/
        0 <= I;                             /# SUBSTITUTION  #/
        I >= 0 BY ARITH, 0 <= I;            /# COMPARISON    #/

        I>=0 => ABS(I)=I BY FUNCTION, ABS(I);
        ABS(I) = I;     /# => ELIMINATION #/
        I > J;          /# SUBSTITUTE INTO ABS(I) > J #/
        I>J | -I>J;     /# | INTRODUCTION #/
    QED;
QED;
```

Figure 4   A Sample Proof

An Example

We now have seen enough rules to write out a proof of an (at least
slightly) interesting assertion, which appears in Figure 4. The parts
enclosed in /# and #/ are not part of the proof; they are there only to
indicate which template has been used. Note the C: that is put before the
conclusion of the proof line on the fourth line of the proof. When a variable is followed by a colon, it is called a "label". A label can be put
before an assertion that is the conclusion of a proof line, or it can be
put before the assumption on an ASSUME or CASE line. On subsequent lines,
whenever that variable is written, it means "insert the assertion labeled
by this variable here". There is such a use of the label C on the fifth
line of the proof.

The amount of work expended to get I>=0 from I>0 is intimidating. However,
we will soon learn about some short cuts that can be used to reduce that
deduction to one line.

```
'0'B introduction      '0'B elimination        ~Introduction

P ...                  '0'B...                 ~P BY INTRO,
  .                      .                      PROOF;
  .                      .                        [ASSUME P;]
  .                      .                          .
~P...                  P;                           .
  .                                                 .
  .                                               '0'B...
  .                                               QED;
'0'B;
```

Figure 5   Rules using '0'B

Rules for '0'B

Figure 5 shows the introduction and elimination rules for '0'B. When first
encountered, '0'B introduction sounds like a crazy idea. How can we <u>prove</u>
'0'B, an assertion that is, by definition, false? Remember though, that we
understand that an assertion in a proof is true only if all of the assumptions accessible to it are true. If the collection of assumptions accessible at some point contains two of the form P and ~P, then it can never happen that every member of the collection is true. We can therefore
correctly assert even '0'B at that point. It should be clear , in fact,
that we can justifiably assert anything at such a point, since the meaning
of the assertion (in the sense of section I) is irrelevant. This observation is exactly the '0'B elimination rule.

The best way to understand the use of '0'B is to realize that proving it is
the formal way of saying that one has made an inconsistent set of assumptions. If it is then necessary to draw the conclusion of an implication or
CASE, it may be asserted without further proof. The fact that '0'B has
been concluded shows that the implication is vacuous, or the CASE impossible.

There is another way of using the derivation of '0'B to gain information
about hypotheses. Suppose we have proven A|~A for some assertion A. Then
if we assume ~A and reach a contradiction, we know that A must be true by
cases. The form of this argument is:

```
A BY CASES, A|~A,
  PROOF;
    CASE ~A;
       .
       .
       .
     '0'B;
     A;
    CASE A;
  QED;
```

```
~(P&Q) => (~P | ~Q) BY INTRO,
PROOF;
   ASSUME ~(P&Q);
   (~P | ~Q) BY CONTRA,
   PROOF;
      ASSUME ~(~P | ~Q);                 ~~(I=I) BY INTRO,
      ~P BY INTRO,                       PROOF;
      PROOF;                                ASSUME ~(I=I);
         ASSUME P;                          I = I;
         ~Q BY INTRO,                       '0'B;
         PROOF;                          QED;
            ASSUME Q;
            P & Q;
            '0'B;
         QED;
         ~P | ~Q;
         '0'B;
      QED;
      ~P | ~Q;
      '0'B;
   QED;
QED;
```

Figure 6   Using the ~ Introduction and Contradiction Rules

Such a form is abbreviated by the CONTRADICTION rule:

```
A BY CONTRA,
 PROOF;
 [ASSUME ~A;]
    •
    •
    •
 '0'B
 QED;
```

Note that this is more than just an abbreviation of the previous form. It
has no reference to the assertion A|~A, and does not need it as a
hypothesis. Classical logic makes the assumption of A|~A for every asser-
tion, and so proof by contradiction is a rule of classical logic. However,
there are many assertions for which we cannot prove A|~A in PL/CV without
using this rule. Systems of logic which do not assume A|~A for every
assertion are called constructive. PL/CV is a constructive system as long
as the rule of contradiction is not used.

The difference between constructive and non-constructive systems and their
relevance is an issue of mathematical philosophy. It seems that all the
mathematics needed for programs can be done using constructive logic, and
we will not use the rule of contradiction in this manual. It is included
for those who may want to do classical mathematics in PL/CV. Figure 6
shows an example of the use of each of these rules. Proofs that use the
contradiction rule are often convoluted, and the one in Figure 6 is no
exception.

```
ALL introduction                ALL Elimination

ALL X type. P BY INTRO,         P{E//I} BY ALLEL, ALL I type. P, E;
PROOF;
    [ARB[ITRARY] X type;]
    .
    .
    .
    P ...
QED;
```
                Figure 7 Introduction and Elimination Rules for ALL

Rules for ALL

Figure 7 shows templates for the ALL introduction and elimination rules.
Let us first consider the ALL introduction rule. When you are using the
rule, substitute either FIXED or BIT for "type" in the template. Recall
that brackets in a template mean that the item is optional. The nested
brackets indicate that we can use ARB or ARBITRARY, or leave the line out
altogether. You may substitute any variable for X in the template.
Although it isn't shown explicitly in the template, the assertion you substitute for P will almost certainly contain the variable you substitute for
X. The part of the proof between the PROOF and QED is a proof block, and
follows all the normal accessibility rules.

The simplest way of explaining the ALL introduction rule is with an example. Suppose we wish to prove the assertion ALL J FIXED. J-1 < J. An
informal argument would be, "Let J be any FIXED value. No matter what J
is, we know by the rules of arithmetic that J-1 is less than J. This argument works for any J." The PL/CV version of this argument is given in figure 8. The purpose of the ARBITRARY line is to introduce a new variable
into the proof. We will call these variables "logic variables." Every
free variable in each assertion we write must be a logic variable. We can
think of ARBITRARY lines as assumptions which are required by any proof
lines that use the logic variables they introduce, and which are true for
any value of those variables. Just as with any other hypothesis, a proof
line may not reach into a proof block to get an ARBITRARY line for its free
variables. Alternatively, we can think of an "ARBITRARY J" line as a kind
of quantifier which says that the following block is a correct proof for
any value substituted for J. We can then think of the proof block as the
scope of the ARBITRARY line, in which all free occurrences of J are bound
by the "quantifier".

This latter interpretation helps us understand a small confusion that can
arise. What if someone tries to introduce the logic variable J at a point
where J is already introduced? This problem is entirely equivalent to
understanding what an assertion like

    ALL J FIXED.((J<0|J>=0) & ALL J FIXED.J<J+1)

means, and in fact would occur in the proof of this assertion. A quantifier binds all _free_ occurrences of its variable inside its scope. The

```
ALL J FIXED. J-1<J BY INTRO,
PROOF;
    ARBITRARY J FIXED;
    J=J;
    J<=J BY ARITH, J=J;                /# weakening #/
    1<=1 BY ARITH;                     /# computation #/
    J-1<=J-1 BY ARITH, J<=J,-,1=1;     /# relation subtraction #/
    J-1<J BY ARITH, J-1<=J-1;          /# comparison #/
QED;
```
Figure 8. Example of ALL-introduction rule

meaning of the above assertion is: any value for J will make J<0|J>=0 true
and ALL J FIXED.(J<J+1) is true. Note that this meaning does not explicitly
involve substituting for the J's bound by the inner quantifier. That comes
up only in determining the truth of that innermost quantified assertion.
Similarly, an ARBITRARY "quantifier" binds only the free occurrences of its
variable inside its scope. Therefore, of all the ARBITRARY lines which are
accessible to some occurrence of a logic variable, it will be that of the
smallest or innermost proof block which binds it.

This situation only rarely happens in actual proofs (usually long ones).
It can always be avoided by careful choice of variable names. (Remember
that ALL J FIXED.J<J+1 means the same thing as ALL FOO FIXED.FOO<FOO+1.)
Nevertheless, to make sure our proofs are correct in the cases where it
does happen, we must add the following restriction to the accessibility
rules: if point A is inside a proof block with an "ARBITRARY X type" line,
then no assertion containing free X outside of that block is accessible
from A.

    Example:

```
        ALL J FIXED. J-1<J BY INTRO,
         PROOF;
            ARB J FIXED;
             .
             .
             .
            J-1<J ...
         QED;
        J-1 <= J BY ARITH, J-1<J;
```

If this section of proof is not inside a proof block with an
ARBITRARY J FIXED line, then the bottom line is incorrect, since it has no
accessible introduction of its free variable. If there is such an enclosing block, then the inner proof of J-1<J cannot use as hypotheses any
assertions with free J that come from outside (because in a sense, it is a
"different" J inside this proof block).

It now should be clear how to find out the type of any variable in a proof.
If the variable is bound, look at the quantifier to which it is bound. If
the variable is free, then look at the ARBITRARY line that introduced it.

(The ARBITRARY line is optional; if it weren't written, just use the ARBITRARY line you would have to write if you were going to write one.) If you think of the ARBITRARY line as a quantifier then every variable we write in our proofs is bound, and its type is determined by its binding.

All the sample proofs shown so far have been incomplete, since they have all contained free variables and no ARBITRARY lines. They have actually been the parts that go inside a proof block of an ALL introduction rule.

Next, look at the ALL elimination rule. In the ALLEL template, I stands for a variable, and E stands for any expression of the appropriate type.

The idea behind the ALL elimination rule is quite simple. Suppose we have proved the assertion ALL J FIXED. J-1 < J. Then we know that the assertion J-1 < J holds for any fixed value given to J. The ALL elimination rule lets us prove that assertion for any particular expression, such as K+2:

    (K+2)-1 < K+2 BY ALLEL, ALL J FIXED. J-1 < J, K+2;

Rules for SOME

Figure 9 contains the templates for the SOME introduction and elimination rules. Both these templates use the new substitution notation introduced with the ALL elimination rule. In the introduction template, I stands for a variable, and E for any expression of the same type. In the elimination rule, both I and J stand for variables.

Suppose we wish to prove as assertion like SOME K FIXED. K>5. This assertion says that there is a FIXED value greater than 5. People from Missouri will like the SOME introduction rule; in essence, it says "show me". In this case, a value for K that will work is 6. The proof is:

    6 > 5 BY ARITH;
    SOME K FIXED. K>5 BY INTRO, 6;

On the other hand, suppose we have a proof that SOME K FIXED. K*K=J. This assertion states that J is a perfect square. The SOME elimination rule lets us assign a name for "the square root of J", and use that name in subsequent proof lines. (This name must not be the same as one from the ARBITRARY line of the smallest proof block containing it, if there is one, nor may it be the same as one used by a previous CHOOSE line in the same block.) For example:

    SOME K FIXED. K*K=J ...
    CHOOSE ROOTJ FIXED WHERE ROOTJ*ROOTJ = J;

The CHOOSE line introduces a new logic variable in the same way that the ARBITRARY line does. Subsequent proof lines can use ROOTJ as a free variable, and ROOTJ*ROOTJ = J as a hypothesis. Naturally, proof lines cannot reach into a proof block to get at ROOTJ.

As with ARBITRARY lines, the CHOOSE line can be thought of as a quantifier. It means that any value for ROOTJ that makes the WHERE assertion true will make the rest of the proof block correct. The scope of a CHOOSE line is

SOME introduction   SOME elimination

P{E//I} ...   SOME I type. P ...
 •   •
 •   •
 •   •
SOME I type. P BY INTRO, E;   CHOOSE J type WHERE P{J//I};

Figure 9   Introduction and Elimination Rules for SOME

not the whole proof block, as with ARBITRARY lines, but only that part of
the block that follows the CHOOSE. Of all the CHOOSE ROOTJ or ARBITRARY
ROOTJ lines that are accessible to an instance of ROOTJ, it is the one of
smallest (innermost) scope that binds it. Assertions with free occurrences
of ROOTJ are not accessible to any point that must "reach through" such a
scope.

Extended Quantifiers
There are some abbreviations you can use when writing quantifiers. Rather
than

     ALL I FIXED. ALL J FIXED. (I<J => I+1<J+1)

you can write

     ALL (I, J) FIXED. (I<J => I+1<J+1)

instead. These two assertions mean the same thing, in the same way that
I<J<K means the same as I<J & J<K & K<J. You can collapse together a
string of any number of ALLs, or a string of any number of SOMEs, but not a
mixed string. For example, in

     ALL I FIXED. SOME J FIXED. I<J

there is no way to collapse the quantifiers. The introduction and elimination rules can be used on extended quantifiers. Use the examples in figure
10 as a guide.

     All introduction:

     ALL (X, Y) FIXED. (X<=Y | Y>X) BY INTRO,
     PROOF;
         ARBITRARY (X, Y) FIXED;
         X<=Y | Y>X BY ARITH;   /# splitting #/
     QED;

     ALL elimination:

     X<=X+1 & X+1<=Z => X<=Z BY ALLEL,
         ALL (I, J, K) FIXED. (I<=J & J<=K => I<=K), X, X+1, Z;

SOME introduction:

```
I < I+1 < J <= K ...
SOME (Y, Z) FIXED. I<Y<Z<=K BY INTRO, I+1, J;
```

SOME elimination:

```
SOME (Q, R) FIXED. A = B*Q+R ...
CHOOSE (Q0, R0) FIXED WHERE A = B*Q0+R0;
```

Figure 10   Introduction and Elimination of Extended Quantifiers

Another abbreviation arises from the very common case of quantifying with ALL over an implication, as in:

```
ALL (I,J) FIXED.(I<J => I+1 < J+1)
```

The straightforward proof of such an assertion generally requires two introductions, one of the quantifier and one of the implication. These can be combined by instead writing the equivalent abbreviation:

```
ALL (I,J) FIXED WHERE I<J. I+1<J+1
```

The first line of the proof block following this is:

```
ARBITRARY (I,J) FIXED WHERE I<J
```

(which does not have to be written). Within the proof block, one may use the FIXED variables I and J, as well as the assumption that I<J. The elimination rule for such an abbreviation is just like that for the usual all elimination, except that the additional WHERE assumption must be proven for the expressions being substituted. Thus the line:

```
(K+2)+1 < (X*X)+1 BY ALLEL,
        ALL (I,J) FIXED WHERE I<J. I+1<J+1, K+2, X*X;
```

is correct only if the assertion K+2<X*X is accessible from where it is written.

One may similarly restrict the existential quantifier. The abbreviation SOME X FIXED WHERE P. Q is equivalent to SOME X FIXED . P&Q. The introduction of this quantifier requires that both P and Q (with proper substitution for X) both be asserted where they are accessible to the introduction. An elimination line would look like:

```
CHOOSE Z FIXED WHERE P{Z//X} & Q{Z//X}
```

Induction
There is another way to introduce an ALL quantifier for FIXED values. If you have an assertion P that depends on a free variable X for which you can show two things:

    1) P is true when X is replaced by some particular value N

2) if P is true for any value M>=N then P is also true for M+1

then you may conclude ALL M FIXED WHERE M>=N.P{M//X} . This method is
called mathematical induction. To see why it is correct consider that, if
you know P{N//X}, then by (2) you know P{N+1//X}, so that by (2) again, you
know P{N+2//X}, ..., etc. up to any value M>=N that you wish. (This also
works "going down". Replace M>=N in (2) by M<=N and M+1 by M-1. You may
then conclude ALL M FIXED WHERE M<=N. P{M//X} by a similar argument.)

The two templates for this rule are:

    P{N//X}...
    •
    •
    •
    •

    ALL M FIXED WHERE $<_{M>=N}^{M<=N}>$. P{M//X} BY INDUCTION

    PROOF;

    [ARBITRARY M FIXED WHERE $<_{M>=N}^{M<=N}>$ & P{M//X};]

        •
        •
        •

        $<_{P\{M+1//X\}...}^{P\{M-1//X\}...}>$

    QED;

where you uniformly choose either the top or bottom expression inside each
set of <>'s. The ARBITRARY line here means just what it does for the usual
ALL-introduction, and is likewise supplied automatically if not explicitly
written.

The extended ARITH rule
If you go back and look at the proof in Figure 4, you will note that we
needed thirteen lines to get from I>0 to I>=0. Although a truly rigorous
proof would require those thirteen lines, we will not be writing proofs
with that level of detail. In fact, in our proofs,

    I>=0 BY ARITH, I>0;

will be sufficient. Many, but not all, simple arithmetic facts can be
written in one ARITH line. The purpose of the next few sections is to give
you a feeling for the sort of things you can do using ARITH.

Transformations

Suppose we have proven the assertion (I+J)+K > 12, and we want to get the assertion I+(J+K) > 12. Using the templates we have seen so far, we would first prove that (I+J)+K = I+(J+K) using the Associative Rule, and then use the Substitution Rule to substitute I+(J+K) for (I+J)+K into (I+J)+K > 12 to get I+(J+K) > 12. Note the pattern here: first use an ARITH template to prove that two expressions, call them A and B, are equal, and then use the Substitution Rule to substitute A for B (or B for A) into one assertion to get a new assertion. We will call this process a "transformation step." We can chain together a series of transformation steps to make a transformation.

Figure 11 shows an example of a transformation. The assertions on the left are the steps of the transformation, and the assertions on the right are the equalities used to go from one step to the next. The equalities can come from the Rule of Computation, the Commutative and Associative Rules, the Distributive Rule, the Rules of Identity, Inverse, Subtraction, Annihilation, and Negation. (See Figure 1, pg. 6.)

A quite reasonable reaction to Figure 11 is, "Look, I believe that you can get to I*J - I*K = 2 from I*(J-K) = 2 using your transformation steps. But I don't want to look at all the details." Fortunately for us, PL/CV is capable of supplying the details. In a proof, all you have to write is each end of the transformation:

I*J - I*K = 2 BY ARITH, I*(J-K) = 2;

and the verifier will supply the intermediate steps (but it won't print them out and make us look at them!).

The Comparison and Shifting Rules of Figure 1 can also be used as transformation steps. The transformation steps allowed by the Comparison Rules have been expressed more compactly in figure 12. Any assertion that looks like a template on the left side of an <--> can be transformed to one that looks like template on the right side of the <-->, and vice versa. And of course, these steps can be combined freely with all the substitution steps. For example, suppose we wanted to transform the assertion H+2 > K to K-2 < H. The steps would be:

H+2 > K
K < H+2
K-1 < H+2-1
K-1-1 < H+2-1-1

and then we would use a bunch of substitution steps to get to K-2 < H. In a proof, we would just write

K-2 < H BY ARITH, H+2 > K;

and let the verifier fill in the details.

So far, all the transformation steps we have seen are reversible. That is, if you can transform assertion P to assertion Q using these steps, then you

```
I*(J-K) = 2              J-K = J+(-K)
I*(J + -K) = 2           I*(J + -K) = I*J + I*(-K)
I*J + I*(-K) = 2         -K = (-1)*K
I*J + I*((-1)*K) = 2     I*((-1)*K) = (I*(-1))*K
I*J + (I*(-1))*K = 2     I*(-1) = (-1)*I
I*J + ((-1)*I)*K = 2     ((-1)*I)*K = (-1)*(I+K)
I*J + (-1)*(I*K) = 2     (-1)*(I+K) = -(I*K)
I*J + -(I*K) = 2         I*J + -(I*K) = I*J - I*K
I*J - I*K = 2
```

Figure 11   A Transformation


```
I<=J       <-->   J>=I
I<J        <-->   J>I
I<J        <-->   I<=J-1
~(I<J)     <-->   I>=J
~(I<=J)    <-->   I>J
~~(I=J)    <-->   I=J
I<J        <-->   I+1<J+1
I<J        <-->   I-1<J-1
```

Figure 12   Comparison and Shifting Transformations

can transform Q back to P using the same steps in reverse. The Weakening
Rules can be used as transformations as well, but these transformations are
not reversible. The Weakening transformations are:

```
I<=J   -->   I<=J+1
I=J    -->   I<=J
```

The --> indicates that you can transform the template on the left to the
template on the right, but you can't transform the one on the right to the
one on the left. For example, repeated applications of the first weakening
transformation will transform H<=K to H<=K+1, H<=K+1+1, H<=K+1+1+1, and
further transformations will give you H<=K+3, so that you can write

```
H<=K+3 BY ARITH, H<=K;
```

but you can't write

```
H<=K BY ARITH, H<=K+3;
```

because the Weakening transformations do not reverse.

Extending Templates
We have seen that if you can use transformations to turn the assertion Q
into the assertion P, then you can write

```
P BY ARITH, Q;
```

in a proof. Also, if you can use transformations to turn an assertion of the form I=I into P, then you can just write

P BY ARITH;

in a proof. For example, you can use transformations to change (K+2)*5 = (K+2)*5 into (K+2)*5 >= 5*K. Therefore, you may write

(K+2)*5 >= 5*K BY ARITH;

in a proof. The rest of the templates shown in Figure 1 (Splitting, Transitivity, Intersection, Relation Addition, Subtraction, and Multiplication and Cancellation) cannot be used as transformation steps. However, transformations can be used to broaden the range of proof lines we can create using these templates. Take, for example, the Transitivity Rule:

I<=K BY ARITH, I<=J, J<=K

Figure 13 shows how we can use transformations to extend this template. The line at the bottom of the figure is an ordinary use of the template, substituting L, M+2, and N+1 for I, J, and K in the template. However, we can use transformations to turn L <= M-1 into L <= M+2, N > M to M+2 <= N+1, and L <= N+1 to L < N+2. Therefore, we can write

L < N+2 BY ARITH, L <= M-1, N > M;

in a proof. The hypotheses we write don't have to match exactly the hypotheses in the template; it is sufficient that the hypotheses that we write can be transformed to the hypotheses in the template. Likewise, the conclusion that we write doesn't have to match exactly the conclusion in the template; it is sufficient that the conclusion in the template can be transformed to the conclusion that we write. The exceptions to this rule are the Relation Multiplication rules and the Cancellation rules. In these rules, the last hypothesis written (K>=0, K<=0, K<0, or K>0) must match the template exactly.

When we are using the template for the Splitting Rule, we can use transformations on each part of the conclusion. For example, the proof line

K+2 <= 5 | K+2 > 5 BY ARITH;

is obtained by substituting directly into the template. But we also get the proof line

K+2 <= 5 | 5 <= K+1 BY ARITH;

by performing a transformation on K+2 > 5.

One more template should be added to the list of ARITH templates, the Rule of Arithmetic Contradiction. This rule is useful in conjunction with the ~ introduction and Contradiction rules.

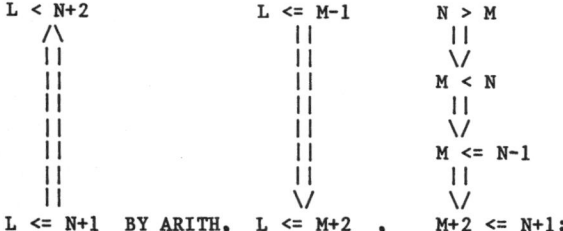

```
L < N+2                  L <= M-1       N > M
   /\                      ||            ||
   ||                      ||            \/
   ||                      ||            M < N
   ||                      ||            ||
   ||                      ||            \/
   ||                      ||            M <= N-1
   ||                      ||            ||
   ||                      \/            \/
L <= N+1   BY ARITH,   L <= M+2  ,    M+2 <= N+1;
```

Figure 13 Using Transformations to extend a template

The Rule of Arithmetic Contradiction
'0'B BY ARITH, I=J, (I~=J);
'0'B BY ARITH, I<J, J<I;

Like all the other ARITH templates, this one can be extended using
transformations. For example, the following is a valid extension of the
Rule of Arithmetic Contradiction:

'0'B BY K<2, K>5;

because K>5 can be transformed to 2<K.

It is very tedious and not very enlightening to work out the transformations for every ARITH proof line. It is much better to have, from experience and playing around with the transformation rules and the other ARITH
templates, a feeling for the kind of things that ARITH will and will not do
for you. In fact, you can bend the rules as presented somewhat, and still
come up with ARITH lines that the proof checker will accept. The following

I=2 | I=3 BY ARITH, 2<=I, I<=3;

is an example of such a line. If you submit an ARITH line to the the proof
checker, and it responds with "INVALID ARITHMETIC INFERENCE," it means that
you tried to do too much in one ARITH line, or that the line is just plain
wrong. After first convincing yourself that your conclusion does follow
from the hypotheses you have given to ARITH, the best course of action is
to try to break the one step into two (or more) that you know from your
experience will work.

Chains of Reasoning
Look at the following piece of a proof. (As usual, three dots indicate a
part of the proof that is missing.)

```
(J<5 | K=2) => ~(H>5) ...
   •
   •
   •
I>2 & H>5 => ~(J<5) BY INTRO,
PROOF;
1)   ASSUME I>2 & H>5;
     ~(J<5) BY INTRO,
     PROOF;
2)       ASSUME J<5;
3)       J<5 | K=2;        /# | introduction      #/
4)       ~(H>5);           /# => elimination      #/
5)       H>5;              /# & elimination       #/
6)       '0'B;             /# '0'B introduction #/
     QED;
QED;
```

In particular, look at the sequence of lines 1, 5, 6. They form a chain of
reasoning, in that each line uses the line before it as one of its
hypotheses. Similarly, the sequence 2, 3, 4, 6 is a chain. Recall that in
the ARITH rule, we only had to write down each end of a long transformation. In the same fashion, we can omit the middle of a long chain of reasoning, writing down only each end, as long as the chain uses only the fol-
lowing rules: & elimination, & introduction, | introduction, => elimina-
tion, <=> introduction, <=> elimination, '0'B introduction, and '0'B elimination. We will call these rules the "immediate" or "automatic" propositional rules. The proof above could be shortened to

```
(J<5 | K=2) => ~(H>5) ...
   •
   •
   •
I>2 & H>5 => ~(J<5) BY INTRO,
PROOF;
     ASSUME I>2 & H>5;
     ~(J<5) BY INTRO,
     PROOF;
         ASSUME J<5;
         '0'B;
     QED;
QED;
```

The Substitution, Transitive, and Reflexive Rules of Equality can also be
used to form chains of reasoning. For example, in the following:

```
X+X = X => X+X+X+X = X BY INTRO,
PROOF;
     ASSUME X+X = X;
     (X+X)+X = X;            /# substitute X+X for leftmost X in X+X=X #/
     ((X+X)+X)+X = X;        /# do it again #/
     (((X+X)+X)+X)+X = X;    /# once more #/
QED;
```

there is chain of reasoning using only the equality rules. As before, the intermediate steps of the chain can be omitted:

```
X+X = X => X+X+X+X = X BY INTRO,
PROOF;
    ASSUME X+X = X;
    (((X+X)+X)+X)+X = X;
QED;
```

There is a third kind of chain of reasoning that can be shortened. In this chain, each link is a transformation that is almost, but not quite like the transformations used in the ARITH rule. We will keep the two kinds of transformations straight by calling one an ARITH transformation and the other an AUTO transformation. With two exceptions, all the rules you can use in ARITH transformations can be used in AUTO transformations. The exceptions are that the Distributive Rule and the Weakening Transformations can not be used. Also, you can take advantage of the fact that the operators & and | are commutative and associative in AUTO transformations, and you may also use the following transformation:

```
I<=J <--> I+K<=I+K
```

for any FIXED expression K. For example, the following proof:

```
(X+2>0 & Y<10) => (10>Y & 2+X>0) BY INTRO,
PROOF;
    ASSUME X+2>0 & Y<10;
    2+X>0 & Y<10;          /# commutativity of + #/
    2+X>0 & 10>Y;          /# change < to >     #/
    10>Y & 2+X>0;          /# commutativity of & #/
QED;
```

can be shortened to

```
(X+2>0 & Y<10) => (10>Y & 2+X>0) BY INTRO,
PROOF;
    ASSUME X+2>0 & Y<10;
    10>Y & 2+X>0;
QED;
```

by removing the two AUTO tranformations

In summary, we have seen three kind of chains of reasoning: propositional, equality, and transformations. In the examples we have seen, each chain has only contained one kind of link. You are allowed to mix the different kinds of links, as long as you don't use a substitution and a transformation link in the same chain. The following:

```
I+J=K & J=5 => I+5=K BY INTRO,
PROOF;
    ASSUME I+J=K & J=5;
    I+J=K; /# & elimination #/
    J=5;   /# & elimination #/
    I+5=K; /# substitution #/
QED;
```

can be shortened to

```
I+J=K & J=5 => I+5=K BY INTRO,
PROOF;
    ASSUME I+J=K & J=5;
    I+5=K;
QED;
```

by taking out the middle of the chain, but the following:

```
I+J=K & J=0 => I=K BY INTRO,
PROOF;
    ASSUME I+J=K & J=0;
    I+J=K; /# & elimination  #/
    J=0;   /# & elimination  #/
    I+0=K; /# substitution   #/
    I=K;   /# transformation #/
QED;
```

contains a chain that has all three kinds of links. That chain cannot be shortened completely. You can shorten the part of the chain that uses only propositional and substitution links, but you must then write the transformation link on another line:

```
I+J=K & J=0 => I=K BY INTRO,
PROOF;
    ASSUME I+J=K & J=0;
    I+0=K;
    I=K;
QED;
```

in order to avoid mixing substitution and transformation in the same shortened chain.

The ability to shorten chains allows us to weaken one of the restrictions on accessibility. Recall that in "reaching back" for a hypothesis, one could not reach out of a scope that re-defined a variable free in that hypothesis. The reason for this restriction was that such an assertion had a different meaning outside the scope than inside. However, if it is the hypothesis to a step that is removed by shortening and does not appear explicitly inside the scope, then the step may be legal. Consider:

```
P => X < 2;
X < 2 => Q;
      •
      •
      •
  PROOF;
  ARBITRARY X FIXED;
      •
      •
      •
    P ...
    Q;    /# BY IMPLICATION ELIMINATION APPLIED TWICE #/
  QED;
```

The conclusion of Q is correct, even though the two outside assertions are not accessible because they contain free occurrences of X. The reason is that the parts of those assertions that mention the different X are not written inside, and so do not interact incorrectly with free X inside the scope.

To allow simple deductions like these in our proofs, we amend the accessibility rules slightly. By "re-naming" a logic variable, we mean changing its name in the ARBITRARY or CHOOSE line that introduced it, and similarly changing all occurrences of it within the scope of that line. The relaxed accessibility rule then is: a proof that reaches back for an assertion out of a scope that re-defines a free variable of that assertion is legal as long as the proof is still correct when the variable is re-named with a name not previously used in the proof. The above proof segment is correct, because the result of re-naming the inner occurrences of X is a correct proof. The following is incorrect:

```
X < 2 => Q;
      •
      •
      •
  PROOF;
  ARBITRARY X FIXED;
      •
      •
      •
    X < 2;
    Q;
  QED;
```

Here, if the inner X were changed to a Y, the "X < 2" inside would become "Y < 2", and the conclusion Q would not follow.

Abbreviations
In the preceding section, we saw how we could shorten chains of reasoning by not writing the intermediate steps, just the first and last steps of the chain. In some cases, we can leave out the ends of the chain as well. For example, we have seen that we are not required to write ASSUME lines, so that if the beginning of a chain of reasoning is an ASSUME, we don't have

to write it. Also, if the beginning of the chain is an instance of the
Reflexive Rule of Equality, or the Rule of Computation, we don't have to
write it.

If a chain ends in the hypothesis to a non-automatic rule, we don't have to
write the end of the chain. For example, in the proof:

```
J = J;  /# reflexive rule #/
~~(J = J); /# transformation #/
SOME K FIXED. ~~(K = J) BY INTRO, J;
```

the first two lines can be omitted. Likewise, if the last line of a chain
is the line that is supposed to appear at the end of a proof block, it can
be omitted. For example, in the following proof,

```
~(I=0 & ~(I=0)) BY INTRO,
PROOF;
    ASSUME I=0 & ~(I=0);
    I = 0;    /# & elimination      #/
    ~(I = 0); /# & elimination      #/
    '0'B;     /# '0'B introduction #/
QED;
```

the beginning, middle, and end of the chain can be omitted, leaving:

```
~(I=0 & ~(I=0)) BY INTRO, PROOF; QED;
```

Anytime a proof block can be abbreviated to just PROOF; QED, it can be left
out altogether as in:

```
~(I=0 & ~(I=0)) BY INTRO;
```

Therefore, we can abbreviate some of the examples from the last section
even more:

```
X+X = X => X+X+X+X = X BY INTRO;
(X+2>0 & Y<10) => (10>Y & 2+X>0) BY INTRO;
I+J=K & J=5 => I+5=K BY INTRO;
```

The same kind of abbreviation can be used in the the Rule of Contradiction,
and the ALL Introduction Rule, as shown in the following examples:

```
~~(I>0) => I>0 BY INTRO,
PROOF;
    ASSUME ~~(I>0);
    I>0 BY CONTRA;
QED;

ALL (X, Y) FIXED. (X+Y = Y+X) BY INTRO;
```

Note that because of these abbreviations, PL/CV is very sensitive to the
mark of punctuation that follows INTRO or CONTRA. If INTRO or CONTRA is
followed by a comma, then a proof block (or a daisy chain-- more about that

later) will be expected; but no proof block is expected when a semicolon is written.

A similar kind of abbreviation can be done when using the | elimination rule. If the proof of any one of the cases can be shortened down to nothing, then that case can be left out. For example:

```
J > I BY CASES, (J+1 > I+1) | (J > I+1),
PROOF;
CASE J+1 > I+1;
    J > I; /# by an AUTO transformation #/
CASE J > I+1;
    J > I BY ARITH, J > I+1;
QED;
```

can be shortened to

```
J > I BY CASES, (J+1 > I+1) | (J > I+1),
PROOF;
CASE J > I+1;
    J > I BY ARITH, J > I+1;
QED;
```

The first case can be proved just with AUTO transformation. However, the second case requires the use of the Weakening Rule that is not an AUTO transformation, so the ARITH rule must be used. If the shortening rule lets you leave out all of the cases, then you can leave out the PROOF and QED as well, as in:

```
J > I BY CASES, (J+1 > I+1) | (J-1 > I-1);
```

Extended ALL Elimination and FUNCTION Rules

The automatic rules give us some leeway in the way ALL elimination and the FUNCTION rules can be applied. The template for ALL elimination is:

```
P{J//I} BY ALLEL, ALL I type. P, J;
```

However, we will often wish to conclude some other formula Q, where Q can be derived from P{J//I} using just automatic rules. We might imagine a template that looks like:

```
?   Q BY ALLEL, ALL I type. P, J,
?   PROOF;
?       [ASSUME P{J//I};]
?       Q;
?   QED;
```

where Q can be proved from P{J//I} using a chain of reasoning that can be shortened down to nothing. The question marks are a reminder that this is an _imaginary_ template; if you try to use it you will get an error message. It is what should be going on in your head when you write:

```
Q BY ALLEL, ALL I type. P, J;
```

which is correct. Here are some examples of the use of extended ALL elimination:

    (J+1)*(J+1) >= 0 BY ALLEL, ALL K FIXED. (K*K >= 0 & -K*K <= 0), J+1;
    J+7 > J+6 BY ALLEL, ALL K FIXED. K+1 > K, J+6;

The same tricks can be played with the FUNCTION rule. For example, you can write:

    ABS(5) = 5 BY FUNCTION, ABS(5);

which is considered an abbreviation for the imaginary proof:

    ? ABS(5) = 5 BY FUNCTION, ABS(5),
    ? PROOF;
    ?   ASSUME 5>=0 => ABS(5) = 5;   /# what the FUNCTION rule gives you #/
    ?   5 >= 0;   /# by the Rule of Computation #/
    ?   ABS(5) = 5;   /# by => elimination #/
    ? QED;

which would get an error message if you tried to write it. Note that you could not write

    MOD(9, 3) = 0 BY FUNCTION, MOD(9, 3);

because the automatic rules would not let you conclude MOD(9, 3)=0 from either of the templates for MOD. This conclusion requires an ALL elimination, which is not done automatically.

Daisy chaining

In the preceding section, we saw that if our shortening rules let us leave out the proof that goes inside a proof block, then we can leave out the proof block. Sometimes, even though the rules won't let us leave out the proof entirely, we can write the proof using just one non-automatic rule. In that case, we can still abbreviate our proof. For example, if we wrote a proof that looked like:

    P => Q BY INTRO,
    PROOF;
        ASSUME P;
        Q BY <some justification>;
    QED;

we could abbreviate it by writing:

    P => Q BY INTRO, <some justification>;

instead. As an example, we could abbreviate the proof:

```
I<J => I<J+1 BY INTRO,
PROOF;
    ASSUME I<J;
    I < J+1 BY ARITH, I<J;
QED;
```

by writing

```
I<J => I<J+1 BY INTRO, ARITH, I<J;
```

instead. This abbreviation can be also be used with the ~ Introduction and ALL introduction rules. For example, we can write:

```
~(I<J & J>I) BY INTRO, ARITH, I<J, J>I;
```

as an abbreviation for:

```
~(I<J & J>I) BY INTRO,
PROOF;
    ASSUME I<J & J>I;
    '0'B BY ARITH, I<J, J>I;
QED;
```

and:

```
ALL (X, Y) FIXED. (X <= Y | Y > X) BY INTRO, ARITH;
```

as an abbreviation for:

```
ALL (X, Y) FIXED. (X <= Y | Y > X) BY INTRO,
PROOF;
    ARBITRARY (X, Y) FIXED;
    X <= Y | Y > X BY ARITH;
QED;
```

The part of the proof represented in the template as <some justification> can contain a proof block. Here is an example of an often-used abbreviation. Instead of writing

```
ALL (X, Y, M) FIXED . (X < Y => X+M < Y+M) BY INTRO,
PROOF;
    ARB (X, Y, M) FIXED;
    X < Y => X+M < Y+M BY INTRO,
    PROOF;
        ASSUME X < Y;
        X+M < Y+M BY ARITH, X < Y, +, M=M;
    QED;
QED;
```

we can write

```
ALL (X, Y, M) FIXED . (X < Y => X+M < Y+M) BY INTRO, INTRO,
PROOF;
    ASSUME X < Y;
    X+M < Y+M BY ARITH, X < Y, +, M=M;
QED;
```

or, we can abbreviate still further by writing

```
ALL (X, Y, M) FIXED . (X < Y => X+M < Y+M) BY
    INTRO, INTRO, ARITH, X < Y, +, M=M;
```

We call this collapsing together of rules "daisy chaining" because of the way that one rule hooks into the next like a chain of daisies. The Rule of Contradiction can also be used to build daisy chains, as in:

```
ALL (I, J) FIXED. (~~(I>J) => I+1>J+1))
    BY INTRO, INTRO, CONTRA, ARITH, ~~(I>J), ~(I+1>J+1);
```

which is an abbreviation for:

```
ALL (I, J) FIXED. (~~(I>J) => I+1>J+1)) BY INTRO, INTRO,
PROOF;
    ASSUME ~~(I>J);
    I+1 > J+1 BY CONTRA,
    PROOF;
        ASSUME ~(I+1 > J+1);
        '0'B BY ARITH, ~~(I>J), ~(I+1 > J+1);
    QED;
QED;
```

However, we will generally try to avoid the use of the CONTRA rule. A more reasonable proof of this formula would be:

```
ALL (I, J) FIXED. (~~(I>J) => I+1>J+1)) BY INTRO, INTRO, ARITH, ~~(I>J);
```

because ~~(I>J) is treated as I>J by the ARITH rule.

Daisy chains can be built using the CASES rule as well. If a CASES proof could be written

```
P BY CASES, Q|R,
PROOF;
CASE Q;
P BY <some justification>;
CASE R;
•
•
•
```

then the proof could be abbreviated as

```
P BY CASES, Q|R
PROOF;
CASE Q BY <some justification>;
CASE R;
    .
    .
    .
```

An example of this kind of thing is:

```
ALL X FIXED. X*X>=0 BY INTRO,
PROOF;
    X<=0 | X>=0 BY ARITH;
    X*X >= 0 BY CASES, X<=0 | X>=0,
    PROOF;
        CASE X<=0 BY ARITH, X<=0, *, X<=0;
        CASE X>=0 BY ARITH, X>=0, *, X>=0;
    QED;
QED;
```

Keeping Perspective

Remember, just because all these abbreviations and short cuts exist doesn't mean you have to use them. When writing proofs, you need not write the shortest possible proof using every trick there is to minimize the number of lines. The purpose of the short cuts and abbreviations is to relieve some of the tedium associated with writing out proofs. If a particular abbreviation is more confusing to you than it is helpful, don't use it. As you get more experience with writing proofs, the abbreviations should begin to feel more and more natural.

Writing Proofs

When writing a proof in PL/CV it is important not to let your thoughts become oriented too quickly to the actual text that must be written. Even moderately complex proofs simply contain too much detail to remember if you proceed sequentially. The way to manage such proofs is to think in terms of higher level concepts and refine those concepts into simpler steps, ultimately reaching the level of PL/CV statements.

PL/CV provides mechanisms which facilitate this process by allowing the user to organize proofs into meaningful pieces at a high level of detail. One feature that we have already seen is the ability to label assertions. A variable name followed by a colon (:) may precede a proof line, or the assertion of a CASE or ASSUME line, or the assertion following the WHERE in an ARBITRARY or CHOOSE line. This label may then be used in the proof in place of its assertion. By selecting mnemonic names, one can provide a high-level outline of the proof that allows much potentially uninteresting detail to be ignored.

The other feature that aids in organizing proofs is the DEFINE statement. A definition line contains the following:

the word FOR
a sequence of (at least one) <variable-list, type> pairs, where
    variable-list is one or more variable names separated by commas,
    and type is either FIXED or BIT
the word DEFINE
a variable, followed by a variable-list in parentheses
an equals sign (=)
an assertion

Examples:

    FOR X FIXED DEFINE SPLIT(X) = ALL Y FIXED.(X<=Y | X>Y);
    FOR P BIT (Q,R) FIXED DEFINE FOO(Q,R,P) = P => Q<R;
    FOR Y FIXED DEFINE GREATER_THAN_X(Y) = Y > X;

The meaning of a definition is that at any point from which the DEFINE is
accessible, the defined identifier (with an argument list) may be used in
place of an assertion. The assertion it represents is that of the defining
statement, with the variables of the variable-list replaced by the
corresponding arguments (which must be of the correct type). For example,
SPLIT(SUM) would be the same as

    ALL Y FIXED.(SUM<=Y | SUM>Y).

As the last example illustrates, free variables may occur in definitions
(or in labelled assertions). This is correct as long as those variables
are bound in an ARBITRARY or CHOOSE line accessible from the point of
definition. The free variables in the expansion are bound by these lines
whenever the label or definition is used even if the variable name has been
re-used inside some proof block. For example:

        PROOF;
        ARB X FIXED WHERE X < Y;
        FOR B FIXED DEFINE GREATER_THAN_X(B) = B > X;
            •
            •
            •

            PROOF;
            ARB X FIXED WHERE X > Y;
                •
                •
                •

            GREATER_THAN_X(Y);
                •
                •
                •

            QED;
            •
            •
            •
        QED;

The assertion GREATER_THAN_X(Y) is true, even though Y is less than X at that point, because the free X referred to in the definition is that of the outermost ARB line. Care must be taken when using definitions or labels for assertions that contain free variables, to make sure that the meaning is what one intended. Note that cases like this can always be avoided by renaming variables in the inner blocks.

The use of these facilities in developing a proof will be illustrated with an example from number theory. Suppose we wanted to prove the assertion that the greatest common divisor of two numbers A and B is equal to the greatest common divisor of one (B, say) and MOD(A,B). (Note B must be non-zero for this theorem to have meaning.) The first step is to decide how we are to express this. We will see later how to write programs to compute functions in PL/CV, and how we prove assertions regarding those functions. If we want to avoid writing a program, however, the usual technique is to write a definition of an assertion which expresses the property of the function we are interested in. Here for instance, we want a definition GCD_DEF(X,Y,Z) which says that Z is the greatest common divisor of X and Y.

By the gcd of X and Y we mean a number that divides both X and Y, and which is greater than or equal to any number that divides them both. We can write a definition of gcd directly in these terms, which we will later refine.

        FOR (X,Y,Z) FIXED DEFINE GCD_DEF(X,Y,Z) = DIV(Z,X) & DIV(Z,Y) &
                                                    BIG_ENOUGH(X,Y,Z)

By DIV(A,B), we mean that B is an even multiple of A. So:

        FOR (D,N) FIXED DEFINE DIV(D,N) = SOME Q FIXED. D*Q=N

The idea of Z being "big enough" translates pretty directly into PL/CV, given our definition of divisiblity:

        FOR (X,Y,Z) DEFINE BIG_ENOUGH(X,Y,Z) =
                    ALL W FIXED WHERE DIV(W,X) & DIV(W,Y). W<=Z

Since we are using an assertion to define gcd, the equality we want to prove will actually be an equivalence between the corresponding assertions:

        ALL (A,B,C) FIXED WHERE ~(B=0). GCD_DEF(A,B,C) <=> GCD_DEF(B,MOD(A,B),C)

How do we know that this assertion is true? Since we are basically proving an equivalence, we have to show that the implication in both directions holds. Informally, the proof is structured as follows:

        PROOF;
        ARBITRARY (A,B,C) FIXED WHERE ~(B=0);
        "Let Q be the quotient such that A = B*Q + MOD(A,B)."
            ONLY_IF_PART: GCD_DEF(A,B,C) => GCD_DEF(B,MOD(A,B),C) BY INTRO,
              PROOF;
              ASSUME GCD_DEF(A,B,C);
              "C divides A and B, so it certainly divides B. It also divides
              A - B*Q which is just MOD(A,B), so it is a common divisor of B

and MOD(A,B). To show that C is "big enough" let W be any common
divisor of B and MOD(A,B). W then divides B and B*Q + MOD(A,B)
which is just A, so it is a common divisor of A and B as well.
But C is the greatest common divisor of A and B, so C is >= W."
QED;

   IF_PART: GCD_DEF(B,MOD(A,B),C) => GCD_DEF(A,B,C) BY INTRO,
    PROOF;
    ASSUME GCD_DEF(B,MOD(A,B),C);
    "C divides B and MOD(A,B) so it certainly divides B. It also
    divides B*Q + MOD(A,B) which is just A, so it is a common divisor
    of A and B. To show that C is "big enough" let W be any common
    divisor of A and B. W then divides B and A - B*Q which is just
    MOD(A,B), so W is also a common divisor of B and MOD(A,B). But
    C is the greatest common divisor of B and MOD(A,B), so C >= W.
    QED:
QED;

After inspecting this sketch, we see that going from divisibility of A and
B to that of MOD(A,B), and from that of B and MOD(A,B) to A is the justification for most of the steps in the proof. If we could prove these in a
general form at the beginning of the proof, then the content of our ONLY_IF
and IF parts would be simply propositional structure and application of
already defined concepts. Confident that we can prove them later, we
assert the propositions we want and use them to further refine our proof:

   ALL (A,B,C) FIXED WHERE ~(B=0).
             GCD_DEF(A,B,C) <=> GCD_DEF(B,MOD(A,B),C) BY INTRO,
    PROOF;
    ARB (A,B,C) WHERE ~(B=0);
    "Let Q be the quotient such that A = B*Q + MOD(A,B)"
    DIVIDES_A_AND_B: ALL F FIXED WHERE DIV(F,A) & DIV(F,B).
                    DIV(F,MOD(A,B)) ...

    DIVIDES_B_AND_MOD: ALL F FIXED WHERE DIV(F,B) & DIV(F,MOD(A,B)).
                    DIV(F,A) ...

    ONLY_IF_PART: GCD_DEF(A,B,C) => GCD_DEF(B,MOD(A,B),C) BY INTRO,
     PROOF;
     ASSUME GCD_DEF(A,B,C);
     DIV(C,MOD(A,B)) BY ALLEL, DIVIDES_A_AND_B, C;
     BIG_ENOUGH(B,MOD(A,B),C) BY INTRO,
      PROOF;
      ARBITRARY W FIXED WHERE DIV(W,B) & DIV(W,MOD(A,B));
      DIV(W,A) BY ALLEL, DIVIDES_B_AND_MOD, W;
      W <= C BY ALLEL, BIG_ENOUGH(A,B,C), W;
      QED;
     QED;

    IF_PART: GCD_DEF(B,MOD(A,B),C) => GCD_DEF(A,B,C) BY INTRO,
     PROOF;
     ASSUME GCD_DEF(B,MOD(A,B),C);
     DIV(C,A) BY ALLEL, DIVIDES_B_AND_MOD, C;

```
            BIG_ENOUGH(A,B,C) BY INTRO,
              PROOF;
               ARBITRARY W FIXED WHERE DIV(W,A) & DIV(W,B);
               DIV(W,MOD(A,B)) BY ALLEL, DIVIDES_A_AND_B, W;
               W <= C BY ALLEL, BIG_ENOUGH(B,MOD(A,B),C), W;
              QED;
            QED;
          QED;
```

The remaining proofs turn out to be straightforward (with a little arithmetic done on the equation defining Q beforehand). We should also do a
quick check that our labelled assertions involving free variables are used
properly. (They are, since we have no block that redefines A or B.) Note
that much expressiveness comes from the ability to use nested labels and
definitions, building up complex assertions that can be referenced by a
single name. To appreciate the usefulness of these features, consider what
this final result would be like if every definition and label were fully
expanded. (And imagine attempting to derive the proof!):

```
/*/
 FOR (D,N) FIXED DEFINE DIV(D,N) = SOME Q FIXED. D*Q = N;
 FOR (X,Y,Z) FIXED DEFINE BIG_ENOUGH(X,Y,Z) =
                   ALL W FIXED WHERE DIV(W,X) & DIV(W,Y). W <= Z;
 FOR (X,Y,Z) FIXED DEFINE GCD_DEF(X,Y,Z) = DIV(Z,X) & DIV(Z,Y) &
                                           BIG_ENOUGH(X,Y,Z);
 ALL (A,B,C) FIXED WHERE ^(B=0).
                    (GCD_DEF(A,B,C) <=> GCD_DEF(B,MOD(A,B),C)) BY INTRO,
     PROOF;
      ARB (A,B,C) FIXED WHERE ^(B=0);
       SOME Q FIXED. A = B*Q + MOD(A,B) BY FUNCTION, MOD(A,B);
       CHOOSE Q FIXED WHERE A = B*Q + MOD(A,B);
       A - B*Q = MOD(A,B) BY ARITH, A = B*Q + MOD(A,B), -, B*Q = B*Q;


      DIVIDES_A_AND_B: ALL F FIXED WHERE DIV(F,A) & DIV(F,B).
                                   DIV(F,MOD(A,B)) BY INTRO,
         PROOF;
          ARB F FIXED WHERE DIV(F,A) & DIV(F,B);
          CHOOSE Q1 FIXED WHERE F*Q1 = B;
          F*Q1*Q = B*Q;
          CHOOSE Q2 FIXED WHERE F*Q2 = A;
          F*(Q2 - Q1*Q) = A - B*Q BY ARITH, F*Q2 = A, -, F*(Q1*Q) = B*Q;
          DIV(F,MOD(A,B)) BY INTRO, Q2 - Q1*Q;
         QED;


      DIVIDES_B_AND_MOD: ALL F FIXED WHERE DIV(F,B) & DIV(F,MOD(A,B)).
                                   DIV(F,A) BY INTRO,
         PROOF;
          ARB F FIXED WHERE DIV(F,B) & DIV(F,MOD(A,B));
          CHOOSE Q1 FIXED WHERE F*Q1 = B;
          F*Q1*Q = B*Q;
          CHOOSE Q2 FIXED WHERE F*Q2 = MOD(A,B);
```

```
        F*(Q1*Q + Q2) = B*Q + MOD(A,B) BY ARITH, F*Q1*Q = B*Q, +,
                                                F*Q2 = MOD(A,B);
      DIV(F,A) BY INTRO, Q1*Q + Q2;
      QED;


  ONLY_IF_PART: GCD_DEF(A,B,C) => GCD_DEF(B,MOD(A,B),C) BY INTRO,
      PROOF;
       ASSUME GCD_DEF(A,B,C);
       DIV(C,MOD(A,B)) BY ALLEL, DIVIDES_A_AND_B, C;
       BIG_ENOUGH(B,MOD(A,B),C) BY INTRO,
         PROOF;
         ARBITRARY W FIXED WHERE DIV(W,B) & DIV(W,MOD(A,B));
         DIV(W,A) BY ALLEL, DIVIDES_B_AND_MOD, W;
         W <= C BY ALLEL, BIG_ENOUGH(A,B,C), W;
         QED;
      QED;


  IF_PART: GCD_DEF(B,MOD(A,B),C) => GCD_DEF(A,B,C) BY INTRO,
      PROOF;
       ASSUME GCD_DEF(B,MOD(A,B),C);
       DIV(C,A) BY ALLEL, DIVIDES_B_AND_MOD, C;
       BIG_ENOUGH(A,B,C) BY INTRO,
         PROOF;
          ARBITRARY W FIXED WHERE DIV(W,A) & DIV(W,B);
          DIV(W,MOD(A,B)) BY ALLEL, DIVIDES_A_AND_B, W;
          W <= C BY ALLEL, BIG_ENOUGH(B,MOD(A,B),C), W;
         QED;
      QED;
  QED;      */
```

IV PROOF RULES

4.1 Substitutions

Substitutions of expressions for variables in assertions and arguments is critical to the description of rules for writing correct arguments. Variables play essentially two different roles in assertions and arguments. In ALL X FIXED . X**2 >= 0 the variable X is simply part of the quantifier serving to relate that quantifier to the assertion on which it operates. In this role it is similar to x in $\int_0^1 x^2 \, dx$.

Such variable occurrences are <u>bound</u>. In the assertion X**3+27=0 the variable X purports to name an integer with a certain property. It should make sense to SUBSTITUTE for this X other names for integers. Such variable occurrences are <u>free</u>.

<u>Definition</u>: If P is an assertion, then P{exp//x} is the assertion obtained by replacing every free occurrence of x in P by the expression exp. $P\{exp_1//x_1,\ldots,exp_n//x_n\}$ is the result of simultaneously substituting exp_i for every free occurrence of x_i. This operation should not be confused with making the substitutions consecutively, which would be represented by $P\{exp_1//x_1\}\{exp_2//x_2\}\ldots\{exp_n//x_n\}$.

> Example:
> Let P be X>Y. Then P{X+Y//X, X+1//Y} is X+Y>X+1 and
> P{X+Y//X}{X+1//Y} is X+Y>Y{X+1//Y}, which is X+(X+1)>X+1.

The intuitive meaning of substitution is that P{exp//x} says about exp the same thing that P said about x. But this intuition can fail because of the dual use of variables as names and as place markers. For example, if we let P(X) be
> SOME Y FIXED . Y>X,

then P(X) is saying there is some integer larger than X, which should be true for all X. If we substitute Y for X we have the absurdity:
> SOME Y FIXED . Y>Y.

The problem is that the expression Y changes meaning when it is substituted. We say that Y has been <u>captured</u> by the quantifier SOME Y FIXED. Therefore, we put the following restrictions on substitution that prevents capture.

<u>Definition</u>: Expression exp is <u>free for x in P</u> if and only if no free occurrence of a variable in exp becomes bound in P{exp//x}.

<u>Hereafter we assume that an expression is free for the variable for which it is being substituted.</u> We can arrange to have any expression free in P if we first rename any binding occurrences of variables that also occur in the expression. We will always be explicit about such

renaming.

4.2 Macro substitutions

Labels from labelled assertions and definitions which are introduced by define statements are treated as programming language macros.
That is, their subsequent appearances in the proof are replaced syntactically by the assertions they represent. Free variables in these
assertions are bound at the point of definition (labelling), not at the
point of substitution. For instance:

```
/*/  ALL (X,Y) FIXED WHERE X < Y. '1'B BY INTRO,
        PROOF;
        ARB (X,Y) FIXED WHERE L: X < Y;
        FOR B FIXED DEFINE GREATER_THAN_X(B) = B > X;
        ALL X FIXED WHERE X > Y. '1'B BY INTRO,
         PROOF;
          ARB X FIXED WHERE X > Y;
          L;
          GREATER_THAN_X(X) BY ARITH, X > Y, L;
         QED;
        QED;     */
```

Both assertions in the inner proof block are true, because the free X in
"L" and "GREATER_THAN_X" is that of the outermost proof block, for which
X < Y. Note that labels and definitions are always accessible through
any ARBITRARY or CHOOSE scope even if their assertions are not because
of re-using of free variables.

Parameters to definitions are replaced by the arguments at the
point of substitution. They are implicitly parenthesized to avoid any
confusion due to precedence of operators that might arise in a strict
textual substitution. In addition, bound variables that might conflict
with (i.e. capture) variables in the arguments are implicitly renamed.
For example, given the definition:

```
FOR X FIXED DEFINE SPLIT(X) = ALL Y FIXED. (X<Y | X>=Y);
```

the assertion SPLIT(Y) is treated as if it were:

```
ALL Y1 FIXED.(Y<Y1 | Y>=Y1)
```

The user therefore has no need to worry that his arguments to a definition might be captured. There is a problem however, in trying to prove
such an occurrence of a definition by ALL introduction. Any "Y" that
appears in the proof block will be bound by the (possibly implicit)
ARBITRARY Y FIXED line that begins it. There will therefore be no way
to explicitly mention the argument to SPLIT in the proof block. This is
the only case where the user might have to change a variable name to use
a definition. Alternatively, the equivalent assertion:

```
ALL Z FIXED. (Y<Z | Y>=Z)
```

may be proven, and SPLIT(Y) asserted afterward.

4.3 Format of rules

An argument is essentially a sequence of assertions which compels
rational agreement to its conclusion. This agreement is based on prior
acceptance of certain rules for using assertions. These rules describe
how to add new assertions to an argument provided certain assertions are
already present. In PL/CV these rules can be classified into two types,
INTRODUCTION and ELIMINATION, depending on whether the new assertion is
formed by introducing a logical symbol to connect assertions or by elim-
inating a logical symbol to disconnect parts of an existing assertion.**

The format for presenting the predicate calculus rules is to show
how new assertions can be brought into an argument on the basis of
assertions already present in the argument. The presentation of most
rules obeys the following scheme:

$$\frac{A_1, A_2, \ldots, A_n}{C \text{ BY justification}}$$

which is an abbreviation for: If $A_1, A_2, \ldots, A_n$, called the hypotheses,
are assertions that are accessible from the point in the argument where
we wish to write assertion C (or are immediate from accessible assertions), then C may be added to the argument by writing C BY justification. The justification identifies the rule being applied, making it
easier to confirm the correctness of the proof mechanically. The exact
form of a justification is specified with each rule that requires one.
If a rule requires no explicit justification, the format is

$$\frac{A_1, \ldots, A_n}{C}$$

Some rules require as hypotheses an entire subargument in the form
of a proof group. This proof group is included in the justification so
that the rule has the form
C BY justification

and the justification contains PROOF;...;QED. In conventional natural
deduction systems this type of rule is called a deduction rule and is
written with the proof-group as a hypothesis,

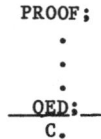

Some steps of reasoning in an argument, such as the introduction of
X>0 & Y>=0 from X>0 and Y>=0, are so obvious that they can be performed
automatically without writing anything down in the argument.

** Logical systems organized in this way are called natural
deduction systems. The PL/CV logic is modeled after the system of
Dag Prawitz, [18].

Conclusions drawn by such steps are _immediate_. However, in crder to describe these steps, we must know exactly what rules are being applied automatically. Therefore, in the list of rules given below there will occur some for which no justification is provided. In place of a syntactic form for justification, the phrase _immediate_ appears. The manner in which these immediate rules are applied is described in the definition of proof.

4.4 Enumeration of rules

INTRODUCTION	ELIMINATION
AND (immediate)	AND (immediate)

$$\frac{A_1,\ldots,A_n}{A_1 \& \cdots \& A_n} \qquad \frac{A_1 \& A_2 \& \cdots \& A_n}{A_i}$$

OR (immediate)   OR

$$\frac{A_i}{A_1 | \cdots | A_i | \cdots | A_n}$$

Q BY CASES, $A_1 | \cdots | A_n$,

```
PROOF;
   CASE A₁;
      argument
      Q;
      .
      .
      .
   CASE Aₙ;
      argument
      Q;
   QED;
```

IMPLICATION   IMPLICATION (immediate)

$$\frac{A => B, A}{B}$$

```
A => B BY INTRO,
   PROOF;
   [ASSUME A;]
      .
      .
      .
   B;
   QED;
```

Note, it is allowable but not necessary to write ASSUME A, so the statement is bracketed.

INTRODUCTION	ELIMINATION

EQUIVALENCE (immediate)

$$\frac{A \Rightarrow B, \; B \Rightarrow A}{A \Leftrightarrow B}$$

EQUIVALENCE (immediate)

$$\frac{A \Leftrightarrow B}{A \Rightarrow B} \qquad \frac{A \Leftrightarrow B}{B \Rightarrow A}$$

NOT

```
~A BY INTRO,
   PROOF;
   [ASSUME A;]
      .
      .
      .
   '0'B;
   QED;
```

NOT (immediate)

$$\frac{A, \; \sim A}{'0'B}$$

FALSE (immediate)

$$\frac{A, \; \sim A}{'0'B}$$

FALSE (immediate)

$$\frac{'0'B}{A}$$

ALL

```
ALL(x1,....,xn) type

[WHERE Q].P BY INTRO,
   PROOF;
[ARB x1,....,xn type

   [WHERE Q];]
      .
      .
      .
   P;
   QED;
```

ALL

$$[Q\{exp_1//x_1,....,exp_n//x_n\}],$$

$$ALL(x,....,x_n) \text{ type}$$

$$\frac{[WHERE\ Q].P}{P\{exp_1//x_1,....,exp_n//x_n\}}$$

BY ALLEL, ALL(x_1,....,x_n) type [WHERE Q].P,exp_1,....,exp_n;

In fact, the conclusion may be any that follows from P and accessible assertions by immediate rules.

SOME

$$[Q\{exp_1//x_1,....,exp_n//x_n\}],$$

$$\frac{P\{exp_1//x_1,....,exp_n//x_n\}}{SOME(x_1,....,x_n)\ [WHERE\ Q]\ type.P}$$

BY INTRO, exp_1,....,exp_n

SOME

$$\frac{SOME(x_1,....,x_n)\ type\ [WHERE\ Q].P}{CHOOSE(y_1,....,y_n)\ type}$$

WHERE P$\{y_1//x_1,....,y_n//x_n\}$

[& Q$\{y_1//x_1,....,y_n//x_n\}$]

Provided the y_i are new for the smallest block containing the choose statement.

> Both ALL and SOME may have more than one variable list,
> not necessarily of the same type, separated by commas.

The above rules are called **constructive**. The final rule is not and
is not permitted in constructive proofs.

                CLASSICAL CONTRADICTION RULE
                      A BY CONTRA,
                        PROOF;
                        [ASSUME ~A;]
                            .
                            .
                            .
                          '0'B
                        QED;

4.5 Immediate rules

The rules marked immediate in the above table are called **immediate
rules of inference**. (The introduction rules: AND, OR, EQUIVALENCE and
FALSE, the elimination rules: AND, IMPLICATION, EQUIVALENCE, FALSE.)
In addition the following special cases of implication introduction are
immediate.[+]

$$\frac{~A}{A \Rightarrow B} \qquad \frac{B}{A \Rightarrow B} \qquad \frac{A}{~A \Rightarrow B}$$

Given a set of assertions S, we say assertion B is **immediate from S**
if and only if

(1) B is in S or

(2) $A_1, \ldots, A_n$ are immediate from S and B follows from them by an
     immediate rule of inference.

4.6 Accessibility

In an argument without proof-groups, an assertion may be inferred
if it follows from lexically previous lines of the proof by a rule of
inference. However, in arguments with block structure the availability
of previous assertions as hypotheses depends on their relative positions. For example, consider:

[+] In classical logic, where A => B is equivalent to ~A|B, these
are instances of OR introduction, which is immediate.

```
((A => B) & A|B) => B BY INTRO,
PROOF;
    ASSUME (A => B) & A|B;
    B BY CASES, A|B;
    PROOF;
      CASE A;
       B;
       QED;
QED;
```

At this point, although B is a previous line in the argument, we cannot assert B because it occurs inside a proof block.

A similar "scope problem" arises with qualifiers. For example, the following argument is fallacious (where P(X) and Q(X) represent assertions containing free X).

```
(P(X) => Q(X)) => ALL X FIXED WHERE P(X).Q(X) BY INTRO,
PROOF;
ASSUME P(X) => Q(X);
ALL X FIXED WHERE P(X).Q(X) BY INTRO,
    PROOF; ARBITRARY X FIXED WHERE P(X);
    Q(X) /# by implication elimination #/
      QED;
QED;
```

The innermost conclusion of Q(X) by implication elimination is wrong, since X has a different meaning inside the proof block than outside. Consider that an assertion like X>2 might be known for the outside X, but does not hold inside.

To eliminate these scope errors, we must say precisely when an assertion at one point p in a proof is accessible from another point q.

Definition: A predicate calculus **proof block** is a proof group. (In part VI a proof block achieves a more general status.)

Definition: An occurrence of an assertion A at position p with variables $x_1, \ldots, x_n$ free in A is **accessible** from a position q in a Predicate Calculus argument if and only if

(0) q does not occur in the justification of this occurrence of A, and

(1) A at p occurs lexically before q, and

(2) any proof block containing p also contains q, and

(3) Either A is the same at p and q, that is the variables x_i have the same scope at p and q (thus if q is in the scope of any binding occurrence of an x_i, then so is p), or else A is used as a hypothesis to an immediate rule at q in such a way that the step would still be correct if all binding occurrences of

any x_i that contain q and not p were systematically changed to variable names not used in the original proof. (See p.42)

Definition: A proof is an argument in which every assertion is either an assumption or follows from accessible lines, immediate assertions and proof groups by a rule of inference.

Note: We can simplify the definitions of proof and accessibility somewhat if we think of writing the justification lexically before the line being justified. Then we do not need line (0) of accessibility, and it is easier to think of a proof in linear order (no assertion is justified by lines occurring lexically beyond it).

4.7 Undefined and well-defined expressions

The PL/CV2 Proof Checker is based on a semantics which assigns meaning to assertions containing undefined expressions. For example,

/*/ EX: ALL (A,B) FIXED. MOD(A,B) = MOD(A,B) ...
.
.
.
MOD(5,0) = MOD(5,0) BY ALLEL, EX, 5, 0; */

is a valid argument even though MOD(5,0) is an undefined expression. The details of this semantics are discussed in **A Programming Logic**.

An alternative semantics for assertions containing undefined expressions is discussed in **A Programming Logic**. It may appear more natural, so we mention it for the user who wants his arguments to remain consistent with the alternative semantics.

An expression, exp, is said to be well-defined if and only if all functions are applied only to elements of their domains. (After part V, we must also insist that all array indices are in the domain of the array.) An assertion involving expressions is valid only if all expressions are well-defined and the assertion is true for their values. This approach introduces the anomaly that MOD(5,0) = MOD(5,0) can be false and MOD(5,0) ~= MOD(5,0) can be false as well (as they are in the EX example). (Note ~(MOD(5,0) = MOD(5,0)) and ~(MOD(5,0) ~= MOD(5,0)) are both true.)

To conform to this semantics, one must change the all elimination rule to:

ALL ELIMINATION

$$[Q\{exp_1//x_1,....,exp_n//x_n\}]$$

$ALL(x_1,....,x_n)$ type [WHERE Q].P

$\{exp_i$ are well-defined$\}$

$P\{exp_1//x_1,....,exp_n//x_n\}$ BY ALLEL, $ALL(x_1,....,x_n)$ type [WHERE Q].P;

As new rules are introduced, we will discuss any changes needed to make them conform to the alternative semantics.

4.8 Equality

Until rules are provided for the relational operators, =, ~=, <, <=, etc., we can deduce only facts about them which would be true of any binary relator. Thus we can prove ALL X FIXED . X=X => 0=0 but not ALL X FIXED . X=X. Since equality is such a primitive concept, regardless of the type of the objects, rules for the equality relator, =, are usually given as part of the underlying logic. Thus, we treat equality here rather than in part 4.11

The specific equality rules are:

REFLEXIVITY	TRANSITIVITY
$exp = exp$	$\dfrac{exp_1 = exp_2,\ exp_2 = exp_3}{exp_1 = exp_3}$

SYMMETRY	SUBSTITUTION
$\dfrac{exp_1 = exp_2}{exp_2 = exp_1}$	$\dfrac{t_1 = t_2}{A\{t_2/x\}}$

In the substitution template we extend the notion of substitution slightly. $A\{t_2/t_1\}$ represents any assertion that can be obtained from A by substituting t_2 for some occurrences of t_1. (Note that it is not uniquely defined.) The instances of t_1 substituted for may not contain any bound variables, nor may any variables of t_2 become bound after the substitution (for reasons given in 4.1). This may be expressed in the previous notation by requiring $A'\{t_1//x\}$ as a hypothesis to the rule, and allowing $A'\{t_2//x\}$ as the conclusion. Here A' is the same as A with certain occurrences of t_1 replaced by some new (free) variable x. The conclusion is therefore A with those t_1's replaced by t_2's, and the rules from 4.1 restricting t_1 and t_2 to be free for x in A insure that the meaning of $A\{t_1//x\}$ is the same as $A\{t_2//x\}$.

The equality relation on boolean expressions is equivalent to <=>, i.e., $bexp_1$ = $bexp_2$ iff $bexp_1$ <=> $bexp_2$. Thus, the equality axioms provide a more powerful treatment of <=>. This treatment extends to arbitrary assertions in place of expressions on either side of an <=>, for which all the above rules hold. In addition, there is the following rule for assertions:

> RE-NAMING OF BOUND VARIABLES
> ALL I type.P <=> ALL J type.P{J//I}
> SOME I type.P <=> SOME J type.P{J//I}

Ideally the equality rules would all be immediate. Unfortunately, it is not decideable whether an assertion follows from a given set of assertions by the rules for equality and the other immediate rules. In some cases where the unwritten derivation uses both a substitution and an AUTO transformation (see pp. 40-41). PL/CV will report an incomplete proof. Supplying either one of these steps explicitly enables the proof-checker to verify the deduction. For further discussion of the immediate rules, see [11].

Note: in the restricted predicate calculus rules of 4.7 we must write the reflexivity rule as:

> REFLEXIVITY
>
> {exp well-defined}
> exp = exp

4.9 Array equality

Arrays (introduced in section V) have a special axiom for equality.

ARRAY EXTENSIONALITY: (A and B both have n dimensions)

$LBOUND(A,i_j)$ = $LBOUND(B,i_j)$, $HBOUND(A,i_j)$ = $HBOUND(B,i_j)$, $1 \le j \le n$

$ALL(i_1,....,i_n)$ FIXED $A(i_1,....,i_n)$ = $B(i_1,....,i_n)$

A=B BY EXTEN[SIONALITY];

Note: we also have from the equality axioms that $\dfrac{A=B}{A(I)=B(I)}$.

4.10 Examples

Here is a variety of examples to illustrate the development of basic logical facts in the PL/CV predicate calculus with equality. Shielding and file formatting are excluded to save space.

```
(i)    ALL (A,B) BIT. ( (A => B) => (~B => ~A)) BY INTRO.
       PROOF;
        (A => B) => (~B => ~A) BY INTRO.
       PROOF;
          ~B => ~A BY INTRO.
         PROOF;
           ~A BY INTRO.
           PROOF;
           ASSUME A;
                   B;   /# IMMEDIATE FROM A => B AND A #/
                  ~B;   /# ASSUMED IN ~B => ~A BLOCK #/
                '0'B;
             QED;
           QED;
         QED;
       QED;
```

This argument can be compressed using the feature that the argument inside a proof block may be eliminated when it consists entirely of immediate assertions. The keyword INTRO is left to indicate what happened. This results in:

```
       ALL (A,B) BIT. ( (A => B) => (~B => ~A)) BY INTRO,INTRO.
         PROOF;
           ~B => ~A BY INTRO,
         PROOF;
            ~A BY INTRO;
         QED;
         QED;
```

The proof can be further collapsed to:

```
       ALL (A,B) BIT. ( (A => B) => (~B => ~A)) BY INTRO,INTRO,INTRO,INTRO;
```

The converse, (~B => ~A) => (A => B) requires the classical rule CONTRADICTION.

```
(ii)  ALL (A,B,C) BIT. (A & (B|C) => (A&B | A&C)) BY INTRO,INTRO,CASES,B|C,
         PROOF;
         CASE B;
            A&B;
         CASE C;
            A&C;
         QED;
```

This compresses to:

```
        ALL (A,B,C) BIT. (A & (B|C) => (A&B | A&C)) BY INTRO,INTRO,CASES,B|C;
```

In the following examples, let A and B be any assertion with free X, and
let C be an assertion with no free occurrences of X.

```
        (iii)   ALL X FIXED.(A(X) => B(X)) => SOME X FIXED.(A(X) => B(X)) BY INTRO,
                  PROOF;
                  ASSUME H: ALL X FIXED.(A(X) => B(X));
                  A(0) => B(0) BY ALLEL, H, 0;
                  SOME X FIXED.(A(X) => B(X)) BY INTRO, 0;
                  QED;
                QED;
```

```
        (iv) SOME X FIXED.(A(X) => C) => (ALL X FIXED.A(X) => C) BY INTRO,
                PROOF;
                ASSUME SOME X FIXED. (A(X) => C);
                CHOOSE X0 FIXED WHERE A(X0) => C;
                ALL X FIXED.A(X) => C BY INTRO,
                  PROOF;
                  ASSUME H: ALL X FIXED.A(X);
                  A(X0) BY ALLEL, H, X0;
                  C;
                  QED;
                QED;
```

```
        (v) SOME X FIXED.~A(X) => ~ALL X FIXED.A(X) BY INTRO,
                PROOF;
                ASSUME SOME X FIXED.~A(X);
                CHOOSE X0 FIXED WHERE ~A(X0);
                ~ALL X FIXED.A(X) BY INTRO,
                    PROOF;
                    ASSUME H: ALL X FIXED.A(X);
                    A(X0) BY ALLEL, H, X0;
                    '0'B;
                    QED;
                QED;
```

4.11 Arithmetic

To reason about the basic data types of integers and booleans we need axioms and rules of inference for their constants, operations, and relations. Elementary arithmetic arguments are requisite to reasoning about programs. Termination proofs and computational complexity analyses of almost any algorithm involve properties of integers. Fortunately, this indispensible theory has been thoroughly studied and we can draw upon the labors of others to frame the PL/CV theory of integers. This theory, to be described below, is very powerful and useful, but provides only the first steps toward a convenient workaday theory. (The theory of booleans is already provided by the propositional logic.)

1. <u>Ordinary axioms of number theory</u>

There is one main rule of arithmetic in PL/CV called ARITH. To explain it we need to classify the ordinary axioms of number theory as follows:

(0) Constant arithmetic

$$1+1 = 2$$
$$2+1 = 3$$
$$3+1 = 4$$
$$\cdot$$
$$\cdot$$
$$\cdot$$

(1) Ring axioms and the definition of minus, -. For all integers x,y,z:

(i)	x+y=y+x x*y=y*x	commutativity
(ii)	(x+y)+z=x+(y+z) (x*y)*z=x*(y*z)	associativity
(iii)	x*(y+z)=(x*y)+(x*z)	distributivity
(iv)	x+0=x	additive identity
(v)	x*1=x	multiplicative identity
(vi)	x+(-x)=0	additive inverse
(vii)	x-y=x+(-y)	subtraction

(2) Discrete linear order. For all integers x,y,z:

67

(i)   ~(x<x)   irreflexivity

(ii) x<y ∨ y<x ∨ x=y   trichotomy

(iii) x<y & y<z => x<z   transitivity

(iv) ~(x<y<x+1)   discreteness

(3) Definitions of order relations and inequality. For all integers, x,y,z:

(i)   x≤y <=> x<y ∨ x=y

(ii) x>y <=> y<x

(iii) x≥y <=> x>y ∨ x=y

(4) Monotonicity of + and *. For all integers w,x,y,z:

(i)   x≥y & z≥w => x+z≥y+w monotonicity of +

If z,w are constants, this is called an instance of **trivial monotonicity**.

(ii) x≥y & z≤w => x-z≥y-w monotonicity of -

If z and w are constants, this is called an instance of **trivial monotonicity**.

(iii) x≥0 & y≥z => x*y≥x*z monotonicity of *

(iv) x>0 & x*y≥x*z => y≥z cancellation (factoring)

2. Variants of basic axioms

To make the proof system more powerful, many variants of the above axioms are incorporated into the arithmetic proof rule. These variants modulo the ring axioms, are given in the following tables, in which each entry contains the conclusion from the hypotheses corresponding to its row and column.

Addition

	z>w	z≥w	z=w	z≠w
x>y	x+z≥y+w+2	x+z≥y+w+1	x+z≥y+w+1 & x+w≥y+z+1	--------
x≥y	x+z≥y+w+1	x+z≥y+w	x+z≥y+w & x+w≥y+z	--------
x=y	x+z≥y+w+1 & y=z≥x+w+1	x+z≥y+w & y+z≥x+w	x+z=y+w & x+w=y+z	x+z≠y+w & x+w≠y+z
x≠y	--------	--------	x+z≠y+w & x+w≠y+z	--------

Subtraction

	z>w	z≥w	z=w	z≠w
x>y	x-w≥y-z+2	x-w≥y-z+1	x-w≥y-z+1 & x-z≥y-w+1	--------
x≥y	x-w≥y-z+1	x-w≥y-z	x-w≥y-z & x-z≥y-w	--------
x=y	x-w≥y-z+1 & y-w≥x-z+1	x-w≥y-z & y-w≥x-z	x-w=y-z & y-w=x-z	x-w≠y-z & x-z≠y-w
x≠y	--------	--------	x-w≠y-z & x-z≠y-w	--------

Multiplication (using xy for x*y)

	y≥z	y>z	y=z	y≠z
x>0	xy≥xz	xy>xz	xy=xz	xy≠xz
x≥0	xy≥xz	xy≥xz	xy=xz	--------
x=0	xy=xz & xy=0	xy=xz & xy=0	xy=xz & xy=0	xy=xz & xy=0
x≤0	xy≤xz	xy≤xz	xy=xz	--------
x<0	xy≤xz	xy<xz	xy=xz	xy≠xz
x≠0	--------	xy≠xz	xy=xz	xy≠xz

Cancellation (factoring using xy for x*y)

	xy>xz	xy≥xz	xy=xz	xy≠xz
x>0	y>z	y≥z	y=z	y≠z
x<0	y<z	y≤z	y=z	y≠z
x≠0	y≠z	--------	y=z	y≠z

3. The arithmetic proof rule ARITH

Definition: A trivial application of monotonicity is an application of
a monotonicity axiom for addition, with one of the hypotheses given in
the form

$$a \; \rho \; b$$

where a,b are integer constants, and ρ is any infix arithmetic relational operator. Any other application of a monotonicity axiom will be
called nontrivial.

Intuitively, a trivial application of monotonicity corresponds to
adding constants to both sides of a relation, in a meaningful way. Thus

we can conclude x+3≠y+4 from x=y, but from x≠y we cannot make any conclusion about x+3 and y+4, since x≠y does not preclude any of the 3 possibilities x+3>y+4, x+3=y+4, x+3<y+4. These two cases are, respectively, an example and a non-example of a trivial application of monotonicity.

The proof system is designed so that whenever the arithmetic proof
rule ARITH is invoked, any necessary applications of the arithmetic
axioms, <u>other than nontrivial application of monotonicity</u>, will be supplied automatically. Only nontrivial applications of monotonicity need
be specified explicitly.

All arithmetic steps in PL/CV arguments have the following restricted form. First, all inferences involve only <u>quantifier free</u> arithmetic relations, i.e., of the form $[\sim]^*t_1<t_2$, $[\sim]^*t_1 \le t_2$, $[\sim]^*t_1>t_2$,
$[\sim]^*t_1=t_2$, $[\sim]^*t_1 \ge t_2$, $[\sim]^*t_1 \ne t_2$ for t_i expressions. Second, each step
involves drawing a conclusion in the form of a disjunction of arithmetic
relations, $C_1|C_2|...C_m$ from a finite set of arithmetic relations
$H_1,...,H_n$. (When m=0 the disjunct is regarded as '0'B, i.e., false.)
We write $H_1,...,H_n \underset{RA}{\vdash} C_1|C_2| \cdot \cdot \cdot |C_m$ if and only if the conclusion can
be deduced from the hypotheses using the rules of the propositional cal-
culus, restricted equality rules, plus the rules in classes 1,2,3 and
trivial monotonicity. We call this a restricted arithmetic (RA) inference. Such an inference, which may be very complex, can be written in
PL/CV as a single step justified in the form:

Rule 1:   C BY ARITH, $H_1,...,H_n$;

C is the disjunction, $C_1|C_2|...|C_m$.

The second type of inference allowed is a single application of
nontrivial monotonicity, specified precisely in the justification, followed by an application of restricted arithmetic inference. The justification has one of these three forms:

Rule 2,3:   Addition/Subtraction

        C BY ARITH, rel, $\{^+_-\}$, rel {,rel}*

The second relation is added to/subtracted from the first relation,
yielding a relation according to the table of axioms.

Rule 4: Multiplication

$$C \text{ BY ARITH, } rel_1, *, rel_2, \{,rel\}^*$$

Here rel_2 gives the sign of the multiplier and must be of the form exp ρ 0 where ρ is any arithmetic relational operator, and rel_1 gives the relation to be multiplied by the multiplier on both sides.

Rule 5: Cancellation (factoring)

$$C \text{ BY ARITH, } rel_1, /, rel_2, \{rel\}^*$$

Here rel_2 or integer refers to the factor to be factored out of the relation given by rel_1. Conventions are as for multiplication. As in all rules, labels may be used in place of relations.

4. **Examples**

Here are isolated examples of PL/CV arithmetic reasoning:

1. X+2 > 0 BY ARITH, X>0;

2. X*X > 0 BY ARITH, X>0, *, X>0;

3. (A-B)+B <= I-1 BY ARITH, A+B <= I, -, B >= 1;

4. A < B BY ARITH, A <= B, A ~= B;

5. A+2 < A+3 BY ARITH;

6. A+B >= 2 BY ARITH, A >= 1, +, B >= 1;

7. 2 <= X | X<0 BY ARITH, X < X*X, /, X ~= 0;

8. Z>0 BY ARITH, Z>W, W>0;

9. X*Z > Y*Z BY ARITH, X>Y, *, Z>0;

10. X*Z > W*Y BY ARITH, Z>W, *, Y>0, X*Z > Y*Z;

11. 3*X + Y >= 2*Z - 1 BY ARITH, X+Y > Z, +, 2*X >= Z;

12. X=Y | Y=Z | Z=X BY ARITH, X-1 <= Y <= X+1, X-1 <= Z <= X+1, Y-1 <= Z <= Y+1;

4.12 Special Functions

The functions /, **, ABS, MAX, MIN, MOD, and SIGN are basic number theoretic functions built into PL/I, but they are not treated by the proof rule ARITH. IN PL/CV they are treated as value-returning procedures verified to have properties that completely characterize the function. Any of the conjuncts in the ATTAIN sections below may be indepently asserted with FIXED expressions substituted for the parameters of the procedure. (See sections IX and IX for more about functions.)

1. Enumeration of special functions

```
ABS: PROCEDURE(X) RETURNS(FIXED);
DECLARE X FIXED /*: READONLY */;
/*/ ASSUME '1'B;                                              */
/*/ ATTAIN X >= 0 => ABS(X) = X,                             */
/*/        X <= 0 => ABS(X) = -X,                            */
/*/        X  = 0 => ABS(X) = 0;                             */


MOD: PROCEDURE(A, B) RETURNS(FIXED);
DECLARE (A, B) FIXED /*: READONLY */;
/*/ ASSUME B ~= 0;                                           */
/*/ ATTAIN ALL (Q, R) FIXED .                                */
/*/           ((A = B * Q + R & 0 <= R < ABS(B))             */
/*/              => R = MOD(A, B)),                          */
/*/        SOME Q FIXED . A = B * Q + MOD(A, B),             */
/*/        0 <= MOD(A, B) < ABS(B);                          */


SIGN: PROCEDURE(X) RETURNS(FIXED);
DECLARE X FIXED /*: READONLY */;
/*/ ASSUME '1'B;                                             */
/*/ ATTAIN X < 0 <=> SIGN(X) = -1,                           */
/*/        X = 0 <=> SIGN(X) = 0,                            */
/*/        X > 0 <=> SIGN(X) = 1;                            */


MAX: PROCEDURE(A, B) RETURNS(FIXED);
DECLARE (A, B) FIXED /*: READONLY */;
/*/ ASSUME '1'B;                                             */
/*/ ATTAIN MAX(A, B) >= A,                                   */
/*/        MAX(A, B) >= B,                                   */
/*/        MAX(A, B) = A | MAX(A, B) = B;                    */


MIN: PROCEDURE(A, B) RETURNS(FIXED);
DECLARE (A, B) FIXED /*: READONLY */;
/*/ ASSUME '1'B;                                             */
/*/ ATTAIN MIN(A, B) <= A,                                   */
/*/        MIN(A, B) <= B,                                   */
/*/        MIN(A, B) = A | MIN(A, B) = B;                    */
```

```
EXP: PROCEDURE (B, E) RETURNS(FIXED);
DECLARE (B, E) FIXED /*: READONLY */;
/*/ ASSUME B ~= 0 & E >= 0;                                        */
/*/ ATTAIN E = 0 => B ** E = 1,                                    */
/*/        E >= 1 => ((B ** E = B * (B ** (E - 1))) & */
/*/                   ((B ** E) / B = B ** (E - 1))); */


DIVISION: PROCEDURE(A, B) RETURNS(FIXED);
DECLARE (A, B) FIXED /*: READONLY */;
/*/ ASSUME B ~= 0;                                                 */
/*/ ATTAIN A >= 0 => A = B * (A / B) + MOD(A, B),                  */
/*/        A <= 0 => A = B * (A / B) - MOD(A, B),                  */
/*/        (A > 0 & 0 < B <= A)  => A / B > 0,                     */
/*/        (A < 0 & A <= B < 0)  => A / B > 0,                     */
/*/        (A > 0 & -A <= B < 0) => A / B < 0,                     */
/*/        (A < 0 & 0 < B <= A)  => A / B < 0,                     */
/*/        A = 0                 => A / B = 0,                      */
/*/        (A ~= 0 & 0 < ABS(A) < ABS(B))                          */
/*/                              => A / B = 0,                      */
/*/        ALL (Q, R) FIXED . (                                    */
/*/        (A >= 0 => ((A = B * Q + R & 0 <= R < ABS(B))           */
/*/                   => (Q = A / B & R = MOD(A, B)))) &            */
/*/        (A <= 0 => ((A = B * Q - R & 0 <= R < ABS(B))           */
/*/                   => (Q = A / B & R = MOD(A, B))))             */
/*/                        );                                      */
```

Note, when division appears in commands, it must be the outermost operator, i.e. it cannot appear in subexpressions. This restriction is
needed because PL/I division is not ordinary integer division; instead
of truncating the fractional part of an integer division, it retains the
fraction. Thus 2/3 is .666666 rather than 0. 2. Applying the axioms

For convenience these axioms can all be applied in a simple format.
One gives the function being referred to, and the expressions used as
arguments. (This will be the format for user defined functions in parts
IX-X.)

```
ABS(2) = 2      BY FUNCTION, ABS(2);
SIGN(-1) = -1   BY FUNCTION, SIGN(-1);
5*X/5 = X       BY FUNCTION, DIVISION(5*X,5)
```

4.13 Induction

PL/CV provides a simple form of induction so that the arithmetic
rules include Peano and Heyting arithmetic (see Kleene [7]).

INDUCTION

        P(K/N);

        ALL N FIXED WHERE $\{^{N<=K}_{N>=K}\}$

        PROOF; [ARBITRARY N FIXED WHERE $\{^{N<=k+1}_{N>=k+1}\}$ & P;]

            .

            .

        $\{^{\bullet P(N-1/N)}_{P(N+1/N)}\}$

      QED;

The braces show two possible forms, increasing and decreasing induction.

Procedures

Up to now, we have been looking at how to prove assertions. Our aim has always been to produce a proof that some assertion is true. However, we are now going to shift our emphasis, and look at programming. From now on, our aim will be to give precise instructions for some task to a computer. The logic we have learned will be used as a tool to help us build programs and to assure ourselves that they specify the tasks we want done.

Procedures are the basic building blocks used by programmers. We imagine a procedure as a calculating machine, such as the one shown in Figure 13. The boxes at the top of the machine, named A, B, C and D, each hold a number. The numbers are stored in the boxes in such a way that both we and the procedure can change them. When we want to perform a calculation, we load new numbers into the boxes, and press the button marked "GO." The procedure grinds and churns a bit, changing the numbers in the boxes. Finally, the numbers stop changing, the "DONE" light comes on, and the numbers left in the boxes are our answers.

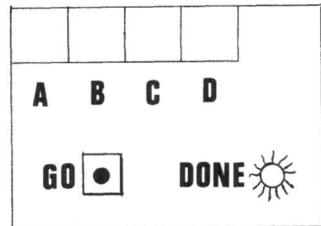

Figure 13 An imaginary picture of a procedure

What is the relationship of such objects to the PL/CV logic? It involves the resemblance between the "boxes" of a procedure and the variables of an assertion. Variables have names and represent values of a certain type; boxes have names and contain values of a certain type. Recall that an assertion with free variables is true or false depending on the values given to those variables. If there are boxes around with the same names (and types) as the free variables, then one rule for assigning values is to give each free variable the value that is contained in the box with the same name. Using this convention, we can write assertions about the values contained in the boxes of a procedure.

In the following sections we will introduce different "program statements" which will allow us to specify how the values in the boxes of a procedure are to be changed. Along with each kind of program statement, we will give rules for assertions which are needed in order to use the statement, as well as the assertions which may be concluded as a result of the actions of the statement. The context of such intermingling of program statements and assertions is always a procedure. The goal is to use the assertions to prove that the program statements of the procedure perform a certain task.

The description of the task itself is given by certain assertions which
appear in the heading of the procedure.

As a simple example, suppose we want the machine in figure 13 to put in box
C the quotient of the values in A and B, and put in box D any number
greater than the product of those two values (we don't care how much
greater). What if the value in box B is zero? Then we can't take the quotient. In that case, the result of executing the procedure is undefined.
Here is how we would write the specification in PL/CV:

```
SAMPLE: PROCEDURE(A, B, C, D);
DECLARE (A, B) FIXED /*/ READONLY */;
DECLARE (C, D) FIXED;
/*/ ASSUME B ~= 0;
    ATTAIN C = A/B & D > A*B;   */
```

The first line gives a name (SAMPLE) to the procedure, tells how many
"boxes" it has, and gives a name to each box. The next two lines indicate
what type value goes in each box.

"Boxes" will henceforth be called program variables, because we will be
referring to them in assertions inside procedures together with the bound
and free variables that we have used up to now. Just as every bound variable has a quantifier, and a free variable an ARBITRARY or CHOOSE line,
every program variable that appears must be introduced by a DECLARE line
that gives its type. All of the program variables that appear on the first
line (the "parameters" of the procedure) must be declared in the lines
immediately following. In addition, most programs will use internal or
"local" program variables that do not appear in the specification. These
must be declared before any of the program statements of the procedure, and
after the ASSUME and ATTAIN lines. (Note: to stay compatible with PL/I,
program variables of type BIT are declared as BIT(*) if they are parameters, and BIT(1) if local.)

The purpose of the ASSUME and ATTAIN lines is to indicate what the procedure does. When the "GO" button is pressed, the procedure, if it is to
meet the specification, must change the program variables in such a way as
to make the assertion on the ATTAIN line true when the "DONE" light comes
on. The ASSUME line is a way of hedging bets. In order to meet its
specification, the procedure need only work on input values that make the
assertion on the ASSUME line true. If the values in the variables do not
make that assertion true, then the behavior is undefined, and no guarantee
is made about the effects of executing the program statements. Note that
in our example, it is necessary to assume B ~= 0, since it is not even
clear what the ATTAIN assertion means when B = 0. Our proof that a program
satisfies the specification is allowed to use the ASSUME assertion at the
start. By following the rules for the statements in the procedure body, we
must establish the ATTAIN assertion at the end.

Sometimes more than one procedure will meet a specification. In the example above, a procedure that set D to A*B+1 would meet the specification, as
would a procedure that set D to A*B + A*A + 5. Another possible way of
satisfying the ATTAIN condition of our example would be a procedure that

completely ignored whatever values the variables started with, and just set
A to 6, B to 3, C to 2, and D to 1000. This is not what we had in mind
when we decided what we wanted the procedure to do. The way we disallow
this kind of "cheating" is to put /*/ READONLY */ on the DECLARE line for A
and B. Then, in order to meet the specification, a procedure must make the
ATTAIN assertion true without changing any of the READONLY variables.

At this point, you may be wondering about the use of the /*/ and */ brackets. Parts of the specification are enclosed in these brackets, and some
are not. The reasons for these brackets is that the programs we write will
be processed by both a proof checker and a compiler. The proof checker
will look at our specification, program, and a proof that we write, and
determine that the program meets the specification. The compiler totally
ignores the specification and just does what the program tells it to. The
parts of the procedure that are ignored by the compiler are enclosed in /*/
and */ brackets, or "shielded." Ideally, we could write our procedure in
two colors of ink. The part of the procedure looked at by the compiler
would be written in black ink, and the rest of the procedure would be written in red ink. However, since most computer equipment does not distinguish colors, we use the brackets instead. Read /*/ as "switch to red ink"
and */ as "switch back to black." The actual placement of the /*/ and */
makes no difference as long as each part of the procedure is in the proper
color of ink. For example, the above specification could just as well have
been written:

```
        SAMPLE: PROCEDURE(A, B, C, D);
        DECLARE (A, B) FIXED /*/ READONLY */;
        DECLARE (C, D) FIXED;
        /*/ ASSUME B ~= 0; */
        /*/ ATTAIN C = A/B & D > A*B;   */
```

or as:

```
        SAMPLE: PROCEDURE(A, B, C, D);
        DECLARE (A, B) FIXED /*/ READONLY */;
        DECLARE (C, D) FIXED;
        /*/
        ASSUME B ~= 0;
        ATTAIN C = A/B & D > A*B;
         */
```

One important rule to keep in mind is never to put a character in column
one, except when writing a control card. (*PLCV, *THEOREM, or *PROCESS. See
section 2.7 on files.)

The Assignment Statements
Once the specification for a procedure is written, the next task is to
write the procedure itself. The procedure body is a series of program
statements and proof lines, followed by a line containing END;. The statements of the procedure are executed one by one in sequence, until the
statement RETURN; is encountered. At that point, the "DONE" light is lit,
and the variables should (if the program meets its specification) contain
values that make the ATTAIN assertion true.

We will be looking at several different kinds of statements. The simplest statement, however, is the assignment statement. The assignment statement looks like:

    V = E;

The above is a template, like the templates we have seen for proof rules. To make an assignment statement, substitute a program variable for V, and an expression for E. For example,

    A = B + 2;

is an assignment statement. (Unfortunately the assignment operator, "=", looks just like the equality operator of our assertion language. This is due to a regrettable historical choice in the development of PL/I, and should be regarded as an inconvenience. We can distinguish equality assertions from assignment statements by the fact that the former are always shielded and the latter never are.)

The computer executes an assignment statement by first getting the value of the expression on the right, using the current values of the program variables. It then stores this value in the variable (think "box") on the left, thereby changing the value of the variable. For example, if the variable A and B had the values 4 and 5, after executing the assignment statement:

    A = B + 2;

the variable A would have the value 7. The value of B would not be changed by the assignment.

There are some restrictions on the use of the assignment statement. The type of the expression must be the same as the type of the variable; you must assign FIXED expressions to FIXED variables, and BIT expressions to BIT variables. Expressions used in assignment statements (or anywhere else in a program) cannot contain any quantifiers, or the operators "=>" and "<=>". The expression can only contain program variables; no logic variables are allowed. Cascaded relational operators such as A < B <= C cannot be used in a program expression; instead you must write out A<B & B<=C. If you use division in an expression, it must be the "main connective" of the expression, that is, the one that is done last when evaluating the expression. For example, the division is the main connective in A / (B + 2), but not in 23 +(A / B). Finally, the variable on the left of the assignment statement cannot be declared READONLY.

Between the statements of a procedure we can write and prove assertions. Here is what it means for an assertion inside a procedure to be true: when the computer gets to the assertion (that is, after the computer executes the statement preceding the assertion, but before it executes the statement following the assertion) the program variables will have values that will make the assertion true. It is important to realize that whether or not an assertion is valid depends on where it appears in the procedure. Consider the following example:

```
/*/ P{E//V} ... */
.
.
.
V = E;
/*/ P; */
```

Figure 14   The Assignment Rule

```
J = 3;
/*/ J > 5; */
J = 7;
/*/ J > 5; */
```

The first J > 5 assertion will not be valid, because when the computer gets
to it, J will have the value 3, and ~(3 > 5). In the second position, however, the assertion will be valid. There J will have the value 7.

How are we going to prove assertions that are embedded within programs?
All the the ways we have seen so far of proving assertions will work. For
example, we can write:

```
/*/ J+1 > J BY ARITH; */
```

inside a program. This line does not rely on the statements of the procedure. The assertion will therefore be true no matter what value J has,
including whatever value it has when the computer gets to it in a program.
However, if we wanted to prove this assertion:

```
J = 7;
/*/ J > 5 BY ??? */
```

nothing we have seen so far could be substituted for the ??? to prove
J > 5. In order to prove J > 5, we have to use the fact that the assertion
comes right after the assignment statement.

The Assignment Rule
Figure 14 contains a template for the assignment rule. What it says, is
that if you wish to conclude the assertion P after the execution of the
statement V = E; then you must somehow be able to prove the assertion
P{E//V}, that is P with every occurrence of V replaced by E, before the
assignment statement. Here is how we would use the assignment rule to
prove our above example:

```
/*/ 7 > 5 BY ARITH; */
J = 7;
/*/ J > 5; */
```

Let me put the above proof in words. Before the assignment, (and anywhere
else, for that matter), 7 is greater than 5. The effect of the assignment
statement is to make J a name for 7. Therefore, after the assignment
statement, J is greater than 5.

The effect of the assignment statement J = J+1; is to increase the value of the variable J by one. Let us see how we can prove this with the assignment rule. Suppose we know somehow that before the assignment statement J is equal to some other variable J0. The proof is then:

```
/*/ J = J0 BY ...
        J+1 = J0+1 BY ARITH, J = J0, +, 1=1; */

    J = J + 1;

/*/ J = J0+1;   /# by assignment rule #/ */
```

What the above proof tells us is that if J = J0 before the assignment statement, then J = J0+1 after the assignment statement.

The assignment rule is an automatic rule. Chains of reasoning in which each link is the assignment rule or a substitution rule can be collapsed. You cannot combine the assignment rule and a transformation in one step. The following example shows how this works.

```
/*/  S1: X*(X*2+3)+5 = X*(X*2+3)+5; */
     A = 2;
/*/  S2: X*(X*A+3)+5 = X*(X*2+3)+5; */
     B = X*A + 3;
/*/  S3: X*B+5 = X*(X*2+3)+5; */
     C = X*B + 5;
/*/  S4: C = X*(X*2+3)+5;
     C = 2*X*X + 3*X + 5 BY ARITH, S4; */
```

In the above, S4 is proved using the assignment rule and S3, which is proved using the assignment rule and S2, which is proved using the assignment rule and S1, which is proved using the Reflexive Rule. Because the chain of reasoning uses no transformations, it can be collapsed down to:

```
     A = 2;
     B = X*A + 3;
     C = X*B + 5;
/*/  C = 2*X*X + 3*X + 5 BY ARITH, C = X*(X*2+3)+5; */
```

Well defined expressions
One more slight complication to the assignment rule needs to be mentioned. If, for example, the assignment statement:

```
    A = B/0;
```

was executed by the computer, the machine would immediately stop the execution of the procedure and print an error message. The same thing would happen if the statement:

```
    A = B/C;
```

was encountered when C had the value zero. When an expression is written in an assignment statement, or for that matter, anywhere else in the program, we must prove the expression to be "well defined." For the time being, "well defined" means: (1) if the expression contains I/J, then J ~= 0, (2) if the expression contains MOD(I, J), then J ~= 0, and (3) if the expression contains I**J, then I ~= 0 and J >= 0. Later, when we see more programming language elements, we will expand our definition of "well defined."

For example, the statement:

    A = MOD(I/J, K**L);

requires the assertion:

    J~=0 & K~=0 & L>=1 & K**L~=0

as a hypothesis. The assertion must be accessible to the assignment statement, or provable using automatic rules.

Assignment statements and accessibility

Recall that an assertion P is accessible to a point X in the proof if a proof line at X can reach back for P as a hypothesis. Basically, the assertion P is accessible to X if P comes before X, X is not inside a proof of P, and if reaching to P from X does not require reaching into a proof block. If P contains any program variables, we have to add one more restriction: there must be no assignments to any of the variables of P between P and X. Here is a simple example of a violation of this rule:

    /*/ 5 > 0 BY ARITH; */
    A = 5;
    /*/ A > 0; */
    A = -10;
    /*/ X: A >=0 BY ARITH, A>0; */

The proof line at X cannot reach past the assignment A = -10 to get the hypothesis A > 0. Although the assertion was true at the place in the program where it was proved, it is not true at X. As soon as A is set to -10, the assertion is invalidated. Even if a statement happens to leave an assertion true when assigning to one of its variables, a proof line still cannot reach back past the assignment statement. The assignment rule must be used to __prove__ that the assignment leaves the assertion true, as in:

    /*/ P: A > 0; */
    /*/ 10 > 0 BY ARITH; */
    A = 10;
    /*/ Q: A > 0; */
    /*/ X: A >= 0 BY ARITH, A>0; */

In the above, the proof line at X cannot use the assertion at P as a hypothesis, but it can use the assertion at Q.

The IF statement

Procedures that use only assignment statements are not very flexible; they must do essentially the same thing no matter what values are input to them.

```
/*/ ATTAIN P; */
IF B
THEN DO;
     /*/ B; */
       .
       .
       .
     /*/ P ... */
     END;
ELSE DO;
     /*/ ~B; */
       .
       .
       .
     /*/ P ... */
     END;
/*/ P; */
```

Figure 15   The IF rule

The IF statement gives us the capability to write procedures that can react
to their input, and execute different statements for different input
values.

Figure 15 contains a template for the IF statement. In this template, B
stands for a boolean expression, and P stands for an assertion. The vertical dots stand for a sequence of statements and proof lines.

When the computer gets to the IF statement, it first evaluates the boolean
expression B. If B is true, the sequence of statements after the THEN,
called the THEN-part, are executed, and the sequence of statements after
the ELSE, called the ELSE-part, are skipped over. If B is false, the
THEN-part is skipped and the ELSE-part is executed.

The reason we write program statements is to make some assertion true by
changing the value of program variables. In the case of the IF statement,
we write this assertion, P, on the ATTAIN line preceding the IF. We are
then obliged to prove that P is true at the end of the THEN-part, and at
the end of the ELSE-part. Once we have done this, we are entitled to conclude that P is true after the execution of the IF statement.

Whenever an expression appears outside of /*/ and */ brackets, it must be
proved to be well defined. In the case of the IF statement, assertions
that prove that B is well defined must be accessible to the IF statement.
These assertions are obtained in the same way as they are for the assignment statement. For now, you only need to worry about the well definedness
of B if it contains division, exponentiation, or the MOD function.

Recall that when we write an assertion at a particular point in a program,
it means "whenever the computer gets to this point this assertion will be
true." Certainly, whenever the computer gets to the beginning of the

```
MAXP: PROCEDURE(A, B, M);
DECLARE (A, B) FIXED /*/ READONLY */;
DECLARE M FIXED;
/*/ ASSUME '1'B; */
/*/ ATTAIN MAXFOUND: (M=A | M=B) & M>=A & M>=B; */

/*/ ATTAIN MAXFOUND; */
IF A >= B
THEN DO;
     /*/ A >= A BY ARITH; */
     /*/ A >= B; */
     M = A;
     /*/ M = A;  M >= A;  M >= B; */
     END;
ELSE DO;
     /*/ B >= A BY ARITH, ~(A >= B); */
     /*/ B >= B BY ARITH; */
     M = B;
     /*/ M = B; M >= A; M >= B; */
     END;

RETURN;
END;
```

Figure 16   A procedure that finds the maximum of two values


```
/*/ A < 0; */ <---------------- <-------
.                          |          |
.                          |          |
.                       R  |       |  W
IF C>2                   I  |       |  R
THEN DO;                 G  |       |  O
     A = 5;              H  |       |  N
     END;               T  |       |  G
ELSE DO;                   |          |
     .                     |          |
     .                     |          |
     .                  |  |          |
     /*/ A+1 < 1 BY ARITH, A<0; */    |
     .                        |       |
     .                        |       |
     .                        |       |
     END;                     |       |
.                             |       |
.                             |       |
.                             |       |
/*/ A+1 < 1 BY ARITH, A<0;  ------------
```

Figure 17 Reaching past an assignment statement in an IF statement

THEN-part, B will be true, because if B is false, the computer skips the THEN-part and goes to the ELSE-part. Likewise, at the beginning of the ELSE-part B will be false, so that ~B will be true. Therefore, the assertions B and ~B can be written in the places shown in Figure 15.

As usual, whenever a template would let us write an assertion followed by a semicolon (as opposed to BY some justification), we don't have to actually write the assertion. Later proof lines can use that assertion as a hypothesis, even though it isn't actually written in the proof.

Figure 16 contains an example of the use of the IF rule. Notice how the label MAXFOUND is used to avoid repeating assertions. Also note that the assertion MAXFOUND itself need not appear at the end of the THEN-part and the ELSE-part. Only enough assertions have been written so that MAXFOUND can be proved with the automatic rules & introduction and | introduction. Since the assignment rule is also automatic, this proof could have been abbreviated even more.

The THEN-part and ELSE-part of the IF statement are proof blocks; the DO and END in programs perform the same function as PROOF and QED in proofs. All the restrictions we have seen about reaching into proof blocks for hypotheses also apply to IF statements.

However, IF statements add a new wrinkle to the rule about reaching past assignment statements for hypotheses. Normally, if a hypothesis contains a program variable, you cannot reach past an assignment to that variable, since the assignment statement could invalidate the asssertion. This rule applies, even if the assignment statement you are reaching past is buried inside an IF statement. However, an exception is made when reaching from the ELSE-part of an IF statement, past an assignment statement in the THEN-part of the same IF statement. The reason we can get away with the reference in this case is that the offending assignment statement cannot possibly be executed between the time the assertion is made true and the time it is used as a hypothesis. Figure 17 shows an example of a proper and improper way of reaching past an assignment statement for an assertion.

Indexed Loops
Programs written using the program statements we have seen so far have required the programmer to do as much work as the computer, and as such, have not been all that useful. The advantage of using computers is that we can write short programs that perform large tasks. The DO INDEX statement will allow us to write procedures that repeatedly execute statements, so that the computer does more work than the programmer.

Figure 18 contains a template for this statement. All of our usual conventions hold for this template; lines followed by three dots must be proved at the places shown in the template, and lines followed by semicolons may be used as hypotheses to subsequent proof lines. In the template, I stands for any FIXED program variable (except a READONLY parameter), S and F (short for "start" and "finish") stand for FIXED expressions, and P stands for an assertion. The vertical dots stand for a sequence of program statements and proof lines. These statements are called the "loop body." Within the loop body, assignment statements that modify the variable I, or

```
/*/ S>F => P{F+1//I} ... */
/*/ P{S//I} ... */
DO I = S TO F BY 1;
    /*/ ASSUME P; */
    /*/ S <= I <= F; */
    .
    .
    .
    /*/ P{I+1//I} ... */
END;
/*/ P{F+1//I}; */
```

Figure 18   The DO INDEX Rule

any of the variables in S or F, are not allowed.

Here is how the computer executes a DO INDEX statement. First the variable I, called the "index variable", is set to S, and the body of the loop is executed. Then I is set to S+1, and the body is executed again. The body of the loop is executed repeatedly for I = S+2, S+3, and so on, until the value of I gets up to F. The body of the loop is executed one last time for I = F, and then the execution of the loop is complete.

There are some special cases. If S and F have the same value, then the body of the loop is executed only once, for I = S = F. If S>F, then the body isn't executed at all; the entire statement is skipped.

Next, let's try to make some sense out of the DO INDEX proof rules. The rules all revolve around the assertion P, called the "loop invariant." The loop invariant specifies a relation between the variables changed by the body of the loop, and the index variable. We are obliged to prove that P{S//I} holds before the loop begins execution. Once we prove this, we will know that P holds at the beginning of the first execution of the loop body, since I = S then. Thus, our assumption of P is valid for the first execution.

The body of the loop must be written so that if P is true before the execution of the loop body, then P{I+1//I} must be true afterwards. During the first execution of the loop body, I = S, so that P{S//I} must hold before the execution, and P{S+1//I} must hold afterwards. But after the first execution of the loop body I is set to S+1, so when the computer gets to the top of the loop body for the second execution, P{I//I}, or just P is still true. Therefore, the assumption P is justified for the second execution of the loop body.

As the loop body is executed a second, third, and fourth time, the assertions P{S+2//I}, P{S+3//I}, and then P{S+4//I} are made true, as I is set to S+2, S+3, and S+4. Each time the computer gets to the top of the loop body, the assertion P will be true. During the last execution of the loop body, I has the value F, so that before the last execution, P{F//I} will be true. The loop body is executed one last time, making P{F+1//I} true after

```
01   SQ: PROCEDURE(N, SUM);
02   DECLARE N FIXED /*/ READONLY */;
03   DECLARE SUM FIXED;
04   /*/ ASSUME N >= 1;
05       ATTAIN 2*SUM = N * (N+1);
06   */
06   DECLARE I FIXED;
07   /*/ 2*0 = (1-1)*1;
08       ~(1>N) BY ARITH, N>=1; */
09
10   SUM = 0;
11
12   /*/ 2*SUM = (1-1)*1; */
13   DO I = 1 TO N BY 1;
14       /*/ ASSUME P: 2*SUM = (I-1)*I;
15           2*(SUM+I) = I*(I+1) BY ARITH, P, +, 2*I=2*I; */
16
17       SUM = SUM + I;
18
19       /*/ 2 * SUM = I * (I+1);
20           2 * SUM = (I+1-1) * (I+1); */
21   END;
22   /*/ 2*SUM = (N+1-1) * (N+1); */
23   RETURN;
24   END SQ;
```

Figure 19   Computing sum of the first N integers

the loop body is executed. Thus, after the loop is finished executing, P{F+1//I} will be true.

The assumption is made in the above discussion that the loop body is executed. When S>F, the loop body is not executed at all. In that case, the assertion we will conclude after the execution of the loop had better be true right away. Thus, we are obliged to prove S>F => P{F+1//I} before the execution of the loop. Often we know that the loop body will be executed at least once. In that case, we can prove ~(S>F), and the implication we need to prove is vacuously true, and will follow from automatic rules.

Let us see how all of this works in a simple example. Figure 19 contains a program that uses a DO INDEX statement to compute the sum of the first N integers. That is, the program sets S = 1 + 2 + ... N. It is a fact of algebra that the sum of the first N integers is (N*(N+1))/2. Let us see how we can use the DO INDEX rule to prove this fact. (We use the ATTAIN 2*SUM = N * (N+1) rather than SUM = (N*(N+1))/2 to avoid the complexities of reasoning about division.)

The first thing to get out of the way is to show that the loop works properly if the body is not executed. We don't have to worry about that problem in this example, since we are assuming that N >= 1 on line 04. Thus, line 08 takes care of the S>F => P{F+1//I} part of the template.

The loop invariant, which appears on line 14, is 2*SUM = (I-1)*I. We must make sure the invariant holds when the loop execution begins, that is, when I=1. Performing the substitution, we must make sure 2*SUM = (1-1)*1 is true just before the loop begins execution. We do this by setting SUM to zero at line 10, and using the assignment rule.

The function of the body of the loop is to start with the assertion 2*SUM = (I-1)*I true, and make the assertion 2*SUM = (I+1-1)*(I+1) true by changing the value of SUM. A single assignment statement does the trick, as is shown by the assignment rule, and some arithmetic reasoning on lines 15-20.

As the body of the loop is executed over and over, the value of SUM and I keep changing, but always in a way that keeps 2*SUM = (I-1)*I true. The reason the assertion is called the "loop invariant" is that the truth of the assertion remains constant, even though the values of the variables keep changing. Thus, the following assertions are made true just before the loop body is repeated:

    2*SUM = (1-1)*1   when I=1
    2*SUM = (2-1)*2   when I=2
    2*SUM = (3-1)*3   when I=3
    2*SUM = (4-1)*4   when I=4

The last time through the loop, I=N, so that before the loop body executes, 2*SUM = (N-1)*N is true. The execution of the loop body makes the invariant true for I=N+1, so that after the loop is finished, at line 22, 2*SUM = (N+1-1)*(N+1) must be true. A little arithmetic manipulation turns that assertion into just what we need to prove at the end of the program: that 2*SUM = N*(N+1).

Loops and Accessibility

The DO and END of the DO INDEX statement delimit a proof block, just as the DO and END of IF statements do. All the accessibility rules we have seen about proof blocks hold for the DO index statement. In particular, a proof line cannot reach into a loop body for the hypothesis, but a proof line can reach out of a loop body.

However, there is one special rule about reaching out of the DO INDEX loop (and DO WHILE loop, which we will see soon) that does not apply to any other kind of proof block. We have already seen that if an assertion P contains a program variable V, a proof line cannot reach past an assignment statement that changes V to get P. The new rule is this: a proof line inside a loop body cannot reach outside for a P if the variable V is assigned to anywhere in the loop body.

The reason for this rule is made clear in figure 20. The assertion V>0 is made true at L1 by setting V to 1. Although the assertion will be true the first time the computer gets to L2, since L2 is inside a loop, and the first execution of the loop body sets V to -1, on subsequent executions, the assertion V>0 will no longer be true. Since the assertion V>0 is not true _every_ time the computer gets to L2, it cannot be used as a hypothesis there.

```
V = 1;
/*/ L1: V > 0 BY ... */   <--------
  .                                |
  .                                | W
  .                                | R
DO I = S TO F BY 1;                | O
     .                             | N
     .                             | G
     .                             |
     /*/ L2: 0 < V BY ARITH, V > 0; */
     .
     .
     .
     V = -1;
     .
     .
     .

END;
```

Figure 20   Example of an invalid reference

Arrays

Another use of computer programs is to process large quantities of data.
If we are to write a procedure that takes a list of numbers as input, we
will need some notation for talking about that list. In programming, a
variable that holds a collection of values is called an "array".

Recall that we think of a simple program variable as a box that can hold a
value. In the same fashion, we think of an array as a big box with a bunch
of compartments, each of which holds a value. In order to tell one compartment from another they are numbered with consecutive integers. Do not
confuse these numbers, called "indexes" or "subscripts", with the values
stored in the compartments.

"Compartments" are usually referred to more formally as "elements". We use
function notation to talk about the elements of an array. For example, the
value in the element of array A that is numbered 3, is written A(3). The
real advantage of using arrays in programming is that expressions may be
used as array subscripts. For example, A(I) can refer to any element of
the array, depending on the value in the program variable I.

It is also possible to have arrays with more than one subscript. In this
case, we imagine a box with compartments laid out in the shape of a rec-
tangular matrix. Each compartment, or element, is labeled with two
numbers: a row number and a column number. For example, if B is an array
with two subscripts, then B(3, 5) is the element at row 3 and column 5.
There is no reason to stop at two. We can have arrays with three, four, or
any number of subscripts. However, we will usually use arrays with just
one subscript.

Here is how we indicate in our procedures that a parameter is an array:

DECLARE (A(*), B(*, *), C) FIXED /*/ READONLY */;

In the above, A is an array with one subscript, B is an array with two subscripts, and C is just a simple variable, with no subscripts. For the time being, all the arrays we use will be READONLY, that is, input to programs. Later we will see how to modify the values of arrays.

The elements of an array are numbered consecutively, and there is always a largest and smallest subscript. For example, an array with four elements might have elements A(3), A(4), A(5), and A(6). In that case, we say that 3 is the "lower bound" of the array, and that 6 is the "upper bound". There are two functions, LBOUND and HBOUND, that tell us what the bounds of the array are. In this example, LBOUND(A, 1) = 3 and HBOUND(A, 1) = 6. The second argument to LBOUND and HBOUND identifies the subscript in arrays with more than one subscript. For example, if B is an array with two subscripts, then LBOUND(B, 1) is the lowest row-number in B, and LBOUND(B, 2) is the lowest column-number in B. When we are dealing with arrays with just one subscript, the second argument of LBOUND and HBOUND will always be 1. Also, the lower bounds of the arrays in our programs will usually be 1.

If LBOUND(A, 1) = 3 and LBOUND(A, 1) = 6, the expression A(9) doesn't make any sense. A(9) is an element that doesn't exist, and we cannot write A(9) any more than we could write J/0. Thus, whenever we write A(I) in a program, (that is, outside of /*/ and */ brackets), we are obliged to prove that LBOUND(A, 1) <= I <= HBOUND(A, 1). Also, we know that every array contains at least one element, so that we may always write LBOUND(A, 1) <= HBOUND(A, 1) in a proof without any justification.

An example: The Maximum of an Array

The DO INDEX statement is very handy for manipulating arrays. In this section, we will develop a sample procedure that uses the DO INDEX rules and arrays. The procedure takes as its input an array, and will find the largest element in that array. It is important to notice how we use the proof rules to help us develop a procedure and its proof.

The method of successive refinement illustrated in the development of the proof in section 3 ("Writing Proofs) is also useful for writing proofs of a programs. Procedures can be very intricate constructs, and attempting to proceed sequentially in understanding them, rather than in an organized top-down fashion, is very likely to lead to an error. It is a much more manageable and comprehensible process to write a program and its proof in stages, initially expressing ideas informally and gradually becoming more specific as "higher level" enclosing pieces are completed in terms of their constituent parts.

Before we can go any farther, we need a specification for the procedure we are going to write. An approximate specification is:

```
AMAX: PROCEDURE(A, N, M);
DECLARE (A(*), N) FIXED /*/ READONLY */;
DECLARE M FIXED;
/*/ ASSUME LBOUND(A, 1) = 1 & HBOUND(A, 1) = N; */
/*/ ATTAIN M is the largest of A(1), A(2), ... A(N); */
```

The reason the specification is approximate is that the ATTAIN assertion is written in English rather than in PL/CV. We will worry about how to say that "M is the largest of A(1), A(2), ... A(N)" in PL/CV later. Remember, this is only a sketch of the proof.

If we are to solve this problem with a DO INDEX statement, we will need a loop invariant. This is the creative part of computer programming. There is no recipe for coming up with loop invariants for every problem. The only guidelines are an understanding of the requirements for invariants and the conclusion the loop is supposed to attain.

The loop we will write will look like this:

```
DO I = S TO F BY 1;
    /*/ ASSUME P; */
    •
    •
    •
END;
```

It is our job to come up with S, F, and P. Where do we start? We know the following things:

(1) From P{F+1//I}, which will be true after the loop, it must be easy to make "M is the largest of A(1), A(2), ... A(N) true.
(2) It must be easy to make P{S//I} true, which we have to prove before the loop starts.
(3) If P is true at the beginning of the body of the loop, it must be easy to make P{I+1//I} true after the body of the loop.

Looking at (1), above, we try using N for F, and making P the assertion "M is the largest of A(1), A(2), ... A(I-1)." This is not the only choice of F and P that will work, but it does lead to a solution.

We don't have S yet. We figure out what S should be by looking at (2). A value for S must be chosen so that the assertion "M is the largest of A(1), A(2), ... A(S-1)" is easy to make true. If we make S = 2, we must make the assertion "M is the largest of A(1), ... A(1)" true before the loop, which we do with the assignment statement S = A(1).

Next, we have to figure out what the body of the loop should be. This we do by looking at (3). The body of the loop must take the assertion "M is the largest of A(1), A(2), ... A(I-1)" and change it to "M is the largest of A(1), A(2), ... A(I+1-1)." This can be done using the assignment

```
AMAX: PROCEDURE(A, N, M);
DECLARE (A(*), N) FIXED /*/ READONLY */;
DECLARE M FIXED;
/*/ ASSUME LBOUND(A, 1) = 1 & HBOUND(A, 1) = N; */
/*/ ATTAIN M is the largest of A(1), A(2), ... A(N); */
DECLARE I FIXED;

M = A(1);

/*/ M is the largest of A(1); */
/*/ 2<N => M is the largest of A(1), A(2), ... A(N) BY INTRO,
    PROOF;
        ASSUME 2<N;
        N=1, since 1 and N are array bounds;
        M is the largest of A(1), ... A(1);
    QED;
 */

DO I = 2 TO N BY 1;
    /*/ ASSUME M is the largest of A(1), A(2), ... A(I-1); */
    M = MAX(M, A(I));
    /*/ M is the largest of A(1), A(2), ... A(I+1-1); */
END;

/*/ M is the largest of A(1), A(2), ... A(N+1-1); */
RETURN;
END;
```

Figure 21   A sketch of the proof of MAX.

statement M = MAX(M, A(I)).

Finally, we should think about the case in which the loop executes zero
times. Forgetting about this case will often lead a programmer to produce
an incorrect program. We must show before the loop begins that 2>N => "M
is the largest of A(1), A(2) ... A(N)." But we know that
N = HBOUND(A, 1) >= LBOUND(A, 1) = 1, or N>=1. If N<2 and N>=1, then N=1.
But we know that just before the loop begins, "M is the largest of A(1),
... A(1)," which is to say, M is A(1).

Putting it all together, we get the sketch of the proof shown in figure 21.
Now we have to translate the English assertions into PL/CV. The key to
doing this is the use of DEFINE statements. We notice that in the sketch,
we often say something like "M is the largest of A(1), A(2), ... A(K)." We
code this notion into a DEFINE as follows:

```
FOR K FIXED DEFINE MAX_TO(K) =
    ALL J FIXED. (1<=J<=K => M>=A(J)) &
    SOME L FIXED. (1<=L<=K & M=A(L));
```

which says, that M is greater or equal to every element in the array from 1
to K, and that M appears somewhere in that part the array.

```
AMAX: PROCEDURE(A, N, M);
DECLARE (A(*), N) FIXED /*/ READONLY */;
DECLARE M FIXED;
/*/ ASSUME LBOUND(A, 1) = 1 & HBOUND(A, 1) = N; */
/*/ FOR K FIXED DEFINE MAX_TO(K) =
        ALL J FIXED.  (1<=J<=K => M>=A(J)) &
        SOME L FIXED. (1<=L<=K &  M=A(L)); */
/*/ ATTAIN MAX_TO(N); */
DECLARE I FIXED;

/*/ LBOUND(A, 1) <= 1 <= HBOUND(A, 1); /# PROOF? #/ */
M = A(1);

/*/ MAX_TO(1); /# PROOF? #/ */
/*/ 2<N => MAX_TO(N) BY INTRO,
    PROOF:
        N=1 BY ARITH, N<2, N>=1;
    QED;
 */

DO I = 2 TO N BY 1;
    /*/ ASSUME MAX_TO(I-1); */
    /*/ LBOUND(A, 1) <= I <= HBOUND(A, 1); /# PROOF? #/ */
    M = MAX(M, A(I));
    /*/ MAX_TO((I+1)-1); /# PROOF? #/ */
END;

/*/ MAX_TO((N+1)-1); */
/*/ MAX_TO(N); */
RETURN;
END;
```

Figure 22 A more refined sketch

The next step is to refine our sketch a bit, using the MAX_TO definition in
place of the English phrases. Also, this is a good time to put in the
assertions that are needed to show that subscripts are in bounds. The
result appears in Figure 22. Some of the lines can be proved with
automatic rules. The lines we need a proof for are marked /# PROOF? #/.

All that is left is to write proofs for those lines. The proofs for the
array bounds consist of just some easy arithmetic and substitutions.
Notice that the other two lines we need to prove follow assignment statements. The patterns for both these proofs is the same. First write out
what MAX_TO is an abbreviation for. Then perform the substitution indicated by the assignment rule to get a formula that must be proved before
the assignment statement. For example, to the proof line after M = A(1),
the assertion you need to prove before the assignment statement is:

```
ALL J FIXED. (1<=J<=1 => A(1) >= A(J)) &
SOME L FIXED. (1<=L<=1 & A(1) = A(L))
```

```
AMAX: PROCEDURE(A, N, M);
DECLARE (A(*),N) FIXED /*/ READONLY */;
DECLARE M FIXED;

/*/ ASSUME LBOUND(A,1)=1 & HBOUND(A,1)=N; */

/*/ FOR K FIXED DEFINE MAX_TO(K) =
        ALL J FIXED. (1<=J<=K => M>=A(J)) &
        SOME L FIXED. (1<=L<=K & M=A(L)); */
/*/ ATTAIN MAX_TO(N); */

DECLARE I FIXED;

/*/ 1<=1<=N;
    LBOUND(A,1) <= 1 <= HBOUND(A,1); */

M=A(1);

/*/ ALL J FIXED.(1<=J<=1 => M>=A(J)) BY INTRO,INTRO,
    PROOF;
        J = 1 BY ARITH, 1<=J<=1;
        M>=A(1) BY ARITH, M=A(1);
        M>=A(J);
    QED;

    1<=1<=1 & M=A(1);
    SOME L FIXED.(1<=L<=1 & M=A(L)) BY INTRO,1;
    MAX_TO(1);    */

/*/ N<2 => MAX_TO(N) BY INTRO,
    PROOF;
        N=1 BY ARITH,N<2,N>=1;
    QED; */
```

Figure 23 The complete proof (part 1)

Each half of the assertion is proved using ALL introduction, and SOME introduction, respectively. The final product, ready to be submitted to the proof checker appears in Figure 23.

The RETURN statement
Let us look at another problem that can be solved using the DO INDEX state-ment. Suppose we are given an array A whose bounds are 1 and N, a value K, and we are given that K appears at least once in the array. Our job is to find an M such that A(M) = K. The specification for this program is:

```
FIND: PROCEDURE(A,N,K,M);
DECLARE (A(*),N,K) FIXED /*/ READONLY */;
DECLARE M FIXED;
/*/ ASSUME LBOUND(A,1) = 1 & HBOUND(A,1)=N &
           SOME C FIXED.(1<=C<=N & A(C)=K);
    ATTAIN 1<=M<=N & A(M)=K;   */
```

```
DO I = 2 TO N BY 1;
   /*/ ASSUME MAX_TO(I-1); */
   /*/ 2<=I<=N; */

   /*/ 1<=I BY ARITH, 2<=I;
       LBOUND(A,1) <= I <= HBOUND(A,1); */

   /*/ ALL J FIXED.(1<=J<=I => MAX(M,A(I)) >= A(J)) BY INTRO,INTRO,
       PROOF;
            ASSUME 1<=J<=I;
            C: J<=I-1 | J=I BY ARITH, J<=I;
            MAX(M,A(I)) >= A(J) BY CASES,C,
            PROOF;
            CASE J <= I-1;
                E: M >= A(J) BY ALLEL,
                         ALL JJ FIXED.(1<=JJ<=I-1 => M>=A(JJ)),J;
                F: MAX(M,A(I)) >= M BY FUNCTION, MAX(M,A(I));
                MAX(M,A(I)) >= A(J) BY ARITH,E,F;
            CASE J = I;
                MAX(M,A(I)) >= A(I) BY FUNCTION, MAX(M,A(I));
            QED;
       QED;   */

   /*/ CC: MAX(M,A(I)) = M | MAX(M,A(I)) = A(I) BY FUNCTION, MAX(M,A(I));
       S: SOME L FIXED.(1<=L<=I & MAX(M,A(I)) = A(L)) BY CASES,CC,
       PROOF;
       CASE MAX(M,A(I)) = M;
            CHOOSE LL FIXED WHERE 1<=LL<=I-1 & A(LL)=M;
            LL <= I BY ARITH,LL<=I-1;
            S BY INTRO,LL;
       CASE MAX(M,A(I)) = A(I);
            S BY INTRO,I;
       QED;   */

   M = MAX(M,A(I));

   /*/ MAX_TO(I);
       MAX_TO((I+1)-1);   */
   END;

/*/ MAX_TO((N+1)-1);
    MAX_TO(N);   */

RETURN;
END;
```

Figure 23, continued

One program we can write for this specification is:

```
DECLARE I FIXED;
DO I = 1 TO N;
    IF A(I) = K
    THEN DO; M = I; END;
    ELSE DO;        END;
END;
```

To prove this program we need an invariant. From the ASSUME line of our specification, we know there is at least one C such that $1 <= C <= N$, and $A(C) = K$. Let C0 be a name for one such value. Looking at the above loop, we see that once the variable I gets past C0, M will always have a value that will make the ATTAIN line true. Translating this statement into PL/CV gets us our invariant:

$$I > C0 => 1<=M<=N \ \& \ A(M)=K$$

Let us check to see that we can use this invariant in a proof. First, if we substitute 1 for I in the invariant, we should get an assertion that is easy to establish before the loop:

$$1 > C0 => 1<=M<=N \ \& \ A(M)=K$$

This assertion is vacuously true, since one of the things we know about C0 is that $1<=C0$.

Next, let's check that substituting N+1 for I in the invariant makes it easy to prove the ATTAIN line of the specification. The result is:

$$N+1 > C0 => 1<=M<=N \ \& \ A(M)=K$$

and, since we know $C0<=N$, we get the ATTAIN line by arithmetic, and => elimination.

The tricky part is to show the loop body maintains the invariant, that after the execution of the body of the loop:

$$I+1 > C0 => 1<=M<=N \ \& \ A(M)=K$$

In order to show that the above is true after the body of the loop, we must show it is true at the end of both the ELSE part and the THEN part of IF statement. The THEN part is easy. We know that $1<=I<=N$ from the DO INDEX rule, and that $A(I)=K$ from the IF rule. Therefore, if we set M = I, from the assignment rule we get $1<=M<=N \ \& \ A(M)=K$. Since the conclusion is true, the implication (our invariant) is trivially true.

The proof that goes in the ELSE part is a little confusing. Inside the ELSE part, we know:

(1)	$I > C0 => 1<=M<=N \ \& \ A(M)=K$	the loop invariant
(2)	$A(I) \ \sim= K$	from the IF rule
(3)	$A(C0) = K$	from what we know about C0

and we have to prove $I+1 > C0 => 1<=M<=N \ \& \ A(M)=K$. Suppose $I+1 > C0$. Then

```
FIND: PROCEDURE(A,N,K,M);
DECLARE(A(*),N,K) FIXED /*/ READONLY */;
DECLARE M FIXED;
/*/ ASSUME LBOUND(A,1) = 1 & HBOUND(A,1)=N &
            SOME C FIXED.(1<=C<=N & A(C)=K);
    ATTAIN 1<=M<=N & A(M)=K;  */
DECLARE I FIXED;
/*/ CHOOSE C0 FIXED WHERE 1<=C0<=N & A(C0)=K; */
/*/ 1 > C0 => (1<=M<=N & A(M)=K) BY INTRO.
    PROOF;
       '0'B BY ARITH. 1 > C0, C0 >= 1;
    QED;   */

/*/ ~(1 > N) BY ARITH. N >= 1;

DO I = 1 TO N BY 1;
    /*/ ASSUME I > C0 => (1<=M<=N & A(M)=K); */
    /*/ 1<=I<=N; */
    /*/ ATTAIN I+1>C0 => (1<=M<=N & A(M)=K); */
    IF A(I)=K
    THEN DO;
         /*/ A(I)=K; */
         M = I;
         /*/ I+1 > C0 => (1<=M<=N & A(M)=K) BY INTRO; */
         END;
    ELSE DO;
         /*/ A(I)~=K;
             A(C0)=K;
             I+1 > C0 => (1<=M<=N & A(M)=K) BY INTRO,
             PROOF;
                 ASSUME I+1 > C0;
                 ~(I=C0) BY INTRO,
                 PROOF;
                   ASSUME I=C0;
                   A(C0)~=K;
                   '0'B;
                 QED;
                 I>C0 BY ARITH. I+1>C0,I~=C0;
                 1<=M<=N & A(M)=K; /# BY "=>" ELIMINATION #/
             QED;    */
         END;
END;
/*/ N+1 > C0 => (1<=M<=N & A(M)=K);
    N+1 > C0 BY ARITH. C0<=N;
    1<=M<=N & A(M)=K;    */
RETURN;
END;
```

Figure 24 A procedure to search an array

I >= C0. From (2) and (3) above, we can conclude that I ~= C0. Therefore,

I>C0, and by => elimination and (1) above, 1<=M<=N & A(M)=K.

The above sketch can be refined to the PL/CV proof in figure 24. But the proof is not as clear as it could be; this business inside the ELSE part is a little mysterious.

Note that as soon as the computer executes the THEN part of the IF, the ATTAIN line for the proof will be satisfied. At that point, a perfectly good "answer" is in M, and the procedure might as well stop. In fact, we can write our procedure so that it does just that, by putting a RETURN statement at the end of the THEN part of the IF. The computer executes the RETURN statement by just stopping (don't be confused by the name "RETURN"; for the time being, think of it as "stop") and, if you remember our imaginary picture of a procedure, turns on the DONE light, indicating that the values currently in the program variables satisfy the ATTAIN line.

Up to now, we have been putting a RETURN statement at the end of every procedure we write, and proving that the ATTAIN assertion holds at the end of every procedure. In fact, we can put a RETURN statement anywhere at all, so long as just before the RETURN statement we prove the ATTAIN assertion for the procedure.

What assertion can we conclude after a RETURN? First, remember what it means to prove an assertion P at a particular place in a program: if the computer gets to that place, the program variables will have values that will make P true. What would it mean to prove the assertion '0'B somewhere in a program? When the computer gets to that place, the variables will have values that make '0'B true. But '0'B can never be true, no matter what values any variables have. Therefore, the only way we can prove '0'B at a place in a program is if <u>the computer can never get to that place</u>.

Therefore, '0'B is precisely the right thing to conclude after a RETURN. The computer can never get to the place just after the RETURN statement, because it will bump into the RETURN first, and stop right there.

There is a place in procedures where we need to prove '0'B, and that is right at the very end. We must prove that the computer cannot get to the END that terminates a procedure, since the action of the computer is then undefined. The usual way of establishing '0'B is to make the last statement of the procedure a RETURN statement, but there are other ways, as shown by the next example.

Suppose we amend procedure FIND, by inserting a RETURN statement:

```
DECLARE I FIXED;
DO I = 1 TO N;
   IF A(I) = K
   THEN DO;
         M = I;
         RETURN;
         END;
   ELSE DO;
         END;
END;
```

How does this change in the program simplify the proof? Now, as soon as
the variable I gets to a value that satisfies the ATTAIN line of the
specification, the procedure stops. Since C0 is one such value, the variable I can never get any bigger than C0. In fact, the invariant I<=C0 is
sufficient.

Once again, let us go through the steps that show this. Substituting 1 for
I in the invariant gives us 1<=C0, which is something we know at the beginning of the procedure.

Substituting N+1 for I in the invariant yields N+1<=C0, which is what will
be true after the loop finishes. Since we also know that C0<=N, this new
invariant will allow us to conclude '0'B at the end of the procedure, so
that we will not need a RETURN statement at the end. Essentially, what we
are proving is that the only way the procedure can stop is by executing the
RETURN statement that is in the THEN part of the IF statement.

Finally, let us see how to prove I+1<=C0 at the end of the body of the
loop. We do this by proving the assertion at the end of the THEN part and
the ELSE part of the IF. The THEN part is easy. After the RETURN statement, we are allowed to conclude '0'B, and from '0'B, we can conclude anything at all, including I+1<=C0. This may look like sleight-of-hand. Can
we prove anything anywhere just by writing a RETURN statement? Yes, but we
are only allowed to write RETURN statements in places where we can prove
the ATTAIN line of the procedure.

The proof in the ELSE part is also simplified. We prove I+1<=C0 using the
following statements:

    (1) I<=C0   (the loop invariant)
    (2) A(I) ~= K   (from the IF rule)
    (3) A(C0) = K   (what we know about C0)

From (2) and (3) we conclude that I ~= C0, and using this assertion and
(1), we conclude that I+1 <= C0. This sketch leads us to the PL/CV proof
in Figure 25.

```
FIND: PROCEDURE(A,N,K,M);
DECLARE(A(*),N,K) FIXED /*/ READONLY */;
DECLARE M FIXED;
/*/ ASSUME LBOUND(A,1) = 1 & HBOUND(A,1)=N &
          SOME C FIXED.(1<=C<=N & A(C)=K);
    ATTAIN 1<=M<=N & A(M)=K;  */
DECLARE I FIXED;
/*/ CHOOSE C0 FIXED WHERE 1<=C0<=N & A(C0)=K; */
/*/ ~(1 > N) BY ARITH, N >= 1;    */

DO I = 1 TO N BY 1;
    /*/ ASSUME I <= C0; */
    /*/ 1<=I<=N; */
    /*/ ATTAIN I+1 <= C0; */
    IF A(I)=K
    THEN DO;
            /*/ A(I)=K; */
            M = I;
            RETURN;
            END;
    ELSE DO;
            /*/ A(I)~=K;
                A(C0)=K;
                ~(I = C0) BY INTRO;
                I+1 <= C0 BY ARITH, I <= C0, ~(I=C0); */
            END;
END;
END FIND;
```

Figure 25 Searching an array using a RETURN statement

The DO WHILE Rule

Figure 26 shows a new kind of loop that is more flexible than the DO INDEX
loop. Remember that the DO INDEX loop executes a series of statements a
specified number of times, using an index variable to keep track of how
many times the loop body has been executed. In constrast, the body of the
DO WHILE loop can be executed an arbitrary number of times.

When the computer gets to the DO WHILE statement, it first finds the value
of the boolean expression B. If B has the value '0'B, the DO WHILE statement, including the body of the loop, is skipped. But if B has the value
'1'B, then the body of the loop is executed. The execution of the loop
body should change some of the program variables in B. The value of B is
found a second time. If B is '0'B, then the execution of the statement is
complete, and the computer goes on the the statement after the END. But if
the value of B is still '1'B, the body of the loop is executed another
time. As implied by the name of the statement, the loop body is executed
over and over, so long as the value of B is '1'B. After each execution of
the loop body, the value of B is found, and as soon as the value of B is
'0'B, the execution of the loop is complete.

```
/*/ P ... */
/*/ SOME S0 FIXED. (S0>=0 & T{S0//S}) ... */
DO WHILE(B);
    /*/ ASSUME P; */
    /*/ ARB[ITRARY] S FIXED WHERE T; */
    /*/ B; */
    /*/ ~T{0//S} ... */
    .
    .
    .
    /*/ P ... */
    /*/ T{S-1 // S} ... */
END;
/*/ P & ~B; */
```

Figure 26   The DO WHILE Rule

In one sense, the proof rules for the DO WHILE loop are simpler than those
for the DO INDEX rule. In order to prove something about the DO WHILE
rule, you must first come up with a loop invariant P. We prove two things
about P. First, we prove that it is true just before the loop begins execution. Second, we show that if P is assumed true at the beginning of the
loop body, then P can be proved true at the end of the loop body, that is,
that the loop body "leaves P invariant." Note that the loop invariant P is
allowed to be false inside the body of the loop, but by the time the loop
body is finished, the invariant must be made true again. If we know these
two facts, then no matter how many times the loop body is executed, we know
the loop invariant must be true after the loop completes execution. Also,
we know that the Boolean expression B must be true at the beginning of the
loop body, since if B is false, the loop body is not executed. Likewise,
when the loop completes, we know ~B, since the loop does not finish until B
is false.

The aspect of the DO WHILE loop that makes it more complicated than the DO
INDEX loop is that it is possible to write DO WHILE loops that never finish. The purpose of the proof lines involving S and T is to show that the
loop you have written does finish.

In the template for the DO WHILE rule, S represents a logic variable, and T
represents an assertion. The assertion T will involve both S and one or
more program variables that are changed inside the body of the loop. (The
loop body should change at least one variable; if you write a DO WHILE loop
whose body does not change any program variables, the loop body will executed either zero times, or the loop will be executed forever, depending on
whether B is false or true.) For the sake of simplicity, let us assume that
T involves only one program variable, V. We will write T(V, S) to
emphasize that T is asserting that there is some relationship between V and
S.

Initially, we must show that there is some S0 >= 0 such that T(V, S0)
holds. That is, the initial value of V must be related (by T) to some

non-negative value S0. We also show that if V is related to S at the beginning of the loop body, then the body will change the value of V in such a way that V is related to S-1 at the end of the loop body. Let's think about the implications of this proof. If initially, V is related to S0, then after one execution of the loop body, V will be changed so that it is related to S0-1. After two executions V will be related to S0-2. After three executions, S0-3, and so on. Now remember that S0 is greater than or equal to zero. Therefore, successive executions of the loop body change V so that it is related to smaller and smaller non-negative values. But, at the top of the loop body, we show that it is impossible for V to be related to zero inside the loop body. Therefore, the loop must finish when or before V gets to be related to zero; it cannot go on forever. Of course the loop does not "know" whether V is related to zero. It simply goes around again as long as B is true. We are the ones who know that P and B together imply that V is not related to zero, so that if V is related to zero at the end of the loop, then B must be false there and the loop does not execute again.

Let's see how this all comes together in an example. We will write a procedure that divides X by Y using a DO WHILE loop, putting the quotient in Q and the remainder in R. The specification for this program is:

```
DIVP: PROCEDURE(X, Y, Q, R);
DECLARE (X, Y) FIXED /*/ READONLY */;
DECLARE (Q, R) FIXED;
/*/ ASSUME X>=0 & Y>0; */
/*/ ATTAIN X = Y*Q + R & 0 <= R < Y; */
```

We perform the division using the method of repeated subtraction. We subtract Y from X over and over, until what is left is less than Y. What is left is the remainder, and the number of subtractions we did is the quotient. The body of the loop is going to consist of a statement that does a subtraction, and the statement Q = Q + 1, which counts in Q the number of subtractions we do.

Notice that if X = Y*Q + R is true, and if we increase Q by one, and decrease R by Y, the assertion remains true. This suggests that X = Y*Q + R is a good choice for an invariant. Now the loop invariant must be true before the loop begins. Because we wish to use Q to count the number of subtractions we do, we want Q to begin with value 0. Thus, in order to make the invariant start out true, we must begin by setting R to X. So far, our program looks like:

```
Q = 0;
R = X;
DO WHILE(???)
    /*/ ASSUME X = Y*Q + R; */
    Q = Q + 1;
    R = R - Y;
END;
```

What do we use for B, the stopping condition for our loop? We know we want the loop to stop when R gets small. But just how small? Well, we know that when the loop finishes, we will get to conclude ~B. One assertion that we want to be true when the loop finishes is that R < Y. One way we can make this assertion true after the loop completes is to use its negation, R >= Y for the stopping condition of the loop.

The final assertion we need to show at the end of the loop is that 0 <= R. But looking at the body of the loop, we see that R is non-negative throughout the execution of the loop. So we just add the condition 0 < R to the loop invariant. This gives us:

```
Q = 0;
R = X;
DO WHILE(R >= Y)
    /*/ ASSUME X = Y*Q + R & 0 <= R; */
    Q = Q + 1;
    R = R - Y;
END;
```

Next, we must show that the loop finishes. In order to do this, we must come up with a termination assertion T. There is a trick for finding a T that almost always works. All you have to do is make up some expression E that has the following properties:

(1) At the beginning of the body of the loop, the expression always has a value that is greater than zero.
(2) An execution of the loop body always decreases the value of the expression.

The expression E does not have to appear anywhere is the program. Usually you cobble it together using program variables that are changed by the body of the loop. Sometimes you have to negate a variable that the loop body increases, to make sure the value of the expression E decreases. Other times, you have to add a constant onto a variable to make sure the value of the expression is greater than zero. In this program, there is an easy expression that meets our needs: R. It is clear that an execution of the loop body decreases R; it is decreased by Y, which is greater than zero. It may not be immediately obvious that R must always be greater than zero at the top of the loop body. But notice that we always know B at the top of the loop body. In this program, B is R >= Y, and we know Y > 0.

Once we have found the expression E, then the termination assertion T is simply E <= S, or in this case, R <= S. The nice thing about using an assertion of the form E <= S for T is that the scary-looking assertion SOME S0 FIXED. (S0 >= 0 & T{S0//S}) is very easy to prove. Usually, as is the case in this program, you will be able to prove that E >= 0 just before the loop begins execution. We just write:

```
SOME S0 FIXED. (S0 >= 0 & R <= S0) BY INTRO, R;
```

That is, the value we pick for S0 is just R; since we know that R >= 0 and R <= R, everything is fine.

```
DIVP: PROCEDURE(X, Y, Q, R);
DECLARE (X, Y) FIXED /*/ READONLY */;
DECLARE (Q, R) FIXED;
/*/ ASSUME X>=0 & Y>0; */
/*/ ATTAIN X = Y*Q + R & 0 <= R < Y; */
/*/ X = Y * 0 + X BY ARITH; */
/*/ 0 <= X; */

Q = 0;
R = X;

/*/ X = Y*Q + R & 0 <= R; */
/*/ SOME S0 FIXED. (S0 >= 0 & R <= S0) BY INTRO, R; */

DO WHILE(R >= Y);
    /*/ ASSUME X = Y*Q + R & 0 <= R; */
    /*/ ARB S FIXED WHERE R <= S; */
    /*/ ~(R <= 0) BY ARITH, R>=Y, Y>0; */

    /*/ X = Y*(Q+1) + (R-Y) BY ARITH, X = Y*Q + R; */
    /*/ 0 <= R - Y BY ARITH, R >= Y, -, Y=Y; */
    /*/ R - Y <= S-1 BY ARITH, R <= S, -, Y > 0; */

    Q = Q + 1;
    R = R - Y;

    /*/ X = Y*Q + R; */
    /*/ 0 <= R; */
    /*/ R <= S-1; */
END;

/*/ X = Y*Q + R & 0 <= R; */
/*/ R < Y BY ARITH, ~(R >= Y); */
RETURN;
END;
```

Figure 26   A procedure to divide X by Y

Occasionally you may run into an involved program in which you will find an
expression E that will meet conditions (1) and (2) above, but you won't be
able to prove that E >= 0 just before the loop begins. There is still a
relatively simple proof:

```
E <= 0 | E >= 0 BY ARITH;
SOME SO FIXED. (SO >= 0 & E <= SO) BY CASES, E <= 0 | E >= 0,
PROOF;
CASE E <= 0 BY INTRO, 0;
CASE E >= 0 BY INTRO, E;
QED;
```

That is, if E <= 0, let SO be 0, and if E >= 0, let SO be E. In either
case, there exists an SO that works.

Let us take a quick look at the two other things we need to prove to show
the loop terminates. At the top of the loop body, we need to show that
~T{0//S}, or ~(R<=0), which is the same as R > 0. We also need to show
that if R <= S at the beginning of the loop body, then R <= S-1 at the end
of the loop body. In other words, we need to show that the loop body
decreases the value of R. This is easily done using the assignment rule
and some arithmetic. The complete proof is shown in Figure 26.

WHILE loops and accessibility
The accessibility rules for WHILE loops are just the same as those for DO
INDEX loops. The body of the loop is a proof block, and proof lines outside the loop cannot reach inside the loop body for hypotheses. Proof
lines inside the loop body can reach outside the loop for hypotheses, but
not if a program variable in the hypothesis is changed anywhere in the loop
body. See the section "Loops and accessibility" on pg. 87 for more
details.

WHILE loops and well-defined expressions
Suppose you have a reference to an array element in the Boolean expression
of a WHILE loop. As usual, you must prove the subscript in bounds just
before the reference:

```
/*/ LBOUND(A, 1) <= I <= HBOUND(A, 1) ... */
DO WHILE(A(I) > 0);
    .
    .
    .
/*/ LBOUND(A, 1) <= I <= HBOUND(A, 1) ... */
END;
```

But you also must prove the array subscript in bounds at the end of the
loop body. The reason you must write this proof in two places is that the
value of the boolean expression is found when the loop first begins, and
after every execution of the body. In both these cases, you must show that
the expression is well-defined. Typically, the assertion you must prove to
show the boolean expression is well-defined will be a consequence of the
loop invariant, and you can use exactly the same proof in both places.

The GOTO statement
Figure 27 contains a template for the GOTO statement. The template
involves at least two statement, the GOTO statement, and the label statement. Whenever the computer gets to a GOTO L statement, it immediately

```
/*/ P ... */
GOTO L;
/*/ '0'B; */
.
.
.
/*/ P ... */
GOTO L;
/*/ '0'B; */
.
.
.
/*/ P ... */
/*/ ATTAIN P; */
L:;
/*/ P; */
```

Figure 27   The GOTO statement

stops executing the statement of the program that contained the GOTO. The
next statement it will execute is the statement after the L:, the label
statement.

In the template in Figure 27, L stands for any label. A label looks just
like a variable. Labels are not declared, and must be different from every
variable in the procedure. There can be more than one GOTO statement for
each label, but each label must appear in just one label statement.

The GOTO statement is very similar to the RETURN statement. It is impossible for the computer to get to the point in the program just after a GOTO
or RETURN statement, because as soon as it gets to one of these statements,
it goes somewhere else. Therefore, after a GOTO or RETURN, we may conclude
'0'B. Remember, if we assert P at a place in a program, we are saying,
"whenever the computer gets to that place, P will be true." To assert '0'B
at a place is to say, "the computer will never get to that place."

The ATTAIN line that comes just before the label statement is used to indicate the assertion P that we want to be true whenever we reach the label
statement. In order to make sure this assertion will be true, we have to
look at all the ways of getting to the label statement. The first way of
getting there is by executing the preceding statement. Therefore, we must
prove that just before the label statement, the assertion P holds. The
other ways of getting to the label statement are by way of any GOTOs that
reference that label. Therefore, before each GOTO, we must be able to
prove that P holds.

There are some restrictions on the use of the GOTO statement. First, the
label statement referenced in the GOTO statement must come after the GOTO
itself. A GOTO that violates this restriction is called a "backwards
GOTO". Programs that contain backwards GOTOs can get into endless loops.
Instead of using a backwards GOTO, use a DO WHILE statement. Then you can

```
GOTO IN_BLOCK;
.
.
.
IF B
THEN DO;
    .
    .
    .
    IN_BLOCK:;
    .
    .
    .
    END;
```

Figure 28   An improper use of the GOTO statement

use the DO WHILE rule to prove that your program does not get into an end-less loop.

The second restriction on the GOTO statement is that it may not be used to enter a proof block. Remember that within programs, a proof block is the THEN part or ELSE part of an IF statement, or the body of a loop. The reason for this restriction is that this kind of GOTO is simply poor programming style. Figure 28 shows an example of a violation of this restriction.

In recent years, the GOTO statement has fallen into disrepute. There are some computer languages, such as FORTRAN and BASIC, in which the THEN part of an IF statement is limited to a single statement, and the ELSE part is required to be empty. Also, these languages have no equivalent of the DO WHILE statement. A programmer using these languages who wants to write a reasonable IF statement or a DO WHILE statement must "construct" them using simple IF statements and GOTO statements. This type of programming is to be avoided in PL/C.

One way of preventing people from writing FORTRAN-style programs in PL/C is to forbid the use of the GOTO statement entirely. Any program that can be written in PL/C can be written without the use of the GOTO statement, and some programmers have given up (voluntarily or otherwise) the use of the statement. However, there are programming problems for which the GOTO-free solution is more awkward than a solution using the GOTO. As long as you follow the two restrictions mentioned above (these restrictions are enforced by the proof checker, but not by the compiler), the only consideration should be whether the GOTO simplifies your program and its proof.

The most common use of the GOTO statement is to branch out of a DO WHILE loop. Sometimes a GOTO statement is the only way that a DO WHILE loop can finish, as in the following example.

```
SP = K;
DO WHILE('1'B);
/*/ ASSUME K<=SP and (all J such that K<J<=SP. J is composite); */
/*/ Let GP be any prime greater than K.  This loop body reduces
    the value of GP-SP.  GP-SP starts out positive, and can never
    get to zero, since if GP-SP=0, then GP=SP, which by the above
    invariant would imply GP is composite, which is a contradiction. */

    SP = SP+1;

    /*/ (all J such that K<J<SP. J is composite) and K<SP; */

    [ Set the variable PRIME to '1'B if SP is prime, and
      set it to '0'B if SP is composite]

    IF PRIME
    THEN DO;
         /*/ all J such that K<J<SP are composite, and SP
             is prime and greater than K, therefore SP is the
             smallest prime greater than K.  */
         GOTO FOUND;
         END;
    ELSE DO;
         /*/ SP is composite, so the invariant is re-established. */
         END;
END;
/*/ '0'B -- the computer can never get here. */

/*/ ATTAIN SP is the smallest prime greater than K; */
FOUND:;
```

Figure 29 Finding the smallest prime greater than K

There is no largest prime number. That is, if you give me any number K,
there is always a prime number greater than K (this fact was first proved
by Euclid). Therefore, it makes sense to write a program that, given K,
produces the smallest prime number that is greater than K. One step in
solving this problem is to write a piece of program that given P, deter-
mines whether or not P is prime. This task can be easily performed with a
DO INDEX loop; let's presume we can do this. Then, Figure 29 shows how we
would write the program to find the smallest prime greater than K. To get
a complete program, we would have to refine the instructions in brackets
down to a DO INDEX loop that performs the function described.

Notice how the rules for '0'B make the proof work. In order to show that
the loop invariant holds at the end of the loop, we have to show that it
holds at both the end of the THEN part and ELSE part of the loop. Since
the statement inside the THEN part is a GOTO, we can conclude '0'B at that
point, and from '0'B, we can infer anything, including the loop invariant.

Likewise, to satisfy the GOTO rule, we must prove that SP is the smallest
prime greater than K just before the GOTO and just before the label

```
/*/ Q BY ... */        <---------
                                |
IF B1                           |
THEN DO; GOTO L; END;  (Say this is the first GOTO L)
                                |
/*/ R BY ... */   <-----        |  R
                       |        |  I
IF B2                  |        |  G
THEN DO; GOTO L; END;  | W      |  H
                       | R      |  T
/*/ S BY ... */   <----| O      |
                       | | N    |
L:;           WRONG    | | G    |
                       | |      |
/*/ P BY ... S, R, Q ... */
```

Figure 30 Valid and Invalid references past GOTO statements

statement. The proof just before the label statement is easy, because
after the DO WHILE('1'B) loop we can conclude ~'1'B, or '0'B, and from that
we can infer anything.

GOTO statements and accessibility
The GOTO statement and its corresponding label statement behave somewhat
like the opening and closing of a proof block. When a proof line reaches
past a label statement for a hypothesis, it must reach back past all GOTO
statements that refer to that label as well. Figure 30 shows some examples
of valid and invalid references involving GOTO statements. The references
to R and S are not valid, since one of the GOTO statements could cause the
statements that make R and S true to be skipped. The reference to Q is
correct, assuming accessibility rules about assignment statements have been
followed.

Variations
There are a number of generalizations and/or minor variants of the programming constructs and rules given thus far. There are no new concepts, only
straightforward extensions of what has been done. To the extent that these
new features may be duplicated using the system already given, they are
redundant. However, certain combinations of program constructs and certain
patterns of proofs occur frequently enough in actual programming to justify
explicit and simple forms for their use.

SELECT
One may take three different courses in a program, depending on
whether the value of a FIXED variable is > 0, = 0, or < 0, by nesting
one IF statement inside another. The proofs for this and for similar
constructs tend to have a great deal of repetition of the same ATTAIN
condition. In addition, this method rapidly becomes unwieldy and
hard to read or understand as the number of options to be distinguished increases. Multi-branch decisions are best done using the
SELECT statement, as follows:

```
SELECT;
  WHEN (bexpl) DO; ... END;
  WHEN (bexp2) DO; ... END;
  .
  .
  .
  WHEN (bexpn) DO; ... END;
  OTHERWISE    DO; ... END;
END;
```

When control reaches a SELECT, the boolean expressions are evaluated
in order until one is reached whose value is '1'B. The corresponding
branch is then executed, after which control passes to the first
statement following the SELECT. If none of the boolean expressions
evaluates to '1'B, the OTHERWISE branch is the one taken. (Note:
SELECT is recognized by the PL/CS compiler, but is not a part of the
PL/C language.)

The proof rules for SELECT are entirely analogous to those for IF.
It is necessary to show that each of the boolean expressions is
well-defined, the line "/*/ ATTAIN P; */" must immediately precede
the "SELECT" line, and the assertion P must be established at the end
of each branch. If this is done, the assertion P is true after the
SELECT is executed. At the beginning of each branch, one is allowed
to assume that its corresponding boolean expresion is true, and that
all previous ones are false. So, in the i-th branch, the assertion:

$$\sim bexpl \ \& \ \sim bexp2 \ \& \ .... \ \& \ \sim bexpi\text{-}1 \ \& \ bexpi$$

is true. In the OTHERWISE branch, one may assume that all of the
boolean expressions appearing are false.

The rule for accessiblity of assertions inside a branch of the SELECT
is similar to that for those inside the ELSE-branch of an IF statement. That is, you may reach from inside a branch to an assertion
appearing before the SELECT, even though a previous branch contains
an assignment to one of the variables in the assertion you are reaching for. Such an assignment could not affect the truth of the assertion inside the later branch, since only one branch of the SELECT is
chosen to be executed.

No-ELSE IFs
There is another minor variation on the IF statement that is used
mainly for aesthetic purposes. Sometimes the ELSE-branch does not
contain any programming statements, but only proof text establishing
P (the ATTAIN of the IF) from the assumption $\sim B$ (where B is the
boolean expresiion of the IF). Many programmers feel that an empty
programming block is inelegant. In such cases therefore, the ELSE-
branch may be eliminated entirely, as long as $\sim B \Rightarrow P$ is proven
before the IF. Should B evaluate to '0'B in such an elseless IF, control simply skips over the THEN-branch to the first statement following the IF.

Downward DO-index loops

The DO-index loop described earlier increased the value of a variable
on each iteration. One can, in effect, "run it backwards" by using
the negation of the index variable. E.g. to look at the elements of
an array of size N in reverse order:

```
DO I = 0 TO N-1 BY 1;
   .
   .
   .
   ... A(N - I) ...
   .
   .
END:
```

A more direct and natural way is available, however. To decrease the
index variable on each iteration, change the "BY 1" to "BY -1". The
above then becomes:

```
DO I = N TO 1 BY -1;
   .
   .
   .
   ... A(I) ...
   .
   .
END:
```

Execution stops when the index variable becomes less than the final
value. If the starting expression you use is <u>already</u> less than the
final expression, the body of the loop is simply skipped.

The proof rule for this case of the DO-INDEX is the same as for the
increasing index case, with the obvious changes needed to account for
the index decreasing. It is as follows (see p. 84 for a fuller
explanation):

```
/*/ S < F => P{F-1//I} ... */
/*/ P{S//I} ... */
    DO I = S TO F BY -1;
    /*/ ASSUME P; */
    /*/ S >= I >= F; */
      .
      .  < body >
      .
    /*/ P{I-1//I} ... */
    END:
/*/ P{F-1//I}; */
```

General ATTAINs on DO-loops

We have defined the conclusion of a DO-index loop to be P{F+1//I} (or
P{F-1//I} for the downward case). The template for this rule is not
really so restrictive. The conclusion may be any assertion E, as

long as it can be shown that E holds when the loop index reaches its final value. To use this form, the old rule must be modified in the following ways:

1) The loop must be immediately preceded by the line "/*/ ATTAIN E; */".
2) The assertion S > F => E (or S < F => E in the downward case) must be true just before the loop, to guard against the case where the body is not executed even once.
3) At the end of the loop body, the two assertions
   a) I ~= F => P{I+1//I} (or P{I-1//I} in the downward case)
   b) I = F => E
   must be true. The first insures that the invariant will still be true if there is another iteration. The second guarantees that E will be true when the loop finishes executing (since I=F on the last iteration). Note that if E is P{F+1//I} (or P{F-1//I}), then this is just the same as the old rule.

There is one restriction on the form of the conclusion. E may not contain the loop index program as a free variable, as the definition of the action of a DO-index loop does not specify the value of this variable after completion of the loop. Even if such an E is provable from this rule, it is not valid as a conclusion since, in this case, the rule would not accurately reflect the meaning of the programming construct.

A DO-WHILE loop can similarly have a general conclusion E. This time, two modifications to the old rule are needed.

1) /*/ ATTAIN E; */ must immediately precede the loop.
2) The invariant must be of the form P & (~B => E), where B is the boolean expression for termination of the loop.

Since the DO-WHILE rule requires the invariant to be true just before entering the loop, and at the end of each iteration, then whenever the loop finishes executing ~B => E and ~B will both be true, and therefore E will be as well.

DO UNTIL
The execution of a DO WHILE loop can be informally described as

1) Test the boolean condition. If true
2) execute the body of the loop.

This sequence of actions is performed until the boolean condition evaluates to '0'B.

There are circumstances when it is more natural to make a test _after_ each execution of a loop instead of before. I.e.

1) execute the body of the loop
2) test the boolean condition, and quit if true.

where the above is repeated while the boolean condition evaluates to
'0'B. Such a sequence could be built out of a DO WHILE('1'B) with an
IF at the end of the body that has a GOTO. PL/CV, however, provides
a more direct means called the DO UNTIL loop:

```
DO UNTIL(B)
    .
    . < body >
    .
END;
```

This operates just as described above. (Note in particular that the
body is executed at least once regardless of the value of B upon
first encountering the loop.)

The rule that insures that such loops will terminate is exactly like
the corresponding rule for DO WHILE's and needs no further explanation. The form required is as follows:

```
/*/ SOME S0 FIXED. S0 >= 0 & T{S0//S} ... */
    DO UNTIL (B);
    /*/ ARB S FIXED WHERE T; */
    /*/ ~T{0//S} ... */
        .
        . < body >
        .
    /*/ T{S-1//S} ... */
    END;
```

The rules for drawing conclusions from the DO UNTIL are basically the
same as for the DO WHILE, but with some modifications to acount for
the test coming afterwards:

```
/*/ P ... */
/*/ ATTAIN E; */
    DO UNTIL (B);
    /*/ ASSUME P; */
        .
        . < body >
        .
    /*/ B => E ... */
    /*/ ~B => P ... */
    END;
/*/ E; */
```

There is no option about the line /*/ ATTAIN E; */. It must immediately precede the DO UNTIL line. Note that one need not prove that
the invariant holds at the bottom of the loop, but only that it holds
if the loop is going to execute again (so that the assumption of P at
the top will be true). In the DO WHILE rule, the assumption that B
is true just inside the loop is often critical in showing that the
invariant holds at the end. In the body of the DO UNTIL, however, one
cannot assume that B is false (or anything else about it) since it is

not tested until after the first iteration. Its proof rule therefore
does not require that P always hold at the end of the loop body. One
must show, however, that if execution is about to halt (because B is
true) then the exit assertion is true. If this is done, then E will
be true just after the loop and may be asserted there.

If the boolean expression B contains an array reference or a division, then it must be shown to be well defined just as in a DO WHILE
loop. However, since the B of a DO UNTIL is only evaluated after
each iteration, a proof that it is well defined is only required at
the end of the loop body. It need not be shown at the entrance to
the loop as with the DO WHILE rule.

LEAVE

One of the most common uses of the GOTO statement is to exit a loop
if its conclusion has already been attained. In such a case, one
typically wants to exit to a point just outside the loop. Because of
the frequency of this construct, a slightly abbreviated form is provided by the PL/CS compiler and checked by the PL/CV proof checker.
(It is not a part of PL/C however.)

If a loop (of any kind) is labelled (by "L:", say) just before it,
then the programming statement "LEAVE L;" may appear anywhere inside
the body of the loop. The effect is the same as a GOTO statement to
a label at the point just after the loop. (Note that the two restrictions on the use of GOTO's are automatically satisfied in this
case. The transfer of control is in a forward direction and does not
enter a proof block.) If E is the conclusion to be attained by the
loop labelled "L", then E must be true at each occurence of a "LEAVE
L" statement. If this is shown, then E may be asserted just after
the loop. (Since the loop L terminates either normally - in which
case the usual proof rules for loops guarantee that E holds - or
through one of the LEAVE's, at which point we have shown E to be
true.)

E may be either the explicit ATTAIN of a loop, or the default P & ~B
or P{F+1//I} of the DO WHILE and DO-index cases respectively. In
actual programming, it is rarely the case that the loop invariant is
true at a point where premature termination of the loop is desired.
Most often then, LEAVE is used in conjunction with a general exit
condition.

Shielded Program Text

In the section on the assignment rule, an example was given using the
statement "J = J+1". The proof segment showed that J's value after the
assignment was one more than its previous value. It required the assumption that "before the assignment statement ... J is equal to some other
variable J0." The variable J0 is needed to be able even to express the
relationship of J's new value to the old one. Such a variable could be
obtained prior to the assignment by the following two statements:

```
/*/ SOME X FIXED. X=J BY INTRO, J;
    CHOOSE J0 FIXED WHERE J0 = J;  */
```

In general, however, in our proofs of programs we may wish to talk about
the relationship of the current value of a variable to several previous
values, or to previous values of other variables. We may even want to
express a conditional relationship between the current values and previous
ones. While these things may be done in the logic using logical variables
as above, such proofs get very long for only moderately complex problems,
and are hard to read and understand. It is usually more concise and under-
standable to use program variables to keep track of old values and to main-
tain expressions that will be useful in describing the relations we want.

However, the space to store such variables, and the time needed to execute
the statements that update them are both resources that we may not be willing to spend on operations that are not necessary for the program to work
properly. For this reason, we shield the declarations of these variables,
as well as all statements involving them, from the compiler in the same way
that we shield our proof text. As far as the logic is concerned, such
statements are treated just as if they were part of the program. All rules
for introducing program statements must be followed, and all conclusions
allowed by the rules may be asserted. When it comes time to execute the
program though, all of these statements are ignored.

If we could distinguish program statements from logical assertions, then we
could simply use the same shielding that we have already introduced to
separate proofs from programs. Recall however, that the assignment operator "=" of the programming language is (regrettably) identical to the
boolean equality operator of our logic. If "D" were a shielded program
variable, we could not distinguish the assertion /*/ D = 0; */ from the
shielded assignment of 0 to D. We therefore use a different kind of
shielding for program statements. Declarations of shielded program variables, and all statements using them are delimited by "/*:" and "*/"
instead of by "/*/" and "*/".

Program variables that are declared shielded may not appear in a non-
shielded program statement. Because the compiler ignores anything
shielded, it would not see the declaration and would report an erroneous
use of an undeclared variable in the program. Non-shielded program variables may of course appear inside shielded program text: one of the things
we wanted shielded variables for was to represent values from the course of
the computation. However, we also want our programs to have the property
that the values in the non-shielded variables are the same whether or not
the shielded statements are executed. We therefore require that shielded
program statements may not change the values of non-shielded variables
(i.e. non-shielded variables may not appear on the left hand side of
shielded assignment statements).

If a shielded variable is a parameter to the procedure it is in, then it
must appear in the parameter list as well as in a shielded declaration.
The occurrences of shielded parameters in parameter lists are shielded as
well, e.g.

```
FOO: PROCEDURE( A, B /*:,C */ ,D /*:,E(*) ,F*/);
     DECLARE (A,B,D) FIXED;
   /*: DECLARE (C,E(*),F) FIXED; */
```

One of the most common uses of shielded variables is as parameters to help express the assume and attain conditions of a procedure. For example, a procedure that put the sum of two of its parameters back into one of them could be specified as:

```
ADD_INTO: PROCEDURE( X, Y /*:, XOLD, YOLD */);
           DECLARE (X, Y) FIXED;
    /*: DECLARE (XOLD, YOLD) FIXED READONLY; */
    /*/ ASSUME X = XOLD & Y = YOLD; */
    /*/ ATTAIN X = XOLD + YOLD; */
```

For a slightly more complex example, consider a procedure that takes a fixed array and exchanges the largest value in the array with the value in the first (lowest numbered) position. This could be specified as follows:

```
MOVE_MAX_TO_FIRST: PROCEDURE( A(*)  /*:, AOLD(*) */ );
           DECLARE A(*) FIXED;
    /*: DECLARE AOLD(*) FIXED READONLY; */
    /*/ ASSUME LBOUND(A,1) = LBOUND(AOLD,1) &
               HBOUND(A,1) = HBOUND(AOLD,1) &
               ALL J FIXED WHERE LBOUND(A,1) <= J <= HBOUND(A,1).
                                 A(J) = AOLD(J); */

    /*/ ATTAIN SOME K FIXED WHERE LBOUND(A,1) <= K <= HBOUND(A,1).(
        ALL L FIXED WHERE LBOUND(A,1) <= L <= HBOUND(A,1).
                                 AOLD(K) >= AOLD(L)
    &    A(1) = AOLD(K)
    &    A(K) = AOLD(1)
    &    ALL M FIXED WHERE M~=1 & M~=K. A(M) = AOLD(M));  */
```

As an example that would use shielded assignments, assume that you want to prove of an array parameter that the values upon return are a permutation of the original values. A straightforward way to state that one array is a permutation of another is to assert that a permutation of the indices of one gives the other. This can be expressed by means of a third array which records that permutation of the indices.

```
PERM: PROCEDURE(A(*) /*:, AOLD(*), P(*) */);
           DECLARE A(*) FIXED;
    /*: DECLARE AOLD(*) FIXED READONLY; */
    /*: DECLARE P(*) FIXED; */
    /*/ ASSUME  LBOUND(A,1) = LBOUND(AOLD,1) = LBOUND(P,1) &
               HBOUND(A,1) = HBOUND(AOLD,1) = HBOUND(P,1) &
               ALL J FIXED WHERE LBOUND(P,1) <= J <= HBOUND(P,1).
                 SOME K FIXED.( LBOUND(P,1) <= K <= HBOUND(P,1)
                         & P(K) = J
                         & A(P(K)) = AOLD(K) ); */
    /*/ ATTAIN  ALL J FIXED WHERE LBOUND(P,1) <= J <= HBOUND(P,1).
                 SOME K FIXED.( LBOUND(P,1) <= K <= HBOUND(P,1)
                         & P(K) = J
                         & A(P(K)) = AOLD(K) ); */
```

The attain and assume conditions both contain clauses that assert that P is a permutation of the indices of the array A that makes it equal to AOLD (the readonly original values). In the body of the procedure, whenever two elements of A are exchanged, the corresponding elements of P may be exchanged (in shielded assignment statements) to preserve this property. The proof that the desired clauses are still true of P may be derived from the array assignment rules and the fact that the clauses were true prior to the assignments.

Rules for Arrays

In the last two examples, we considered procedures whose bodies contained assignments to array elements. Until then, we had only used arrays as readonly parameters to a procedure. As such, arrays follow all the same rules as any other variable. When they appear on the left-hand side of assignment statements however, some subtleties arise which require a little more complexity in the proof rules to describe properly.

Individual elements of an array, say A(I), are sometimes called <u>subscripted variables</u>. They are thought of as variables with special access via subscripts. From this point of view, we would expect to be able to treat them as simple variables, e.g. use them in expressions like 2+A(I). In particular, if they are program variables, we expect to be able to modify them by assignment as in

    A(I) = 2;

Suppose at this point I has the value 4. Then the meaning is that location A(4) gets the value 2. We can represent this pictorially with boxes as:

```
A   |_?_|_?_|_?_|_?_|_?_|_?_|_...          I   |_4_|
     1   2   3   4   5   6   ...

    A(I) = 2;


A   |_?_|_?_|_?_|_2_|_?_|_?_|_...
     1   2   3   4   5   6   ...
```

We can reference a subscripted variable by an expression, as in A(I+J), A(MOD(I,10)), or even A(A(I)). This gives us considerable power.

One might expect that the rule for for reasoning about assignment to subscripted variables would be the same as for simple variables, i.e.

$$P\{exp1 \mathbin{//} A(exp2)\};$$

$$A(exp2) = exp1;$$

$$\overline{}$$

$$P$$

But consider the case A(A(I)) = 2 and the assertion 2 > 0. We expect to conclude A(A(I)) > 0, but suppose A and I are:

A |_1_|_0_|_...   I |_1_|
    1   2 ...

Then after the assignment A(A(I)) = 2 we have A(1) = 2, so A(A(I)) =
A(A(1)) = A(2) and A(2) = 0, so the falsehood 0 > 0 would result from this
rule. (Note that if A(I) ~= I, we could not derive 0 > 0.)

The difficulty here is that an array is more than a collection of simple
variables. The array name A refers to an entire structure, a mapping from
indices to values. The assignment A(I) = 2 affects the meaning of A.
Thus, in the expression A(A(I)) both occurrences of A must be accounted for
in the rule.

If we know each element of A before the assignment, then there is sufficient information to describe the effect of assignment. The situation is
similar to that encountered in describing the effect of X = X + 1. There
we wrote:

```
/*: X0 = X;  */
    X = X + 1;
/*/ X = X0 + 1;  */
```

In the array case, suppose we know A0 = A, so that A0(I) = A(I) for all I.
We can say after the assignment A(A(I)) = 2 that we know A(A0(I)) contains
the value 2, because we must be indexing the same location that we just
assigned to. To determine the value of A(A(I)) after the assignment, we
must first know A(I). If we know A0(I) = A(I), then we have
A(A(I)) = A(A0(I)). But to know this we need to know A(I) was not changed
by the assignment A(A(I)) = 2. To know this we must know A(I) ~= A(A(I)),
that is, I ~=A(I). So if we know A0(I) ~=I, we should be able to conclude
A(A(I)) = 2. The array assignment rule allows us to draw the desired conclusion easily in such "natural" cases, while preventing us from being
fooled when something trickier is going on:

```
B' = B, t' = t, exp' = exp
   (where t', exp', B'
     cannot contain B)

   B(t) = exp
```

```
   B(t') = exp'    &

ALL I FIXED WHERE  I ~= t.
   B'(I) = B(I)
```

So to conclude A(A(I))=2 from this rule, we take A0 for A', A0(I) = A(I)
for t' = t. (To get these equalities, we may use a shielded assignment:

```
/*: A0 = A;  */
```

whose meaning is described below.) We then have A(A0(I)) = 2 and

(*)   ALL J FIXED WHERE J~=A0(I). A(J) = A0(J);

so if we know A0(I) ~= I, we can apply ALL-elimination with I in place of
J. This gives us A(I) = A0(I), so by equality substitution we get the
desired conclusion A(A(I)) = 2.

If we want to analyse the assignment when A(I)=I (as in the case above
where A(1)=1) then we first note that A0(2)=0 and A0(1)=1. Thus we have
A0(I)=I since I=1, and A0(I) ~= 2. Again we get A(A0(I)) = 2 as one part
of the conclusion, hence A(I) = 2. This time we use (*) above with J
replaced by 2 (which is fine, since A0(I) ~= 2). The result is that
A(2) = A0(2) = 0, so we can show that A(A(I)) = 0.

This short example illustrates how complex reasoning about statements
involving arrays can be. The basic idea is straigtforward: when you assign
to an element of an array, that element has the value you gave it, and
everything else stays the same. As we have seen though, the representation
of this simple action in our formal language requires careful handling. In
some sense, this is the price we pay for the powerful ability to reference
array elements by arbitrary expressions.

There is a further complicating feature of the array assignment rule that
may be overlooked at first. When an assignment is made to any element of
an array, assertions which use that array name are no longer accessible
after the assignment. If you know that B(1)=0, and you make the assignment
B(2)=3, then you must re-prove B(1)=0 by all-elimination from the rule
given above (and the fact that 2~=1). In programs involving much manipulation of arrays, a great deal of proof text must be used to re-establish
assertions which are, in some sense, obvious. This is probably the biggest
obstacle to using PL/CV to verify large programs. As a result of further
research, a new array rule has been developed (but not yet implemented)
which reduces the amount of proof text needed.

Local Array Declarations

A (one-dimensional) array name is introduced into a procedure by a declaration of the form:

DECLARE A(L:U) type;

The FIXED expressions L and U determine the upper and lower bounds of the
array. The domain of the array is the interval L<=X<=U. It must be the
case that the domain of a PL/I array is non-empty, thus the above declaration requires a proof that L<=U.

When a (one-dimensional) array is a parameter to a procedure, we have seen
that it is declared as

DECLARE A(*) type;

because the upper and lower bounds are determined by the actual array
passed as an argument. In order to speak about the domain in this case,

PL/I provides the functions LBOUND(A,1) and HBOUND(A,1). In the procedure that declares A locally, the assertions

LBOUND(A,1) = L   and   HBOUND(A,1) = U

are immediate. When A is a parameter, the requirement that the domain be non-empty allows one to make the assertion

LBOUND(A,1) <= HBOUND(A,1)

anywhere in the procedure.

Assignment of Entire Arrays

There are simple assignment axioms for arrays when we want to set an entire array to a some fixed value, or when we want to copy one array into another. If A and B are the following:

A |_1_|_2_|_3_|_4_|_5_| B |_5_|_4_|_3_|_2_|_1_|

then the assignment A = 0 results in

A |_0_|_0_|_0_|_0_|_0_|

while A = B yields

A |_5_|_4_|_3_|_2_|_1_|

The rule for the latter is really a special case of the equality substitution rule. After the assignment, A(exp) = B(exp) may be asserted for any fixed expression exp. From this, one can quickly derive

ALL I FIXED. A(I) = B(I) BY INTRO;

For the single-value assignment, the rule is that, after the statement A = C, the assertion

ALL I FIXED. A(I) = C

holds. From this, one may show A(exp) = C for any particular fixed expression by all-elimination.

Both of these rules speak about arrays having values for all fixed indices, with no distinction made as to whether they are in the domain of the array. The PL/CV semantics for these "elements" is the same as for the result of a function being applied outside of its domain, or for an uninitialized program variable. That is, they are considered to have an unspecified, but unique value of the proper type. Thus, one may prove assertions about them which are true for any value of the given type. For instance, one can show

$$MOD(A,0) = MOD(A,0) \quad \text{or} \quad A(6) < 0 \mid A(6) = 0 \mid A(6) > 0$$

(where A has a high bound of 5). An assertion which contains such "undefined" components is regarded as true if it is true for any consistent association of values to the undefined terms. This is intended to be a convenience for the user, enabling him or her to ignore domain constraints under certain circumstances. Such terms may only occur in proof text, never in a program statement. (The user who wishes to consider arrays as finite objects may personally impose the restriction of proving all expressions used are well-defined, but this is not checked by PL/CV.)

The assignment of a single value to an array does have the effect of giving that value to the locations which are out of bounds. Subsequent assertions involving the array must reflect this. That is, they regarded as true only if they are true when the undefined terms are given the indicated value. An array so assigned to may have its value changed by subsequent similar assignments. It may also "pass along" its acquired value by being assigned to another array. For this reason, assignment of one array to another may only take place when the domain of both is the same.

Array Equality

There is an axiom for asserting the equality of two arrays when it has been shown that their domains match, and their values are equal for every integer subscript (whether in the mutual domain or not). If one has accessible the assertions:

$$LBOUND(A,1) = LBOUND(B,1) \qquad HBOUND(A,1) = HBOUND(B,1)$$
$$\vdots \qquad\qquad\qquad\qquad \vdots$$
$$LBOUND(A,N) = LBOUND(B,N) \qquad HBOUND(A,N) = HBOUND(B,N)$$

(where N is the number of dimensions of A and B)

$$ALL \ (I1, \ \ldots, \ IN) \ FIXED. \ A(I1, \ \ldots, \ IN) = B(I1, \ \ldots, \ IN)$$

then one may assert

    A = B BY EXTEN;

where EXTEN is short for extensionality.

6.1 Introduction

PL/I is an Algol-like programming language organized around the concept of a command acting on a state through variables. To reason about these commands, they must be allowed in arguments. Their free use in arguments creates a logic far more expressive than the predicate calculus.

The logic of commands described in this section is the heart of the PL/CV asserted program logic. There are three new ideas which must be mastered. First, commands introduce new types of binding, new block structure, and, with gotos, a nonlinear order among statements. The added complexity appears in 6.3. Second, proof rule formats must now display information about positions of the hypotheses and conclusion in the program, especially concerning their lexical order. This added complexity appears in the presentation of rules in 6.4. Third, commands are allowed as part of the purely logical structure of a program, as inside proof-groups. These commands are not meant to be executed. To indicate this fact, they are shielded (from the compiler) just as assertions are. Special rules for shielding commands must be stated.

6.2 Syntax

(i) Shielding

To insure that PL/CV programs are compatible with dialects of PL/I, all PL/CV assertions occurring in programs are enclosed in special PL/I comment delimiters, /*/ and */. Therefore, a PL/CV procedure is actually a program which will compile under either the PL/I, PL/C or PL/CS compiler depending on which commands are used (e.g., PL/C release 7 does not include DO UNTIL, LEAVE, SELECT, whereas PL/I does not include READONLY, etc.).

Commands are, of course, essential in the part of the argument which we intend to execute, the program. But they may also be valuable in the purely logical part of the argument; for instance, to construct an object exclusively for the sake of the proof or to preserve relationships among the logical variables and various program variables, whose values may be changing. These commands, which we do not intend to execute, must be shielded. But since = is both the equality and assignment symbol, /*/ A=0; */, is ambiguous. Is it the assertion "A equals 0" or the command "A gets 0"? The command is written as /*: A=0; */, resolving the ambiguity but necessitating two kinds of left-hand shielding delimiters /*/ and /*:.

To be more precise about shielding, we define the notion of program, program variable, logic variable, and shielding.

<u>Definition</u>: Given a PL/CV procedure, the associated <u>program</u> is the
sequence of statements not enclosed in comment delimiters. All variables and statements in the program are called <u>program variables</u> and
<u>program statements</u> respectively.   Any token enclosed in the special
comments which begin /*/ or /*: and end */ is called <u>shielded</u>.   Any
variable declared in shielded declarations is called an <u>auxiliary vari-
able</u>. Any shielded command is called an <u>auxiliary command</u>. A variable
not appearing in a declaration is <u>logical</u>.

Note 1: Ordinary PL/I comments may not be used inside PL/CV shielded
text because the */ will prematurely close the shield, e.g., /*: DCL
(A(*)/*PERMUTATION ARRAY */, B); */. To include a comment inside
shielded text, use the delimiters /#, #/, as in /*: DCL (A(*) /# PERMU-
TATION ARRAY #/, B); */.

Note 2: Comments cannot cross a card boundary in PL/CS. Hence to submit
a verified program to PL/CS, all shielding delimiters must be closed on
one line and reopened on the next.

     To describe the shielding rules in the syntax below, the following
definitions are useful. Let T be a piece of an argument.

T is completely shielded iff every token in T is shielded.

T is completely unshielded iff no token in T is shielded.

T is partially shielded iff there is at least one shielded and one unshielded
token.

(ii) <u>Grammar of commands</u>

Note, "stmt" is used throughout to abbreviate "statement" and "boolean"
or "bexp" are sometimes used to abbreviate "boolean_exp". (a)   general
categories

```
command  →  unit
         →  compound
         →  branching
         →  iteration
         →  control_punctuation
         →  input_output


unit                    →  assignment_stmt
branching               →  if_stmt
                        →  select_stmt
iteration               →  do-index_stmt
                        →  do-while_stmt
                        →  do-until_stmt
control_punctuation     →  leave_stmt
                        →  goto_stmt
input_output            →  get_stmt
                        →  put_stmt
```

Note: In all categories, the ATTAIN statements must be shielded.

proof_stmt → define_stmt
        → choose_stmt
        → assertion [justification];

stmt → proof_stmt
    → command

(b) unit commands

assignment_stmt → identifier [(integer_exp {, integer_exp}*)] = expression;

Assignments must be completely shielded or unshielded. The left
side of a shielded assignment may not contain a variable declared
in an unshielded declaration.

(c) compound commands

compound → DO;{stmt} $^{+}$END;

(d) branching commands

if_stmt → [ATTAIN assertion;] IF(boolean_exp) THEN stmt [ELSE stmt]

Note: Conditional or select in proofs are preceded by an ATTAIN

select_stmt → [ATTAIN assertion ;]
              [label :] SELECT;
                      {WHEN (boolean_exp) stmt} $^{+}$
                      OTHERWISE stmt END [label];

Note: the select_stmt is not compatible with PL/C version 7.

(e) iteration commands

do-index_stmt → [ATTAIN assertion ;]
               [label :]
               DO identifier = integer_exp TO integer_exp
                 BY {+1,1,-1};
               ASSUME assertion ;
               argument
               END [label] ;

do-while_stmt → [ATTAIN assertion;]
               [label:]
               DO WHILE (boolean_exp);
                 ASSUME assertion;
                 proof_stmt*
               {ARBITRARY,ARB}identifier
                 FIXED WHERE assertion;
                 proof_stmt*
                 argument
               END [label];

```
do-until_stmt → [ATTAIN assertion ;]
              [label :]
              DO UNTIL (boolean_exp)
              ASSUME assertion;
              {ARBITRARY,ARB} identifier FIXED WHERE
               assertion;
               argument
              END [label];
```

(f) punctuation

   goto_stmt → GOTO identifier;   leave_stmt → LEAVE identifier;

   Note: The labeled statement must lie lexically beyond the goto itself,
          but not inside any block not containing the goto.

We do not provide syntax for input-output statements since we have no
rules for them in this version of the system.

6.3 Substitutions

      Program variables have free occurrences in arguments just as logi-
cal variables have free occurrences in assertions. For example, in the
assignment Y=X+1, X is a free variable and Y is bound. We do not need
the concept of substitution for free program variables at this point,
but the concept of a bound program variable is useful in describing the
rules of accessibility, so we define it here.

Definition: Any of the following occurrences of a variable x are binding occurrences (the first six were defined in II 2.8 (ii)).

      1. SOME...x   ALL...x

      2. ARBITRARY...x (or ARB...x)

      3. CHOOSE...x

      4. FOR...x

      5. DEFINE x

      6. x: (as a label of an assertion)

      7. DO x= ...

      8. x=exp (in an assignment)

A nonbinding occurrence of the variable x in an argument A is said to be
bound in A (tightly bound in A) if and only if any of the following
hold:

1. The occurrence is in a subassertion P within the assertion

    ALL...x... .P or SOME...x... .P

2. A is qualified by ARIBTRARY...x or ARB...x or the occurrence is in a subargument B within an argument qualified by ARIBTRARY...x or ARB...x.

3. A contains the statement CHOOSE...x or the occurrence is in a subargument B containing CHOOSE...x.

4. The occurrence is within the assertion or expression following = in FOR...x DEFINE...=.

5. A contains DEFINE x or the occurrence is within a subargument B containing the definition DEFINE x.

6. The occurrence is lexically below the label x: on an assertion in A or in a subargument B of A.

7. The occurrence is within the do-index loop DO $x=exp_1$ to exp_1...END.

8. The occurrence is in an assertion or command L of A for which there is an assignment x=exp on **some** execution path (on **every** execution path) from the beginning of A to L

Remark. A bound variable which is not tightly bound is called **loosely bound**. Such variables arise when one execution path binds x and another does not. For instance X is loosely bound in

                IF X>0 THEN X=5;
                       ELSE Y=7;
        /*/ X-1≥0   */

It would be tightly bound if Y=7 were replaced by X=7.

The next definition tells exactly which binding occurrence of x binds which other occurrences of x. Intuitively, a variable is bound by each binding occurrence which might affect its meaning.

Definition: Every free or loosely bound occurrence of a variable x in argument segments α, β, γ is bound by the binding occurrence of x in

1. ALL...x α; SOME...x α;

2. ARBITRARY...x α QED;

3. CHOOSE...x α QED;

4. FOR...x DEFINE α;

5. FOR...DEFINE x α QED;

6. x: assertion α QED;

7. DO x=exp$_1$ TO exp$_2$ α END;

8. (a) x=exp; α or

   (b) IF bexp THEN DO; ... x=exp α end; ELSE DO; ...END; β or

   (c) DO index = exp$_1$ TO exp$_2$ BY {+,-}1; α; x=exp; β END; γ

   (d) DO WHILE(bexp);α; x=exp; β; END; γ or

   (e) DO UNTIL(bexp);α; x=exp; β; END; γ

For instance, in line 1, α is any well formed part of an assertion up to the first semi-colon. So in ALL N FIXED WHERE N>0 . F(N) = 0 the occurrences of N in N>0 and F(N) =0 are bound by ALL N. In line 8, clause (a) means that after x=exp any free or loosely bound occurrence of x in the rest of the argument is bound by this assignment. Thus in X=0; IF Y>0 THEN X=2; ELSE Y=2; P(X) the loosely bound occurrence of x in IF Y>0 THEN X=2; ELSE Y=2; P(X) is bound by X=0. Assignments x=exp inside loops bind all free or loosely bound occurrence of x in the body.

All other occurrences of x in A are _free_ in A.

6.4 Proof Rules

(i) _Rule formats_

Proof rules for commands require a more complex format than those for the predicate calculus. The rule must show relative lexicographic order of hypotheses. This is done by making vertical order significant, e.g., if hypothesis H$_i$ occurs vertically above hypothesis H$_j$ then H$_i$

must occur lexically before H$_j$ in the argument (unless there is an

explicit remark to the contrary). Some rules must show even more about the relative position of hypotheses and conclusion; this is done by including segments of commands such as conditionals and loops to indicate context. In the case of the loop introduction rules, the loop body is a hypothesis to the introduction of the entire loop (which, of course, contains the body), so sometimes the conclusion must be specified in words.

In all rules, certain hypotheses need only be implicitly known, that is they may be immediate from other assertions appearing previously. Such hypotheses are enclosed in braces.

In some cases, special provisions must be stated to indicate accessibility relationships among hypotheses and conclusions. Subject to these conclusions and the syntactic rules, the hypotheses of any rule can be separated by other commands and assertions _provided that for positions not separated by ellipses_ (...), _the first is accessible to_ the second.

(ii) Well-defined expressions

For each rule involving the evaluation of an expression which may contain defined functions (including arrays), and for each occurrence of a defined function application, there must be an hypothesis guaranteeing that the function application is defined. (When any partial infix operators, such as division, are allowed, then we require also that its arguments are in its domain, e.g. non-zero.) The programming languages PL/C and PL/CS guarantee that any variable uninitialized by the programmer is initialized by the compiler, so an expression is undefined only if array indices are out of bounds.

An expression exp is well-defined if and only if every function application occurring in it is defined. Thus an expression is well-defined only if for each array A in it and for each $A(exp_1, \ldots, exp_n)$ the assertion $LBOUND(A,i) <= exp_i <= HBOUND(A,i)$ is true.

In the proof rules, the phrase "exp is well-defined" will mean the conjunction of all assertions that each function application in exp is defined. For example, the expression
$$(A(2,X)+Z) * B(MOD(A(X,Y),Z))$$

is well-defined means

$LBOUND(A,1) <= 2 <= HBOUND(A,1)$ & $LBOUND(A,2) <= X <= HBOUND(A,2)$ &

$LBOUND(A,1) <= X <= HBOUND(A,1)$ & $LBOUND(A,2) <= Y <= HBOUND(A,2)$ &

$LBOUND(B,1) <= MOD(A(X,Y),Z) <= HBOUND(B,1)$ & $Z \sim= 0$.

(iii) Accessibility

In order for an assertion A at position p to be accessible in an argument at position q, it must mean the same thing at q and p, and it must be visible from q. Commands may cause an assertion A to become inaccessible after the command by changing the meaning of free variables in A. For instance,

1. /*/ Y>0 */

2. /*/ X>2 */

3. /*: X=-3 */

4. /*/ X*Y>2*Y BY ARITH, X>2, *, Y>0 ; */

Line 4 is false because the command at 3 changed the meaning of X. The same thing can happen even though the command lies beyond the assertion, as in this illustration:

```
1.  /*/  X>0;  */

2.     DO WHILE Y>0;

3.        Y=Y-1;

4.  /*/  X>0;  */

5.  /*:  X=X-1; */

6.     END;
```

The assertion X>0 at line 4 may be false although no command changes X in the <u>lexical segment</u> from 1 to 4.

In order for an assertion A at position p to be accessible in an argument at position q, it must be the case that any way of getting to position q passes through position p. Here is an example where this fails:

```
1.  GOTO L;

2.  /*/  X>0;  */

3.  L: ;

4.  /*/  Y>0;  *

5.  /*/  X+Y>0 BY ARITH, X>0,+,Y>0;  */
```

For the purpose of determining accessibility, we use a generalization of the concept of an execution path. This generalization affords a fast check of accessibility.

First we examine the apparently <u>possible</u> execution paths. To define these, ignore the actual values of any boolean and consider execution for both possible values. Replace any unconditional goto, GOTO L, by IF _____ THEN GOTO L ELSE ; and consider both possible paths. (Thus the goto will be ignored in one case.) We say that execution paths determined this way are <u>execution paths in the general sense</u>.

<u>Definition</u>: A position p in an argument <u>dominates</u> position q if and only if every execution path in the general sense from start to q must pass through p. (This is a generalization of lexical order.)

<u>Definition</u>: A <u>proof-block</u> is either a proof-group, a THEN clause, an ELSE clause, a WHEN clause, a WHILE loop, an UNTIL loop, or a DO-index loop.

Let $A(x,...,x)$ indicate that $x_1,...,x_n$ are <u>all</u> the variables free in A.

<u>Definition</u>: An occurrence of an assertion $A(x_1,...,x_n)$ at position p in an argument with commands is <u>accessible</u> from position q if and only if:

(0) q does not occur in a proof block used as justification for the occurrence of $A(x_1,\ldots,x_n)$ at p,

(1) position p **dominates** position q, and

(2) any proof-block containing p also contains q (say, p is **visible** from q), and

(3) $A(x_1,\ldots,x_n)$ is the same at q and p, that is:

    (a) the x_i have the same scope at p as at q.

    (b) no x_i is changed on any execution path (in the general sense) from p to q.

Note: Using the concept of a bound variable of an argument, we can simplify (3) to case (a) since $x_i = exp$ is a binding of x_i which changes its scope.

(iv) **Proofs**

Definition: A **proof** in the language of PL/CV programs is an argument in which every occurrence of an assertion at a position p is either an assumption or follows from accessible lines and immediate assertions by a rule of inference.

Note: Logical variables CANNOT be modified by commands. They are **readonly**.

(v) **Enumeration of command rules**

(1) ASSIGNMENT INTRODUCTION (immediate)

$$\frac{\{exp \text{ is well-defined}\}}{x = exp}$$

If x is an array, exp must be a scalar or an array with the same domain as x.

$$\frac{\{exp, t_1,\ldots,t_n \text{ are well-defined}\}}{\{<t_1,\ldots,t_n> \text{ is in the domain of } A\}}$$
$$A(t_1,\ldots,t_n) = exp$$

(2) ASSIGNMENT ELIMINATION (immediate)

$$P\{exp//x\} \qquad \frac{A=C \qquad C \text{ a constant}}{ALL \ (I_1,\ldots,I_n) \ FIXED.A(I_1,\ldots,I_n)=C}$$

$$x = exp$$
$$P$$

(3) ARRAY ASSIGNMENT ELIMINATION

$$B'=B, \ t'_1=t_1, \ \ldots \ , t'_n=t_n, \ exp'=exp$$

(where t'_i, exp', B'
cannot contain B)

$$\frac{B(t_1, \ \ldots \ , t_n) = exp}{B(t'_1, \ \ldots \ , t'_n) = exp' \ \&}$$

ALL$(I_1, \ \ldots \ , I_n)$ FIXED WHERE $\sim(I_1=t'_1 \& \ldots \& I_n=t'_n)$.

$$B'(I_2, \ \ldots \ , I_n) = B \ (I_1, \ \ldots \ , I_n)$$

(4) CONDITIONAL INTRODUCTION (immediate)

$$\frac{\{bexp \ is \ well\text{-}defined\}}{IF(bexp)THEN \ \ \cdots \ \ [ELSE...]}$$

The content of the branches must be filled in by other introduction
rules.

(5) SELECT INTRODUCTION (immediate)

$$\frac{\{all \ bexp_i \ are \ well\text{-}defined\}}{[label :] \ SELECT;}$$

WHEN $(bexp_1)$ ...

.
.
.

WHEN $(bexp_n)$ ...

OTHERWISE ... END [label];

(6) BOOLEAN EXPRESSION INTRODUCTION (immediate)

conditional

$$\frac{\text{IF (bexp) THEN} \quad \cdots \quad \text{[ELSE } \ldots]}{\text{IF (bexp) THEN DO; bexp} \quad \bullet \bullet \bullet \quad \text{END; [ELSE } \sim\text{bexp} \ldots]}$$

select

SELECT;
    .
    .
    .
WHEN (bexp_i) ...
    .
    .

$$\frac{\text{OTHERWISE} \quad \cdots \quad \text{END;}}{\begin{array}{l} \text{WHEN (bexp}_i) \text{ DO; } \sim\text{bexp}_1 \& \ldots \& \sim\text{bexp}_{i-1} \& \\ \qquad\qquad\qquad\quad \text{bexp}_i \ldots \text{ END;} \\ \quad . \\ \quad . \\ \quad . \\ \text{OTHERWISE DO; } \sim\text{bexp}_1 \& \ldots \& \sim\text{bexp}_n \ldots \text{ END;} \end{array}}$$

END;

The above rules describe which boolean expressions can be introduced as assertions at which points inside conditional and select statements governed by these boolean expressions.

(7) CONDITIONAL ELIMINATION

{bexp is well-defined}
ATTAIN E;

IF (bexp) THEN [DO;] ... E ; [END;]
$$\frac{\qquad\qquad \text{ELSE [DO;]} \quad \bullet \bullet \bullet \quad \text{E ; [END;]}}{E}$$

{bexp is well-defined}
$\sim$bexp => E
ATTAIN E;

$$\frac{\text{IF (bexp) THEN [DO;]} \quad \bullet \bullet \bullet \quad \text{E ; [END;]}}{E}$$

(8) SELECT ELIMINATION

> {bexp$_i$ are well-defined}
>
> ATTAIN E;
> SELECT;
>   WHEN (bexp$_1$) [DO;] ... E ; [END;]
>   .
>   .
>   .
>   WHEN (bexp$_n$) [DO;] ... E ; [END;]
>
>   OTHERWISE [DO;] ... E ; [END;]
>
> <u>END;   </u>
>   E

These rules describe which boolean expressions can be introduced as assertions at which points inside conditional and select statements governed by these boolean expressions.

(9) DO-INDEX INTRODUCTION (immediate)

> <u>{the expressions lower, upper are well-defined}</u>
> DO index = lower TO upper BY {+1,1,-1}; ...END;

(10) DO-INDEX BOUNDS INTRODUCTION (immediate)

> D index = lower TO upper   DO index = upper TO lower
> BY {+1,1};   BY -1;
> lower <= index <= upper;   upper >= index >= lower;
>   .   .
>   .   .
>   .   .
> END;   END;

(11) DO-INDEX ELIMINATION

> upward form
>
> > P{lower//i};
> > [ATTAIN E ;] [lower > upper => E ;]
> >   DO index = lower TO upper BY {+1,1};
> >   ASSUME P{index//i};
> >   .
> >   .
> > <u>   END   .   </u>
> >   E

Note 1: P{upper +1//i} is the default for E if the attain statement is

missing, in which case the last two hypotheses are replaced by
P{upper+1//i}.

Note 2: Index and all variables in upper and lower are readonly inside
the do block.

Note 3: E may not depend on index, which has an arbitrary value upon
exit from the block.

Note 4: The downward form is similar, and is not given here.

(12) DO WHILE INTRODUCTION

```
{bexp is well-defined}
SOME n FIXED . (n>=0 & T);
DO WHILE (bexp);
ARBITRARY n FIXED WHERE T;
~T{0//n};
        .
        .
        .
body
        .
        .
        .
T{n-1//n}; {bexp is well-defined}
END;
```

The loop itself is the conclusion. The rule is used to justify introducing loops into a proof. They can only be introduced if they terminate.

(13) DO WHILE BOOLEAN INTRODUCTION (immediate)

```
DO WHILE (bexp);
        .
        .
        .
END;  .
_____
DO WHILE (bexp);
    ASSUME P;
    bexp;
        .
        .
        .
END;
```

This rule indicates where the boolean expression governing the loop can
be introduced into a loop body, after ASSUME.

(14) DO WHILE ELIMINATION

```
{bexp is well-defined}
P[& (~bexp => E)];
[ATTAIN E;]
DO WHILE (bexp);
   ASSUME P[& (~bexp => E)& {bexp is well-defined}
      .
      .
      .
   body
      .
      .
      .
   {P[ & (~bexp => E)];}
END; {bexp is well-defined}
─────────────────────────────
E
```

Note 1: If the exit condition E is missing, the default is P & ~bexp, in which case ~bexp => E is not necessary

Note 2: If ATTAIN E is present, then ~bexp => E must be part of the invariant P, or derivable from P by immediate rules.

(15) DO UNTIL INTRODUCTION

```
SOME i FIXED . (i>=0 & T);
DO UNTIL (bexp);
   ARBITRARY i FIXED WHERE T;
   ~T{0//i};
      .
      .
      .
   body
      .
      .
      .
   {bexp is well-defined}
   T{i-1//i};
END;
```

The loop itself is the conclusion.

(16) DO UNTIL ELIMINATION

```
P,
ATTAIN E;
DO UNTIL (bexp);
   ASSUME P;
      .
      .
      .
   body
      .
      .
      .
   bexp => E;
   ~bexp => P;
END;
E
```

Note 1: The attain statement is necessary for the until loop.

(17) CONTROL PUNCTUATION

<u>GOTO label;</u>   <u>LEAVE label;</u>
      A   A

This rule permits the introduction of an arbitrary assertion A immediately after (accessible to) GOTO and LEAVE.

(18) LABEL

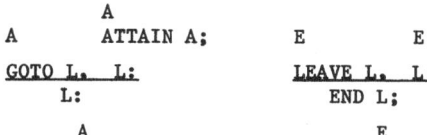

Where A is accessible to each occurrence of GOTO L, and E is the exit condition of the loop labeled L.

PL/CV and Mathematics

The logic presented in sections I-IV is based on the first-order predicate
calculus. This is a formalism capable of expressing much mathematics on
its own. As we have seen, our version can be used to specify the task of a
program and describe the meaning of assignment, sequential execution, conditional execution and iteration which underlie the PL/C and PL/CS programming languages. In defining the assertion language, especially the format
of proof rules, our main concern has been to facilitate the merging of the
logic with program statements, as discussed in section V.

We have primarily used PL/CV to unite assertions and programs, but it
should not be thought that the resulting formal system is merely an application of the first-order predicate calculus which neglects the ability to
do mathematics. All strictly logical proofs are as valid in PL/CV as in
any other formulation of the calculus. In addition, one has directly
available the notions of construction and algorithm that are a part of many
informal proofs. It would be more accurate, and more fruitful, to think of
PL/CV as an augmented first-order logic in which algorithms are very naturally expressible.

There are some limitations in the PL/CV2 implementation of assertions and
programs. For example, we have not defined a meaning for program statements appearing inside theorems. It is possible to meaningfully interpret
declared variables and/or program statements inside assertions, but PL/CV2
does not implement this. There are also features missing from the first-
order logic part of the system that would constitute a real lack if it were
not possible to use the procedure context. For instance, the logic provides no way of asserting the existence of an array by simply listing its
elements. For such a demonstration, an array of the desired size must be
declared in a procedure and assigned the given values.

Because this latter method is sufficient, and in most cases more elegant
than the strictly logical formulation would be, and because our motivation
is interest in programs, we do not add explicit non-procedural axioms for
creating arrays. Rather, we understand that procedures are our most general context, in which the full power of PL/CV may be called upon to
express and prove our mathematical ideas.

Procedure Calls

One may think of the "meaning" of a procedure as: if a set of values
satisfies the ASSUME, then executing the body of the procedure with those
values will change them so as to satisfy the ATTAIN. Just as one may use
previously verified theorems in a proof, so one may use existing verified
procedures in the body of a new procedure. This is further reason for
thinking of procedures as our most general context, since they may reference theorems, but theorems may not contain procedures.

Just how does one procedure call upon another? In our original description
of the operation of a procedure, we assumed that prior to pushing the "GO"

button, somebody put values into its boxes. That someone is another procedure (we'll see later where it all gets started). The reason that one
procedure gives values to another is to be able to use the new values it
produces. However, since the procedure doing the calling can only reference its own variable names, we need some way of transferring values
between procedures. For the sake of discussion let us assume we have two
procedures A and B. A wants to make a call on B, whose specification
begins:

```
B: PROCEDURE(W, X, Y(*), Z);
   DECLARE (W,X,Y(*)) FIXED;
   DECLARE Z BIT(1);
```

The first rule for calling procedure B is that A must provide the proper
number of "arguments" of the correct type (in the correct order). An argument may itself be a variable of A, or an expression made up of constants
and/or variables of A. A typical call on B might look like:

```
CALL B(SUM+1, TEMP, ARRAY, ON);
```

where SUM and TEMP are FIXED variables of A, ARRAY is a fixed array, and ON
is a BIT(1) variable. (These may be locally declared in A or themselves
parameters to it).

When a CALL statement is encountered in the execution of A, the compund
expressions in the argument list (SUM+1 in this case) are evaluated and
placed in the corresponding boxes of B. For those arguments which are just
variables (TEMP, ARRAY and ON), B is given instructions as to where those
boxes are located. Execution of A pauses, and that of B begins. During
this time, whenever B wants to use one of its parameters for which it was
give the location of another box, it actually reads from or writes to that
box. When B returns, any changes made to these borrowed boxes will still
be there. For instance, in the above call, if B assigns 3 to X just before
returning, TEMP will have a value of 3 when A resumes execution after the
call.

The behavior of a procedure is only guaranteed when the initial values of
its parameters satisfy the ASSUME condition. Before the call therefore, A
must prove the ASSUME of B is true, with SUM+1 substituted for W, TEMP for
X, etc.. If B requires

$$Z \Rightarrow Y(X) = 1$$

for example, A must show that

$$ON \Rightarrow ARRAY(TEMP) = 1$$

We must be a little more careful about drawing conclusions in A from the
call to B. B guarantees its ATTAIN condition to hold for _its_ parameters
when it is finished executing. Since not all of these values are necessarily available to A, we cannot simply substitute A's actual arguments for
their corresponding parameters in the ATTAIN of B. Thus, from X=1 in B's
ATTAIN we may conclude TEMP=1 in A just after the call, but from W=1 we

could not say SUM+1=1. In this case, changes made to the parameter W by B are entirely local and do not affect A, since the argument is not a simple variable.

In general then, it is the simple variable arguments in the call which may be changed. For this reason, procedure calls restrict accessibility of assertions in the same way as assignment statements. Recall that after assigning to a variable (VAR, say), no assertions involving VAR are accessible afterwards. Even if the assignment does not actually change the value in VAR, such assertions must be re-proven using the assignment rule. Similarly, even if B does not actually change the values of X, Y or Z, assertions in A involving TEMP, ARRAY, and ON are not accessible after the call to B (unless they are re-proven from the ATTAIN).

There are two ways around this. Remember that a READONLY parameter is one for which the called procedure guarantees that the value in the box will not change. PL/CV enforces this guarantee by checking that no assignments are made to READONLY variables. Such variables also may not be passed as arguments to other procedures, again unless it is in place of a READONLY parameter. (For instance, if W in B were declared READONLY, the statement CALL C(W) could not appear in B unless C's parameter were also declared READONLY.) Since the value of a variable passed to a readonly parameter is not changed, assertions involving that variable will be accessible after the call.

An argument in the place of a readonly parameter may, therefore, always be substituted into the ATTAIN of the procedure, even if it is an expression. For example, if W were declared READONLY in B and W=Y(X) were part of the ATTAIN, we could conclude

        SUM+1 = ARRAY(TEMP)

after our call above. As we have seen , this is not allowed if W is an ordinary read-write parameter to B, but being READONLY means that it must still have the same value as the original argument when B terminates.

The other method for ensuring that the value of an argument remains unchanged by a procedure call is a little tricky, and is usually not needed in good programming. We can make up expressions out of single variables that have the same value as the variable. (VAR + 1) - 1 is an example. Even simpler, (VAR) is treated as an expression by the compiler. So by enclosing any variable name in parentheses, one may hand it as an argument for a readwrite parameter without fearing that its value will be changed. Unfortunately, no conclusions about VAR may then be drawn from the ATTAIN of the procedure (just as for all expression-arguments). This will make no difference if the called procedure does not mention the corresponding parameter in the ATTAIN, or if the calling procedure does not have to use the part of the ATTAIN that does. Either case is a little unusual, and probably indicates that more concise procedures could be used that do not pass unused parameters around. Nevertheless, we mention them here for the sake of completeness.

Aliasing

We must take note of one further restriction on passing variables. From
the sample call given earlier there seems to be no reason why the same
variable name may not be included twice in one procedure call, i.e. CALL
B(TEMP,TEMP,ARRAY,ON). This does lead to trouble though. The procedure
called (B) will be unknowingly referencing the same box under two different
names (W and X in this case). Assignments made to either name will change
the value of the other as well, since it is the same box. This situation
is not properly described by the assignment rule, and so the logical
description of the procedure's behavior would be invalid.

There is a problem even if one of the occurrences is in a READONLY position. In this case, B may unknowingly violate its promise not to change
the value of the readonly parameter by assigning to it under a different
name for which there is read-write access. These problems are instances of
what is called aliasing, i.e. one variable box appears under two different
names in procedure B. For simple variables, it is easy for the verifier to
check that no procedure calls will lead to either of these cases. There is
no further proof necessary, merely an obligation on the part of the programmer not to write such procedure calls. (Note that it is alright to
pass the same variable more than once in a call if every corresponding
parameter is readonly. It is read-write access to a variable which must be
unique.)

When elements of an array are passed as arguments to a procedure, a
subtlety arises. Because they are specified by an expression (the index
into the array), aliasing may occur if the expressions give the same value.
To make sure this is avoided we require a proof from the programmer that
the two expressions are unequal. For instance, to use the statement:

CALL B(ARRAY(I+1), ARRAY(J-1), ...);

the assertion I+1 ~= J-1 must be accessible at the point of call. Such a
proof of non-aliasing is required of every procedure call which has two
elements from the same array in the argument list (unless they are both for
READONLY parameters). In addition, it is forbidden to hand an entire array
and one of its elements separately in an argument list if either is in a
read-write position.

Shielded Parameter Passing

Remember that shielded program text must be written so that its removal
does not affect execution in any way. If a procedure has a shielded parameter, then any call to it must contain a shielded argument in the
corresponding position. This may be either an expression or a shielded
variable of the calling procedure. It may not be an unshielded variable of
the procedure unless the parameter is READONLY. In addition, a shielded
variable of the calling procedure may never appear as an argument in an
unshielded position, either by itself or as part of an expression. All the
other rules governing aliasing and drawing conclusions from the ATTAIN are
the same as for non-shielded parameters.

External Variables

There is another way in which procedures may communicate values to one
another. A program variable may be declared to be common to a number of
procedures. It must be declared in each of them with the keyword "EXTER-
NAL". For instance:

                DCL RECORDS(10) FIXED EXTERNAL READONLY;
and   DECLARE COUNT FIXED EXTERNAL;

are valid external declarations. We imagine such a variable to be a box
accessible to all of the procedures which declare it, but not inside any of
them (hence the name). It may be used in program statements just as any
other variable by any of the procedures. If anyone changes the value of an
external variable then the next procedure to use it will find the new
value. A READONLY external declaration means just the same as a readonly
parameter declaration: the procedure promises not to change the value
inside the external box, only look at it.

External variables are declared in a procedure after the parameters, but
before the ASSUME and ATTAIN conditions. They may therefore appear in the
specification. There they act just like a parameter with regard to the
conventions of calling, except that there is no need of substitution of
names since the name of an external variable is the same in every procedure
where it is declared. The principle motivation for external variables is
to keep the size of parameter lists short among procedures which have to
exchange a lot of information.

External variables may be passed as arguments in a procedure call by a procedure which has access to them. Care must be taken however, for this can
lead to very intricate forms of aliasing. Consider, for example, that an
external variable may be passed to a procedure which does not otherwise
have access to it. This procedure may in turn pass that parameter in a
call to a second procedure which **does** access the original external variable. This second procedure will then have access to the same box under
two different names. This case, and others like it, are of the type which
may be simply checked for and need no additional proof. The programmer only
has to avoid writing procedures which pass arguments around in such a way
as to give read-write access to the same box under two names, or read-write
and readonly access under two names.

Input-Output and Main Procedures

When we write and execute a program, we usually want its behavior to depend
on input that is provided from the outside in some way. We also want to
observe that behavior through output that the program makes available. The
PL/C and PL/CS programming statements for a procedure to receive input
values of variables, or to produce values for output are GET and PUT resec-
tively. In the PL/CV assertion language there is no way to talk about the
input and output streams implied by these statements, and consequently no
proof rules for them. As a result, PL/CV is more useful for developing
one's understanding of program correctness than for verifying complete programs which are actually to be run. (Of course, certain procedures of a
program may not contain GET or PUT statements. Verifying these can
increase one's confidence in the correctness of the whole program.)

When it comes time to execute a set of procedures which call one another, there has to be a starting point. In PL/C and PL/CS, exactly one procedure out of each such set is designated as the MAIN procedure. It is the beginning of the sequence of execution and procedure calls, and may not itself have parameters. In the absence of GET and PUT statements, and because it is "called" unconditionally, a MAIN procedure could have no other ASSUME than '1'B. Because there are no parameters, its ATTAIN could have only EXTERNAL variables. While such procedures could be verified, their limited description would bear little resemblance to the actual behavior and usefulness of programs where input and output were permitted. Accepting the limitations of our formalism therefore, we do not support in PL/CV the verification of MAIN procedures.

Recursive Procedures

In the preceding sections we have seen how one procedure may make use of another previously written. We extended our informal model of computation to include a description of procedure calls and provided proof rules that enabled us to make conclusions about their execution. We are now going to extend our model again to allow for a construct which is elegent mathematically and which has a corresponding usefulness in writing programs. This is definition by recursion.

In trying to solve a problem, say ATTAIN $A(x)$, with a procedure P, it frequently happens that a subproblem of the form $A(y)$ arises. If so, it is natural to use the procedure P which we are writing to solve the subproblem. Thus, in defining P, we use P. The resulting form is

```
P: PROC(X);
   .
   .
   .
   ...CALL P(Y)...
   .
   .
   .
   END P;
```

Consider this concrete example. Assume that $IN(L, H, X)$ is

SOME Y FIXED WHERE L<=Y<=H. B(Y) = X

and let the attain statement $A(L, H, X)$ be

ATTAIN   X = B(Y) & L<=Y<=H .

We can start writing a procedure to find Y as follows

```
P: PROC(L, H, X, B, Y);
   DCL (L, H, X, B(*)) FIXED READONLY;
   DCL Y FIXED;
   ASSUME IN(L, H, X) & LBOUND(B,1) <= L & H <= HBOUND(B,1);
   ATTAIN A(L, H, X);
```

```
    IF B(L) = X THEN Y=L;

        ?

END P;
```

After testing B(L)=X, we either have solved the problem or have a simpler
problem of the same form to solve, namely A(L+1, H, X). In the latter
case, we can just use P itself. To the procedure already written, we need
only add the clause:

```
    ELSE P(L+1, H, X, B, Y);
```

The structure of the result is charecteristic of recursion, and syntactically the concept is very natural; in fact we wwould have to explicitly
rule out such procedures if we did not want to allow them, because the most
straightforward syntax (see sec. 8.2) permits them. The meaning (or semantics) of recursive procedures is a more subtle matter. We consider this
next.

In our model for procedure calls, we had procedures pause in their execution, to wait for the return from the procedure they issued the call to.
Since the procedure which is called may make a call of its own, and so on,
there may be several suspended procedures at any time. What happens if,
while suspended, a procedure is called again? We could say that it takes
the new values into its parameters, executes as usual, and upon returning,
resumes its waiting for the procedure that it had called previously. This
is clearly wrong though, since the values in the boxes (local variables and
parameters) may have been changed by the "recursive" call so that they no
longer satisfy the assertions that the procedure makes about them. From
this point on then, the proof of the program will no longer be valid.

The most obvious solution to this problem is the one that is actually used.
The values in the local variables and parameters of the procedure that is
called recursively (i.e. while waiting) are saved somewhere. When the execution of the recursive call is finished, the saved values are put back
into the correct boxes and the procedure resumes its waiting. (Remember
that the contents of a parameter will not always be a value. Sometimes
they are the instructions for where to find the variable box that was
handed as an argument. In this case, it is these instructions that are
saved.) It may happen that, during the execution of the recursive call,
the procedure again issues some call itself. If it then receives yet
another recursive call while waiting, both sets of values must be saved.
In general there will be a list of saved values. Upon returning from a
recursive call, the most recent set of values saved is restored and waiting
is resumed.

Fortunately, as programmers we do not have to concern ourselves with the
details of the above process. It is simply a description of how the compiler treats recursive calls. The advantage to this method is that it
preserves the truth of assertions made according to the rules we have
described up to now. Therefore, when we write recursive procedure calls,
we only have to follow the same rules we always do for satisfying the

```
SET_ZERO: PROCEDURE(X);
   DECLARE X FIXED;
   /*/ ASSUME X>=0;
       ATTAIN X=0; */

       /*/ ATTAIN '0'B; */
       IF X=0 THEN RETURN;
              ELSE DO;
                   /*/ X>0 BY ARITH, X>=0, ~(X=0);
                       X-1 >= 0 BY ARITH, X>0; */

                   X = X - 1;
                   CALL SET_ZERO(X);

                   /*/ X = 0; */

                   RETURN;
              END;
   END;
```

Fig. 31   Proposed recursive procedure proof

ASSUME, avoiding aliasing, etc. .

Let us illustrate this with a simple example. (In fact the following is
trivial, and one would never use recursion to solve such an easy problem.
Unfortunately, those problems for which recursion is natural and useful
tend to have a complex structure and long proofs. In this section, we will
confine ourselves to programs which are easy to understand so that the
application of the recursive proof rules is obvious.) Say that we wanted a
procedure of one parameter to set that parameter to zero and return. The
specification might look like:

```
SET_ZERO: PROCEDURE(X);
   DECLARE X FIXED;
   /*/ ASSUME X >= 0;
       ATTAIN X = 0;  */
```

We could just set X to zero and return, but that would not lead to any
recursive calls. Instead, we will reason as follows: if X already is zero
we are done and may return. This could be one branch of an IF statement.
What of the other, where X is not zero? Well, subtracting one from it is a
step in the right direction, making the value closer to zero. Since we
know X >= 0 from the ASSUME and X ~= 0 from the ELSE branch of the IF, we
know X > 0 before the subtraction and X >= 0 after it. At this point we
have a variable (X) which is >= 0, and which we want to set to zero. But
this is exactly the specification of SET_ZERO itself! That is, we have
satisfied the ASSUME of SET_ZERO, and so may call it and conclude X = 0
afterwards. This satisfies our own ATTAIN, so we may RETURN. A proposed
proof of this procedure is given in figure 31.

```
SET_ZERO: PROCEDURE(X);
  DECLARE X FIXED;
  /*/ ASSUME X>=0;
      ATTAIN X=0; */

        IF X=0 THEN RETURN;
              ELSE DO;

                    CALL SET_ZERO(X);
                    RETURN;
                  END;
  END;
```

Fig. 32   Questionable Recursive Procedure

Upon second consideration, it may seem like something questionable is being done here. The fact that we subtract one from X before the recursive call is not necessary to the reasoning we have employed. Would not the program in figure 32 satisfy the same proof? In fact it would, but is nevertheless incorrect. The problem is that we have left out an important part of the proof of our first program. We have neglected to show that its sequence of recursive calls will eventually terminate. That is, at some point a recursive call to SET_ZERO is going to take the first branch of the IF and not make another call. It will return, leaving the value 0 in the box it was handed as a parameter. The previous waiting call will then have its values restored (actually there is only X, and it stays the same throughout the sequence of calls, but this is not generally true). It will then return, leaving X in its parameter, and so on up the chain of waiting calls. Finally the top is reached and SET_ZERO returns to the original calling procedure, leaving zero in the argument as promised. For the second procedure, unless the initial value of the input were zero, each call would take the same branch of the IF, producing an endless sequence of recursive calls. A correctness proof for recursive calls has, therefore, the requirement of showing termination in addition to following the usual rules for procedure calls.

This is very similar to another construct we have already seen - the DO WHILE statement. Its proper use also involved proving "correctness" (i.e. maintaining the invariant) and termination. The termination proof came in three parts:

(1) showing the existence of a number greater than zero (i.e. that satisfied the "termination predicate" of the loop)
(2) a proof at the beginning of the loop that zero did not satisfy the termination predicate
(3) a proof that if a number N satisfied the termination predicate at the beginning of the loop, then N-1 satisfied it after one iteration

From these three facts, we argued that the number shown to exist in (1) was in fact an upper bound on the number of times the loop could execute. Since such a number existed, the loop eventually had to terminate.

The basic idea for proving termination of a sequence of recursive calls is the same. We again will have a number N >= 0 which can never be zero at the beginning of one of the calls, and which is decreased by each call in the sequence. N will therefore be an upper bound on the length of the sequence of recursive calls (or the "depth of recursion" as is sometimes said). Since such a number exists, the recursion can not go on forever.

Before explaining how we prove these things about N, we must introduce a slightly different terminology. Up to now we have been focusing on the property of recursiveness of calls. For the case where a procedure contains a call to itself (as in SET_ZERO) it is clear that every time that that call is executed it will be recursive. When more than one procedure is involved, it is not so obvious when a call statement will be recursive during execution. Consider two procedures P and Q which each contain a call to the other. If a third procedure R calls either one of them (Q, say), then it could happen that Q calls P, P returns, Q returns and R goes on executing. Neither of the mutual calls in this case were recursive. On the other hand, some other call on Q or P with different arguments could lead to the same mutual call statements executing more than once, and so recursively.

The verifier assumes that a collection of programs like P and Q is guilty until proven innocent. That is, it takes each procedure submitted for verification and looks at all the procedure names which appear in CALL statements. It then looks at each of those procedures and who they call etc. Whenever a cycle is discovered in this fashion, all of the procedures in it form what is called a "mutually recursive set." It is the obligation of the programmer to show, in the way we are about to describe, that such a set will not actually make the cyclic series of calls forever, but that any sequence of recursive calls must terminate. Logically speaking, we note that no procedure that belongs to a mutually recursive set can be completely written or understood "first" apart from all the rest. Such a set forms, in some sense, a single mathematical object with a (rather complicated) rule for proving its correctness.

We say that a procedure is recursive if it belongs to a mutually recursive set of procedures. (SET_ZERO belongs to the mutually recursive set with only itself as a member.) A recursive procedure must have the keyword "RECURSIVE" in the first line following the parameter list. It must also specify a termination predicate T, which in general will depend on the parameters, EXTERNAL variables, and a free FIXED variable. T is given in a line following the ASSUME but prior to the ATTAIN, as follows:

     ARBITRARY n FIXED WHERE T;

where "n" is the free fixed variable. This is very similar to the termination predicate for DO WHILE loops, as are the following requirements for a set of mutually recursive procedures:

(1) For any call of a procedure in the set from a procedure <u>not</u> in
    the set we must prove the existence of an N>=0 which satisfies
    the termination predicate of the procedure being called
(2) For each procedure in the set we must prove that zero does not
    satisfy its predicate at the start (this will follow from the
    ASSUME condition)
(3) For each procedure "Q" in the set, we must consider all the calls
    it makes to other procedures "R" in the set. If "n" is the free
    fixed variable appearing in q's termination predicate, then we
    must show that n-1 satisfies the termination predicate of R prior
    to each call of R. (In general there will be more than one "R",
    each with its own predicate.)

If we replace the notion of "the next iteration of the loop" by "the next
recursive call in the sequence" then our argument that the loop termination
rule is correct shows that the above requirements are sufficient to show
that the set of mutually recursive procedures introduced is well defined
(i.e. will not make an endless series of calls). As an example to illustrate the use of these rules, here is a complete proof of SET_ZERO.

```
              SET_ZERO: PROCEDURE(X) RECURSIVE;
                 DECLARE X FIXED;
                 /*/ ASSUME X>=0;
                     ARBITRARY N FIXED WHERE X<N;
                     ATTAIN X=0; */

                 /*/ ~(X<0) BY ARITH, X >= 0; */

                    /*/ ATTAIN '0'B; */
                       IF X=0 THEN RETURN;
                             ELSE DO;
                                 /*/ X>0 BY ARITH, X>=0, ~(X=0);
                                     X-1 >= 0 BY ARITH, X>0;
                                     X-1 < N-1 BY ARITH, X<N, -, 1=1; */

                                 X = X - 1;
                                 CALL SET_ZERO(X);

                                 /*/ X = 0; */

                                 RETURN;
                             END;
                 END;
```

The termination predicate is X < N. Conditions 2 and 3 are a part of the
procedure itself. Condition 1 must be satisfied by any procedure calling
SET_ZERO, i.e. it must be able to prove the assertion

    SOME M FIXED.(M >= 0 & exp <= M) ...

prior to the statement CALL SET_ZERO(exp). This will always be possible,

since the ASSUME of SET_ZERO must be true at that point, therefore exp
itself has the properties required of M.

To illustrate the rule in the case of more than one procedure in the mutually recursive set, we prove the two procedures ADD_ONE and SUBTRACT_ONE.
Their task is to take two parameters, and make the value of the first equal
to that of the second. They accomplish this by, respectively, adding or
subtracting 1 from the appropriate parameter and calling the other. (This
is neither a practical problem nor an efficient solution, but the emphasis
here is on the use of the proof rules, not on a particular problem.)

```
          ADD_ONE: PROCEDURE(X,Y) RECURSIVE;
            DECLARE(X,Y) FIXED;
            /*/ ASSUME X<=Y;
                ARBITRARY N FIXED WHERE Y-X<N;
                ATTAIN X=Y;  */
            /*/ ~(Y-X<0) BY ARITH, X<=Y, -, X=X; */

            /*/ ATTAIN '0'B; */
                IF X=Y THEN RETURN;
                      ELSE DO;
                            /*/ X<Y BY ARITH, X<=Y, ~(X=Y);
                                X+1<=Y BY ARITH, X<Y;
                                Y-(X+1) < N-1 BY ARITH, Y-X<N, -, 1=1; */

                            X=X+1;
                            CALL SUBTRACT_ONE(X,Y);

                            /*/ X=Y;  */

                            RETURN;
                            END;
               END;

          SUBTRACT_ONE: PROCEDURE(W,Z) RECURSIVE;
                  DECLARE (W,Z) FIXED;
              /*/ ASSUME W<=Z;
                  ARBITRARY D FIXED WHERE Z-W<D;
                  ATTAIN W=Z;    */
              /*/ ~(Z-W<0) BY ARITH, W<=Z, -, W=W; */

                  /*/ ATTAIN '0'B; */
                      IF W=Z THEN RETURN;
                            ELSE DO;
                                  /*/ W<Z BY ARITH, W<=Z, ~(W=Z);
                                      W<=Z-1 BY ARITH, W<Z;
                                      (Z-1)-W < D-1 BY ARITH, Z-W<D, -, 1=1; */

                                  Z=Z-1;
                                  CALL ADD_ONE(W,Z);

                                  /*/ W=Z;  */
```

```
                               RETURN;
                          END;
          END;
```

To conclude, we provide a complete proof of a recursive procedure (including one other procedure that it calls non-recursively). The proof uses
most of the ideas that have been discussed in this section. What the procedure does is take an array and reverse its elements by exchanging the
outermost two, then recursively calling itself on the remainder between
those two. The termination predicate is more complicated than those we
have seen thus far. Basically, there are two different termination cases
which must be handled. If the array has an odd number of elements, then
the last recursive call is made with the markers for the upper and lower
bounds equal. If even, then termination happens when those two have passed
each other by one position. It is instructive to check how all the
requirements of the various rules are satisfied by the proof.

```
          REVERSE: PROCEDURE (A,L,U /*:,B */) RECURSIVE;
             DCL A(*) FIXED;
             DCL (L,U) FIXED READONLY;
        /*: DCL B(*) FIXED READONLY;      */

        /*/    ASSUME   LBOUND(A,1)=LBOUND(B,1) & HBOUND(A,1)=HBOUND(B,1) &
               A=B & LBOUND(A,1)<=L<=HBOUND(A,1) & LBOUND(A,1)<=U<=HBOUND(A,1);

               ARBITRARY D FIXED WHERE (U>=L => U-L+1<D)&(U<L => D~=0);

               ATTAIN INNER: ALL I FIXED WHERE 0 <= I <= U-L. A(L+I) = B(U-I),
                     OUTER: ALL I FIXED WHERE (LBOUND(A,1) <= I < L |
                                              U<I<=HBOUND(A,1)). A(I) = B(I); */

        /*: DCL C(LBOUND(A,1):HBOUND(A,1)) FIXED;  */

             /*  ACHIEVE THE REVERSAL OF A BETWEEN L AND U BY EXCHANGING */
             /*  A(L), A(U) AND REVERSING A FROM L+1 TO U-1.            */

             /* BASE CASE OF TERMINATION CONDITION          */
             /*/ ~((U>=L => U-L+1<0)&(U<L => 0~=0)) BY INTRO,
                  PROOF;
                    U>=L | U<L BY ARITH;
                    '0'B BY CASES, U>=L | U<L,
                       PROOF;
                         CASE U>=L;
                             U-L+1>=1 BY ARITH, U>=L,-,L-1=L-1;
                             U-L+1<0;
                             '0'B BY ARITH, U-L+1>=1, U-L+1<0;
                         CASE U<L;
                       QED;
                    QED;                                      */

        /*/    ATTAIN INNER & OUTER;    */
```

```
IF (U<=L) THEN DO;

            /* ATTAIN INNER:  SINCE U <= L, I=0, RESULT IS DIRECT  */
            /*/ ALL I FIXED WHERE 0<=I<=U-L.  A(L+I)=B(U-I)
                BY INTRO,
                PROOF;
                ARBITRARY I FIXED WHERE 0<=I<=U-L;
                    U-L<=0 BY ARITH, U<=L,-,L=L;
                    U-L = 0 BY ARITH, 0<=I<=U-L<=0;
                    I=0 BY ARITH, 0<=I<=U-L<=0;
                    L+0=L BY ARITH;
                    U-0=L BY ARITH, U-L=0,+,L=L;
                    A(L+I)=B(L+I);
                QED;                                               */

            /* ATTAIN OUTER: NO CHANGE TO A, RESULT IMMEDIATE. */
            /*/ OUTER BY INTRO; */

                END;

        ELSE DO;
            /*/ L < U BY ARITH, ~(U<=L); */

            /* INITIAL INFORMATION FOR SWAP */

            /* ARRAY SUBSCRIPTS IN BOUNDS */
            /*/ L<=HBOUND(A,1) BY ARITH, L<U, U<=HBOUND(A,1);
                LBOUND(A,1)<=U BY ARITH, L<U, LBOUND(A,1)<=L; */

            /* SUBSTITUTIONS ARE FREE - NO ALIASING */
            /*/ L~=U BY ARITH, L<U;  */

            /* NOTE THAT INPUT CONDITIONS ARE SATISFIED. */
            /* A(L) = B(L) AND A(U) = B(U) SINCE A = B.  */

            CALL SWAP(A(L),A(U) /*:,(B(L)), (B(U)) */);
            /* CONCLUSIONS OF SWAP LEMMA     */
            /*/ C1: A(U)=B(L) & A(L)=B(U);  */
            /*/ C2: ALL J FIXED WHERE J~=L & J~=U. A(J)=B(J)
                    BY INTRO,
                        PROOF;
                            A(J)=B(J) BY ALLEL,
                ALL K FIXED WHERE K~=U & K~=L. B(K) = A(K), J;
                        QED;                 */

            /* INITIAL INFORMATION FOR REVERSE        */

            /* INDICES IN BOUNDS   */
            /*/ L+1 <= HBOUND(A,1) BY ARITH, L<U, U<=HBOUND(A,1);
                LBOUND(A,1) <= L+1 BY ARITH, LBOUND(A,1) <= L;
                U-1 <= HBOUND(A,1) BY ARITH, U <= HBOUND(A,1);
                LBOUND(A,1) <= U-1 BY ARITH, L<U, LBOUND(A,1)<=L; */
```

```
                    /* DEPTH PARAMETER SATISFIES INPUT ASSUMPTION */
                    /*/   U-1>=L+1 => U-1-(L+1)+1<D-1  BY INTRO,
                          PROOF;
                             U-L>=2 BY ARITH, U-1>=L+1,-,L-1=L-1;
                             U>=L BY ARITH, U-L>=2,+,L=L;
                             U-1-(L+1)+1<D-1 BY ARITH, U-L+1<D,-,1=1;
                          QED;
                          U-1<L+1 => D-1~=0 BY INTRO,
                           PROOF;
                             U-L<2 BY ARITH, U-1<L+1,-,L-1=L-1;
                             U-L=1 BY ARITH, U-L<2, U-L>0;
                             U>=L BY ARITH, U-L=1,+,L=L;
                             D>2 BY ARITH, U-L+1<D, U-L=1;
                             D^=1 BY ARITH, D>2;
                          QED;                                           */

                    /* CURRENT VALUES OF A HELD IN C */
                    /*: C=A;                          */

                    /* RELATE B AND C                             */
                    /*/ C(U)=B(L) & C(L)=B(U);                    */
                    /*/ CB: ALL J FIXED WHERE J~=L & J~=U. C(J)=B(J); */

                    CALL REVERSE(A,L+1,U-1 /*:,(C) */);

                    /* INDUCTION HYPOTHESES    */
                    /*/ IND1: ALL J FIXED WHERE 0<=J<=(U-1)-(L+1).
                                      A(L+1+J)=C(U-1-J);            */
                    /*/ IND2: ALL K FIXED WHERE (LBOUND(A,1)<=K<L+1 |
                                             U-1<K<=HBOUND(A,1)).
                                      A(K)=C(K);                     */

            /* CONCLUSIONS FROM INDUCTION HYPOTHESES */

            /*   CONCLUDE OUTER   */
            /*/ ALL J FIXED WHERE (LBOUND(A,1)<=J<L | U<J<=HBOUND(A,1)).
                A(J)=B(J) BY INTRO,
                 PROOF;
                  A(J)=B(J) BY CASES, LBOUND(A,1)<=J<L | U<J<=HBOUND(A,1),
                          PROOF;
                          CASE LBOUND(A,1)<=J<L;
                             J<L+1 BY ARITH, J<L;
                             A(J)=C(J) BY ALLEL, IND2, J;
                             J~=L BY ARITH, J<L;
                             J~=U BY ARITH, J<L<U;
                             C(J)=B(J) BY ALLEL, CB, J;
                          CASE U<J<=HBOUND(A,1);
                             U-1<J BY ARITH, U<J;
                             A(J)=C(J) BY ALLEL, IND2, J;
                             J~=U BY ARITH, U<J;
                             J~=L BY ARITH, L<U<J;
                             C(J)=B(J) BY ALLEL, CB, J;
                          QED;
```

```
        QED;                                                                    */

   /*    CONCLUDE INNER    */
   /*/   ALL I FIXED WHERE 0<=I<=U-L. A(L+I)=B(U-I)
            BY INTRO, PROOF;
      /#   CONSIDER THE CASES I=0, 1<=I<=(U-L)-1, I=U-L.          #/
      /#   CASE 1<=I<=(U-L)-1 IS TREATED AS 0<=I<=(U-1)-(L+1). #/
      /#   THE CASES MUST BE TREATED INDIRECTLY BECAUSE OF       #/
      /#   LIMITATIONS OF ARITHMETIC RULES.                      #/
      DI:  I=0 | I>0 BY ARITH, I>=0;
          A(L+I)=B(U-I) BY CASES, DI,
          PROOF;
            CASE I=0; /# FIRST MAIN CASE #/
            L<L+1 BY ARITH;
            A(L)=C(L) BY ALLEL, IND2,L;
            A(L)=B(U); /# SUBSTITUTION IN C(L)=B(U) #/
            A(L+0)=B(U-0);
            CASE I>0;
            DUL: I<U-L|I=U-L BY ARITH, I<=U-L;
            A(L+I)=B(U-I) BY CASES, DUL,
            PROOF;
              CASE I<U-L; /# SECOND MAIN CASE    #/
                          /# 1<=I<=(U-L)-1, USE INDUCTION #/
                          /# HYPOTHESIS TO TRANSFORM THE  #/
                          /# INTERVAL TO MATCH INDUCTION  #/
                          /# FORMULA.                     #/
              0<=I-1 BY ARITH, 1<=I;
              I-1<=(U-1)-(L+1) BY ARITH, I<(U-L),-,1=1;
            A(L+1+(I-1))=C(U-1-(I-1)) BY ALLEL, IND1, I-1;
              L+1+(I-1)=L+I BY ARITH;
              U-1-(I-1)=U-I BY ARITH;
              A(L+I)=C(U-I);
              L<U-I BY ARITH, I<U-L,+,L-I=L-I;
              U-I ~= L BY ARITH, L<U-I;
              U-I ~= U BY ARITH, U=U,-,I>0;
              C(U-I)=B(U-I) BY ALLEL, CB, U-I;
              CASE I=U-L;  /# THIRD MAIN CASE #/
              L+(U-L)=U BY ARITH;
              U-(U-L)=L BY ARITH;
              L+I=U & U-I=L;
              C(L+I)=B(U-I); /# BY SUBST IN C(U)=B(L) #/
              U-1<U BY ARITH;
              A(U)=C(U) BY ALLEL, IND2, U;
              A(L+I)=C(L+I);
            QED;
          QED;
                QED;    */

END;
  RETURN;
END REVERSE;

SWAP: PROCEDURE (X,Y /*: ,X0,Y0 */);
```

```
     DCL (X,Y) FIXED;
/*: DCL (X0,Y0) FIXED READONLY; */
/*/ ASSUME X=X0 & Y=Y0 ; */
/*/ ATTAIN Y=X0 & X=Y0 ; */
     DCL T1 FIXED;
     T1 = X;
     X = Y;
/*/ X = Y0; */
     Y = T1;
/*/ X=Y0 & Y=X0 ; */
     RETURN;
END  SWAP;
```

VIII   PROCEDURE RULES

8.1   Introduction

Procedures are as important to proofs as they are to programs. They serve like lemmas in conventional proofs, decomposing the argument into logically separate pieces which may be analyzed and structured independently. They are most useful when parameterized to apply at several different steps of the argument. Adapting them to a particular step usually involves substituting expressions for the parameters. These parameters are program variables as well as logical variables. Thus, the notion of substitution for program variables is critical to the use of procedures. It is a subtle notion requiring even more care than the already delicate matter of substitution of expressions for (logical) variables (discussed in IV 4.1). The fact that we treat only external procedures without static external variables helps keep the presentation of rules simple.

Procedures are especially useful if they can be recursive. However, proofs involving recursive procedures require careful attention because they involve patterns of inductive argument far more intricate than the already error prone simple inductions of 4.13 and of ordinary number theory.

8.2   Syntax

In addition to the components of ordinary PL/CS procedures, PL/CV procedures may have auxiliary (shielded) parameters and logical information in the heading.

```
                    label:  PROCEDURE[(parameter_list)]
                              [RECURSIVE];
                            {declaration, define_statement}*
This portion              ASSUME [label:] assertion;
is called the            [ARBITRARY n FIXED WHERE T;]
heading.                  ATTAIN [label:] assertion;
                            argument
                            END [label];
```

Note: The attribute RECURSIVE is needed on recursive procedures only for compatibility with PL/I.

We add to the old categories as follows:

procedure_call_stmt → CALL identifier[(expression_list)];

unit → procedure_call_statement

control_punctuation → return_statement

```
        return_statement → RETURN;

        expression_list → expression {, expression}*

        declaration → {DCL, DECLARE} variable_list type [EXTERNAL]
                      [READONLY];
```

Note: Actual parameters corresponding to shielded formal parameters must be shielded.

8.3 Substitution

We extend an analysis of substitution for free variables to the case of variables occurring in commands. External variables introduce complex possibilities for binding and aliasing, which the following will be useful in describing:

Definition: The relationship R->S holds between procedures if a call to S appears in the body of R. R->$^+$S holds if there are t_1, ..., t_n such that R->t_1, ..., t_i->t_{i+1}, ..., t_n->S (i.e. the transitive closure of R->S). R->*S means that either R->$^+$S or R=S.

Definition: A procedure P depends upon an external variable E if there is some procedure Q such that P->*Q and Q contains E as a readonly external variable. P potentially modifies E if there is a Q where P->*Q and Q contains E as a readwrite parameter.

Definition: Among the binding occurrences of a variable x enumerated in II 2.8(ii) and VI 6.3 is now included case 9, occurrence as a readwrite parameter to a procedure call (said to be a binding call), i.e.

9.   CALL p(...x...) where the formal parameter corresponding to x is readwrite.

and case 10, implicit occurrence as a potentially modified external (also a binding call), i.e.

10.   CALL q(...) where q potentially modifies x.

An occurrence of a variable is said to be bound in an argument A iff the conditions of the definition in VI 6.3 hold or

9.   The occurrence is in an assertion or command L of A (or of a subargument of A) for which there is some execution path of A to L containing a binding call.

Definition: If $A(x_1, \ldots, x_n)$ is an argument with free variables $x_1, \ldots, x_n$, then expression t_i is _free for_ x_i provided x_i does not occur in the scope of any operators containing binding occurrence of variables in t_i, i.e., no variable of t_i is captured when t_i is substituted for x_i.

For example, in the two line argument

```
/*: Y=X+1; */
/*: Z=Y*Z; */
```

the expression Y+2 is free for X but not for Y or Z.

8.4 Proof Rules

(i) _Declaration rules_

DECLARATION INTRODUCTION

$$\frac{lower_1 <= upper_1, \ldots, lower_n <= upper_n}{DCL\ A(lower_1: upper_1, \ldots, lower_n: upper_n)}$$

If $lower_i = 1$ it (and the separating colon) may be omitted from the conclusion.

ARRAY BOUNDS INTRODUCTION

$$\frac{DCL\ A(lower_1: upper_1, \ldots, lower_n: upper_n)}{LBOUND(A,i) = lower_i,\ HBOUND(A,i) = upper_i)}$$

Note if i is not between 1 and n, no conclusion can be drawn from the declaration. When these functions are used in commands they must be well-defined.

BOUNDS AXIOM

$$\frac{A\ is\ variable\ of\ array\ type}{LBOUND(A,i) <= HBOUND(A,i)}$$

(ii) Procedure rules

In describing the procedure rules it will be convenient to have these definitions.

Definition: The **apparent domain** of a procedure is the cartesian product of the types of the parameters in order of appearance. The (**real**) **domain** is the subset of the apparent domain on which the procedure halts. The **assumed domain** is the subset of the apparent domain which satisfies the input assumption.

The proof rules must guarantee that the assumed domain is a subset of the real domain.

NONRECURSIVE PROCEDURE INTRODUCTION

A procedure definition can be introduced when we know that its body is a correct argument from the input assumption. The following rule says this. (The tokens PROOF, QED are enclosed in < > to indicate that they are not actually present.)

```
    <PROOF;>
       ASSUME A;
       argument
          where B before each
          RETURN
          '0'B

    <QED;>_____
    p: PROCEDURE (parameter_list);

       {declaration, definition}*
       ASSUME A;
       ATTAIN B;
       argument
       END p;
```

RECURSIVE PROCEDURES INTRODUCTION

A set of mutually recursive procedures can be introduced if and only if they each terminate on their assumed domains (these are the completed procedures of A Programing Logic). An argument involving these procedures can be (simultaneously) introduced if it is a correct induction argument. Namely (using function notation to indicate substitutions):

p: PROCEDURE $(\bar{v}, \bar{w})$ [RECURSIVE];

$\bar{v}$	READONLY
$\bar{w}$	READWRITE
$\bar{x}$	EXTERNAL

ASSUME IN_p $(\bar{v}, \bar{w}, \bar{x})$;

[ARBITRARY n FIXED WHERE $T_p(n, \bar{v}, \bar{w}, \bar{x})$;]

ATTAIN OUT_p $(\bar{v}, \bar{w}, \bar{x})$;

$\sim T_p(0, \bar{v}, \bar{w}, \bar{x})$;

.
.
.

$T_q(n-1, \bar{t}, \bar{u}, \bar{x})$

$IN_q(\bar{t}, \bar{u}, \bar{x})$ for each call of a procedure q in the set

CALL q $(\bar{t}, \bar{u})$;

.
.
.

OUT_p $(\bar{v}, \bar{w}, \bar{x})$;

before each RETURN;

.
.
.

END p;

The conclusion is the set of procedures itself and the mutually recursive argument.

The arbitrary statement is needed only for recursive procedurer.

Variables external to q which appear in its T or IN predicate must also be external to p (i.e. they must appear in $\bar{x}$).

PROCEDURE CALL(PROCEDURE ELIMINATION)

p: PROCEDURE$(\bar{v},\bar{w})$;

$\bar{v}$ READONLY

$\bar{w}$ READWRITE

$\bar{x}$ EXTERNAL

ASSUME $IN_p(\bar{v},\bar{w},\bar{x})$;

ARBITRARY n FIXED WHERE $T_p(n, \bar{v},\bar{w},\bar{x})$;

ATTAIN $OUT_p(\bar{v},\bar{w},\bar{x})$;

.
.
.

$OUT_p(\bar{v},\bar{w},\bar{x})$; $\Big\{$ for each return   SOME m FIXED.(m>=0 &

RETURN;   in the body $T_p(m,\bar{t},\bar{u},\bar{x}))$

.
. $IN_p(\bar{t},\bar{u},\bar{x})$
.

END:

CALL $p(\bar{t},\bar{u})$;

$OUT_p(\bar{t},\hat{u},\bar{x})$;

This rule may only be used subject to certain provisos. Let Z be the set of external variables which p depends upon, and W the set which it

potentially modifies (note that all variables in $\bar{x}$ are in either Z or W). We must have:

1.   If $\bar{u}$ consists entirely of simple variables, then $\hat{u}=\bar{u}$. But if an

array element $a(exp_1, \ldots, exp_n)$ occurs in $\bar{u}$, then in $\hat{u}$ that element

is replaced by $a(exp'_1, \ldots, exp'_n)$ as described in ARRAY ACCESSIBILITY.

2.   No variable of $\bar{u}$ or W occurs in either $\bar{t}$ or Z.

3.   All variables in $\bar{u}$ are distinct and do not belong to W.

This means that if $a(exp_1,\ldots,exp_n)$ and $a(exp'_1, \ldots, exp'_n)$ appear as

parameters in $\bar{t},\bar{u}$ or $\bar{x}$ and if the proviso requires that these variables be distinct, then there must be a hypothesis that $\sim(exp_1=exp'_1 \&\ldots\& exp_n=exp'_n)$.

These provisos are simple, sufficient ways to guarantee that no capture of variables occurs in the substitution. Because of the restrictons on READONLY parameters, they ensure that no set of variables can be handed as arguments to a procedure call if they would even potentially lead to capture. A less stringent set of resctrictions, involving the notion of substitution for bound program variables, can be found A Programming Logic. They are syntactically checkable, and amount to saying that no actual capture occurs in the substitution of parameters.

When array elements are passed to a procedure as in CALL P(A(I), A(J), I, J) we would like to conclude by general accessibility conditions that A(K) for $K{\neq}I$, $K{\neq}J$ are not changed. The current version of the implemented system does not allow this generality, but as a temporary measure it allows the user to easily deduce it using the following accessibility axiom.

ARRAY ACCESSIBILITY

for each list of (m) occurrences of an array A of dimension n as a readwrite parameter

$$IN_p(...A(e_1), ..., A(e_m)...), A'=A, e'_1=e_1 , ... , e'_m=e_m$$
$$CALL\ p(...A(e_1), ..., A(e_m)...)$$
$$\overline{\rule{0pt}{0pt}\hspace{3cm}}$$
$$OUT_p(...A(e'_1),...,A(e'_m)...)\&$$

$$ALL\ (i_1,...,i_n)\ FIXED\ WHERE\ ''{\sim}(i_1,...,i_n) = e'_1''\ \&...\&$$
$$''{\sim}(i_1, . . . , i_n) = e'_m'' .$$
$$A(i_1,...,i_n) = A'(i_1,...,i_n)$$

where e_j is a list of n expressions, say $exp_{j1},...,exp_{jn}$. The phrase

$''{\sim}(i_1, . . . , i_n) = e'_j''$ abbreviates ${\sim}(i_1=exp'_{j1}\&...\&i_n=exp'_{jn})$.

For completeness we also need the RETURN RULE

RETURN
A

which allows any conclusion at a position from which RETURN is accessible.

(iii) Proofs

The definition of proof is as in IV.4 except that the definition of accessibility must now be additionally restricted to include the changes to the concept of bound variable introduced in 8.3.

Motivation

One common use for procedures is to take the values of some parameters and
return in another parameter a function of these values. For instance, we
can write a procedure that returns in Z the sum of the squares of X and Y.
It would have the following specification:

```
            SUM_OF_SQUARES: PROCEDURE(X,Y,Z);
                   DCL (X,Y) FIXED /*/ READONLY */;
                   DCL Z FIXED;
              /*/ ASSUME '1'B;
                   ATTAIN Z = X*X + Y*Y; */
```

Usually the parameter used for returning the function value (Z in this
case) serves no other purpose than to communicate the value to the calling
procedure. This is done so frequently that a special form has been provided which eliminates the need for the "storage" variable, thereby removing superfluous details from the calling procedure and its proof. A
defined function is a value-returning procedure. That is, it takes all of
its parameters readonly, and may be used by name as an operator to build up
expressions (either in the logic or in program statements). As an operator, it gives as a value a function of its arguments which is defined by
the ATTAIN statement. Here is how we would make SUM_OF_SQUARES a function:

```
            SUM_OF_SQUARES: PROCEDURE(X,Y) RETURNS(FIXED);
                   DCL (X,Y) FIXED;
              /*/ ASSUME '1'B;
                   ATTAIN SUM_OF_SQUARES(X,Y) = X*X + Y*Y; */
```

The two differences from an ordinary procedure specification are that the
type of value returned is given, and the procedure name itself is used in
the ATTAIN. Note that all parameters and external variables are assumed to
be READONLY and need not be explicitly designated as such.

In the procedure version of SUM_OF_SQUARES we would assign the desired
value to Z and return. In the function version, we include the value as
part of the return statement. The above specification in fact, could have
as a program the single statement:

```
            RETURN(X*X + Y*Y);
```

A procedure which called the SUM_OF_SQUARES as a function instead of a procedure could replace the two statements:

```
            CALL SUM_OF_SQUARES(A,B,C);
            FOO = 2*C - 1
```

with just

```
            FOO = 2*SUM_OF_SQUARES(A,B) - 1;
```

As with procedures, we have proof rules for both the definition and use of functions.

Rules For Using Functions

Defined functions are used exactly the same way that the special functions like ABS and MOD are. MOD(I,J), for instance, is a function with J~=0 as its ASSUME. Its ATTAIN is the conjunction of the assertions given in figure 2 (sec. III). Reviewing briefly, there are three ways to use functions:

(1) A function name may appear in a program statement as part of an expression to be evaluated. The ASSUME for the function must be proven at that point for the arguments used.

(2) A function application may appear in assertions wherever it could be replaced by an arbitrary expression of the same type. For example, given a FIXED function F(X,Y), the following may be written anywhere:

```
F(1,2) = F(1,2);        ALL (W,Z) FIXED. F(W,Z) > 2
                                => F(W,Z) > 1 BY INTRO, INTRO,
                        PROOF;
                        F(W,Z) > 1 BY ARITH, F(W,Z) > 2;
                        QED;
```

See section 4.7 for more on the PL/CV semantics of function applications.

(3) The ATTAIN of a function (for given arguments) may be asserted anywhere that its ASSUME (for the same arguments) is true. The justification is BY FUNCTION, followed by the function name and arguments. For instance, we may write

```
0 <= MOD(I,J) < ABS(J)  BY FUNCTION, MOD(I,J);
```

wherever J~=0 is accessible. Similarly, we may assert

```
SUM_OF_SQUARES(W,Z) = W*W + Z*Z BY FUNCTION, SUM_OF_SQUARES(W,Z);
```

anywhere, since the ASSUME for this function ('1'B) is always true.

As the MOD example shows, the ATTAIN of a function may do more than simply state what the value of the function is. Any assertion using the function name and/or parameters may appear in the ATTAIN. Note that, unlike procedures, functions may be used via the FUNCTION rule in strictly logical theorems. This can often be an effective means for providing theorems with access to algorithmic notions of construction.

(Functions that take BIT(*) parameters may be applied to boolean expressions made up of logical variables, but not to assertions. This restriction is to keep PL/CV a constructive logic.)

Verifying Functions

There are three differences between the proof rules for functions and for
procedures. The first is a restriction: functions return a value and do
nothing else. They may not have any side effects. A side effect is
defined as changing the value of any variable other than the functions own
local variables. We have alreay mentioned that the parameters and EXTERNAL
variables of a function are assumed to be readonly. In addition, the function may not make any procedure calls which will produce side effects.
(I.e. only the function's local variables may be read-write arguments to a
procedure, and no procedure called may assign to EXTERNAL variables.) The
motivation for this restriction comes from our desire to use function names
as operators. If they were allowed to change their arguments, or otherwise
alter the environment they were evaluated in, the logic for making correct
assertions would become vastly more complicated.

The second difference is in the rule for RETURN statements. The basic idea
is still the same: the ATTAIN must be proven at any point where the function returns. We simply have to modify what this means to account for the
fact that a value is being returned. Let F be a function of one argument,
X. In general, its ATTAIN condition will contain occurrences of F(X) to
describe the value returned. When a RETURN(exp) statement is encountered
during execution, the value of exp will be the value that is returned for
the function. Therefore, the ATTAIN must be proven with all occurrences of
F(X) replaced by exp. This must be done for each RETURN statement in the
function.

Finally, we must recognize a subtle form of recursion that can occur in
function definitions. Any time an assertion is justified BY FUNCTION,
F(exp), it must be the case that evaluation of F(exp) is possible at that
point. What if an assertion in the body of F is justified this way? This
will be correct only if the call is a proper one, but clearly it will be a
recursive call. The rules for termination of recursive function applications are the same as for procedure calls. In particular, the termination
predicate for F(exp) must be satisfied by N-1 before any occurrence of
F(exp) in a program statement or any assertion justified BY FUNCTION,
F(exp). Note that this means that two functions may be mutually recursive
just by mentioning each other in their proofs, without actually executing
an expression that contains the other. (Note: it is not permitted for a
function and a procedure to be mutually recursive.)

The ability to recursively refer to functions in their own proofs can be
very useful. A good example is the function FACT(X), which returns the
factorial of X as a value. There is no easy way to express the relation of
FACT(X) to X in our assertion language without using recursion. Note that
saying that every number less than or equal to X divides FACT(X) is not
enough, since other numbers besides the factorial of X have that property.
The most elegent ATTAIN for the function FACT(X) is

$$X=0 \implies FACT(X)=1 \quad \& \quad X > 0 \implies FACT(X) = X * FACT(X-1)$$

This ATTAIN can actually be proven for a function body which proceeds in
the straightforward iterative manner, multiplying together all the numbers
less than X and returning the answer. The proof however, contains two uses

of the function rule on FACT itself, both times with arguments which are smaller than X. (See the last example below.) It is probably less complex than anything that could be done using a non-recursive ATTAIN. Moreover, once this description of FACT is shown, other desirable properties of the function may be proven by induction (for example, the fact that FACT(X) is divisible by all numbers less than or equal to X).

Examples
Here is the proof for the built-in function ABS, which returns the absolute value of its argument:

```
        ABS: PROCEDURE(X) RETURNS(FIXED);
        DECLARE X FIXED /*: READONLY */;
        /*/ ASSUME '1'B;                                     */
        /*/ ATTAIN X >= 0 => ABS(X) = X,                     */
        /*/        X <= 0 => ABS(X) = -X,                    */
        /*/        X  = 0 => ABS(X) = 0;                     */

        /*/ ATTAIN '0'B;                                     */
        SELECT;

        WHEN(X > 0)
            DO;
            /*/ X >= 0 BY ARITH, X > 0;                  */
            /*/ ~(X <= 0) BY ARITH, X > 0;               */
            /*/ ~(X = 0) BY ARITH, X > 0;                */
            RETURN(X);
            END;

        WHEN(X < 0)
            DO;
            /*/ ~(X >= 0) BY ARITH, X < 0;               */
            /*/ ~(X = 0) BY ARITH, X < 0;                */
            /*/ X <= 0 BY ARITH, X < 0;                  */
            RETURN(-X);
            END;

        OTHERWISE
            DO;
            /*/ X = 0 BY ARITH, ~(X< 0), ~(X > 0);           */
            /*/ X >= 0 BY ARITH, X = 0;                       */
            /*/ X <= 0 BY ARITH, X = 0;                       */
            /*/ -X = 0 BY ARITH, X = 0, *, -1 < 0;            */
            RETURN(X);
            END;
        END;
        END ABS;
```

The built-in function EXP contains a recursive call to itself in the procedure body. (It returns as a value B raised to the power E.)

```
        EXP: PROCEDURE (B, E) RETURNS(FIXED);
        DECLARE (B, E) FIXED /*: READONLY */;
```

```
/*/ ASSUME B ~= 0 & E >= 0;                                   */
/*/ ARBITRARY D FIXED WHERE D > E;                             */
/*/ ATTAIN E = 0 => EXP(B, E) = 1,                              */
/*/        E >= 1 => ((EXP(B, E) = B * EXP(B, E - 1)) & */
/*/                   (EXP(B, E) / B = EXP(B, E - 1))); */

/*/ ~(0 > E) BY ARITH, E >= 0;                                */

/*/ ATTAIN '0'B;                                              */
IF E = 0
THEN DO;
     /*/ ~(E >= 1) BY ARITH, E = 0;                           */
     RETURN(1);
     END;
ELSE DO;
     /*/ E >= 1 BY ARITH, E >= 0, ~(E = 0);                 */
     /*/ D - 1 > E - 1;                                      */
     /*/ E - 1 >= 0 BY ARITH, E >= 1;                        */
     /*/ B <= 0 | B >= 0 BY ARITH;                           */
     /*/ ABS(B) > 0 BY CASES, B <= 0 | B >= 0,               */
     /*/ PROOF;                                              */
     /*/ CASE B <= 0;                                        */
     /*/     ABS(B) = -B BY FUNCTION, ABS(B);                */
     /*/     -B > 0 BY ARITH, B <= 0, B ~= 0;                */
     /*/ CASE B >= 0;                                        */
     /*/     ABS(B) = B BY FUNCTION, ABS(B);                 */
     /*/     B > 0 BY ARITH, B >= 0, B ~= 0;                 */
     /*/ QED;                                                */
     /*/ B * EXP(B,E-1) = EXP(B,E-1)*B + 0;                  */
     /*/ MOD_RESULT: ALL (Q, R) FIXED .                      */
     /*/     ((B*EXP(B,E-1) = B*Q+R & 0<=R<ABS(B*EXP(B,E-1))) */
     /*/     => R = MOD(B*EXP(B,E-1), B))                      */
     /*/     BY FUNCTION, MOD(B*EXP(B,E-1), B);              */
     RETURN(B * EXP(B, E-1));
     END;
END EXP;
```

Here is a proof of the factorial function, which was given as an example of
a function with recursive reference to itself in an assertion.

```
FACT: PROCEDURE(X) RETURNS(FIXED);
     DECLARE X FIXED;
     /*/ ASSUME X>=0;
         ARBITRARY N FIXED WHERE X < N;
         ATTAIN (X=0 => FACT(X)=1) & (X>0 => FACT(X)=X*FACT(X-1)); */
     DECLARE (PROD,I) FIXED;
         /*/  ~(X < 0) BY ARITH, X>=0; */

         PROD = 1;

         /*/ 1>X => ( (X>0 => PROD=X*FACT(X+1-2)) &
                      (X=0 => PROD = 1)) BY INTRO.
             PROOF;
```

```
                   ~(X>0) BY ARITH, 1>X;
                   PROD = 1;
                   QED;      */
         /*/ (X+1)-1 = X BY ARITH; */
         /*/ ~(0>0) BY ARITH; */

            DO I = 1 TO X BY 1;
            /*/ ASSUME (I-1=0 => PROD=1) & (I-1>0 => PROD=(I-1)*FACT(I-2)); */
            /*/ X>=1 BY ARITH, X>=I>=1; */
            /*/ I-1=0 | I-1>0 BY ARITH, I>=1,-,1=1; */
            /*/ PROD*I = I*FACT(I-1) BY CASES, I-1=0 | I-1>0,
                   PROOF;
                   CASE I-1=0;
                     0>=0 BY ARITH;
                     1 < N BY ARITH, X<N, X>=1;
                     0 < N-1 BY ARITH, 1<N, -, 1=1;
                     FACT(0)=1 BY FUNCTION, FACT(0);
                     I=1 BY ARITH, I-1=0, +, 1=1;
                   CASE I-1>0;
                     I-1 >= 0 BY ARITH, I-1>0;
                     I < N BY ARITH, X<N, X>=I;
                     I-1 < N-1 BY ARITH, I<N, -, 1=1;
                     FACT(I-1)=(I-1)*FACT(I-2) BY FUNCTION, FACT(I-1);
                     I>0 BY ARITH, I-1>0;
                     PROD*I = I*FACT(I-1) BY ARITH, PROD=FACT(I-1), *, I>0;
                   QED;  */

              PROD = PROD*I;

            /*/ ~(I=0) BY ARITH, I>=1; */
            /*/ (I+1)-1 = I BY ARITH;
                   (I+1)-2 = I-1 BY ARITH;  */
            /*/ (I=0 => PROD=1) & (I>0 => PROD=I*FACT(I-1)); */

            END;

          /*/ (X=0 => PROD=1) & (X>0 => PROD=X*FACT(X-1)); */

            RETURN(PROD);
         END;
```

X FUNCTION RULES

10.1 Introduction

Rules for introducing recursive and nonrecursive function definitions are nearly identical to the corresponding rules for recursive and
nonrecursive procedures. However, since functions play an entirely different role in the logic than do assignments and their generalization to
procedures, the rules for using defined functions have an entirely different character than the rules for using procedures. The first difference is that functions affect the most basic level of the logic, the
predicate calculus. Secondly, all arguments to functions (including
external variables) are readonly, so the intricate problem of substitution for bound variables does not arise. Thirdly, defined functions
occur in every type of expression, so their use complicates every rule
which mentions expressions, that is every rule except the goto and label
rules.

10.2 Syntax

```
            f:   PROCEDURE(parameter_list) RETURNS(type) [RECURSIVE];
                 {declaration, define_statement}*
                 ASSUME assertion;
                 [ARBITRARY variable FIXED WHERE assertion;]
  heading        ATTAIN assertion;
                 proof_stmt *
                 declaration*
                 argument
                 END f;
```

Note 1: f is any label. It is the function name. The attain statement
may involve f itself

Note 2: A function in PL/CS may not contain input/output statements, or
calls to procedures which may modify either EXTERNAL variables or the
function's parameters. This is to guarantee that function evaluations
produce no side effects.

Note 3: External variables and all parameters are readonly.

10.3 Proof Rules

In order to introduce a set of mutually recursive function definitions, we must know that each halts on its assumed domain. This is
demonstrated almost exactly as in the case of procedures.

RECURSIVE FUNCTION INTRODUCTION

$\quad$ f: $\quad$ PROCEDURE$(\bar{v})$;

$\qquad \bar{v}$ READONLY

$\qquad \bar{x}$ EXTERNAL

$\qquad$ ASSUME $IN_f(\bar{v},\bar{x})$;

$\qquad$ ARB d FIXED WHERE $T_f(d,\bar{v},\bar{x})$;

$\qquad$ ATTAIN $OUT_f(\bar{v},\bar{x}, f(\bar{v}))$;

$\qquad \sim T_f(0,\bar{v},\bar{x})$;

$\qquad \quad \cdot$
$\qquad \quad \cdot$
$\qquad \quad \cdot$

$$\left\{ \begin{array}{l} T_g(d-1, \ \bar{u},\bar{x}), \ IN_g(\bar{u},\bar{x}) \\[4pt] \text{before any occurrence} \\[4pt] \text{of } g(\bar{u}) \text{ for any g in} \\ \text{the set of mutually} \\ \text{recursive definitions} \\ \qquad \cdot \\ \qquad \cdot \\ \qquad \cdot \\ \quad \text{'0'B} \end{array} \right. \quad \left\{ \begin{array}{l} OUT_f(\bar{v},\bar{x},\exp) \quad \text{before} \\[4pt] \text{each occurrence of} \\ \qquad \text{RETURN(exp)} \end{array} \right.$$

$\qquad$ END f;

Note, not all externals need be mentioned in IN_f, IN_g.

$\quad$ A function definition in PL/CV comprises an algorithm and a lemma about the defined function. This lemma has the form

$$IN_f(\bar{v},\bar{x}) \ \& \ T_f(d,\bar{v},\bar{x}) \Rightarrow OUT_f(\bar{v},\bar{x},f(\bar{v}))$$

where $\bar{v}$ can be considered universally quantified (and $\bar{x}$ are parameters of definition). The lemma is proved by a form of induction, so we call it the **recursive function induction rule**. The invocation rule is simply called **function lemma invocation**.

FUNCTION LEMMA INVOCATION

    f: PROCEDURE($\overline{v}$) RETURNS(atype);

        $\overline{v}$ READONLY;

        $\overline{x}$ READONLY EXTERNAL;

        ASSUME $IN_f(\overline{v},\overline{x})$;

        ARBITRARY d FIXED WHERE $T_f(d,\overline{v},\overline{x})$;

        ATTAIN $OUT_f(\overline{v},\overline{x},f(\overline{v}))$;

          .   SOME m FIXED $.m>=0\&T_f(\overline{m},\overline{u},\overline{x})$;

          .

          . $IN_f(\overline{u/v},\overline{x})$

        END f ───

            $OUT_f(\overline{u},\overline{x},f(\overline{u}))$ BY FUNCTION, $f(\overline{u})$;

For completeness we also need the rule

RETURN RULE

      <u>RETURN(exp)</u>
        A

APPENDIX A

Producing Verified Files Under CMS

General Comments About Errors

The sample developments of proofs in the manual are meant to illustrate how one's thoughts should be organized and guided by using PL/CV. The very reason that we need a verifier however, is that people make mistakes. The actual process of obtaining a verified file almost always requires several iterations of finding errors (using the output of the proof checker) and re-submitting the corrected proof.

In the case where a file contains no errors (i.e. all statements are justified according to the rules of PL/CV) the output is simply a copy of the file with the statements numbered. (There is also some accounting information about the execution of the check at the bottom of the output.) If errors are found, they are signalled by the presence of additional lines in the output. An error line begins with four asterisks and contains a message indicating the nature of the error that caused it.

The location of such a line classifies the error as being of one of two types. A syntax error is the failure to follow PL/CV syntax properly, i.e. the input is not in the form of a proof. It is indicated by an error line in the numbered text of the proof, following the line at which the error was detected. A logical error occurs when all of the statements, assertions and expressions are formed properly and are type correct, but some rule is violated in the use of a statement. The error line for a logical error occurs at the end of the output (just before the execution information) and contains the line number of the incorrect statement.

We may think of a syntax error as the failure of the user to communicate his or her ideas properly. The error is a logical one when the ideas are expressed correctly in the formalism, but are themselves wrong. For example, if the verifier expects an assertion and gets

      1) X+1 > A, BY ARITH, X=A, +, 1>0;

then confusion arises because of the lack of meaning (note the extra comma before "BY"). If instead the next line is

      2) X+1 > A BY ARITH;
or   3) X+1 < A BY ARITH, X=A, +, 1>0;

then the user's intended assertion and justification are clear, but inadequate to the PL/CV rules. (Note the last two examples illustrate, respectively, the cases where the justification is insufficient and where the conclusion is wrong.)

Naturally the proof checker does not quit upon discovering the first error, but attempts to continue processing the file to uncover further mistakes. As with error recovery in a compiler, the basic idea is to make some assumption about what was really meant, and proceed on the basis of that assumption. The distinction between syntactic and semantic errors made in

the last paragraph is the motivation for the corresponding different means
by which the verifier does this.

Its recovery from syntax errors is not very sophisticated. No attempt is
made to discern the user's intent from an improperly formed statement.
Rather, further processing is done on the assumption that the incorrect
line does not exist. (A "line" is from the last semicolon up to and
including the next one.) One consequence of this approach is that syntax
errors tend to generate further messages beyond that of the original mistake. For example, after line (1) above, any justification which uses
X+1>A as a hypothesis will be flagged with a logical error message for
using an unproven assumption. The verifier may also generate spurious syntax error messages by ignoring a line this way (if, for example, the line
ignored ends in "PROOF").

By comparison, logical errors are fairly well contained. Though they may
arise for a number of reasons, the immediate cause of any logical error
message is that some statement in the proof is not justified correctly.
The verifier's assumption for the purposes of proceeding is that the statement was properly introduced. I.e. after (2) above, the assertion X+1>A
may be used as a hypothesis. Where one simply has neglected some part of
an otherwise correct proof, this approach works nicely. It may happen,
however, that the justification is inadequate because the assertion is in
fact false. In certain cases where the automatic rules apply, this can
have the effect of suppressing further logical error messages. For
instance, if one mistakenly typed I=0 where I~=0 was meant, and if I~=0 was
true by an immediate rule of inference, then both would be asserted. This
would yield a contradiction, from which all subsequent assertions follow
immediately.

This last case seems to happen only rarely in practice. It is worthwhile
knowing though, that there is no relation between the number of error messages and the "correctness" of a file (unless that number is zero). A single misplaced semicolon can have a cascading effect, producing frightful
looking output for an almost perfect proof, while a mistake-ridden file may
be flagged only by an error in the justification of a statement near the
beginning. All error messages must be eliminated before PL/CV makes any
guarantees about the correctness of a file.

Syntax errors produce the most confusing output, and are less subtle than
most logical errors. For this reason, it is best to work on them
separately, so as to later be able to focus on any _real_ logical errors in
one's proof. To aid in this two-step approach to correction, PL/CV provides the option of just performing a syntax check on a file. (In addition
to making a separation of concerns possible, this option is much less
expensive to run than the full check.) This is done by adding "SYNTAX" to
the first line of the file e.g.

    *PLCV SYNTAX
    *THEOREM
       •
       •
       •

Once the output from the verifier contains no error messages, the "SYNTAX" option should be removed and the full verifier used until all errors have been eliminated. The following sections will describe some errors that have arisen fequently in practice, and how to recognize and correct them.

Syntax Errors

Since syntax error messages may appear on correct lines because of the cascading effect mentioned, how does one go about tracking down the real errors in a systematic way? This is partly a talent that is acquired after encountering the more common errors enough to be able to recognize the patterns of messages that they generate. For the beginner, there is one hard and fast rule: the first error message that appears in the proof is for real. Beyond this, one must rely on experience as a guide to which messages genuinely require attention. If an error message seems to be irrelevant to the line it appears at, or if it claims a mistake which clearly is not true, or if you don't understand what it means, it is probably a good idea just to correct whatever other errors you can, and hope that it goes away as a result.

When you have decided that a message corresponds to a real error (as you must for at least the first one appearing), the first step is to check the line in question for simple typos. Many a "TYPE INCONSISTENCY" or "UNDECLARED" variable is the result of writing A=B instead of A+B, or of misspelling a variable name. Enclosing parentheses, shielding, and PROOF-QED's should also be carefully examined to make sure that they both match and correctly structure the assertions and proof blocks. Having somebody else do this kind of checking is often more effective than doing it yourself.

The usual message for a mistake of this kind is "ERROR AT END OF", followed by a string of characters from the line. This means that somewhere near the end of that string, the verifier found something it did not expect and could not make sense of. In addition to mis-matched parentheses, this message may be generated by misspelt keywords and incorrect or missing punctuation. It also appears when certain syntactic forms are not followed. For instance, declaring a program variable of type "BIT" instead of "BIT(1)" will cause it. So will attempting to prove an assertion "BY INTRO" which does not have a principal connective that can be introduced by a proof block. This last case can happen when daisy chaining is used improperly, e.g.

    ALL X FIXED. (X>2 => X>1) BY INTRO, INTRO, INTRO,

Because of the extra introduction, the verifier sees an attempt to prove "X>1 BY INTRO", for which there is no rule. Remember too, that immediate rules do not have explicit justifications. (You cannot prove A&B BY INTRO.)

Syntax errors may come from finger slips or miscounting. They may also happen because of a faulty recollection of the form of a rule. One of the main purposes for the reference sections of this manual is to help you remember where the commas and semicolons belong and in what order the different parts of rules go. Until you are thoroughly familiar with the PL/CV syntax, it will pay to check the forms of rules used in the vicinity of an error message. The usual effect of, say, putting a comma before the "BY" of a justification, or forgetting the dot in a quantifier, or leaving out the variables to be substituted in an "ALLEL", is an "ERROR AT END OF" message. However, a few cases have more obscure consequences, as follows.

Putting a semicolon instead of a comma after either "BY INTRO" or "BY CASES" happens frequently. This error is not detected immediately because it is in fact a legitimate form of the rule. The verifier assumes that you think the proof is trivial and will follow from immediate rules. When it encounters the keyword "PROOF" immediately afterwards, it reports that you are using it as an undeclared variable. (In general, when you get error messages complaining that your keywords are being used as variables, it means that the structure of your written proof is not what you had in mind. Check punctuation, and delimiters like parentheses and PROOF-QED's.)

Messages near the beginning of a procedure that mention the declarations and/or the ASSUME and ATTAIN probably come from not strictly following the form of a procedure heading. The name of the procedure and its parameters comes first, followed by, in this order, the declarations of the parameters, the ATTAIN, ASSUME and ARBITRARY (if there is one) assertions, and the declarations of local parameters. Once the first program statement is encountered, no more declarations are permitted.

Mistaking the precedence of operators is usually signalled by a logical error message (because a statement doesn't say what you thought it did) or an "ERROR AT END OF" (because the justification is for the wrong quantifier). The major exception is also the case which is most often written incorrectly. Remember that quantifiers have a higher precedence than any logical operator. Consequently, if you quantify an assertion that contains a logical operator, the intended scope of the quantifier must be enclosed in parentheses to be grouped properly. If this is not done, any "bound" variables that appear after the first logical connective will in fact be outside the real scope of the quantifier, and so will not be declared. In addition, if the quantifier was an "ALL" being introduced, the introduction will instead apply to some other connective, possibly causing the quantified variables to be undeclared in a subsequent proof group. This is a very common error which one learns to look for when "undeclared variable" messages appear. (Such messages may also be caused by syntax errors on an ARBITRARY or CHOOSE line. In general they mean that the variables in question are not accessible to their DECLARE, ARBITRARY, CHOOSE, or quantifier.)

The ARITH Rule
Arith lines are subject to the same sorts of syntax errors as any other line. To understand some of the logical errors that may arise however, it is worthwhile to understand how these lines are processed.

First, each of the hypotheses listed is checked to see if it is accessible or follows from accessible assertions by immediate rules. Every one that cannot be so validated generates the error message

        ARITH INTRO: HYPOTHESIS NOT PROVEN -- NUMBER

followed by the number of the questionable hypothesis. Then, all of the
hypotheses, whether verified or not, are used in an attempt to verify the
conclusion of the ARITH application according to the rules given for arithmetic deductions. If the conclusion cannot be proven from the hypotheses,
the mesage

INVALID ARITHMETIC INFERENCE

is generated.

One common error is to expect that the necessary hypotheses are known simply because they are accessible to the arith line. This is the error of
example 2 above, and result in an "INVALID" message. Only the hypotheses
listed on the ARITH line are used in trying to derive the conclusion.

The ARITH processor considers all subscripted variables and function applications to be simple variables for the purpose of verifying the conclusion
from the hypotheses. So, for instance, the line

F(A+2-C) = F(B+1-C) BY ARITH, A+2 = B+1, -, C=C;

is invalid, since the subscripts in the conclusion are not looked at. The
correct way to reach this conclusion from the hypotheses would be to assert
the equality of the index expressions BY ARITH. The conclusion would then
follow automatically from the substitution rule of equality.

The hypotheses of an ARITH statement must each be a conjunction of (one or
more) simple arithmetic relations. (A simple arithmetic relation is one of
the form exp1 = exp2, exp1 < exp2, ^(exp1 > exp2), etc.) Therefore the
line

X*Y = 0 BY ARITH, X=0 | Y=0;

is incorrect. Similarly, the conclusion to an ARITH statement must be a
disjunction of (one or more) simple arithmetic relations. The most frequent temptation to offend in this regard seems to be to draw a cascaded
relation like "0 < X < 10" as a conclusion from ARITH. Of course this is
an abbreviation for a conjunction, not a disjunction of the simple relations involved, which therefore must be established by separate ARITH
lines. Depending on how these two rules are violated, one gets an "ERROR
AT END OF" message, or a more specific syntax error message.

One last error to avoid in the use of ARITH is the tendency we all have of
doing something to both sides of an equation freely. With the single
exception of adding/subtracting an integer to both sides, such steps
require an explicit application of the monotonicity axioms, and only one
such application is permitted on each ARITH line.

Logical Errors
As we have said, the immediate cause of any logical error message is that
some assertion or program statement is not justified properly. Sometimes
this happens because we have left out part of a rule, e.g. we have forgot-
ten to show that our loop conclusion follows from the no-iterations case,

or that our subscripts are in bounds, or that we are not aliasing with our
array arguments in a procedure call. When this happens, the user usually
needs only to be reminded of what he has left out. The straightforward
messages like "ARRAY ALIASING NOT DISPROVEN", "INVARIANT NOT PROVEN AT LOOP
ENTRY", and "LOOP HALTING => ATTAIN CONDITION NOT PROVEN" do this ade-
quately. (There is one possibly obscure message: in an ALL elimination or
a SOME introduction, the error message "BOUND AFTER SUBSTITUTION NOT PRO-
VEN" means that the variables listed to be substituted for the bound variables have not been shown to satisfy the "WHERE" part of the quantifier.)

At times, however, you get such messages when you think that you have proven what is required. You may also get messages that say that your proof
blocks do not prove what they are supposed to ("OR ELIM: CONCLUSION NOT
PROVEN", or "IMPLICATION INTRO: CONCLUSION NOT PROVEN FROM HYPOTHESIS",
etc.), or that your assertions are not justified ("JUSTIFICATION: ASSERTION
NOT IMMEDIATE"). These situations can be divided into two types: those
where you have actually written out the assertion that the verifier claims
is missing, and those where you thought that it would follow by immediate
rules.

In the former case, the first thing you should do is find out what the
required assertion is, i.e. what the verifier is looking for. There will
be some clue from the error message itself, but it usually pays to go back
to the rule involved (use the reference sections of the manual if you need
to) to see the exact form the verifier wants. If you think that what you
have written is of exactly this form, check the precedence of the logical
operators used, and make sure your parentheses are nested properly; you may
not be saying what you thought you were. Also, make sure you are using the
right rule. This means checking any daisy chains carefully, and in general
examining each of your BY INTRO's to see what you have assumed and what you
are required to prove. Finally, check the accessibility of the assertion
you have written with respect to the point where it is needed. Have you,
in between, made an assignment to any of the variables (especially if
arrays are involved)? Have you passed any of them as parameters to a procedure? Have you re-declared (by ALL-introduction or a CHOOSE statement)
any of the variable names? Are your proof blocks nested the way you think
they are, and is the hypothesis that is needed inside all blocks containing
the assertion which uses it?

If you haven't written the needed assertion explicitly, but think that it
follows from accessible assertions by immediate rules, then all of the
above steps should still be followed. In addition, you ought to examine
the chain of immediate deductions that leads to the hypothesis. A general
way to proceed in doing this is to explicitly insert steps of the chain,
and see what messages result. If only the original messages are still generated, then the faulty step is between what you have inserted and the
assertion that caused the error message. If that assertion becomes properly justified, but the step you inserted causes an error, then you've
still narrowed down the location of the problem.

You should watch out for certain "obvious" conclusions like X<0 | X>=0 or
2*X < 0 from X<0, which have to be proven BY ARITH. However, most errors
in chains of immediate rules are a result of trying to do both substitution

and normalization automatically. You should read the manual sections on this problem until you understand it thoroughly and can identify it, because it occurs so frequently and arises so easily from our natural mathematical ways of thinking. It most often occurs when the step of normalization is one that we have come to regard as trivial, such as commutativity of equality or a mathematical identity like X*0=0 or X+0=X. Thus, from "A=B" and "C=A" it follows immediately that "C=B", but not that"B=C" (when this occurs as a subformula). Similarly, from "A=0", it does not follow immediately that "A+A=0". The intermediate step of "0+0=0" must be inserted. The general cure for all problems of this sort is to introduce an intermediate step which breaks the chain into two parts, neither of which contain both a substitution and a normalization step.

There is one particularly hard to identify instance of the substitution and normalization problem which is worthwhile mentioning explicitly. In the rule for assignment to arrays we said that an assertion was generated as a conclusion, which said basically that all the unchanged elements of the array were still the same. (The same thing happens when array elements are passed as arguments to a procedure.) The form of the conclusion was:

ALL I FIXED WHERE ~(I=J). A'(I) = A(I)

A' is an internally generated name for the array A before the assignment. The user cannot access this name directly, but only by equality substitution of some array which was shown to be equal to A before the assignment (B, say). Thus, the user may assume that he has the assertion

(*) ALL I FIXED WHERE ~(I=J). B(I) = A(I)

accessible. However, it is accessible as part of a chain which already contains the substitution step of B for A', and so any further step of normalization will not be justified immediately. In particular, if instead of (*), the user writes

ALL I FIXED WHERE ~(I=J). A(I) = B(I)

then this will be flagged as an unproven assertion, because it requires a normalization of the inner equality from (*) to derive. Such problems can be easily avoided by writing (*) explicitly after array assignments.

Sample Session
What follows is a typical derivation of a verified file using PL/CV under CMS. The user's typed commands are in lower case, and the machine response in upper. Comments are to the right, separated by angle brackets. The session begins after the user has logged on, and is typing in a file containing a division procedure that he or she would like verified.

```
ed div plcv
NEW FILE:
EDIT:
i
INPUT:
*plcv syntax
*proc
   divide: procedure (a,b,q,r)
      dcl (a,b) readonly;
      dcl (q,r) fixed;
      /*/ assume a >= 0, b > 0;
          attain a = b*q+r, 0 <= r < b;    */
      r = a;
      q = 0;
      /*/ a = b*q+r;  */
      /*/ some i fixed. I >=0 & r <= i by intro, r;  */
      do while (r-b >= 0);
         /*/ assume a = b*q+r, r >= 0;
             arb i fixed where r <= i;
             ^(r <= 0) by arith, r-b >= 0, +, b > 0;
             a = b*(q+1) + (r-b) by arith  a = b*q+r;
             r-b <= i-1 by arith, r <= i;
             r = r-b;
             q = q+1;
         end;
      /*/ r < b by arith, ^(r-b >= 0), +, b=b;  */
      return;
   end divide;
EDIT:
file
R; T=0.05/0.30 21:33:17

plcv div          <if no filetype is specified, "plcv" is assumed>
DMSLIO109S VIRTUAL STORAGE CAPACITY EXCEEDED.    < oops, forgot to >
DMSLIO109S VIRTUAL STORAGE CAPACITY EXCEEDED.    < allow enough    >
DMSABN148T SYSTEM ABEND 15A CALLED FROM 1D3D24.   < memory          >
CMS
def stor 1m                      < one megabyte usually is enough >
STORAGE = 01024K
CP ENTERED; DISABLED WAIT PSW '00020000 00000000'
CP
ipl cms
CORNELL CMS 6.8              < the response at this point >
Y (19E) R/O                 < will vary somewhat         >
C (29F) R/O
E (199) R/O
G (29E) R/O
- THE 370/168 SYSTEM WILL BE DOWN FROM 4 AM - 6 AM .. 1/28/80
BULLETIN TYPE:
R; T=0.20/0.43 21:34:12


plcv div
```

```
R; T=1.07/1.73 21:37:08

type div listing          < where the output ends up >

PL/CV PROOF CHECKER   VERSION 8010A

*PLCV SYNTAX
*PROC
0001     DIVIDE: PROCEDURE (A,B,Q,R)
0001        DCL (A,B) READONLY;
****  MISSING SEMICOLON              < we see in fact that we are missing >
0002        DCL (Q,R) FIXED;      < a semicolon two lines up           >
0003        /*/ ASSUME A >= 0, B > 0;
0004           ATTAIN A = B*Q+R, 0 <= R < B;   */
0005        R = A;
0006        Q = 0;
0007        /*/ A = B*Q+R; */
0008        /*/ SOME I FIXED. I >=0 & R <= I BY INTRO, R; */
****  "I" HAS NOT BEEN DECLARED              < mis-parenthesized the >
****  ERROR AT END OF     " <= I BY INTRO,"  < quantifier again      >
0009        DO WHILE (R-B >= 0);
0010           /*/ ASSUME A = B*Q+R, R>=0;
0011              ARB I FIXED WHERE R<=I;
0012              ^(R <= 0) BY ARITH, R-B >=0, +, B > 0;
0013              A = B*(Q+1) + (R-B) BY ARITH  A=B*Q+R;
****  ERROR AT END OF      "-B) BY ARITH  A"    < left a comma out >
0014              R-B <= I-1 BY ARITH, R <= I;
0015              R = R-B;
0016              Q = Q+1;
0017           END;
****  "END" HAS NOT BEEN DECLARED              < something is wrong with >
****  RESERVED WORD BEING USED AS VARIABLE    < the structure of things >
0018           /*/ R < B BY ARITH, ^(R-B >= 0), +, B=B; */
****  ERRONEOUS SHIELDING                 < aha! we forgot to close the >
0019           RETURN;                      < shielding at line 14        >
0020        END DIVIDE;
****  LABEL ON END DOES NOT MATCH LABEL ON DO        < probably due to >
****  END OF TEXT REACHED BEFORE LOGICAL END OF PROGRAM < the shielding  >
LOCAL CONTEXT CHECKING            0.606 SEC           < error          >
VCODE INTERPRETATION              0.000 SEC
TOTAL EXECUTION TIME              0.776 SEC
END PLCV

R; T=0.02/0.14 21:37:35

ed div plcv               < we have four syntax errors to correct and >
EDIT:                     < we hope the last message will go away      >
do3
   DIVIDE: PROCEDURE (A,B,Q,R)
c/)/);                            < add a semicolon >
   DIVIDE: PROCEDURE (A,B,Q,R);
do8
     /*/ SOME I FIXED. I >=0 & R <= I BY INTRO, R;   */
```

```
c/. /. (                                                    < add parentheses >
        /*/ SOME I FIXED. (I >=0 & R <= I BY INTRO, R;  */
c/i b/i) b
        /*/ SOME I FIXED. (I >=0 & R <= I) BY INTRO, R;  */
do5
            A = B*(Q+1) + (R-B) BY ARITH  A = B*Q+R;
c/arith/arith,                                             < add comma >
            A = B*(Q+1) + (R-B) BY ARITH,  A = B*Q+R;
do
            R-B <= I-1 BY ARITH, R <= I;
c0;0;  */                                                 < close shielding >
            R-B <= I-1 BY ARITH, R <= I;  */
file
R; T=0.05/0.21 21:38:53

plcv div          < try again >
<BLIP>

R; T=1.08/1.74 21:39:50

type div listing

PL/CV PROOF CHECKER   VERSION 8010A

*PLCV SYNTAX
*PROC
 0001     DIVIDE: PROCEDURE (A,B,Q,R);
 0002     DCL (A,B) READONLY;
 0003     DCL (Q,R) FIXED;
 0004     /*/ ASSUME A >= 0, B > 0;
 0005         ATTAIN A = B*Q+R, 0 <= R < B;   */
 0006     R = A;
 0007     Q = 0;
 0008     /*/ A = B*Q+R;  */
 0009     /*/ SOME I FIXED. (I >=0 & R <= I) BY INTRO, R;  */
 0010     DO WHILE (R-B >= 0);
 0011         /*/ ASSUME A = B*Q+R, R >= 0;
 0012             ARB I FIXED WHERE R <= I;
 0013             ^(R <= 0) BY ARITH, R-B >= 0, +, B > 0;
 0014             A = B*(Q+1) + (R-B) BY ARITH,  A = B*Q+R;
 0015             R-B <= I-1 BY ARITH, R <= I;  */
 0016             R = R-B;
 0017             Q = Q+1;
 0018         END;
 0019         /*/ R < B BY ARITH, ^(R-B >= 0), +, B=B;  */
 0020     RETURN;
 0021     END DIVIDE;
LOCAL CONTEXT CHECKING              0.610 SEC
VCODE INTERPRETATION                0.000 SEC
TOTAL EXECUTION TIME                0.781 SEC
END PLCV
                                    < great! no more syntax errors   >
R; T=0.02/0.11 21:40:10             < now let's get the logical ones >
```

```
ed div plcv
EDIT:
do
*PLCV SYNTAX
c/syntax//                              < remove the syntax check option >
*PLCV
file
R; T=0.04/0.12 21:40:25

plcv div                      < and let'er rip >
<BLIP>


R; T=1.85/2.48 21:46:59

type div listing

PL/CV PROOF CHECKER   VERSION 8010A

*PLCV
*PROC
0001     DIVIDE: PROCEDURE (A,B,Q,R);
0002       DCL (A,B) READONLY;
0003       DCL (Q,R) FIXED;
0004       /*/ ASSUME A >= 0, B > 0;
0005           ATTAIN A = B*Q+R, 0 <= R < B;   */
0006       R = A;
0007       Q = 0;
0008       /*/ A = B*Q+R; */
0009       /*/ SOME I FIXED. (I >=0 & R <= I) BY INTRO, R; */
0010       DO WHILE (R-B >= 0);
0011          /*/ ASSUME A = B*Q+R, R >= 0;
0012              ARB I FIXED WHERE R <= I;
0013              ^(R <= 0) BY ARITH, R-B >= 0, +, B > 0;
0014              A = B*(Q+1) + (R-B) BY ARITH,  A = B*Q+R;
0015              R-B <= I-1 BY ARITH, R <= I;   */
0016          R = R-B;
0017          Q = Q+1;
0018       END;
0019       /*/ R < B BY ARITH, ^(R-B >= 0), +, B=B;   */
0020       RETURN;
0021     END DIVIDE;
****     8 JUSTIFICATION: ASSERTION NOT IMMEDIATE
****    15 INVALID ARITHMETIC INFERENCE
NUMBER OF VCODE INSTRUCTIONS        80
LENGTH OF ASSERTIONS PROCESSED     772
LOCAL CONTEXT CHECKING          0.606 SEC
VCODE INTERPRETATION            0.786 SEC
TOTAL EXECUTION TIME            1.561 SEC
END PLCV
                < Not bad, only two errors. A little cosideration shows   >
                < that we're subtacting from the inequality in line       >
                < 15, so must need a monotonicity application.  Since      >
```

```
                < everything else seems all right with line 8, we check if >
                < we're having substitution - normalization problems. In   >
                < fact that's the case. Convince yourself that its true,    >
                < and consider why the change we make works                 >
R;  T=0.02/0.16  21:47:38


ed div plcv
EDIT:
do 10
        /*/ A = B*Q+R;  */  < our new assertion will normalize to something  >
c/q/0/                      < immediately true by the assignment "R = A", and >
        /*/ A = B*0+R;  */  < will satisfy the do-rule by substitution of Q   >
do7
            R-B <= I-1 BY ARITH, R <= I;  */    < note, B>0 is the same as >
c/;/, -, b>0;                                   < B <= 1                    >
            R-B <= I-1 BY ARITH, R <= I, -, B>0;  */
file
R;  T=0.04/0.16  21:52:31


plcv div
<BLIP>


R;  T=1.86/2.53  21:52:57


type div listing

PL/CV PROOF CHECKER   VERSION 8010A

*PLCV
*PROC
 0001      DIVIDE: PROCEDURE (A,B,Q,R);
 0002          DCL (A,B) READONLY;
 0003          DCL (Q,R) FIXED;
 0004          /*/ ASSUME A >= 0, B > 0;
 0005              ATTAIN A = B*Q+R, 0 <= R < B;    */
 0006          R = A;
 0007          Q = 0;
 0008          /*/ A = B*0+R;  */
 0009          /*/ SOME I FIXED. (I >=0 & R <= I) BY INTRO, R;  */
 0010          DO WHILE (R-B >= 0);
 0011              /*/ ASSUME A = B*Q+R, R >= 0;
 0012                  ARB I FIXED WHERE R <= I;
 0013                  ^(R <= 0) BY ARITH, R-B >= 0, +, B > 0;
 0014                  A = B*(Q+1) + (R-B) BY ARITH,  A = B*Q+R;
 0015                  R-B <= I-1 BY ARITH, R <= I, -, B>0;  */
 0016              R = R-B;
 0017              Q = Q+1;
 0018          END;
 0019          /*/ R < B BY ARITH, ^(R-B >= 0), +, B=B;  */
 0020          RETURN;
 0021      END DIVIDE;
NUMBER OF VCODE INSTRUCTIONS         81
LENGTH OF ASSERTIONS PROCESSED      774
```

```
LOCAL CONTEXT CHECKING          0.607 SEC
VCODE INTERPRETATION            0.796 SEC
TOTAL EXECUTION TIME            1.571 SEC
END PLCV
                                < the proof is complete and correct >
R; T=0.02/0.10 21:53:31
```

Appendix B

Known Bugs in PL/CV2

Alias checking

The current version of the verifier does not properly check for aliasing
involving EXTERNAL variables passed as parameters. Thus it is possible to
write a set of procedures using external variables, verify the proof and
receive no error messages, and still have errors remaining because of
aliasing.

Solution: Do not use external variables, but rather pass all variables that
would otherwise be made external as parameters. (Using externals but not
passing them as parameters is safe as long as one does not reference the
externals in a function.) Since alias checking works for elements of arrays
passed as parameters and for duplicate parameters, all possible aliasing
errors will be caught.

Functions calling procedures
The restriction that functions not have side effects was originally
enforced by not allowing a function to call a procedure of any description.
This restriction was later lifted to allow functions to call procedures
which themselves change only their parameters (i.e. access all externals
READONLY). Checking of this restriction is flaky; use it at your own risk.
Making a recursive loop from a procedure to a function and back to the procedure is not checked at all, and is liable to cause an abort with very
strange error messages.

Solution: To obtain a function/procedure recursion, translate the function
into the appropriate procedure and use procedure/procedure recursion.

Readonly variables in DO loops
The semantics of PL/CS demand that all variables referenced in an indexed
do-loop be READONLY within the body of the loop. The verifier checks that
the index variable is readonly within the loop body, but variables occurring in the expressions for the lower and upper bounds of the loop, are not
checked. Assignments to these variables within the loop will not generate
error messages, and will likely cause logical errors later in the proof.

Solution: Be careful when using indexed do-loops.

Syntax errors
The parser for PL/CV was not designed to be tolerant of syntax errors. A
lot of syntax errors may result in the parser "losing track" of its place
in a proof, with the subsequent generation of a multitude of (erroneous, or
at least useless) error messages.

Solution: Fix the worst of the syntax errors and try again.

Passing non-auxiliary variables as auxiliary variables
The verifier erroneously allows one to pass a non-auxiliary variable, by
reference, as an auxiliary parameter. The semantics of auxiliary variables

is meant to be such that the removal of all auxiliary statements and references to auxiliary variables should not make any difference in the execution of a program. By allowing a non-auxiliary variable to, in effect, become an auxiliary variable, we have lost this part of the semantics.

Solution: Be careful in passing values to auxiliary parameters. The actual parameter, if it contains non-auxiliaries, should be passed readonly, either as an expression or to a READONLY auxiliary parameter.

The Fundamental Theorem of Arithmetic

PL/CV PROOF CHECKER   VERSION 8002A

```
*PLCV
*THEOREM
 0001    /*/
 0001    /# NUMBER THEORY: SECTION                                            #/
 0001    /# THIS IS THE DIRECTORY FOR PLCV NUMBER THEORY.  SECTIONS ARE LABELED #/
 0001    /# BY THEIR FILE NAMES.                                             #/
 0001
 0001    /#  0. BUILT-IN FUNCTIONS    (BLTNHDRS)     -- LINE 1               #/
 0001
 0001    /#      ABS,DIVISION,EXP,MAX,MIN,MOD,SIGN                           #/
 0001
 0001    /#  1. BASIC FUNCTIONS                      -- LINE 36              #/
 0001
 0001    /#      ABS_LEMMA  (B^=0 => ABS(B)>0 )                              #/
 0001    /#      LOG PROCEDURE                                               #/
 0001    /#      DIVISION LEMMA  (MOD(N,P) => N/P>1 )                        #/
 0001
 0001    /#  2. DIVISION THEORY BASICS  (DIVTHY)     -- LINE 114             #/
 0001
 0001    /#      DEFINITION  DIV(X,Y)  AS   X = Q*Y                          #/
 0001    /#      DIV_MOD_EQUIVALENCE                                         #/
 0001    /#      DIVISOR_SIZE                                                #/
 0001    /#      TRANSITIVITY_OF_DIVIDE                                      #/
 0001    /#      DIVIDE_SUM_DIFFERENCE                                       #/
 0001    /#      DIVIDE_PRODUCT                                              #/
 0001
 0001    /#  3. PRIME NUMBER THEORY (PRIMETHY)       -- LINE 173             #/
 0001
 0001    /#      DEFINITION OF PRIME, INT_PRIME, NO_PROPER_DIVISORS          #/
 0001    /#      PRIME_EQUIVALENCE                                           #/
 0001    /#      PRIMEQ_EQUIVALENCE                                          #/
 0001    /#      LEAST_PRIME_FACTOR PROCEDURE                                #/
 0001    /#      PRIMENESS  ( IS DECIDABLE )                                 #/
 0001
 0001    /#  4. GREATEST COMMON DIVISORS  (GCDTHY)  -- LINE 312              #/
 0001
 0001    /#      DEFINITION OF GCD  (GCDDEF)                                 #/
 0001    /#      EUCLIDS_GCD_THEOREM                                         #/
 0001    /#      GCD PROCEDURE                                               #/
 0001    /#      LINEAR_COMBINATION PROCEDURE                                #/
 0001    /#      GCD_OF_RELATIVELY_PRIME                                     #/
 0001    /#      MONUS FUNCTION                                              #/
 0001    /#      ARITHEQ                                                     #/
 0001
 0001    /#  5. PRODUCT THEORY  (PRODTHY)            -- LINE 472             #/
 0001
 0001    /#      PROD PROCEDURE                                              #/
```

```
0001    /#        PROD_SPLIT_LEMMA, PROD_SPLIT                                #/
0001    /#        PROD_INCREASING PROCEDURE                                   #/
0001    /#        *** PART OF GCD THEORY ***                                  #/
0001    /#        LINEAR_COMBINATION_THEOREM  (A FUNCTION)                    #/
0001    /#        GCD_OF_RELATIVELY_PRIME2                                    #/
0001    /#        ***                     ***                                #/
0001    /#        PRIME_DIVIDES_PRODUCT                                       #/
0001    /#        PROD_TERMINATION FUNCTION                                   #/
0001    /#        PROD_POSITIVE                                               #/
0001    /#        DEFINITION  DIVIDES_A_FACTOR                                #/
0001    /#        PRIME_DIVIDES_LONG_PRODUCT                                  #/
0001
0001    /# 6. MORE ABOUT BASIC FUNCTIONS           -- LINE 879               #/
0001
0001    /#        (THESE FACTS ARE NEED FOR THE FACTORIZATION PROCEDURE)      #/
0001    /#        LOG_POSITIVE                                                #/
0001    /#        EXP_POSITIVE                                                #/
0001    /#        EXP_ADDITIVE                                                #/
0001    /#        EXP_MONOTONE                                                #/
0001    /#        LOG_MONOTONE                                                #/
0001    /#        LOG_EXACT                                                   #/
0001    /#        LOG_OF_PRODUCT                                              #/
0001
0001    /# 7. ADVANCED DIVISION THEORY (DIVTHY2)  -- LINE 1069               #/
0001
0001    /#        PRIME_FACTORIZATION PROCEDURE                               #/
0001    /#        DEFINITIONS: PRIME_FACTORS,ORDERED,FACTORIZATION            #/
0001    /#        FTA_LEMMA FUNCTION                                          #/
0001    /#        FTA_UNIQUENESS FUNCTION                                     #/
0001
0001    /# PARTS 1,2,3,4,5,7  WERE WRITTEN IN THE FALL OF 1978.  PARTS 1 AND  #/
0001    /# 2 WERE CHECKED AS OF SEPT. 28 1979.  PARTS 3 AND 4 WERE CHECKED AS #/
0001    /# OF JANUARY 4 1980.  PART 5 WAS CHECKED AS OF JANUARY 20 1980.  PART #/
0001    /# 6 WAS WRITTEN AND CHECKED AS OF FEBRUARY 3 1980.  PART 7 WAS CHECKED #/
0001    /# AS OF 17   FEBRUARY 1980.                                         #/
0001
0001
0001    */
0001    /* ******** THIS IS THE FILE OF BUILT-IN FUNCTIONS ********          */
*PROCESS ABS
0001    ABS: PROCEDURE(X) RETURNS(FIXED);
0002    DECLARE X FIXED /*: READONLY */;
0003    /*/ ASSUME '1'B;                                                      */
0004    /*/ ATTAIN X >= 0 => ABS(X) = X,                                      */
0004    /*/        X <= 0 => ABS(X) = -X,                                     */
0004    /*/        X  = 0 => ABS(X) = 0;                                      */
0005    END ABS;
*PROCESS MOD
0006    MOD: PROCEDURE(A, B) RETURNS(FIXED);
0007    DECLARE (A, B) FIXED /*: READONLY */;
0008    /*/ ASSUME B ^= 0;                                                    */
0009    /*/ ATTAIN ALL (Q, R) FIXED .                                        */
0009    /*/             ((A = B * Q + R & 0 <= R < ABS(B))                    */
```

```
0009   /*/                         => R = MOD(A, B)),                      */
0009   /*/         SOME Q FIXED . A = B * Q + MOD(A, B),                   */
0009   /*/            0 <= MOD(A, B) < ABS(B);                             */
0010   END MOD;
*PROCESS SIGN
0011   SIGN: PROCEDURE(X) RETURNS(FIXED);
0012   DECLARE X FIXED /*: READONLY */;
0013   /*/ ASSUME '1'B;                                                    */
0014   /*/ ATTAIN X < 0 <=> SIGN(X) = -1,                                  */
0014   /*/        X = 0 <=> SIGN(X) = 0,                                   */
0014   /*/        X > 0 <=> SIGN(X) = 1;                                   */
0015   END SIGN;
*PROCESS MAX
0016   MAX: PROCEDURE(A, B) RETURNS(FIXED);
0017   DECLARE (A, B) FIXED /*: READONLY */;
0018   /*/ ASSUME '1'B;                                                    */
0019   /*/ ATTAIN MAX(A, B) >= A,                                          */
0019   /*/        MAX(A, B) >= B,                                          */
0019   /*/        MAX(A, B) = A | MAX(A, B) = B;                           */
0020   END MAX;
*PROCESS MIN
0021   MIN: PROCEDURE(A, B) RETURNS(FIXED);
0022   DECLARE (A, B) FIXED /*: READONLY */;
0023   /*/ ASSUME '1'B;                                                    */
0024   /*/ ATTAIN MIN(A, B) <= A,                                          */
0024   /*/        MIN(A, B) <= B,                                          */
0024   /*/        MIN(A, B) = A | MIN(A, B) = B;                           */
0025   END MIN;
*PROCESS EXP
0026   EXP: PROCEDURE (B, E) RETURNS(FIXED);
0027   DECLARE (B, E) FIXED /*: READONLY */;
0028   /*/ ASSUME B ^= 0 & E >= 0;                                         */
0029   /*/ ATTAIN E = 0 => B ** E = 1,                                     */
0029   /*/        E >= 1 => ((B ** E = B * (B ** (E - 1))) &               */
0029   /*/                   ((B ** E) / B = B ** (E - 1)));               */
0030   END EXP;
*PROCESS DIVISION
0031   DIVISION: PROCEDURE(A, B) RETURNS(FIXED);
0032   DECLARE (A, B) FIXED /*: READONLY */;
0033   /*/ ASSUME B ^= 0;                                                  */
0034   /*/ ATTAIN A >= 0 => A = B * (A / B) + MOD(A, B),                   */
0034   /*/        A <= 0 => A = B * (A / B) - MOD(A, B),                   */
0034   /*/        (A > 0 & 0 < B <= A)   => A / B > 0,                     */
0034   /*/        (A < 0 & A <= B < 0)   => A / B > 0,                     */
0034   /*/        (A > 0 & -A <= B < 0)  => A / B < 0,                     */
0034   /*/        (A < 0 & 0 < B <= A)   => A / B < 0,                     */
0034   /*/        A = 0                  => A / B = 0,                     */
0034   /*/        (A ^= 0 & 0 < ABS(A) < ABS(B))                          */
0034   /*/                               => A / B = 0,                     */
0034   /*/           ALL (Q, R) FIXED . (                                  */
0034   /*/        (A >= 0 => ((A = B * Q + R & 0 <= R < ABS(B))            */
0034   /*/                 => (Q = A / B & R = MOD(A, B)))) &               */
0034   /*/        (A <= 0 => ((A = B * Q - R & 0 <= R < ABS(B))            */
```

```
0034    /*/                     => (Q = A / B & R = MOD(A, B))))              */
0034    /*/                         );                                        */
0035    END DIVISION;
0036    /* ********** THIS IS THE FILE BASIC FUNCTIONS PLCV ********          */
0036    /* DERIVED PROPERTIES OF BUILT-IN FUNCTIONS AND OF DEFINED FUNCTIONS  */
*THEOREM
0036    /*/
0036    ABS_LEMMA_1: ALL B FIXED WHERE B^=0. ABS(B)>0 BY INTRO,
0036    PROOF;
0037      TRI: B<0 | B=0 | B>0 BY ARITH;
0038      ABS(B)>0 BY CASES,TRI,
0038      PROOF;
0039        CASE B<0;
0040        B <= 0 BY ARITH, B < 0;
0041        ABS(B)=-B BY FUNCTION,ABS(B);
0042        -B > 0 ;
0043        CASE B=0;
0044        CASE B>0;
0045        B >= 0 BY ARITH, B > 0;
0046          ABS(B)=B BY FUNCTION,ABS(B);
0047      QED;
0048    QED; /# END OF LEMMA                                                  #/
0049    */
*PROCESS
0049        LOG: PROCEDURE(B,N) RETURNS(FIXED);
0050            DECLARE(B,N) FIXED;
0051            /*/ ASSUME B>1,N>0;                                           */
0052            /*/ ATTAIN B**LOG(B,N)<=N, LOG(B,N)>=0,
0052                      B**(LOG(B,N)+1) > N;                                 */
0053            /*/ ARBITRARY D FIXED WHERE N<=D;                             */
0054            /*/ ^(N <= 0) BY ARITH, N > 0;                                */
0055            /*/ B ^= 0 BY ARITH, B>0;                                     */
0056            /*/ ATTAIN '0'B;                                              */
0057        IF N < B
0057        THEN DO;
0058            /*/ ABS(B)=B BY FUNCTION,ABS(B);                              */
0059            /*/ B ** 0 = 1 BY FUNCTION, EXP(B, 0);                        */
0060            /*/ 1 <= N BY ARITH, N > 0;                                   */
0061            /*/ B ** (0 + 1) = B * (B ** 0) BY FUNCTION, EXP(B,1);        */
0062            /*/ B * 1 > N BY ARITH, N < B;                                */
0063        RETURN(0);
0064        END;
0065        ELSE DO;
0066            /*/ DEFINE R = MOD(N, B);                                     */
0067            /*/ 0 <= R < ABS(B) BY FUNCTION, MOD(N, B);                   */
0068            /*/ ABS(B) = B BY FUNCTION, ABS(B);                           */
0069            /*/ (N / B) * B + R = N BY FUNCTION, DIVISION(N, B);          */
0070            /*/ N >= B BY ARITH, ^(N<B);                                  */
0071            /*/ N / B > 0 BY FUNCTION, DIVISION(N, B);                    */
0072
0072            /*  PROVE TERMINATION */
0072
0072            /*/ S1: N / B < (N / B) * B BY ARITH, 1 < B, *, N / B > 0;    */
```

```
0073          /*/ S2: (N / B) * B <= N BY ARITH, (N / B) * B + R = N,-,R >= 0;*/
0074          /*/ N / B <= D - 1 BY ARITH, S1, S2, N <= D;                      */
0075
0075          /* PROVE FIRST ATTAIN */
0075
0075          /*/ T0: LOG(B, N/B) >= 0 BY FUNCTION, LOG(B, N/B);                */
0076          /*/ LOG(B, N/B) + 1 >= 0 BY ARITH, T0;                            */
0077          /*/ LOG(B,N/B)+1 >= 1 BY ARITH,T0,+,1=1;                          */
0078          /*/ T1:   B ** (LOG(B, N/B) + 1) = B * (B ** (LOG(B, N/B)+1-1)) */
0078          /*/            BY FUNCTION, EXP(B, LOG(B, N/B)+1);                 */
0079          /*/ T2: B ** LOG(B, N/B) <= N/B BY FUNCTION, LOG(B, N/B);         */
0080          /*/ T3: B * B ** LOG(B, N/B) <= (N/B) * B BY ARITH, T2, *, B > 0*/
0081          /*/ B ** (LOG(B, N/B) + 1) <= N BY ARITH, T1, T3, S2;             */
0082          /* PROVE SECOND ATTAIN --- ALREADY DONE   *                       */
0082
0082          /* PROVE THIRD ATTAIN                                             */
0082
0082          /*/ LOG(B,N/B)+1+1 >= 1 BY ARITH, T0;                             */
0083          /*/ U1:  B ** (LOG(B, N/B) + 1 + 1) = B * B ** (LOG(B, N/B)       */
0083          /*/            + 1) BY FUNCTION, EXP(B, LOG(B, N/B)+1+1 );         */
0084          /*/ U2: B ** (LOG(B, N/B) + 1) > N/B BY FUNCTION, LOG(B, N/B);   */
0085          /*/ U3: B ** (LOG(B, N/B) + 1) >= N/B + 1 BY ARITH, U2;           */
0086          /*/ U4: B * B ** (LOG(B, N/B) + 1) >= (N/B) * B + B               */
0086          /*/              BY ARITH, U3, *, B > 0;                          */
0087          /*/ U5: (N/B)*B + B > N BY ARITH,                                 */
0087          /*/      (N/B)*B = (N/B)*B,+,B>R, N=(N/B)*B + R;                   */
0088          /*/ B **(LOG(B, N/B) + 1 + 1) > N BY ARITH, U1, U4, U5;          */
0089        RETURN(LOG(B, N/B) + 1);
0090        END;
0091      END LOG;
```

*THEOREM

```
0092   /*/
0092        DIVISION_LEMMA: ALL (N,P) FIXED WHERE N>0 & P>0.(MOD(N,P)=0 => N/P>=1)
0092        BY INTRO,INTRO,
0092        PROOF;
0093            DEFINE FALSE = '0'B;
0094            P ^= 0 BY ARITH, P>0;
0095            P^=0 BY ARITH,P>0;
0096            N = (N/P)*P + MOD(N,P) BY FUNCTION,DIVISION(N,P);
0097            C: N/P < 0 | N/P >=0 BY ARITH;
0098            N/P >= 0 BY CASES,C,
0098                PROOF;
0099                CASE N/P < 0;
0100                (N/P)*P+0 < 0 BY ARITH,N/P<0,*,P>0;
0101                N = (N/P)*P+0;
0102                N<0;
0103                FALSE BY ARITH, N<0, N>0;
0104                QED;
0105            D: N/P = 0 | N/P > 0 BY ARITH,N/P>=0;
0106            N/P > 0 BY CASES,D,
0106            PROOF;
0107              CASE N/P = 0;
0108              N = 0*P + MOD(N,P);
```

```
0109                N = MOD(N,P);
0110                N = 0;
0111                '0'B BY ARITH, N=0,N>0;
0112           QED;
0113        QED;
0114    */
*THEOREM
0114    /*/
0114    /# ********** THIS IS THE FILE DIVTHY PLCV, BASIC DIVISON THEORY *****    #/
0114    /# BASIC DIVISIBILTY CONCEPTS                                            #/
0114    FOR (X,Y) FIXED DEFINE DIV(Y,X)=SOME Q FIXED.X=Q*Y;
0115    /# DIV(Y,X) IS READ "Y DIVIDES X" AND IS EQUIVALENT TO MOD(X,Y)=0.       #/
0115    /# WITH INFIX OPERATORS IN PLCV WE WOULD WRITE 'Y DIVIDES X' TO MATCH     #/
0115    /# THE MATHEMATICAL NOTATION Y|X.                                        #/
0115    /# WE ESTABLISH NEXT THE PRECISE RELATIONSHIP BETWEEN DIV AND MOD.        #/
0115    /# *************************************************************          #/
0115    DIV_MOD_EQUIVALENCE:
0115      ALL (A,B) FIXED WHERE B^=0. ( DIV(B,A) <=> MOD(A,B)=0 )  BY INTRO,
0115      PROOF;
0116      ONLY_IF_PART: DIV(B,A) => MOD(A,B)=0 BY INTRO,
0116        PROOF;
0117        CHOOSE Q0 FIXED WHERE A=B*Q0;
0118        A=B*Q0+0;
0119        0<ABS(B) BY ALLEL,ABS_LEMMA_1,B;
0120        0<=0<ABS(B);
0121        MOD_FACT: ALL (Q,R) FIXED.(A=B*Q+R & 0<=R<ABS(B) => R=MOD(A,B) )
0121        BY FUNCTION,MOD(A,B);
0122        0=MOD(A,B) BY ALLEL,MOD_FACT,Q0,0;
0123        QED; /# END OF ONLY IF PART                                          #/
0124      IF_PART: MOD(A,B)=0 => DIV(B,A) BY INTRO,
0124        PROOF;
0125        SOME Q FIXED.(A=B*Q+MOD(A,B)) BY FUNCTION,MOD(A,B);
0126        SOME Q FIXED.(A=B*Q+0);
0127        DIV(B,A);
0128        QED; /# END OF IF PART                                              #/
0129      QED; /# END OF DIV_MOD_EQUIVALENCE                                     #/
0130    */
*THEOREM
0130    /*/
0130    DIVISOR_SIZE:
0130    /# FOR D>=0, A>0, IF D DIVIDES A THEN D<= A                              #/
0130    ALL (D,A) FIXED WHERE D>=0 & A>0 . (DIV(D,A) => D<=A)
0130    BY INTRO, INTRO,
0130    PROOF;
0131        CHOOSE M FIXED WHERE M*D=A;
0132        M<=0 | M>=1 BY ARITH;
0133           D = 0 | D > 0 BY ARITH, D>=0;
0134           D<=A BY CASS =0 | D>0,>
0134           PROOF;
0135             CASE D=0;
0136             D<=A BY ARITH,D=0,0<=A;
0137             CASE D>0;
0138             D<=A BY CASES, M<=0 | M>=1,
```

```
0138              PROOF;
0139                CASE M<=0;
0140                  M*D<=0 BY ARITH, M<=0, *, D>=0;
0141                  '0'B BY ARITH, 1 <= A = M*D <= 0;
0142                CASE M>=1;
0143                  M*D>=D BY ARITH, M>=1, *, D>=0;
0144              QED;
0145            QED;
0146    QED;
0147    */
*THEOREM
0147    /*/
0147    TRANSITIVITY_OF_DIVIDE:
0147    /# TRANSITIVITY OF DIVIDES                                         #/
0147    ALL (A, B, C) FIXED .(DIV(A,B) & DIV(B,C) => DIV(A, C))
0147    BY INTRO, INTRO,
0147    PROOF;
0148        CHOOSE M1 FIXED WHERE M1*A = B;
0149        CHOOSE M2 FIXED WHERE M2*B = C;
0150        M2*(M1*A) = C; /# BY SUBSTITUTION                              #/
0151        (M2*M1)*A = C; /# BY ASSOCIATIVITY OF *                        #/
0152        DIV(A,C) BY INTRO, M2*M1;
0153    QED;
0154    */
*THEOREM
0154    /*/
0154        DIVIDE_SUM_DIFFERENCE:
0154        ALL (X,S1,S2) FIXED.(DIV(X,S1)&DIV(X,S2) => DIV(X,S1+S2)&DIV(X,S1-S2) )
0154        BY INTRO,INTRO,
0154        PROOF;
0155          CHOOSE Q1 FIXED WHERE S1 = Q1*X;
0156          CHOOSE Q2 FIXED WHERE S2 = Q2*X;
0157          S1 + S2 = (Q1+Q2)*X BY ARITH,S1=Q1*X,+,S2=Q2*X;
0158          DIV(X,S1+S2) BY INTRO,(Q1+Q2);
0159          S1 - S2 = (Q1-Q2)*X BY ARITH,S1=Q1*X,-,S2=Q2*X;
0160          DIV(X,S1-S2) BY INTRO,(Q1-Q2);
0161        QED;
0162    */
*THEOREM
0162    /*/
0162        DIVIDE_PRODUCT:
0162        ALL (X,P,Q) FIXED.(DIV(X,P) => DIV(X,P*Q))
0162        BY INTRO,INTRO,
0162        PROOF;
0163          CHOOSE F FIXED WHERE P = F*X;
0164          /# A NASTY FEATURE OF ARITH                                  #/
0164          Q<0 | Q>=0 BY ARITH;
0165          P*Q = (F*Q)*X BY CASES,Q<0|Q>=0,
0165          PROOF;
0166            CASE Q<0; Q*P=Q*(F*X) BY ARITH,P=F*X,*,Q<0;
0168            CASE Q>=0; P*Q=(F*Q)*X BY ARITH,P=F*X,*,Q>=0;
0170          QED;
0171          DIV(X,P*Q) BY INTRO,(F*Q);
```

```
0172      QED;
0173   */
0173      /* END OF DIVISION THEORY BASICS                              */
*THEOREM
0173   /*/
0173   /# ****** THIS IS THE FILE PRIMETHY PLCV, BASIC FACTS ABOUT PRIMES ***** #/
0173   FOR P FIXED DEFINE PRIME(P) = P>1 & ALL D FIXED WHERE D>1 & DIV(D,P). D=P;
0174   FOR N FIXED DEFINE INT_PRIME(N) = PRIME(ABS(N));
0175   FOR X FIXED DEFINE NO_PROPER_DIVISORS(X) =
0175               ALL Z FIXED WHERE 1<Z<X. ^DIV(Z,X);
0176   PRIME_EQUIVALENCE: ALL X FIXED.(PRIME(X) <=> NO_PROPER_DIVISORS(X) & X>1 )
0176   BY INTRO. PROOF; ARBITRARY X FIXED;
0178     IF_PART: NO_PROPER_DIVISORS(X) & X>1 => PRIME(X) BY INTRO,
0178     PROOF;
0179     X>1;
0180     ALL D FIXED WHERE D>1 & DIV(D,X). D=X BY INTRO,
0180       PROOF; ARBITRARY D FIXED WHERE D>1 & DIV(D,X);
0182       /# ALL DIVISORS ARE LESS EQUAL X                           #/
0182       D<=X BY ALLEL.DIVISOR_SIZE,D,X;
0183       D<X | D=X BY ARITH.D<=X;
0184       /# DIVISOR D MUST BE X SINCE WE ASSUME NO D<X DIVIDES X.    #/
0184       D=X BY CASES,D<X|D=X,
0184       PROOF;
0185         CASE D<X;
0186         1<D<X;
0187         ^DIV(D,X) BY ALLEL.NO_PROPER_DIVISORS(X),D;
0188         DIV(D,X); /# FROM DEFINITION OF D                         #/
0189       QED;
0190     QED; /# END OF ALL INTRO FOR DEF OF PRIME                      #/
0191   QED; /# END OF INTRO FOR IF_PART                                 #/
0192   ONLY_IF_PART: PRIME(X) => NO_PROPER_DIVISORS(X) & X>1 BY INTRO,
0192   PROOF; ASSUME PRIME(X);
0194   X>0 BY ARITH,X>1;
0195   NO_PROPER_DIVISORS(X) BY INTRO,
0195   PROOF; ARBITRARY Z FIXED WHERE 1<Z<X;
0197     /# ANY PROPER DIVISOR Z MUST BE X SO IT CAN'T BE LESS THAN X. #/
0197     /# THUS FOR Z AS CHOSEN, NOT DIV(Z,X).                        #/
0197     ^DIV(Z,X) BY INTRO,
0197     PROOF; ASSUME DIV(Z,X);
0199       Z=X BY ALLEL, ALL D FIXED WHERE D>1&DIV(D,X).D=X,Z;
0200       '0'B BY ARITH,Z=X,Z<X;
0201     QED;
0202   QED; /# END OF ALL INTRO                                         #/
0203   QED; /# END OF ONLY IF PART                                      #/
0204   QED; /# END OF THEOREM.                                          #/
0205   */
*THEOREM
0205   /*/
0205   /# THE FOLLOWING DEFINITION OF PRIME IS CONVENIENT FOR ALL ELIMINATION. #/
0205   FOR P FIXED DEFINE PRIMEQ(P) =
0205        ALL Z FIXED.( P>1 & (1<Z & DIV(Z,P) => Z=P) );
0206   /# THE NOTION IS EQUIVALENT TO THE DEFINITON OF PRIME.          #/
0206   PRIMEQ_EQUIVALENCE: ALL P FIXED. ( PRIME(P) <=> PRIMEQ(P) ) BY INTRO,
```

```
0206    PROOF;
0207    IF_PART: PRIMEQ(P) => PRIME(P) BY INTRO,
0207    PROOF;
0208    P>1 BY ALLEL,PRIMEQ(P),1;
0209    ALL Z FIXED WHERE 1<Z & DIV(Z,P). Z=P BY INTRO,
0209    PROOF; Z=P BY ALLEL,PRIMEQ(P),Z; QED;
0212    QED;  /# END OF IF PART                                        #/
0213    ONLY_IF_PART: PRIME(P) => PRIMEQ(P) BY INTRO,
0213    PROOF;
0214    PRIMEQ(P) BY INTRO,
0214    PROOF;
0215    P>1;
0216    1<Z & DIV(Z,P) => Z=P BY INTRO,
0216    PROOF;
0217    LL1: ALL Z FIXED WHERE 1<Z & DIV(Z,P). Z=P; /# FROM DEF OF PRIME   #/
0218    Z = P BY ALLEL,LL1,Z;
0219    QED;
0220    QED;
0221    QED;
0222    QED;
0223    */
*PROCESS
0223    LEAST_PRIME_FACTOR: PROCEDURE(X) RETURNS(FIXED);
0224        DECLARE X FIXED;
0225        /* THIS FUNCTION SHOWS THAT FOR EVERY POSITIVE INTEGER, X,      */
0225        /* GREATER THAN 1, WE CAN FIND A LEAST PRIME FACTOR.            */
0225        /*/ ASSUME X>1;                                                */
0226        /*/ ATTAIN /# RESULT IS PRIME                                  #/
0226            PRM: PRIME(LEAST_PRIME_FACTOR(X)),
0226            /# RESULT DIVIDES X                                        #/
0226            DIVIDES_X: DIV(LEAST_PRIME_FACTOR(X),X),
0226            /# RESULT IS THE LEAST DIVISOR                             #/
0226            LEAST_FACTOR: ALL Z FIXED WHERE 1<Z<LEAST_PRIME_FACTOR(X).
0226                    ^DIV(Z,X);
0227        */
0227        /* LOOK FOR THE SMALLEST DIVISOR OF X  STARTING WITH 2.  SINCE X   */
0227            /* DIVIDES ITSELF, THE SEARCH IS BOUNDED.  IN A MATURE      */
0227            /* PROGRAMMING THEORY, THE PROOF WOULD SIMPLY BE :          */
0227            /* ATTAIN ALL Z FIXED WHERE 1<Z<P.MOD(X,Z)^=0 & DIV(P,X)   */
0227            /* BY ITERATION,DO I=2 TO X;                                */
0227            /*               IF MOD(X,I)=0                              */
0227            /*                  THEN DO; P=I; LEAVE; END;               */
0227            /*               END;                                      */
0227            /* FILL IN THE DETAILS OF THE 'BY ITERATION' HIGH LEVEL     */
0227            /* PROOF STEP                                               */
0227            DECLARE (P,I) FIXED;    /* THE FUNCTON VALUE                */
0228            /*/ FOR K FIXED DEFINE INVARIANT(K)=
0228                ALL Z FIXED WHERE 1<Z<K. MOD(X,Z)^=0;                  */
0229            /*/ FOR K FIXED DEFINE EXIT(K) =
0229                DIV(K,X) & INVARIANT(K) & K>1 ;                        */
0230            /*/ INVARIANT(2) BY INTRO, ARITH,1<Z<2;                    */
0231            /*/ ^(X<2) BY ARITH,X>1;                                   */
0232            /*/ X<2 => EXIT(2);                                        */
```

```
0233                /*/ ATTAIN EXIT(P) ;                                             */
0234                LOOP: DO I = 2 TO X BY 1;
0235                   /*/ ASSUME INVARIANT(I);                                      */
0236                   /*/ I^=0 BY ARITH,2<=I<=X;                                    */
0237                   /*/ ATTAIN INVARIANT(I+1);                                    */
0238                   IF MOD(X,I)=0
0238                   THEN
0238                      DO;
0239                      P = I;
0240                      /*/
0240                      MOD(X,P)=0;
0241                      P ^= 0 BY ARITH, 2<=I,P=I;
0242                      P>1 BY ARITH,2<=I,P=I;
0243                      DIV(P,X) BY ALLEL,DIV_MOD_EQUIVALENCE,X,P;
0244                      EXIT(P);
0245                      */
0245                      LEAVE LOOP;
0246                      END;
0247                   ELSE
0247                      DO;
0248                      /*/
0248                      MOD(X,I)^=0;
0249                      /# ROUTINE DOMAIN EXTENSION TO SHOW INVARIANT(I+1)          #/
0249                      /# THIS SHOULD BE AUTOMATIC IN A MATURE THEORY              #/
0249                      INVARIANT(I+1) BY INTRO,
0249                      PROOF;
0250                      Z<I | Z=I BY ARITH, Z<I+1;
0251                      MOD(X,Z)^=0 BY CASES, Z<I | Z=I,
0251                      PROOF;
0252                      CASE Z<I;
0253                      1<Z<I;
0254                      MOD(X,Z)^=0 BY ALLEL,INVARIANT(I),Z;
0255                      CASE Z=I;
0256                      MOD(X,Z)^=0;
0257                      QED; /# END OF CASES                                        #/
0258                      QED; /# END OF INTRO                                        #/
0259                      */
0259                      END;
0260                      P=I;
0261                   /*/ P>1 BY ARITH,2<=I,P=I;                                     */
0262                   /*/ I^=X => INVARIANT(I+1); /# TRIVIAL SINCE INVARIANT     #/ */
0263                   /*/ I=X => EXIT(P) BY INTRO,
0263                      PROOF; X=1*X BY ARITH; DIV(X,X) BY INTRO,1; QED;           */
0267                END LOOP;
0268                /*/ EXIT(P);                                                     */
0269                /* CLAIM P IS PRIME BECAUSE ANY DIVISOR OF P IS A DIVISOR        */
0269                /* OF X, AND NO NUMBER BETWEEN 1 AND P DIVIDES X.                */
0269                /*/
0269                ALL Z FIXED WHERE 1<Z<P.^DIV(Z,P) BY INTRO,
0269                PROOF;
0270                   Z ^= 0 BY ARITH, 1<Z;
0271                   ^DIV(Z,P) BY INTRO,
0271                   PROOF;
```

```
0272                    DIV(Z,X) BY ALLEL,TRANSITIVITY_OF_DIVIDE.Z,P,X;
0273                    MOD(X,Z)^=0 BY ALLEL,INVARIANT(P),Z;
0274                    ^DIV(Z,X) BY ALLEL,DIV_MOD_EQUIVALENCE,X,Z;
0275                  QED;
0276                QED; /# END OF ALL INTRO                                  #/
0277                PRIME(P) BY ALLEL,PRIME_EQUIVALENCE,P;
0278                ALL Z FIXED WHERE 1<Z<P.^DIV(Z,X) BY INTRO,
0278                PROOF;
0279                  Z ^= 0 BY ARITH, 1<Z;
0280                  MOD(X,Z)^=0 BY ALLEL,INVARIANT(P),Z;
0281                   ^DIV(Z,X) BY ALLEL,DIV_MOD_EQUIVALENCE,X,Z;
0282                QED;
0283                */
0283                /*/ PRIME(P) & DIV(P,X) & ALL Z FIXED WHERE 1<Z<P.^DIV(Z,X);    */
0284                RETURN(P);
0285           END LEAST_PRIME_FACTOR;
*THEOREM
0286      /*/
0286           PRIMENESS: ALL X FIXED WHERE X>=0.(PRIME(X) | ^PRIME(X)) BY INTRO,
0286           PROOF;
0287             /# ONLY POSITIVE INTEGERS GREATER THAN ONE ARE INTERESTING          #/
0287             D1: X<=1 | X>1 BY ARITH;
0288             PRIME(X) | ^PRIME(X) BY CASES,D1,
0288             PROOF;
0289              CASE X<=1;
0290              ^PRIME(X) BY INTRO, PROOF; '0'B BY ARITH,X<=1,X>1; QED;
0293              CASE X>1;
0294              /# LOOK AT THE LEAST PRIME FACTOR OF X. IF THIS IS X ITSELF         #/
0294              /# THEN X IS PRIME, OTHERWISE IT IS NOT.                           #/
0294              DEFINE P = LEAST_PRIME_FACTOR(X);
0295              PRIME(P) & DIV(P,X) BY FUNCTION,LEAST_PRIME_FACTOR(X);
0296              LEAST: ALL Z FIXED WHERE 1<Z<P.^DIV(Z,X)
0296              BY FUNCTION,LEAST_PRIME_FACTOR(X);
0297              D2: P=X | P^=X BY ARITH;
0298              PRIME(X) | ^PRIME(X) BY CASES, D2,
0298              PROOF;
0299              CASE P=X;
0300               /# NO NUMBER IN RANGE 1 TO X DIVIDES X                            #/
0300               NO_PROPER_DIVISORS(X);
0301               PRIME(X) BY ALLEL,PRIME_EQUIVALENCE,X;
0302              CASE P^=X;
0303               /# X IS NOT A PRIME SINCE P IS A PROPER DIVISOR                   #/
0303               ^PRIME(X) BY INTRO,
0303                 PROOF;
0304                 ASM: ALL Z FIXED WHERE 1<Z & DIV(Z,X). Z=X; /# DEF OF PRIME   #/
0305                 P>1 & DIV(P,X);
0306                 P=X BY ALLEL,ASM,P;
0307                 P^=X; /# THE CONTRADICTION                                      #/
0308               QED; /# END OF NOT INTRO                                          #/
0309             QED; /# END OF CASES ON D2                                          #/
0310            QED; /# END OF CASES ON D1                                           #/
0311          QED; /# END OF BOUNDED ALL INTRO                                       #/
0312      */
```

```
*THEOREM
0312    /*/
0312    /# ********** THIS IS THE FILE GCDTHY PLCV ************            #/
0312    /# THIS FILE CONTAINS BASIC INFORMATION ABOUT THE GREATEST COMMON DIVISOR#/
0312    /# OF POSITIVE INTEGERS: DEFINITION, EUCLIDS THEOREM, EXISTENCE, ... #/
0312    /# THE GREATEST COMMON DIVISOR OF A AND B IS A NUMBER C WHICH DIVIDES #/
0312    /# BOTH A AND B AND IS LARGER THAN ANY OTHER NUMBER WHICH DIVIDES    #/
0312    /# THEM BOTH.                                                        #/
0312    FOR (A,B,C) FIXED DEFINE GCDDEF(A,B,C) =
0312         DIV(C,A) & DIV(C,B) &
0312         ALL D FIXED WHERE DIV(D,A)&DIV(D,B). D<=C;
0313    */
0313    /*/
0313    EUCLIDS_GCD_THEOREM:
0313    ALL (A,B,C) FIXED WHERE 0<B<=A.(GCDDEF(A,B,C) <=> GCDDEF(B,MOD(A,B),C))
0313    BY INTRO,
0313    PROOF;
0314      B ^= 0 BY ARITH,0<B;
0315      SOME Q FIXED . A = B*Q + MOD(A,B) BY FUNCTION,MOD(A,B);
0316      CHOOSE Q FIXED WHERE A = B*Q + MOD(A,B);
0317      MOD(A,B) = A-B*Q BY ARITH, A = B*Q + MOD(A,B),-,B*Q = B*Q;
0318      ONLY_IF_PART: GCDDEF(A,B,C) => GCDDEF(B,MOD(A,B),C) BY INTRO,
0318      PROOF;
0319        DIV(C,B*Q) BY ALLEL,DIVIDE_PRODUCT,C,B,Q;
0320        DIV(C,MOD(A,B)) BY ALLEL,DIVIDE_SUM_DIFFERENCE,C,A,B*Q;
0321        ALL D FIXED WHERE DIV(D,B)&DIV(D,MOD(A,B)). D<=C BY INTRO,
0321        PROOF;
0322          DIV(D,B*Q) BY ALLEL,DIVIDE_PRODUCT,D,B,Q;
0323          DIV(D,A) BY ALLEL,DIVIDE_SUM_DIFFERENCE,D,B*Q,MOD(A,B);
0324          D<=C BY ALLEL,ALL W FIXED WHERE DIV(W,A)&DIV(W,B). W<=C,D;
0325        QED;
0326      QED; /# END OF ONLY IF PART                                        #/
0327      IF_PART: GCDDEF(B,MOD(A,B),C) => GCDDEF(A,B,C) BY INTRO,
0327      PROOF;
0328        DIV(C,B*Q) BY ALLEL,DIVIDE_PRODUCT,C,B,Q;
0329        DIV(C,A) BY ALLEL,DIVIDE_SUM_DIFFERENCE,C,B*Q,MOD(A,B);
0330        ALL D FIXED WHERE DIV(D,A)&DIV(D,B). D<=C BY INTRO,
0330        PROOF;
0331          DIV(D,B*Q) BY ALLEL,DIVIDE_PRODUCT,D,B,Q;
0332          DIV(D,MOD(A,B)) BY ALLEL,DIVIDE_SUM_DIFFERENCE,D,A,B*Q;
0333          D<=C BY ALLEL,ALL W FIXED WHERE DIV(W,B)&DIV(W,MOD(A,B)). W<=C,D;
0334        QED; /# END OF ALL INTRO                                         #/
0335      QED; /# END OF IMPLICATION INTRO FOR IF PART                       #/
0336    QED; /# END OF EUCLIDS THEOREM                                       #/
0337    */
*PROCESS
0337    GCD: PROCEDURE(A,B) RETURNS(FIXED);
0338    /* THIS FUNCTION PICKS OUT THE GCD OF POSITIVE INTEGERS A, B.        */
0338    /* IT DOES NOT ASSUME NOR PROVE THAT THE GCD IS UNIQUE, BUT THE      */
0338    /* FUNCTION IS PROOF THAT THE GCD EXISTS.  FOR A PROOF OF THIS       */
0338    /* FACT IN PURE NUMBER THEORY, USING INDUCTION, SEE THE FILE         */
0338    /* GCDDEF.                                                           */
0338    /* THE ORDER OF ARGUMENTS IS CRITICAL TO THE STATEMENT              */
```

```
0338          /* OF THE RESULT, TO THE TERMINATION PROOF, AND TO THE                */
0338          /* CHOICE OF ARGUMENTS TO MOD.                                         */
0338             DECLARE (A,B) FIXED;
0339             /*/ ASSUME  0 < B <= A ;                                            */
0340             /*/ ATTAIN GCDDEF(A,B,GCD(A,B)),
0340                   GCD(A,B)>0,
0340                   MOD(A,B)=0 => GCD(A,B)=B,
0340                   MOD(A,B)^=0 => GCD(A,B)=GCD(B,MOD(A,B));                       */
0341             /* THE DEFINITION IS RECURSIVE FOLLOWING THE ATTAIN                  */
0341             /*/ ARBITRARY D FIXED WHERE A+B<D;                                  */
0342             /*/ 0<A BY ARITH,0<B<=A;
0343                A+B > 0 BY ARITH,0<B,+,0<A;
0344                ^(A+B < 0) BY ARITH,A+B>0;
0345                0<A BY ARITH, 0<B<=A;
0346                A^=0 BY ARITH, 0<A;
0347                B^= 0 BY ARITH, 0<B;                                             */
0348             /*/ ATTAIN '0'B;                                                    */
0349          IF MOD(A,B)=0
0349          THEN
0349             DO;
0350             /*/
0350             DIV(B,A) BY ALLEL,DIV_MOD_EQUIVALENCE,A,B;
0351             DIV(B,B) BY INTRO,1;
0352             ALL Z FIXED WHERE (DIV(Z,A) & DIV(Z,B)) . Z<=B
0352             BY INTRO,PROOF;
0353             Z<0 | Z>=0 BY ARITH;
0354             Z<=B BY CASES, Z<0 | Z>=0,
0354             PROOF;
0355                CASE Z<0; Z<=B BY ARITH,Z<0,0<B;
0357                CASE Z>=0; Z<=B BY ALLEL,DIVISOR_SIZE,Z,B;
0359             QED;
0360             QED;  /# END OF PROOF THAT DIVISOR IS GREATEST                       #/
0361             ^(MOD(A,B) ^= 0) BY INTRO;
0362             0 <= B BY ARITH,0<B; /# SHOULD BE UNNECESSARY                        #/
0363             */
0363             RETURN(B);
0364             END;
0365          ELSE
0365             DO;
0366             /*/
0366             ^(MOD(A,B) = 0);
0367             /# BY EUCLID'S GCD THEOREM WE KNOW THAT THE GCD OF A AND B          #/
0367             /# IS THE SAME AS THE GCD OF B AND MOD(A,B) AND THE SIZE OF         #/
0367             /# B + MOD(A,B) IS LESS THAN  A + B.                                #/
0367             0<=MOD(A,B) BY FUNCTION, MOD(A,B);
0368             0<MOD(A,B) BY ARITH,0<=MOD(A,B),MOD(A,B)^=0;
0369             ABS(B) = B BY FUNCTION,ABS(B);
0370             MOD(A,B)<B BY FUNCTION,MOD(A,B);
0371             0<MOD(A,B)<=B;
0372             /# SHOW THAT RECURSIVE CALL OF GCD TERMINATES                       #/
0372             B+MOD(A,B)<A+B BY ARITH,B<=A,+,B>MOD(A,B);
0373             B+MOD(A,B)<D-1 BY ARITH,B+MOD(A,B)<A+B,A+B<D;
0374             /# USING FACT THAT GCD(B,MOD(A,B)) IS THE GCD OF                    #/
```

```
0374              /# B AND MOD(A,B), SHOW GCD(A,B) IS GCD OF A AND B              #/
0374              GCDDEF(B,MOD(A,B),GCD(B,MOD(A,B))) BY FUNCTION,GCD(B,MOD(A,B));
0375              GCDDEF(A,B,GCD(B,MOD(A,B))) BY ALLEL,EUCLIDS_GCD_THEOREM,
0375                           A,B,GCD(B,MOD(A,B));
0376              GCD(B,MOD(A,B))>0 BY FUNCTION,GCD(B,MOD(A,B));
0377              */
0377              RETURN(GCD(B,MOD(A,B)));
0378              END;
0379         END GCD;
*PROCESS
0380         LINEAR_COMBINATION: PROCEDURE(A,B,S,T);
0381         /* THIS PROCEDURE EXPRESSES THE GCD OF A AND B AS A LINEAR            */
0381         /* COMBINATION OF A AND B, NAMELY GCD(A,B) = S*A + T*B                */
0381              DECLARE (A,B) FIXED /*: READONLY */ ;
0382              DECLARE (S,T) FIXED;
0383              /*/ ASSUME 0<B<=A;  */
0384              /*/ ATTAIN GCD(A,B) = S*A + T*B;                                 */
0385              /*/ ARBITRARY D FIXED WHERE A+B <= D;                           */
0386              DECLARE (S1,T1,DD) FIXED;
0387              /*/ B ^= 0 BY ARITH,0<B;                                        */
0388              /*/ ABS(B) = B BY FUNCTION,ABS(B);                             */
0389              /*/ 0<= MOD(A,B)< B  BY FUNCTION,MOD(A,B);                      */
0390              /*/ 0 < A BY ARITH,0<B<=A;                                      */
0391              /* FOR TERMINATION, SHOW D CANNOT BE 0                          */
0391              /*/ ^(A+B <= 0) BY ARITH,0<B,+,B<=A;                           */
0392              /*/ 0 <= (A+B)+1 BY ARITH,0<B,+,0<A;                           */
0393                  A+B <= (A+B)+1 BY ARITH;
0394                  SOME D FIXED. (D>=0 & A+B < D) BY INTRO,(A+B)+1;           */
0395              /*/ ATTAIN '0'B;                                               */
0396              IF MOD(A,B)=0
0396              THEN
0396                DO;
0397                /*/ B = 0*A + 1*B BY ARITH;                                  */
0398                S = 0; T = 1;
0400                /*/ GCD(A,B) = B BY FUNCTION,GCD(A,B);                       */
0401                /*/ GCD(A,B) = 0*A + 1*B;                                    */
0402                /*/ GCD(A,B) = S*A + T*B;                                    */
0403                RETURN;
0404                END;
0405              ELSE
0405                DO;
0406                /*/  /# NOW WE FIND S AND T RECURSIVELY                      #/
0406                MOD(A,B)^=0;
0407                0 < MOD(A,B) BY ARITH,0<=MOD(A,B),MOD(A,B)^=0;
0408                0<MOD(A,B)<=B;
0409                B + MOD(A,B) >=0 BY ARITH,0<B,+,MOD(A,B)>=0;
0410                GCD(A,B) = GCD(B,MOD(A,B)) BY FUNCTION,GCD(A,B);
0411                /# FOR TERMINATION, SHOW THAT D DECREASES                    #/
0411                MOD(A,B)<B BY FUNCTION, MOD(A,B);
0412                B+MOD(A,B)<A+B BY ARITH,B<=A,+,MOD(A,B)<B;
0413                B+MOD(A,B)<=D-1 BY ARITH,B+MOD(A,B)<A+B,A+B<=D;
0414                */  /* NOW FIND LINEAR COMBINATION FOR B,MOD(A,B)            */
0414                CALL LINEAR_COMBINATION((B),MOD(A,B),S1,T1);
```

```
0415            /*/   /# COMPUTE S AND T FROM S1 AND T1                          #/
0415            GCD(B,MOD(A,B)) = S1*B + T1*MOD(A,B);
0416            /# NOW RELATE MOD(A,B) TO A AND B                                 #/
0416            EQN1: A = (A/B)*B + MOD(A,B) BY FUNCTION,DIVISION(A,B);
0417            MOD(A,B) = A - (A/B)*B BY ARITH,EQN1,-, (A/B)*B = (A/B)*B;
0418            EQN2: GCD(A,B) = S1*B + T1*MOD(A,B);
0419            EQN3: S1*B+T1*(A-(A/B)*B) = T1*A+(S1-T1*(A/B))*B
0419               BY ARITH;
0420            EQN4: S1*B + T1*MOD(A,B) = S1*B +T1*(A-(A/B)*B);
0421            EQN5: GCD(A,B) = T1*A + (S1-T1*(A/B))*B ;
0422            */  /* NOW RETURN THE COMPUTED VALUES OF S AND T                  */
0422            S = T1; DD =  (A/B); T = S1-T1*DD;
0425            RETURN;
0426            END;
0427        END LINEAR_COMBINATION;
0428
*THEOREM
0428    /*/
0428        GCD_OF_RELATIVELY_PRIME: ALL (P,A) FIXED WHERE 0<P<=A.
0428            ( PRIME(P) & ^DIV(P,A) => GCD(A,P)=1 ) BY INTRO,INTRO,
0428        PROOF;
0429
0429            0<A BY ARITH,0<P<=A;
0430            PRIME(P) <=> PRIMEQ(P) BY ALLEL,PRIMEQ_EQUIVALENCE,P;
0431            PRIME(P); /# SHOULD BE UNNECESSARY                                 #/
0432            PRIMEQ(P);
0433               0<= P+A BY ARITH,P>0,+,A>0;
0434               P+A < (P+A)+1 BY ARITH;
0435               SOME D FIXED. ( D>=0 & P+A < D) BY INTRO,(P+A)+1;
0436            GCD(A,P)>0 BY FUNCTION,GCD(A,P);
0437            D1: GCD(A,P)>1 | GCD(A,P)=1 BY ARITH,GCD(A,P)>=1;
0438            GCD(A,P)=1 BY CASES,D1,
0438            PROOF;
0439               CASE GCD(A,P)>1;
0440               DIV(GCD(A,P),P) BY FUNCTION,GCD(A,P);
0441               GCD(A,P) = P BY ALLEL,PRIMEQ(P),GCD(A,P);
0442               DIV(GCD(A,P),A) BY FUNCTION,GCD(A,P);
0443               DIV(P,A);
0444               ^DIV(P,A); /# BY ASSUMPTION                                    #/
0445            QED;
0446        QED;
0447    */
*PROCESS
0447        MONUS:PROCEDURE(X,Y) RETURNS(FIXED);
0448            DCL (X,Y) FIXED /*: READONLY */ ;
0448            /* A FORM OF SUBTRACTION UNDER WHICH NONNEGATIVE INTEGERS         */
0448            /* ARE CLOSED                                                     */
0449            /*/ ASSUME '1'B;
0450               ATTAIN A1: MONUS(X,Y) >= 0,
0450                   A2: X>=Y => MONUS(X,Y) = X-Y,
0450                   A3: X<Y => MONUS(X,Y) = 0;                                 */
0451            /*/ ATTAIN '0'B;                                                  */
0452            IF X >= Y
```

```
0452              THEN DO;
0453              /*/ X-Y >= 0 BY ARITH, X >= Y,-,Y=Y;
0454              ^(X<Y) BY ARITH,X>=Y;                                    */
0455              RETURN(X-Y);
0456              END;
0457              ELSE DO;
0458              /*/ X < Y BY ARITH,^(X>=Y );                             */
0459              RETURN(0);
0460              END;
0461         END;
*THEOREM
0462         /*/ FOR (A(*),I) FIXED DEFINE DOM(A,I) =
0462             LBOUND(A,1)  <=I<=HBOUND(A,1);                            */
*THEOREM
0463         /*/
0463         /#  THIS IS A BASIC ARITHMETIC LEMMA USED TO EXTEND THE      #/
0463         /# CURRENT ARITHMETIC RULE.                                  #/
0463         ARITHEQ: ALL (E1,E2,T) FIXED.( E1=E2 => T*E1 = T*E2 ) BY INTRO,INTRO,
0463             PROOF;
0464             D: T=0 | T^=0 BY ARITH;
0465             E: T*E1 = T*E2 BY CASES,D,
0465                 PROOF;
0466                 CASE T=0;
0467                 E BY ARITH,E1=E2,*,T=0;
0468                 CASE T^=0;
0469                 E BY ARITH,E1=E2,*,T^=0;
0470                 QED;
0471             QED;
0472         */


*PROCESS
0472    /* ********** THIS IS THE FILE PRODTHY PLCV, FACTS ABOUT PROD ********   */
0472         PROD: PROCEDURE(A,L,U) RETURNS(FIXED);
0472             /* PROD(A,L,U) IS THE PRODUCT A(L)*...*A(U)               */
0473             DECLARE (A(*),L,U) FIXED /*: READONLY */ ;
0474             /*/ ASSUME   L<=U => DOM(A,L) & DOM(A,U) ;                */
0475             /*/ ATTAIN ( L<=U => PROD(A,L,U) = A(L)*PROD(A,L+1,U)
0475                                             = PROD(A,L,U-1)*A(U) ),
0475                         L=U => PROD(A,L,U) = A(L),
0475                         U<L => PROD(A,L,U)=1;                         */
0476        /* ALLOWING PROD TO BE DEFINED WHEN U<L REGARDLESS OF WHETHER  */
0476        /* L AND U ARE IN THE DOMAIN OF A IS VERY CONVENIENT.          */
0476             /*/ ARBITRARY D FIXED WHERE MONUS(U+1,L)<D;              */
0477             DECLARE (P,I) FIXED;
0478             /*/ MONUS(U+1,L)>=0 BY FUNCTION,MONUS(U+1,L);            */
0479             /*/ ^(MONUS(U+1,L) < 0 ) BY ARITH,MONUS(U+1,L)>=0;       */
0480             /*/ ATTAIN L<=U;                                         */
0481             IF U<L THEN DO; /*/ ^(L<=U) BY ARITH,U<L; U^=L BY ARITH,U<L;  */
0484                 RETURN(1);
0485                 END;
0486             ELSE DO; /*/ L<=U BY ARITH,^(U<L); */ END;
0489             /*/ MONUS(U+1,L) = (U+1)-L BY FUNCTION,MONUS(U+1,L);     */
0490         P = A(L);
```

```
0491            /*/ ATTAIN L^=U;                                                */
0492            IF L=U THEN DO;
0493                /*/ ^(U<L) BY ARITH,L=U;
0494                U<L+1 BY ARITH,U=L,+,0<1; U+1=L+1 BY ARITH,U=L,+,1=1;
0496                U+1-(L+1) = 0 BY ARITH,U+1=L+1,-,L+1=L+1;
0497                MONUS(U+1,L+1)=0 BY FUNCTION,MONUS(U+1,L+1);
0498                (U+1)-L=1 BY ARITH,(U+1)=L+1,-,L=L;
0499                1<D BY ARITH,(U+1)-L<D,(U+1)-L=1;
0500                0<D-1 BY ARITH,1<D,-,1=1;
0501                MONUS(U+1,L+1)<D-1;
0502                PROD(A,L+1,U)=1 BY FUNCTION,PROD(A,L+1,U);
0503                (U+1)-1 = U; (U-1)+1=U;  U-L=0 BY ARITH,L=U,-,L=L;
0506                MONUS(U,L)=0 BY FUNCTION,MONUS(U,L);
0507                MONUS(U,L)<D-1;
0508                PROD(A,L,U-1) = 1 BY FUNCTION,PROD(A,L,U-1);
0509                A(L)*1 = A(L) = 1*A(L);
0510                A(L) = A(L)*PROD(A,L+1,U) = PROD(A,L,U-1)*A(U);
0511                */
0511            RETURN(A(L));
0512            END;
0513        /*/
0513        L<U BY ARITH, L<=U,^(L=U);  L<U+1 BY ARITH,L<U,U<U+1;
0515        /# TERMINATION OF PROD(A,L,L) IS PROVED                              #/
0515        1<(U+1)-L BY ARITH,L<U,-,L=L;
0516        2<D BY ARITH,MONUS(U+1,L)=(U+1)-L,1<(U+1)-L,MONUS(U+1,L)<D;
0517        MONUS(L+1,L)=1 BY FUNCTION,MONUS(L+1,L);
0518        1<D-1 BY ARITH,2<D,-,1=1;  0<D-1 BY ARITH,0<1,1<D-1;
0520        MONUS(L+1,L)<D-1;
0521        PROD(A,L,L) = A(L) BY FUNCTION,PROD(A,L,L);
0522        P = PROD(A,L,L);
0523        ^(U<L+1) BY ARITH,L<U;
0524        /# TERMINATION OF PROD(A,L+1,L) NEED FOR ATTAIN                      #/
0524        L<L+1 BY ARITH;  L<=L+1;
0526        MONUS(L+1,L+1) = 0 BY FUNCTION,MONUS(L+1,L+1);
0527        MONUS(L+1,L+1)<D-1;
0528        /# INPUT CONDITION FOR PROD                                          #/
0528        L+1<=U BY ARITH,L<U,+,1>0;
0529        LBOUND(A,1)<=L+1 BY ARITH,DOM(A,L),L<L+1;
0530        L+1<=HBOUND(A,1) BY ARITH,DOM(A,U),L+1<=U;
0531        DOM(A,L+1);
0532        PROD(A,L+1,L) = 1 BY FUNCTION,PROD(A,L+1,L);
0533        /# SHOW THE ATTAIN CONDITION FOR LOWER BND OF LOOP                   #/
0533        PROD(A,L,L) = A(L)*1;
0534           PROD(A,L,L) = P = A(L)*PROD(A,L+1,L);  (L+1)-1=L;
0536        P = PROD(A,L,(L+1)-1) = A(L)*PROD(A,L+1,(L+1)-1);
0537        /# **** USE OF (L+1)-1 FOR L SHOULD BE UNNECESSARY                   #/
0537        ATTAIN P = PROD(A,L,U-1)*A(U) = A(L)*PROD(A,L+1,U);
0538        */
0538        DO I = L+1 TO U BY 1;
0539            /*/ ASSUME P = PROD(A,L,I-1) = A(L)*PROD(A,L+1,I-1);
0540            L+1<=I<=U; L<=I<=U; L<=I-1 BY ARITH,L+1<=I,-,1=1; L<=I-1<=U;
0544            L+1<I+1 BY ARITH,L+1<=I;
0545            I+1<=U+1 BY ARITH,I<=U;
```

```
0546            /# TERMINATION OF PROD(A,L+1,I)                              #/
0546            MONUS(I+1,L+1) = I+1-(L+1) BY FUNCTION,MONUS(I+1,L+1);
0547            L<=I BY ARITH,L+1<=I,L<I+1;
0548            MONUS(I+1,L) = I+1-L BY FUNCTION,MONUS(I+1,L);
0549            I+1<=U+1 BY ARITH,I<=U,+,1=1;
0550            I+1-L<D BY ARITH,I+1<=U+1,-,L=L,U+1-L<D;
0551            I+1-(L+1)<D-1 BY ARITH,I+1-L<D,-,1=1;
0552            I<=HBOUND(A,1) BY ARITH,DOM(A,L),DOM(A,U), L<=I<=U;
0553            LBOUND(A,1)<=I BY ARITH,DOM(A,L),DOM(A,U),L<=I<=U;
0554            DOM(A,I);
0555            I-1<=HBOUND(A,1) BY ARITH,DOM(A,L),DOM(A,U),L<=I-1<=U;
0556            LBOUND(A,1)<=I-1 BY ARITH,DOM(A,L),DOM(A,U),L<=I-1<=U;
0557            DOM(A,I-1);
0558            */
0558            P = P*A(I);
0559            /*/
0559            P = PROD(A,L,I-1)*A(I);
0560          /# A TRICKY RECURSIVE CALL NEEDED FOR INVARIANT                 #/
0560          PROD(A,L+1,I) = PROD(A,L+1,I-1)*A(I)
0560          BY FUNCTION,PROD(A,L+1,I);
0561            /# NOW PREPARE TO CALL PROD(A,L,I-1)                          #/
0561            I-L<D-1 BY ARITH,I+1-L<D,-,1=1; /# TERMINATION               #/
0562            DOM(A,I-1); /# INPUT CONDTION FOR PROD                       #/
0563                (I-1)+1 = I;
0564            MONUS(I,L) = I-L BY FUNCTION,MONUS(I,L);
0565            E1: PROD(A,L,I-1) = A(L)*PROD(A,L+1,I-1)
0565            BY FUNCTION,PROD(A,L,I-1);
0566            /# NOW PREPARE TO PROVE SECOND EQUALITY OF INVARIANT          #/
0566            PROD(A,L,I-1)*A(I) = A(L)*(PROD(A,L+1,I-1)*A(I))
0566            BY ALLEL,ARITHEQ,PROD(A,L,I-1),A(L)*PROD(A,L+1,I-1),A(I);
0567            PROD(A,L,I-1)*A(I) = A(L)*PROD(A,L+1,I); /# SUBSTITUTION      #/
0568            /# THE GOAL: #/ P = A(L)*PROD(A,L+1,I);  /# EQUALITY #/
0569            I=U => P = PROD(A,L,U-1)*A(U) = A(L)*PROD(A,L+1,U) BY INTRO;
0570            /# LOOP REPEATING IMPLIES INVARIANT HOLDS AT NEW INDEX, I+1   #/
0570            I^=U => P=PROD(A,L,(I+1)-1)=A(L)*PROD(A,L+1,(I+1)-1) BY INTRO,
0570            PROOF;
0571              /# CALLS TO PROD IN PROOF WILL TERMINATE                    #/
0571              I+1<U+1 BY ARITH,I<=U,I^=U;
0572              I+1-L<U+1-L BY ARITH,I+1<U+1,-,L=L;
0573              I+1-L<D-1 BY ARITH,I+1-L<U+1-L,U+1-L<D;
0574              PROD(A,L,I) = PROD(A,L,I-1)*A(I)
0574              BY FUNCTION,PROD(A,L,I);
0575              PROD(A,L,I) = A(L)*PROD(A,L+1,I)
0575              BY FUNCTION,PROD(A,L,I);
0576              P = PROD(A,L,I);  PROD(A,L,I) = P = A(L)*PROD(A,L+1,I);
0578              (I+1)-1 = I; /# THIS SHOULD BE UNNECESSARY                  #/
0579              P = PROD(A,L,(I+1)-1) = A(L)*PROD(A,L+1,(I+1)-1);
0580            QED;
0581            */
0581          END;
0582      RETURN(P);
0583      END PROD;
*THEOREM
```

```
0584    /*/
0584    /# WE PROVE A BASIC FORMULA ABOUT PRODUCT, THAT                          #/
0584    /#        PROD(A,L,U) = PROD(A,L,I)*PROD(A,I+1,U)                         #/
0584    /# THE PROOF IS BY INDUCTION ON U-L.                                      #/
0584        FOR N FIXED DEFINE STMT(N) = ALL (A(*),L,I,U) FIXED WHERE
0584            L<=I<=U & U-L = N & DOM(A,L) & DOM(A,U) .
0584            PROD(A,L,U) = PROD(A,L,I)*PROD(A,I+1,U);
0585        /# BASIS OF INDUCTIVE PROOF                                           #/
0585        STMT(0) BY INTRO.
0585        PROOF;
0586            L<=U BY ARITH,L<=I<=U;
0587          D: U-L<0 | U-L = 0 BY ARITH,U-L<=0;
0588          PROD(A,L,U) = PROD(A,L,I)*PROD(A,I+1,U) BY CASES,D.
0588          PROOF;
0589            CASE U-L<0; U<L BY ARITH,U-L<0,+,L=L;
0591            '0'B BY ARITH,U<L,L<=U;
0592            CASE U-L = 0;
0593            L=U BY ARITH,U-L=0,+,L=L; L=I BY ARITH,U=L<=I<=U;
0595            /# PREPARE TO CALL PROD(A,L+1,L), NOTE IN THIS CASE               #/
0595            /# L+1 IS NOT IN THE DOMAIN OF A. BUT PROD IS DEFINED.            #/
0595            /# INPUT CONDITION: #/ L<L+1 BY ARITH;
0596            /# TERMINATION OF PROD:                                           #/
0596                0<1; (L+1)-(L+1) = 0;
0598            MONUS(L+1,L+1) = 0 BY FUNCTION,MONUS(L+1,L+1);
0599            SOME D FIXED.(D>=0 & MONUS(L+1,L+1)<D) BY INTRO,1;
0600            PROD(A,L+1,L) = 1 BY FUNCTION,PROD(A,L+1,L);
0601            PROD(A,L,I) = PROD(A,L,U);
0602            PROD(A,I+1,U) = PROD(A,L+1,L);
0603            PROD(A,L,U) = PROD(A,L,U)*1; PROD(A,L,U)=PROD(A,L,I)*1;
0605            PROD(A,L,U) = PROD(A,L,U)*1;
0606            PROD(A,L,U) = PROD(A,L,I)*1 = PROD(A,L,I)*PROD(A,I+1,U);
0607        QED; /# END OF CASES                                                  #/
0608      QED; /# END OF ALL INTRO                                                #/
0609      /# END OF BASIS CASE                                                    #/
0609      PROD_SPLIT_LEMMA: ALL N FIXED WHERE N>=0. STMT(N) BY INDUCTION.
0609      PROOF;
0610        /# ASSUME STMT(N)                                                     #/
0610        STMT(N+1) BY INTRO.
0610        PROOF;
0611            ARBITRARY (A(*),L,I,U) FIXED WHERE L<=I<=U & U-L=N+1 &
0611            DOM(A,L) & DOM(A,U);
0612            L<=U BY ARITH,L<=I<=U;
0613        /# TERMINATION OF PROD(A,L,U)                                         #/
0613        MONUS(U+1,L)>=0 BY FUNCTION, MONUS(U+1,L);
0614        MONUS(U+1,L)<MONUS(U+1,L)+1 ;
0615        SOME D FIXED.(D>=0 & MONUS(U+1,L)<D) BY INTRO,MONUS(U+1,L)+1;
0616
0616        /# TERMINATION OF PROD(A,I+1,U)                                       #/
0616        MONUS(U+1,I+1)>=0 BY FUNCTION, MONUS(U+1,I+1);
0617        MONUS(U+1,I+1)<MONUS(U+1,I+1)+1;
0618        SOME D FIXED.(D>=0&MONUS(U+1,I+1)<D) BY INTRO,MONUS(U+1,I+1)+1;
0619        U-L=N+1; (U-1)-L=N BY ARITH,U-L=N+1,-,1=1; L<=I<=U;
0622        D: I<=U-1 | I=U BY ARITH,I<=U;
```

```
0623              PROD(A,L,U) = PROD(A,L,I)*PROD(A,I+1,U) BY CASES,D,
0623              PROOF;
0624                CASE I<=U-1;
0625                I+1<=U BY ARITH,I<=U-1,+,1=1;
0626                /# ATTAIN DOM(A,I+1) FOR CALL OF PROD                    #/
0626                I+1<=HBOUND(A,1) BY ARITH,DOM(A,U),I+1<=U;
0627                L<=I+1 BY ARITH,L<=I,+,0<1;
0628                LBOUND(A,1)<=I+1 BY ARITH,DOM(A,L),L<=I+1;
0629                DOM(A,I+1);
0630                DD: U-1<L | L<=U-1 BY ARITH;
0631                PROD(A,L,U-1)=PROD(A,L,I)*PROD(A,I+1,U-1) BY CASES,DD,
0631                PROOF;
0632                  CASE U-1<L;
0633                  U-1<I BY ARITH,U-1<L,L<=I;
0634                  '0'B BY ARITH,I<=U-1,U-1<I;
0635                  CASE L<=U-1;
0636                  LBOUND(A,1)<=U-1 BY ARITH,DOM(A,L),L<=U-1;
0637                  U-1<=HBOUND(A,1) BY ARITH,DOM(A,U);
0638                  DOM(A,U-1);
0639                  PROD(A,L,U-1)=PROD(A,L,I)*PROD(A,I+1,U-1)
0639                  BY ALLEL,STMT(N),A,L,I,U-1;
0640                QED;
0641              PROD(A,L,U) = PROD(A,L,U-1)*A(U) BY FUNCTION,PROD(A,L,U);
0642              PROD(A,L,U) = PROD(A,L,I)*PROD(A,I+1,U-1)*A(U);
0643              I+1<=U BY ARITH,I<=U-1,+,1=1;
0644              PROD(A,I+1,U)=PROD(A,I+1,U-1)*A(U) BY FUNCTION,PROD(A,I+1,U);
0645                PROD(A,L,U) = PROD(A,L,I)*(PROD(A,I+1,U-1)*A(U));
0646                PROD(A,L,I)*(PROD(A,I+1,U-1)*A(U)) =
0646                PROD(A,L,I)*PROD(A,I+1,U);
0647              PROD(A,L,U) = PROD(A,L,I)*PROD(A,I+1,U);
0648              CASE I=U;
0649              U<I+1 BY ARITH,I=U,+,1>0;
0650              PROD(A,I+1,U) = 1 BY FUNCTION,PROD(A,I+1,U);
0651              PROD(A,L,U) = PROD(A,L,I);   PROD(A,L,I) = PROD(A,L,I)*1;
0653              PROD(A,L,U) = PROD(A,L,I)*1 = PROD(A,L,I)*PROD(A,I+1,U);
0654            QED; /# END OF CASES                                        #/
0655          QED; /# END OF INTRO                                          #/
0656        QED; /# END OF INDUCTION                                        #/
0657    */
*THEOREM
0657    /*/
0657        PROD_SPLIT: ALL (A(*),L,I,U) FIXED WHERE L<=I<=U & DOM(A,L) & DOM(A,U) .
0657               PROD(A,L,U) = PROD(A,L,I)*PROD(A,I+1,U) BY INTRO,
0657        PROOF;
0658            L<=U BY ARITH,L<=I<=U;
0659            U-L>=0 BY ARITH,U>=L,-,L=L;
0660            STMT(U-L)
0660            BY ALLEL,PROD_SPLIT_LEMMA,U-L;
0661            PROD(A,L,U) = PROD(A,L,I)*PROD(A,I+1,U)
0661            BY ALLEL,STMT(U-L),A,L,I,U;
0662        QED;
0663    */
*PROCESS
```

```
0663        PROD_INCREASING:PROCEDURE(A,L,U) RETURNS(BIT(1));
0664           DECLARE (A(*),L,U) FIXED /*: READONLY */ ;
0665        /* THIS PROCEDURE IS A THEOREM THAT PRODUCT IS INCREASING IN U      */
0665        /* UNDER THE APPROPRIATE CONDITIONS.                                */
0665           /*/ ASSUME ASM1: L<=U, DOM(A,L), DOM(A,U),
0665                      ASM2: ALL I FIXED WHERE L<=I<=U.A(I) > 1;              */
0666           /*/ ATTAIN PROD(A,L,U) = PROD(A,L,L) => U=L,
0666                  PROD(A,L,U) > 1;                                          */
0667           /*/ ARBITRARY D FIXED WHERE U-L<D;                              */
0668        /* ********** BODY OF PROOF **********                             */
0668           /*/
0668        ^(U-L<0) BY ARITH,L<=U,-,L=L;
0669        A(L) > 1 BY ALLEL,ASM2,L;
0670           /# TERMINATION OF PROD(A,L,U)                                  #/
0670           MONUS(U+1,L)>=0 BY FUNCTION,MONUS(U+1,L);
0671           MONUS(U+1,L)<MONUS(U+1,L)+1;
0672           SOME D FIXED.(D>=0 & MONUS(U+1,L)<D)
0672           BY INTRO,MONUS(U+1,L)+1;
0673        ATTAIN L^=U;                                                       */
0674        IF U=L THEN DO;
0675           /*/ PROD(A,L,U)=A(L) BY FUNCTION,PROD(A,L,U);
0676               U=L;                                                         */
0677           RETURN('1'B);
0678           END;
0679           /*/
0679        L<U BY ARITH,L<=U,L^=U;
0680        PROD(A,L,U) = A(L)*PROD(A,L+1,U) BY FUNCTION,PROD(A,L,U);
0681        U-(L+1)<D-1 BY ARITH,U-L<D,-,1=1;
0682        L+1<=U BY ARITH,L<U;
0683        ALL I FIXED WHERE L+1<=I<=U.A(I) > 1 BY INTRO,
0683        PROOF; L<=I BY ARITH,L<L+1<=I; A(I)>1 BY ALLEL,ASM2,I; QED;
0687           /# ATTAIN DOM(A,L+1)                                           #/
0687        L+1<=HBOUND(A,1) BY ARITH,DOM(A,U),L+1<=U;
0688        LBOUND(A,1)<=L+1 BY ARITH,DOM(A,L),L<L+1;
0689        DOM(A,L+1);
0690        LL: PROD(A,L+1,U) >1 BY FUNCTION,PROD_INCREASING(A,L+1,U);
0691           A(L)*PROD(A,L+1,U)>1 BY ARITH,A(L)>1,*,PROD(A,L+1,U)>0;
0692           PROD(A,L,U)>1;
0693        PROD(A,L,U)=PROD(A,L,L) => U=L BY INTRO,
0693        PROOF;
0694           /# TERMINATION OF PROD(A,L,L)                                  #/
0694        MONUS(L+1,L) = 1 BY FUNCTION,MONUS(L+1,L); 1<2; 0<=2;
0697        SOME D FIXED.(D>=0 & MONUS(L+1,L)<D) BY INTRO,2;
0698           PROD(A,L,L) = A(L) BY FUNCTION,PROD(A,L,L);
0699           A(L)*PROD(A,L+1,U)>A(L) BY ARITH,LL,*,A(L)>0;
0700           PROD(A,L,U) > A(L);
0701           '0'B BY ARITH,PROD(A,L,L)>A(L),PROD(A,L,L)=A(L);
0702        QED;
0703        */
0703        RETURN('1'B);
0704     END PROD_INCREASING;
*PROCESS
0705        LINEAR_COMBINATION_THEOREM: PROC(A,B)  RETURNS(BIT(1));
```

```
0706            DCL (A,B) FIXED  /*: READONLY */ ;
0707            /* THIS PROCEDURE IS NEEDED TO CONVERT A PROCEDURE TO A          */
0707            /* THEOREM.  IT PROVIDES INTEGER VARIABLES, S AND T, TO          */
0707            /* BE USED AS PARAMETERS TO A PROCEDURE CALL.  THEY WOULD        */
0707            /* BE UNNECESSARY IF COMMANDS COULD BE USED MORE FREELY IN       */
0707            /* PROOFS.  WE HAD PLANNED TO ALLOW ALL COMMANDS IN PROOFS       */
0707            /* BUT THAT FEATURE IS NOT YET IMPLEMENTED.                      */
0707            /*/ ASSUME 0<B<=A;                                               */
0708            /*/ ATTAIN SOME(S,T) FIXED.(GCD(A,B) = S*A + T*B);               */
0709            DCL (S,T) FIXED; /* THIS IS THE KEY LINE OF THE PROCEDURE        */
0710            /*/
0710            A>0 BY ARITH,0<B<=A;
0711            A+B>=0 BY ARITH,A>0,+,B>0;
0712            A+B<=A+B+1 BY ARITH;
0713            A+B+1>=0 BY ARITH,A+B+1>=A+B>=0;
0714            SOME D FIXED.(D>=0 & A+B<=D) BY INTRO,A+B+1;                      */
0715                CALL LINEAR_COMBINATION((A),(B),S,T);
0716            /*/ GCD(A,B) = S*A + T*B;                                        */
0717            /*/ SOME (S,T) FIXED.(GCD(A,B) = S*A + T*B) BY INTRO,S,T;        */
0718            RETURN('1'B);
0719         END;
*THEOREM
0720         /*/
0720         GCD_OF_RELATIVELY_PRIME2: ALL (P,A) FIXED.
0720             (PRIME(P) & 0<A<=P & ^DIV(P,A) => GCD(P,A) = 1 )  BY INTRO,INTRO,
0720             PROOF;
0721               0<P BY ARITH,0<A<=P; 0<P+A BY ARITH,0<A,+,0<P;
0723               P+A < (P+A)+1 BY ARITH;
0724               SOME D FIXED.(D>=0 & P+A<D) BY INTRO,(P+A)+1;
0725               GCD(P,A)>0 BY FUNCTION,GCD(P,A);
0726               D: GCD(P,A)>1 | GCD(P,A)=1 BY ARITH,GCD(P,A)>0;
0727               GCD(P,A) = 1 BY CASES,D,
0727                  PROOF;
0728                    CASE GCD(P,A)>1;
0729                    DIV(GCD(P,A),P) BY FUNCTION,GCD(P,A);
0730                    AA: ALL Z FIXED WHERE Z>1&DIV(Z,P). Z=P;
0731                    GCD(P,A) = P BY ALLEL,AA,GCD(P,A);
0732                    DIV(GCD(P,A),A) BY FUNCTION,GCD(P,A);
0733                    DIV(P,A); ^DIV(P,A);
0735                 QED;
0736             QED;   */
*THEOREM
0737    /*/
0737         PRIME_DIVIDES_PRODUCT: ALL (P,A,B) FIXED WHERE PRIME(P)&A>0&B>0.
0737                   ( DIV(P,A*B) => DIV(P,A) | DIV(P,B) )
0737         BY INTRO,INTRO,PROOF;
0738           DIV(P,A*B);  A^=0 BY ARITH,A>0;
0740           P^=0 BY ARITH,P>1; /# SINCE PRIME P IMPLIES P>1 #/ '1'B;
0742           /# GOAL: TO PROVE DIV(P,A) | DIV(P,B)                            #/
0742           MOD(A,P)^=0 | MOD(A,P)=0 BY ARITH;
0743           DIV(P,A) <=> MOD(A,P)=0 BY ALLEL,DIV_MOD_EQUIVALENCE,A,P;
0744               ^DIV(P,A) => MOD(A,P)^=0 BY INTRO;
0745               MOD(A,P)^=0 => ^DIV(P,A) BY INTRO;
```

```
0746                 ^DIV(P,A) <=> MOD(A,P)^=0;
0747          D1: ^DIV(P,A) | DIV(P,A);
0748         DIV(P,A) | DIV(P,B) BY CASES,D1,
0748         PROOF;
0749            CASE ^DIV(P,A);
0750               D: A<=P | P<A BY ARITH;
0751               DIV(P,B) BY CASES,D,
0751               PROOF;
0752                  CASE A<=P;
0753            GCD(P,A)=1 BY ALLEL,GCD_OF_RELATIVELY_PRIME2,P,A;
0754            SOME (S,T) FIXED.( GCD(P,A) = S*P + T*A ) BY FUNCTION,
0754              LINEAR_COMBINATION_THEOREM(P,A);
0755            CHOOSE (S,T) FIXED WHERE GCD(P,A) = S*P + T*A;
0756            EQN1: 1 = S*P + T*A;
0757            EQN2: B = B*(S*P) + T*(A*B) BY ARITH,EQN1,*,B>0;
0758            DIV(P,S*B*P) BY INTRO, S*B;
0759            DIV(P,T*(A*B)) BY ALLEL,DIVIDE_PRODUCT,P,(A*B),T;
0760            DIV(P,B) BY ALLEL,DIVIDE_SUM_DIFFERENCE,P,B*(S*P),T*(A*B);
0761                  CASE P<A;
0762                  0<P;  /# BY DEFINITION OF PRIME P                      #/
0763                  ^DIV(A,P) BY INTRO,
0763                    PROOF;
0764                    A<=P BY ALLEL,DIVISOR_SIZE,A,P;
0765                    '0'B BY ARITH,P<A,A<=P;
0766                    QED;
0767                  GCD(A,P)=1 BY ALLEL,GCD_OF_RELATIVELY_PRIME,P,A;
0768                  SOME(S,T)FIXED.(GCD(A,P)=S*A + T*P) BY FUNCTION,
0768                  LINEAR_COMBINATION_THEOREM(A,P);
0769                  CHOOSE(S,T)FIXED WHERE  (GCD(A,P)=S*A + T*P);
0770                  EQN3: 1 = S*A + T*P;
0771                  EQN4: B = B*S*A + B*T*P BY ARITH,EQN3,*,B>0;
0772                  DIV(P,B*T*P) BY INTRO,B*T;
0773                  DIV(P,B*S*A) BY ALLEL,DIVIDE_PRODUCT,P,(A*B),S;
0774                  DIV(P,B) BY ALLEL,DIVIDE_SUM_DIFFERENCE,P,B*S*A,B*T*P;
0775                  QED;
0776            QED; /# END OF CASES                                        #/
0777     QED;
0778     */
*PROCESS
0778        PROD_TERMINATION: PROC(A,L,U) RETURNS(BIT(1));
0779            DCL(A(*),L,U) FIXED;
0780            /*/ ASSUME '1'B;
0781            ATTAIN SOME D FIXED.( D>=0 & MONUS(U+1,L)<D);
0782              MONUS(U+1,L)>=0 BY FUNCTION,MONUS(U+1,L);
0783              MONUS(U+1,L)<MONUS(U+1,L)+1;
0784              SOME D FIXED.(D>=0 & MONUS(U+1,L)<D) BY INTRO,MONUS(U+1,L)+1;
0785            */
0785     RETURN('1'B);
0786     END;
*THEOREM
0787        /*/
0787        FOR N FIXED DEFINE CLAIM(N) =
0787            ALL (A(*),L,U) FIXED WHERE DOM(A,L) & DOM(A,U) & U-L=N>=0.
```

```
0787              (ALL I FIXED WHERE L<=I<=U.A(I)>0 => PROD(A,L,U)>0);
0788         /# BASIS CASE OF INDUCTION TO PROVE CLAIM OR ALL NONNEGATIVE N  #/
0788         BASIS: CLAIM(0) BY INTRO,INTRO,
0788             PROOF;
0789                U-L=0; U=L BY ARITH,U-L=0,+,L=L;
0791                SOME D FIXED.(D>=0 & MONUS(U+1,L)<D)
0791                BY FUNCTION,PROD_TERMINATION(A,L,U);
0792                A(L)>0 BY ALLEL,ALL I FIXED WHERE L<=I<=U.A(I)>0,L;
0793                PROD(A,L,U) = A(L) BY FUNCTION,PROD(A,L,U);
0794                PROD(A,L,U)>0;
0795             QED;
0796         INDUCT: ALL N FIXED WHERE N>=0. CLAIM(N) BY INDUCTION,
0796             PROOF;
0797                /# ASSUME CLAIM(N)                                        #/
0797                /# ATTAIN CLAIM(N+1)                                      #/
0797                CLAIM(N+1) BY INTRO,INTRO,
0797                PROOF;
0798                   U-L = N+1; N+1>0 BY ARITH,N>=0,+,1=1;
0800                   U-L>0; L<U BY ARITH,U-L>0,+,L=L;
0802                L<=L<=U;
0803                   SOME D FIXED.(D>=0 & MONUS(U+1,L)<D)
0803                   BY FUNCTION,PROD_TERMINATION(A,L,U);
0804                   PROD(A,L,U) = A(L)*PROD(A,L+1,U) BY FUNCTION,PROD(A,L,U);
0805                   U-(L+1) = N BY ARITH,U-L=N+1,-,1=1;
0806                   /# ATTAIN DOM(A,L+1)                                   #/
0806                   L+1<=HBOUND(A,1) BY ARITH,DOM(A,U),L<U;
0807                   LBOUND(A,1)<=L+1 BY ARITH,DOM(A,L),L<L+1;
0808                   DOM(A,L+1);
0809                ALL I FIXED WHERE L+1<=I<=U.A(I)>0 BY INTRO,
0809                PROOF;
0810                   L<=I BY ARITH,L+1<=I;
0811                   L<=I<=U;
0812                   A(I)>0 BY ALLEL,ALL I FIXED WHERE L<=I<=U.A(I)>0,I;
0813                QED;
0814                   PROD(A,L+1,U)>0 BY ALLEL,CLAIM(N),A,L+1,U;
0815                   A(L)>0 BY ALLEL,ALL I FIXED WHERE L<=I<=U.A(I)>0,L;
0816                   A(L)*PROD(A,L+1,U)>0 BY ARITH,A(L)>0,*,PROD(A,L+1,U)>0;
0817                   PROD(A,L,U)>0;
0818                QED;
0819             QED;  */
0820
*THEOREM
0820         /*/
0820         PROD_POSITIVE: ALL (A(*),L,U) FIXED WHERE DOM(A,L) & DOM(A,U) & L<=U.
0820             (ALL I FIXED WHERE L<=I<=U.A(I)>0 => PROD(A,L,U)>0)
0820             BY INTRO,INTRO,
0820             PROOF;
0821                U-L>=0 BY ARITH,L<=U,-,L=L;
0822                CLAIM(U-L) BY ALLEL,ALL N FIXED WHERE N>=0.CLAIM(N),U-L;
0823                PROD(A,L,U)>0 BY ALLEL,CLAIM(U-L),A,L,U;
0824             QED;
0825         */
*THEOREM
```

```
0825    /*/
0825    /# THE THEOREM STATES THAT IF A PRIME DIVIDES A PRODUCT OF LENGTH        #/
0825    /# PRECISELY N, THEN IT DIVIDES ONE OF THE FACTORS.  THE PROOF IS BY     #/
0825    /# INDUCTION ON THE PRODUCT LENGTH, E.G. N IN A(L)*A(L+1)*...*A(L+N).    #/
0825    FOR (A(*),L,U,P) FIXED DEFINE DIVIDES_A_FACTOR(A,L,U,P)=
0825      SOME J FIXED WHERE L<=J<=U.DIV(P,A(J));
0826    FOR N FIXED DEFINE STMT2(N) =
0826      ALL P FIXED WHERE PRIME(P). ALL (A(*),L,U) FIXED WHERE L<=U & DOM(A,L)
0826      & DOM(A,U) & U-L=N.(DIV(P,PROD(A,L,U)) & ALL I FIXED WHERE L<=I<=U.A(I)>0
0826      => DIVIDES_A_FACTOR(A,L,U,P));
0827    /# PROVE BASIS CASE, N=0                                                  #/
0827        STMT2(0) BY INTRO,INTRO,INTRO,
0827        PROOF;
0827        /# A(L)=A(U), SO P DIVIDES A(L)                                       #/
0828            SOME D FIXED.(D>=0 & MONUS(U+1,L)<D)
0828            BY FUNCTION,PROD_TERMINATION(A,L,U);
0829          DIV(P,PROD(A,L,U));
0830          L=U BY ARITH,U-L=0,+,L=L;
0831          PROD(A,L,U) = A(L) BY FUNCTION,PROD(A,L,U);
0832          DIV(P,A(L));
0833          L<=L<=U;
0834          DIVIDES_A_FACTOR(A,L,U,P) BY INTRO,L;
0835        QED;
0836      */
*THEOREM
0836        /*/
0836    /# INDUCTION CASE #/
0836        PRIME_DIVIDES_LONG_PRODUCT: ALL N FIXED WHERE N>=0. STMT2(N)
0836        BY INDUCTION,
0836        PROOF;
0837          ARBITRARY N FIXED WHERE N>=0 & STMT2(N);
0838          /# ATTAIN STMT2(N+1);                                              #/
0838          STMT2(N+1) BY INTRO,INTRO,INTRO,
0838          PROOF;
0838          /# ESTABLISH CONDITIONS FOR ANALYSIS OF PROD AT LINE 856           #/
0839              SOME D FIXED.(D>=0 & MONUS(U+1,L)<D)
0839              BY FUNCTION,PROD_TERMINATION(A,L,U);
0840            U-L = N+1;
0841            N+1 > 0 BY ARITH,N>=0,+,1=1;
0842            U-L>0 BY ARITH,U-L=N+1,N>=0;
0843            L<U BY ARITH,U-L>0,+,L=L;   L+1<=U;  L<=L+1;  L<=L+1<=U;
0847            /# ATTAIN DOM(A,L+1)                                             #/
0847            L+1<=HBOUND(A,1) BY ARITH,DOM(A,U),L+1<=U;
0848            LBOUND(A,1)<=L+1 BY ARITH,DOM(A,L),L<L+1;
0849            ALL I FIXED WHERE L+1<=I<=U.A(I)>0 BY INTRO,
0849            PROOF;
0850              L<=I BY ARITH,L+1<=I;
0851              L<=I<=U;
0852              A(I)>0 BY ALLEL,ALL I FIXED WHERE L<=I<=U.A(I)>0,I;
0853            QED;
0854            A(L)>0 BY ALLEL,ALL I FIXED WHERE L<=I<=U.A(I)>0,L;
0855            PROD(A,L+1,U)>0 BY ALLEL,PROD_POSITIVE,A,L+1,U;
0856            PROD(A,L,U) = A(L)*PROD(A,L+1,U) BY FUNCTION,PROD(A,L,U);
```

```
0857                DIV(P,PROD(A,L,U));  DIV(P,A(L)*PROD(A,L+1,U));
0859                D1: DIV(P,A(L)) | DIV(P,PROD(A,L+1,U))
0859                BY ALLEL,PRIME_DIVIDES_PRODUCT,P,A(L),PROD(A,L+1,U);
0860                DIVIDES_A_FACTOR(A,L,U,P) BY CASES,D1,
0860                PROOF;
0861                  CASE DIV(P,A(L));
0862                  L<=L<=U;
0863                  DIVIDES_A_FACTOR(A,L,U,P) BY INTRO,L;
0864                  CASE DIV(P,PROD(A,L+1,U));
0865                  L1: ALL (A(*),L,U) FIXED WHERE L<=U & DOM(A,L) & DOM(A,U)
0865                      & U-L=N.( DIV(P,PROD(A,L,U)) & ALL I FIXED WHERE L<=I<=U.A(I)>0
0865                      => DIVIDES_A_FACTOR(A,L,U,P) ) BY ALLEL,STMT2(N),P;
0866                  U-(L+1) = N BY ARITH,U-L=N+1,-,1=1;
0867                  L+1<=HBOUND(A,1) BY ARITH,L<U,DOM(A,U);
0868                  LBOUND(A,1)<=L+1 BY ARITH,DOM(A,L);
0869                  DOM(A,L+1);
0870                  DIV(P,PROD(A,L+1,U)) => DIVIDES_A_FACTOR(A,L+1,U,P)
0870                  BY ALLEL,L1,A,L+1,U;
0871                  DIVIDES_A_FACTOR(A,L+1,U,P);
0872                  CHOOSE J FIXED WHERE L+1<=J<=U & DIV(P,A(J));
0873                  L<=J BY ARITH,L+1<=J;
0874                  L<=J<=U;
0875                  DIVIDES_A_FACTOR(A,L,U,P) BY INTRO,J;
0876                QED; /# END OF CASE ANALYSIS                            #/
0877              QED; /# END OF ALL INTRO                                  #/
0878            QED; /# END OF INDUCTION                                    #/
0879        */
*THEOREM
0879        /*/
0879        /# ********** MORE ABOUT BASIC FUNCTIONS **********            #/
0879        /# THESE FACTS ARE NEEDED FOR THE FACTORIZATION PROCEDURE      #/
0879        LOG_POSITIVE: ALL (B,N) FIXED WHERE B>1 & N>0.
0879        ( N>=B => LOG(B,N)>=1 )
0879            BY INTRO,INTRO,PROOF;
0880            B^=0 BY ARITH,B>1; N>=0;
0882            SOME D FIXED.(D>=0 & N<=D) BY INTRO,N;
0883            D: LOG(B,N)<1 | LOG(B,N)>=1 BY ARITH;
0884            LOG(B,N)>=1 BY CASES,D,
0884            PROOF;
0885                CASE LOG(B,N)<1;
0886                LOG(B,N)>=0 BY FUNCTION,LOG(B,N);
0887                LOG(B,N)=0 BY ARITH,0<=LOG(B,N)<1;
0888                LOG(B,N)+1 = 1 BY ARITH,LOG(B,N)=0,+,1=1;
0889                B**1 = B*(B**0) BY FUNCTION,EXP(B,1);
0890                B**0 = 1 BY FUNCTION,EXP(B,0);
0891                B**1 = B*1 = B;
0892                B**(LOG(B,N)+1) > N BY FUNCTION,LOG(B,N);
0893                B**1 > N; B>N;
0895                '0'B BY ARITH,B>N,N>=B;
0896            QED;
0897        QED;
0898        */
*THEOREM
```

```
0898        /*/
0898        /# THESE RESULTS LOGICALLY BELONG IN SECTION  1. BASIC FUNCTIONS     #/
0898        BASIS_EXP_POSITIVE: ALL B FIXED WHERE B>0. B**0 > 0  BY INTRO,
0898             PROOF;
0899             B^=0 BY ARITH,B>0;
0900             B**0 = 1 BY FUNCTION,EXP(B,0); B**0 > 0 BY ARITH,B**0=1;
0902             QED;
0903        INDUCTION_EXP_POSITIVE: ALL X FIXED WHERE X>=0.
0903                      ALL B FIXED WHERE B>0.B**X > 0
0903             BY INDUCTION,PROOF;
0904             ASM: ALL B FIXED WHERE B>0.B**X > 0;
0905             ALL B FIXED WHERE B>0.B**(X+1)>0 BY INTRO,
0905              PROOF;
0906             B^= 0 BY ARITH,B>0;
0907             X+1>=1 BY ARITH,X>=0,+,1=1;   (X+1)-1 = X;
0909             B**(X+1) = B*B**X BY FUNCTION,EXP(B,X+1);
0910             B**X > 0 BY ALLEL,ASM,B;
0911             B*(B**X) > 0 BY ARITH,B>0,*,B**X > 0;
0912             B**(X+1) > 0;
0913             QED;
0914             QED;
0915        EXP_POSITIVE: ALL (B,X) FIXED WHERE B>0 & X>=0. B**X > 0
0915             BY INTRO,PROOF;
0916             L1: ALL B FIXED WHERE B>0. B**X > 0
0916             BY ALLEL,INDUCTION_EXP_POSITIVE,X;
0917             B**X > 0 BY ALLEL,L1,B;
0918             QED;
0919        /# SHOW THAT THE EXPONENTIAL, B**X, IS ADDITIVE IN X         #/
0919        BASIS_EXP_ADDITIVE: ALL (B,Y) FIXED WHERE B>0 & Y>=0.
0919                     (B**0)*(B**Y) = B**(0+Y)
0919             BY INTRO,PROOF;
0920                 B^=0 BY ARITH,B>0;
0921                 B**0 = 1 BY FUNCTION,EXP(B,0);
0922                 0+Y = Y; 1*B**Y = B**(0+Y);
0924                 (B**0)*(B**Y) = B**Y;
0925             QED;
0926        INDUCTION_EXP_ADDITIVE: ALL X FIXED WHERE X>=0.
0926                     ALL (B,Y) FIXED WHERE B>0 & Y>=0.
0926                     (B**X)*(B**Y) = B**(X+Y)
0926             BY INDUCTION,
0926             PROOF;
0927                 ASM: ALL (B,Y) FIXED WHERE B>0 & Y>=0.
0927                 (B**X)*(B**Y) = B**(X+Y);
0928                 /# ATTAIN B**(X+1)*(B**Y) = B**(X+1+Y)          #/
0928                 ALL (B,Y) FIXED WHERE B>0 & Y>=0.
0928                   (B**(X+1))*(B**Y) = B**(X+1+Y)
0928                 BY INTRO,PROOF;
0929                 B^=0 BY ARITH,B>0;
0930                 AA: (B**X)*(B**Y) = B**(X+Y) BY ALLEL,ASM,B,Y;
0931                 X+1>=1 BY ARITH,X>=0,+,1=1; (X+1)-1 = X;
0933                 B**(X+1) = B*(B**X) BY FUNCTION,EXP(B,X+1);
0934                 (B**(X+1))*(B**Y) = B*(B**X)*(B**Y)
0934                 BY ALLEL,ARITHEQ,B**(X+1),B*(B**X),B**Y;
```

```
0935                       (B**(X+1))*(B**Y) = B*((B**X)*(B**Y));
0936                       (B**(X+1))*(B**Y) = B*(B**(X+Y));/# FROM AA              #/
0937                       X+Y>=0 BY ARITH,X>=0,+,Y>=0;
0938                       X+1+Y>=1 BY ARITH,X+Y>=0,+,1=1;  (X+1+Y)-1 = X+Y;
0940                       B**(X+1+Y) = B*(B**(X+Y)) BY FUNCTION,EXP(B,X+1+Y);
0941                       (B**(X+1))*(B**Y) = B**(X+1+Y);
0942                   QED;
0943               QED;
0944         */
```
*THEOREM
```
0944         /*/
0944             EXP_ADDITIVE: ALL (B,X,Y) FIXED WHERE B>0 & X>=0 & Y>=0.
0944             ((B**X)*(B**Y) = B**(X+Y) )
0944                   BY INTRO,PROOF;
0945                   E1: ALL (B,Y) FIXED WHERE B>0 & Y>=0.
0945                   (B**X)*(B**Y) = B**(X+Y)
0945                   BY ALLEL,INDUCTION_EXP_ADDITIVE,X;
0946                   (B**X)*(B**Y) = B**(X+Y) BY ALLEL,E1,B,Y;
0947                   QED;
0948         */
```
*THEOREM
```
0948         /*/
0948         EXP_MONOTONE_BASIS: ALL (B,X) FIXED WHERE B>1 & X>=0.
0948             (X<0 => B**X < B**0)
0948             BY INTRO,INTRO,
0948             PROOF; '0'B BY ARITH,X<0,X>=0;  QED;
0951         EXP_MONOTONE_INDUCTION: ALL Y FIXED WHERE Y>=0.
0951                       ALL (B,X) FIXED WHERE B>1 & X>=0.
0951                       (X<Y => B**X < B**Y)
0951             BY INDUCTION,
0951             PROOF;
0952         ASM: ALL (B,X) FIXED WHERE B>1 & X>=0.(X<Y => B**X<B**Y);
0953         ALL (B,X) FIXED WHERE B>1 & X>=0.(X<Y+1 => B**X<B**(Y+1))
0953             BY INTRO,INTRO,
0953             PROOF;
0954           Y+1 >= 1 BY ARITH,Y>=0,+,1=1;  Y+1 >= 0;  B^=0 BY ARITH,B>1;
0957           X<Y => B**X < B**Y BY ALLEL,ASM,B,X;
0958           D: X<Y | X=Y BY ARITH,X<Y+1;
0959           E: B**X <= B**Y     BY CASES,D,
0959               PROOF;
0960               CASE X<Y; B**X < B**Y; B**X <= B**Y;
0963               CASE X=Y; B**X = B**Y; B**X <= B**Y BY ARITH, B**X = B**Y;
0966               QED;
0967           (Y+1)-1 = Y;
0968           B**(Y+1) = B*(B**Y) BY FUNCTION,EXP(B,Y+1);
0969           /# ANOTHER WEAKNESS OF THE ARITH RULE                             #/
0969           B**Y > 0 BY ALLEL,EXP_POSITIVE,B,Y;
0970           F: B**Y < B*B**Y BY ARITH,1<B,*,B**Y>0;
0971           B**X < B*(B**Y) BY ARITH,E,F;
0972           B**X < B**(Y+1);
0973         QED; /# END OF ALL INTRO                                            #/
0974         QED; /# END OF INDUCTION                                            #/
0975         */
```

```
*THEOREM
0975     /*/
0975     EXP_MONOTONE: ALL (B,X,Y) FIXED WHERE B>1 & X>=0 & Y>=0.
0975     (X<Y => B**X < B**Y)
0975          BY INTRO,INTRO,
0975          PROOF;
0976            A: ALL (B,X) FIXED WHERE B>1 & X>=0.(X<Y => B**X<B**Y)
0976            BY ALLEL,EXP_MONOTONE_INDUCTION,Y;
0977            B**X < B**Y BY ALLEL,A,B,X;
0978          QED;
0979     */
0979
*THEOREM
0979     /*/
0979     LOG_MONOTONE: ALL (B,X,Y) FIXED WHERE B>1 & X>0 & Y>0 .
0979     ( X <= Y  =>  LOG(B,X) <= LOG(B,Y) )
0979          BY INTRO,INTRO,
0979          PROOF;
0980            /# TERMINATION OF LOG                                        #/
0980            SOME D FIXED.(D>=0 & X<=D) BY INTRO,X;
0981            SOME D FIXED.(D>=0 & Y<=D) BY INTRO,Y;
0982            LOG(B,X) >= 0 BY FUNCTION,LOG(B,X);
0983            LOG(B,Y) >= 0 BY FUNCTION,LOG(B,Y);
0984            D: LOG(B,X) > LOG(B,Y) | LOG(B,X)<=LOG(B,Y) BY ARITH;
0985            LOG(B,X)<=LOG(B,Y) BY CASES,D,
0985            PROOF;
0986              CASE LOG(B,X) > LOG(B,Y);
0987              LOG(B,X) >= LOG(B,Y)+1;
0988              DD: X<Y | X=Y BY ARITH,X<=Y;
0989              '0'B BY CASES,DD,
0989              PROOF;
0990                CASE X<Y;
0991                DDD: LOG(B,X) > LOG(B,Y)+1 | LOG(B,X)=LOG(B,Y)+1
0991                BY ARITH,LOG(B,X)>=LOG(B,Y)+1;
0992                E: B**LOG(B,X) >= B**(LOG(B,Y)+1) BY CASES,DDD,
0992                PROOF;
0993                CASE LOG(B,X)>LOG(B,Y)+1;
0994                  B**LOG(B,X)>B**(LOG(B,Y)+1) BY ALLEL,EXP_MONOTONE,B,
0994                LOG(B,Y)+1,LOG(B,X);
0995                CASE LOG(B,X)=LOG(B,Y)+1;
0996                B**LOG(B,X)=B**(LOG(B,Y)+1);
0997                QED;
0998              IEQ1: X>= B**LOG(B,X) BY FUNCTION,LOG(B,X);
0999              IEQ2: B**(LOG(B,Y)+1)>Y BY FUNCTION,LOG(B,Y);
1000              X>Y BY ARITH,IEQ1,IEQ2,E;
1001              '0'B BY ARITH,X>Y,X<=Y;
1002              CASE X = Y;
1003              LOG(B,X) = LOG(B,Y);
1004              '0'B BY ARITH,LOG(B,X)=LOG(B,Y),LOG(B,X)<LOG(B,Y);
1005            QED; /# END OF CASES ON X<=Y                                  #/
1006            CASE LOG(B,X)<=LOG(B,Y);  /# IMMEDIATE                        #/
1007          QED; /# END OF CASES                                           #/
1008          QED;
```

```
1009       */
*THEOREM
1009       /*/
1009       LOG_EXACT: ALL (B,X) FIXED WHERE B>1 & X>=0. LOG(B,B**X) = X
1009            BY INTRO,
1009            PROOF;
1010            B^=0 BY ARITH,B>1;
1011            B**X > 0 BY ALLEL,EXP_POSITIVE,B,X;  B**X >= 0;
1013            T: SOME D FIXED.(D>=0 & B**X<=D) BY INTRO,B**X;
1014            /# A POOR FEATURE OF THE FUNCTION RULE                        #/
1014            /# REQUIRES THAT WE PROVE THIS SILLY TERMINATION              #/
1014            LOG(B,B**X) >= 0 BY FUNCTION,LOG(B,B**X);
1015            LOG(B,B**X)+1 > 0 BY ARITH,LOG(B,B**X)>=0,+,1=1;
1016            D: LOG(B,B**X)>X | LOG(B,B**X)<=X BY ARITH;
1017            I: B**X > 0 BY ALLEL,EXP_POSITIVE,B,X;
1018            E: LOG(B,B**X)<=X BY CASES,D,
1018            PROOF;
1019              CASE LOG(B,B**X)>X;
1020              L1: B**LOG(B,B**X)>B**X BY ALLEL,EXP_MONOTONE,B,X,LOG(B,B**X);
1021              L2: B**LOG(B,B**X)<=B**X BY FUNCTION,LOG(B,B**X);
1022              '0'B BY ARITH,L1,L2;
1023            QED;
1024            DD: LOG(B,B**X)<X | LOG(B,B**X)=X BY ARITH,E;
1025            LOG(B,B**X)=X BY CASES,DD,
1025            PROOF;
1026              CASE LOG(B,B**X)<X;
1027              L3: LOG(B,B**X)+1 <= X;
1028              DDD: LOG(B,B**X)+1 <X | LOG(B,B**X)+1 =X BY ARITH,L3;
1029              A1: B**(LOG(B,B**X)+1) <= B**X BY CASES,DDD,
1029              PROOF;
1030                CASE LOG(B,B**X)+1 < X;
1031                B**(LOG(B,B**X)+1) < B**X BY ALLEL,EXP_MONOTONE,B,
1031                                     LOG(B,B**X)+1,X;
1032                CASE LOG(B,B**X)+1 = X;
1033                B**(LOG(B,B**X)+1) = B**X;
1034              QED;
1035              A2: B**(LOG(B,B**X)+1)>B**X BY FUNCTION,LOG(B,B**X);
1036              '0'B BY ARITH,A1,A2;
1037            QED;
1038            QED;
1039       */
*THEOREM
1039       /*/
1039       /# THIS IS THE RESULT FOR WHICH THE PREVIOUS SEVERAL LEMMAS ABOUT    #/
1039       /# EXP AND LOG WERE PROVED.  IT IS CRUCIAL IN THE PRIME FACTORIZATION#/
1039
1039
1039       LOG_OF_PRODUCT: ALL (B,X,Y) FIXED WHERE B>1 & 0<Y<=X.
1039              LOG(B,X/Y) + LOG(B,Y) <= LOG(B,X)
1039            BY INTRO,
1039            PROOF;
1040            Y^=0 BY ARITH,Y>0;
1041            0<X BY ARITH,0<Y<=X;
1042            B^=0 BY ARITH,B>1;
```

```
1043              EQ1: X = (X/Y)*Y + MOD(X,Y) BY FUNCTION,DIVISION(X,Y);
1044              EQ2: MOD(X,Y)>=0 BY FUNCTION,MOD(X,Y);
1045              IEQ0: X>=(X/Y)*Y BY ARITH,EQ1,-,EQ2;
1046              /# SET UP CONDITIONS FOR MONOTONICITY LEMMAS                    #/
1046
1046              X/Y > 0 BY FUNCTION,DIVISION(X,Y);
1047              (X/Y)*Y > 0 BY ARITH,X/Y>0,*,Y>0;
1048              /# TERMINATION OF LOG #/
1048              SOME D FIXED.(D>=0 & Y<=D) BY INTRO,Y;
1049              SOME D FIXED.(D>=0 & X/Y<=D) BY INTRO,X/Y;
1050              I1: LOG(B,X/Y) >= 0 BY FUNCTION,LOG(B,X/Y);
1051              I2: LOG(B,Y) >= 0 BY FUNCTION,LOG(B,Y);
1052              LOG(B,X/Y) + LOG(B,Y) >= 0 BY ARITH,I1,+,I2;
1053              EZ1: B**LOG(B,X/Y) > 0 BY ALLEL,EXP_POSITIVE,B,LOG(B,X/Y);
1054              EZ2: B**LOG(B,Y) > 0 BY ALLEL,EXP_POSITIVE,B,LOG(B,Y);
1055              IEQ1: B**LOG(B,X/Y) <= X/Y BY FUNCTION,LOG(B,X/Y);
1056              IEQ2: B**LOG(B,Y) <= Y BY FUNCTION,LOG(B,Y);
1057              IEQ3: B**(LOG(B,X/Y)+LOG(B,Y)) > 0
1057                   BY ALLEL,EXP_POSITIVE,B,(LOG(B,X/Y)+LOG(B,Y));
1058              /# BECAUSE OF LOG PROPERTIES WE MUST RAISE LOG TO EXP           #/
1058              /# IN ORDER TO COMPARE ARGUMENTS.                              #/
1058
1058              EQ3: B**LOG(B,X/Y)*B**LOG(B,Y) = B**(LOG(B,X/Y)+LOG(B,Y))
1058                   BY ALLEL,EXP_ADDITIVE,B,LOG(B,X/Y),LOG(B,Y);
1059              /# NOW MULTIPLY IEQ1 BY IEQ2 IN STAGES                         #/
1059              L1: B**LOG(B,X/Y)*B**LOG(B,Y) <= (X/Y)*B**LOG(B,Y)
1059                   BY ARITH,IEQ1,*,EZ2;
1060              L2: (X/Y)*B**LOG(B,Y) <= (X/Y)*Y BY ARITH,IEQ2,*,X/Y>0;
1061              L3: B**LOG(B,X/Y)*B**LOG(B,Y) <= (X/Y)*Y
1061                   BY ARITH,L1,L2;
1062              B**(LOG(B,X/Y) + LOG(B,Y)) <= (X/Y)*Y; /# SUBST IN EQ3         #/
1063              /# NOW TAKE LOGARITHMS AND COMPARE                            #/
1063              LOG(B,B**(LOG(B,X/Y)+LOG(B,Y)))<=LOG(B,(X/Y)*Y)
1063              BY ALLEL,LOG_MONOTONE,B,B**(LOG(B,X/Y)+LOG(B,Y)),(X/Y)*Y;
1064              LOG(B,B**(LOG(B,X/Y)+LOG(B,Y))) = LOG(B,X/Y) + LOG(B,Y)
1064              BY ALLEL,LOG_EXACT,B,LOG(B,X/Y)+LOG(B,Y);
1065              F1: LOG(B,X/Y) + LOG(B,Y) <= LOG(B,(X/Y)*Y);
1066              F2: LOG(B,(X/Y)*Y) <= LOG(B,X)
1066                   BY ALLEL, LOG_MONOTONE,B,(X/Y)*Y,X; /# FROM IEQ0         #/
1067              CONCLUSION: LOG(B,X/Y) + LOG(B,Y) <= LOG(B,X)
1067                   BY ARITH,F1,F2;
1068         QED;
1069         */
*PROCESS
1069         /* **** THIS IS THE FILE DIVTHY2 PLCV. ADVANCED DIVISION THEORY **** */
1069         PRIME_FACTORIZATION: PROCEDURE(N,A,L,U,M  /*: ,AA */);
1070           DECLARE (A(*),M) FIXED;  /* READWRITE PARAMETERS                  */
1071           DECLARE (N,L,U) FIXED  /*/ READONLY */ ;
1072           /*: DECLARE (AA(*)) FIXED  READONLY;                              */
1073           /* FACTOR AN INTEGER GREATER THAN 1 INTO A PRODUCT                */
1073           /* OF PRIMES, PROD(A,L,M).  THE PRIMES APPEAR IN NONDECREASING    */
1073           /* ORDER, A(I)<=A(J) FOR I<=J.  M IS THE COMPUTED NUMBER OF FAC-  */
1073           /* ORS WHILE U IS THE UPPER BOUND OF THE ARRAY A WHICH IS AN      */
```

```
1073        /* ESTIMATE OF THE NUMBER OF FACTORS.  LOG TO THE BASE 2 OF N IS    */
1073        /* THE ESTIMATE (CLEARLY AT LEAST THIS MANY IS REQUIRED FOR N A      */
1073        /* POWER OF 2).  THE NEED TO ESTIMATE THE NUMBER OF FACTORS IS       */
1073        /* DUE TO PL/1'S REQUIREMENT ON ARRAY DECLARATIONS.  THIS IS AN      */
1073        /* ANNOYING FEATURE OF A PL/1 BASED THEORY WHICH WOULD NOT APPEAR    */
1073        /* IN, SAY, A LISP BASED THEORY.                                     */
1073        /*/ ASSUME
1073            DOM(A,L) & DOM(A,U) & U-L >= LOG(2,N) & N > 1, AA = A;           */
1074        /*/ ATTAIN
1074            AT1: N = PROD(A,L,M) & L<=M<=U, DOM(A,M),
1074            AT2: ALL I FIXED WHERE L<=I<=M.(PRIME(A(I)) & DIV(A(I),N) ),
1074            AT3: ALL (I,J) FIXED WHERE L<=I<=J<=M. A(I)<=A(J),
1074            AT4: ALL I FIXED WHERE LBOUND(A,1)<=I<L.AA(I)=A(I);             */
1075        /*/ ARBITRARY D FIXED WHERE U-L < D;                                 */
1076            DECLARE (P,N2) FIXED;
1077            /*: DECLARE AAA(LBOUND(A,1): HBOUND(A,1)) FIXED;                  */
1078            /*: DECLARE AR(LBOUND(A,1):HBOUND(A,1)) FIXED;                    */
1079        /*/ SOME D FIXED.(D>=0 & N<=D) BY INTRO,N;                           */
1080        /*/ LOG(2,N)>=0 BY FUNCTION,LOG(2,N);
1081            U-L>=0 BY ARITH,U-L>=LOG(2,N)>=0;
1082            L<=U BY ARITH,U-L>=0,+,L=L;
1083            ^(U-L<0) BY ARITH,U-L>=LOG(2,N)>=0;
1084            N^=0 BY ARITH,N>1;                                              */
1085        /* FIND THE LEAST PRIME FACTOR OF N, CALL IT P                       */
1085        P = LEAST PRIME_FACTOR(N);
1086        /*/ P = LEAST PRIME FACTOR(N);                                       */
1087        /*/ PRIME(P) & DIV(P,N) & ALL I FIXED WHERE 1<I<P.^DIV(I,N)
1087            BY FUNCTION,LEAST PRIME_FACTOR(N);                              */
1088        /* DIVIDE OUT THE LEAST PRIME FACTOR AND MAKE IT THE FIRST           */
1088        /* FACTOR OF THE PRODUCT, A(L).  IF N IS COMPLETELY FACTORED         */
1088        /* AS A RESULT, THEN STOP, OTHERWISE FACTOR N/P IN THE SAME WAY.     */
1088        /*/ P^=0 BY ARITH,P>1;                                               */
1089        /*/ MOD(N,P) = 0 BY ALLEL, DIV_MOD_EQUIVALENCE,N,P;                  */
1090        /*/ ATTAIN N/P^=1 &  AA = A;                                         */
1091        IF N/P = 1
1091        THEN
1091           DO;
1092            /* N IS COMPLETELY FACTORED. ALL THE REQUIRED PROPERTIES         */
1092            /* AT1,AT2,AT3, CAN BE PROVED TRIVIALLY FROM THE INFORMATION     */
1092            /* THAT P IS PRIME, P DIVIDES N, N/P=1, A(L)=P AND M=L.          */
1092            /* FOR THE ARRAY RULE SAVE A IN AR                               */
1092            /*: AR = A;                                                      */
1093            /*/ AR = A; AR = AA;                                             */
1095            M =L; ;
1097            /*/ M = L; A(L) = P; DOM(A,M); M<=L; M<=L<=U; DOM(A,M);
1103            /# BY ARRAY ASSIGNMENT CONCLUDE:                                 #/
1103            ASGN1: ALL I FIXED WHERE I^=L.AR(I) = A(I);
1104            SOME D FIXED.(D>=0 & N<=D) BY INTRO,N;
1105            SOME D FIXED.(D>=0 & MONUS(M+1,L)<D) BY FUNCTION,
1105            PROD_TERMINATION(A,L,M);
1106             PROD(A,L,M) = A(L) BY FUNCTION,PROD(A,L,M);
1107             N = (N/P)*P + MOD(N,P) BY FUNCTION,DIVISION(N,P);
1108             N = 1*P + 0;
```

```
1109              N = P = PROD(A,L,M);
1110              M <= U;
1111              ALL I FIXED WHERE L<=I<=M.(PRIME(A(I))&DIV(A(I),N)) BY INTRO,
1111              PROOF;
1112              I = L BY ARITH,L<=I<=M,L=M;
1113              A(I) = P;
1114              QED;
1115              ALL (I,J) FIXED WHERE L<=I<=J<=M. A(I)<=A(J) BY INTRO,
1115              PROOF;
1116                I = L BY ARITH,L<=I<=J<=M,L=M;
1117                J = L BY ARITH,L<=I<=J<=M,L=M;
1118                A(I) <= A(J) BY ARITH,A(I)=A(J);
1119              QED;
1120              ALL I FIXED WHERE LBOUND(A,1)<=I<L. AA(I) = A(I) BY INTRO,
1120               PROOF;
1121                 I^=L BY ARITH,I<L;
1122                 AR(I) = A(I) BY ALLEL,ASGN1,I;
1123                 AR(I) = AA(I); /# FROM AR = AA                           #/
1124               QED;
1125              */
1125              RETURN;
1126              END;
1127    /* N IS NOT COMPLETELY FACTORED, SO FACTOR N/P IN THE SAME          */
1127    /* WAY, BY CALLING PRIME_FACTORIZATION.  IT MUST BE SHOWN           */
1127    /* THAT THE INPUT CONDITIONS TO PRIME_FACTORIZATION ARE MET         */
1127    /* WE FIRST SHOW THAT THE ARRAY LENGTH IS ADEQUATE TO CONTAIN       */
1127    /* ALL THE FACTORS.  WE SHOW THIS FIRST BECAUSE IT IS MOST IN-      */
1127    /* TERESTING.  THE PROOF OF THE DOMAIN CONDITIONS IS MOST BORING    */
1127    /* AND IS A PRIME CANDIDATE FOR AUTOMATION IN A THEORY OF SUCC-     */
1127    /* ESSOR.                                                           */
1127         /*/
1127         /# CONDITIONS NEEDED TO USE LOG_OF_PROD                        #/
1127         N>0; P>0;
1129         P<=N BY ALLEL,DIVISOR_SIZE,P,N;
1130         2>1; 0<P<=N;
1132         L0: LOG(2,N/P) + LOG(2,P) <= LOG(2,N)
1132         BY ALLEL,LOG_OF_PRODUCT,2,N,P;
1133       L1: LOG(2,N/P) <= LOG(2,N)-LOG(2,P) BY ARITH,L0,-,LOG(2,P)=LOG(2,P);
1134       P>=2 BY ARITH,P>1;
1135       SOME D FIXED.(D>=0 & P<=D) BY INTRO,P;
1136       L2: LOG(2,P)>=1 BY ALLEL,LOG_POSITIVE,2,P;
1137       L3: LOG(2,N)-LOG(2,P) <= LOG(2,N)-1
1137       BY ARITH,LOG(2,N)=LOG(2,N),-,LOG(2,P) >= 1;
1138       L4: ( LOG(2,N/P) <= LOG(2,N)-1 ) BY ARITH,L1,L3;
1139       U-(L+1)>=LOG(2,N)-1 BY ARITH,U-L>=LOG(2,N),-,1=1;
1140       U-(L+1)>=LOG(2,N/P) BY ARITH,
1140       U-(L+1)>=LOG(2,N)-1>=LOG(2,N/P);
1141    /# SHOW THAT L+1 BELONGS TO THE DOMAIN (THIS DEPENDS ON N )         #/
1141       N>=2;
1142    /# TERMINATION OF LOG(2,N)                                          #/
1142       SOME D FIXED.(D>=0 & N<=D) BY INTRO,N;
1143       N>=0; N>=N;
1145       LOG(2,N)>=1 BY ALLEL,LOG_POSITIVE,2,N;
```

```
1146          0<U-L BY ARITH,U-L>=LOG(2,N)>=1;
1147          L<U BY ARITH,0<U-L,+,L=L;
1148          L+1<=HBOUND(A,1) BY ARITH,L+1<=U,DOM(A,U);
1149     /#  L<L+1 BY ARITH;  DO WE NEED THIS                            #/
1149          LBOUND(A,1)<=L+1 BY ARITH,LBOUND(A,1)<=L,L<L+1;
1150          DOM(A,L+1);
1151     /#  SHOW N/P IS GREATER THAN 1                                  #/
1151          P<=N BY ALLEL,DIVISOR_SIZE,P,N;
1152          N/P >= 1 BY ALLEL,DIVISION_LEMMA,N,P; /# NEED THE LEMMA     #/
1153          N/P > 1 BY ARITH,N/P>=1,N/P^=1;
1154     /#  SHOW U-(L+1)<D-1 FOR TERMINATION                            #/
1154           U-(L+1) < D-1 BY ARITH,U-L<D,-,1=1;
1155     */
1155             /* USE AR TO NAME A BEFORE ASSIGNMENT A(L)=P          */
1155     /*: AR = A;                                                   */
1156             /*/ AR = A; AR = AA;                                  */
1158          N2 = N/P;  A(L) = P;
1160     /*/ N2 = N/P; N2>1; U-(L+1)>=LOG(2,N2);  A(L) = P;           */
1164             /* BY ARRAY ASSIGNMENT:                               */
1164             /*/ ASGN2: ALL I FIXED WHERE I^=L.AR(I)=A(I);         */
1165             /* USE AAA TO KEEP TRACK OF THE AFFECT                */
1165             /* OF PRIME_FACTORIZATION ON A.                       */
1165             /*: AAA = A;                                          */
1166             /*/ TRANSF: ALL I FIXED    . AAA(I) = A(I) BY INTRO;  */
1167          AAA = A;
1168          AAA(L) = A(L) BY ALLEL,TRANSF,L;
1169          AAA(L) = P;
1170             /# RELATE AA TO AAA FOR PROOF OF AT4 BELOW             #/
1170             AA_AAA: ALL I FIXED WHERE I^=L.AA(I) = AAA(I)
1170             BY INTRO,PROOF;
1171               AR(I) = A(I) BY ALLEL,ASGN2,I;
1172               AA(I) = AR(I);
1173             QED;
1174          LBOUND(A,1) = LBOUND(AAA,1);
1175          HBOUND(A,1) = HBOUND(AAA,1);
1176          DOM(AAA,L+1); DOM(AAA,U);                                 */
1178     CALL PRIME_FACTORIZATION( (N2) ,A,L+1,(U),M /*:,(AAA) */);
1179          /* LIST CONSEQUENCES                                      */
1179          /*/
1179          C1: N2 = PROD(A,L+1,M);
1180          C2: L+1<=M<=U;  L<=M; DOM(A,M);
1183          C3: ALL I FIXED WHERE L+1<=I<=M.(PRIME(A(I)) & DIV(A(I),N2));
1184          C4: ALL (I,J) FIXED WHERE L+1<=I<=J<=M. A(I)<=A(J);
1185          C5:  /# TRANSFER CONDITION ALLOWING PROOF THAT A(L) IS UNCHANGED#/
1185              ALL I FIXED WHERE LBOUND(A,1)<=I<L+1.AAA(I)=A(I);
1186              LBOUND(A,1)<=L<L+1 ;
1187              AAA(L) = A(L) BY ALLEL,C5,L;
1188          A(L) = AAA(L) = P;
1189          N = P*(N/P) + MOD(N,P) BY FUNCTION,DIVISION(N,P);
1190          N = A(L)*N2 + 0;  N = A(L)*N2;
1192          N = A(L)*PROD(A,L+1,M);
1193          SOME D FIXED.(D>=0 & MONUS(M+1,L)<D) BY FUNCTION,
1193          PROD_TERMINATION(A,L,M);
```

```
1194              PROD(A,L,M) = A(L)*PROD(A,L+1,M) BY FUNCTION,PROD(A,L,M);
1195         */
1195   /*/ /# ******* PROVE OUTPUT PROPERTIES *********                      #/
1195   /# ALL OUTPUT PROPERTIES EXCEPT THE ORDER OF THE F ARE                #/
1195   /# EASY TO PROVE, FOR EXAMPLE,                                        #/
1195         SOME D FIXED.(D>=0 & MONUS(U+1,L)<D) BY FUNCTION,
1195         PROD_TERMINATION(A,L,U);
1196   PROD(A,L,U) = A(L)*PROD(A,L+1,U) BY FUNCTION, PROD(A,L,U);
1197   M <= U;
1198   /# WE NOW PROVE THAT THE FACTORS ARE ORDERED.                         #/
1198   ALL (I,J) FIXED WHERE L<=I<=J<=M. A(I) <= A(J) BY INTRO,
1198   PROOF;
1199   /# FOR ANY J IN L<=J<=M A(J) IS A PRIME FACTOR OF N, BUT              #/
1199   /# A(L) IS THE LEAST PRIME FACTOR, SO THE RESULT F FROM C4.           #/
1199   D1: L+1<=I | I=L BY ARITH, L<=I;
1200   A(I) <= A(J) BY CASES,D1,
1200   PROOF;
1201     CASE L+1<=I;
1202     L+1<=I BY ARITH,L+1<=I,L<=I<=J<=M;
1203       I<=M BY ARITH,L<=I<=J<=M;
1204     A(I) <= A(J) BY ALLEL,C4,I,J;
1205     CASE I=L;
1206     /# USE THE FACT THAT A(L) IS THE LEAST PRIME FACTOR.                #/
1206     D2: A(I) > A(J) | A(I) <= A(J) BY ARITH;
1207     A(I) <= A(J) BY CASES,D2,
1207     PROOF;
1208     CASE A(J) < A(I);
1209         ( I=J | I^=J ) BY ARITH;
1210       I^=J BY CASES,(I=J | I^=J),
1210       PROOF;CASE I=J;A(I)=A(J);'0'B BY ARITH,A(I)=A(J),A(J)<A(I); QED;
1215       L+1<=J BY ARITH,L<=I<=J,I^=J;
1216       PRIME(A(J)) & DIV(A(J),N2) BY ALLEL,C3,J;
1217       N = P*N2;  N = N2*P;
1219       DIV(A(J),N) BY ALLEL,DIVIDE_PRODUCT,A(J),N2,P;
1220       1<A(J); 1<A(J)<A(I);   A(I) = A(L) = P; 1<A(J)<P;
1224       ^DIV(A(J),N) BY ALLEL,ALL I FIXED WHERE 1<I<P.^DIV(I,N),A(J);
1225       '0'B; /# A(J) BOTH DIVIDES AND DOES NOT DIVIDE N                   #/
1226       QED; /# END OF CASES ON D2                                        #/
1227   QED; /# END OF CASES ON D1                                            #/
1228   QED; /# END OF INTRO                                                  #/
1229   /# NOW ROUTINELY EXTEND THE DOMAIN OF C3.                             #/
1229   ALL. I FIXED WHERE L<=I<=M.( (PRIME(A(I)) & DIV(A(I),N)) ) BY INTRO,
1229   PROOF;
1230     D1: L+1<=I | L=I BY ARITH, L<=I;
1231     PRIME(A(I)) & DIV(A(I),N) BY CASES,D1,
1231     PROOF;
1232       CASE L+1<=I;
1233       L+1<=I<=M;
1234       PRIME(A(I)) & DIV(A(I),N2) BY ALLEL,C3,I;
1235       N = P*N2;  N = N2*P;
1237       DIV(A(I),N) BY ALLEL,DIVIDE_PRODUCT,A(I),N2,P;
1238       CASE L=I; DIV(P,N); DIV(A(L),N); DIV(A(I),N); PRIME(A(I));
1243     QED; /# END OF CASES ON D1                                          #/
```

```
1244          QED; /# END OF BOUNDED ALL INTRO                              #/
1245               /# FINALLY PROVE THE TRANSFER CONDITION, AT4             #/
1245               /# BY RELATING A BEFORE A(L)=P AND CALL OF               #/
1245               /# PRIME_FACTORIZATION TO A AFTER.                       #/
1245               ALL I FIXED WHERE LBOUND(A,1)<=I<L.AA(I)=A(I)
1245               BY INTRO,PROOF;
1246                 I<L+1 BY ARITH,I<L; I^=L BY ARITH,I<L;
1248                 AAA(I) = A(I) BY ALLEL,C5,I;
1249                 AAA(I) = AA(I) BY ALLEL,AA_AAA,I;
1250
1250               QED;                                                      */
1251          RETURN;
1252     END PRIME_FACTORIZATION;
*THEOREM
1253          /*/ FOR (N,F(*),L,U) FIXED DEFINE PRIME_FACTORS(N,F,L,U) =
1253               ALL I FIXED WHERE L<=I<=U.(PRIME(F(I)) & DIV(F(I),N) );
1254               FOR (F(*),L,U) FIXED DEFINE ORDERED(F,L,U) =
1254               ALL (I,J) FIXED WHERE L<=I<=J<=U. F(I)<=F(J);
1255               FOR (N,F(*),L,U) FIXED DEFINE FACTORIZATION(N,F,L,U) =
1255               N = PROD(F,L,U) & L<=U & PRIME_FACTORS(N,F,L,U) & ORDERED(F,L,U);
1256          */
*PROCESS
1256          FTA_LEMMA: PROCEDURE(N,P,F,L,U) RETURNS(BIT(1));
1257               DECLARE (N,P,F(*),L,U) FIXED  ;
1257               /* A LEMMA NEEDED TO SHOW THAT PRIME FACTORIZATION IS UNIQUE   */
1258               /*/ ASSUME N > 1, PRIME(P), DIV(P,N),
1258                   DOMAIN: DOM(F,L) & DOM(F,U),
1258                   FACT: FACTORIZATION(N,F,L,U),
1258                   LESS: ALL I FIXED WHERE L<=I<=U. P < F(I);           */
1259               /*/ DEFINE FALSE = '0'B;                                  */
1260               /*/ ATTAIN FALSE;                                         */
1261               /* SHOW THAT SINCE P DIVIDES N AND IS PRIME, IT MUST DIVIDE   */
1261               /* ONE OF THE F(I) ( A CONSEQUENCE OF PRIME_DIVIDES_LONG_PRODUCT*/
1261               /* SINCE F(I) IS ALSO PRIME, P MUST EQUAL F(I).  BUT THIS IS   */
1261               /* IMPOSSIBLE SINCE P<F(I).                              */
1261               /*/ /# ***** BODY OF THE PROOF *****                     #/
1261               L<=U;
1262               DIV(P,PROD(F,L,U)); /# FROM FACTORIZATION AND DIV(P,N)    #/
1263               ALL I FIXED WHERE L<=I<=U.F(I)>0 BY INTRO,
1263               PROOF;
1264                 L<=I<=U; /# DEFINITION OF DOM(F,I) AND DOMAIN ASSUME    #/
1265                 PRIME(F(I)) BY ALLEL,PRIME_FACTORS(N,F,L,U),I;
1266                 F(I)>0 BY ARITH,F(I)>1; /# FROM DEF OF PRIME            #/
1267               QED;
1268               DIV(P,PROD(F,L,U));
1269               STMT2(U-L)
1269               BY ALLEL,PRIME_DIVIDES_LONG_PRODUCT,U-L;
1270               /# POOR STYLE IN WRITING THE QUANTIFIERS IN              #/
1270               /# PRIME_DIVIDES_LONG_PRODUCT RESULTS IN ALL             #/
1270               /# THIS FUSS TO GET AT THE STATEMENT.                    #/
1270               /# WE NEED TO BE CAREFUL ABOUT CAPTURING U-L             #/
1270               /# SO WE RENAME THE BOUND VARIBLES OF STMT2(U-L)         #/
1270               LA: ALL (A(*),LL,UU) FIXED WHERE LL<=UU & DOM(A,LL) &
```

```
1270                DOM(A,UU) & UU-LL = U-L.(DIV(P,PROD(A,LL,UU))   &
1270                ALL I FIXED WHERE LL<=I<=UU.A(I)>0  =>
1270                DIVIDES_A_FACTOR(A,LL,UU,P)) BY ALLEL,STMT2(U-L),P;
1271           DIVIDES_A_FACTOR(F,L,U,P) BY ALLEL,LA,F,L,U;
1272           SOME J FIXED WHERE L<=J<=U. DIV(P,F(J));
1273           CHOOSE K FIXED WHERE L<=K<=U & DIV(P,F(K));
1274           PRIME(F(K)) BY ALLEL,PRIME_FACTORS(N,F,L,U),K;
1275           P=F(K) BY ALLEL,ALL D FIXED WHERE D>1 & DIV(D,F(K)).D=F(K),P;
1276           L1: P=F(K);
1277           L2: P<F(K) BY ALLEL,LESS,K;
1278           FALSE BY ARITH,L1,L2;
1279           */
1279           RETURN('1'B);
1280           /* A SUBTLE POINT: THE VALUE RETURNED IS IRRELEVANT       */
1280           /* SINCE IT DOES NOT ENTER THE PROOF EXCEPT IN THE        */
1280           /* FORM VALUE=VALUE.  IT IS NOT POSSIBLE TO INTRODUCE     */
1280           /* FALSE INTO A PROOF THIS WAY UNLESS A CONTRADICTION     */
1280           /* IS ACTUALLY PROVED.                                    */
1280       END FTA_LEMMA;
*PROCESS
1281       FTA_UNIQUENESS:   PROCEDURE(N,F1,L1,M1,F2,L2,M2) RETURNS(BIT(1));
1282       DECLARE (N,F1(*),L1,M1,F2(*),L2,M2) FIXED  ;
1282           /* PRIME FACTORIZATION IS UNIQUE                          */
1283           /*/ DEFINE TRUE = '1'B; DEFINE FALSE = '0'B;              */
1285       /* ********** INPUT CONDITIONS **********                     */
1285       /*/ ASSUME N > 1, FACTORIZATION(N,F1,L1,M1), FACTORIZATION(N,F2,L2,M2),
1285                DOM(F1,L1),DOM(F1,M1),DOM(F2,L2),DOM(F2,M2),
1285                L1 = L2;                                             */
1286       /*/ FOR (F(*),G(*)) FIXED DEFINE EQ(F,G) =
1286           ALL I FIXED WHERE L1<=I<=M1. F(I) = G(I);                */
1287       /*/ ATTAIN OUT: M1 = M2 & EQ(F1,F2);                          */
1288       /*/ ARBITRARY D FIXED WHERE N<=D; /#D IS THE TERMINATION PARAMETER#/ */
1289       /* ********** BODY OF THE PROOF ************                  */
1289       /*/
1289       ^(N<=0) BY ARITH,N>1;
1290         DEFINE L = L1; L =L2 = L1;
1292           /# TERMINATION FOR VARIOUS USES OF PROD                 #/
1292           SOME D FIXED.(D>=0 & MONUS(M1+1,L+1)<D)
1292           BY FUNCTION,PROD_TERMINATION(F1,L+1,M1);
1293           SOME D FIXED.(D>=0 & MONUS(M2+1,L+1)<D)
1293           BY FUNCTION,PROD_TERMINATION(F2,L+1,M2);
1294           SOME D FIXED.(D>=0 & MONUS(M1+1,L)<D)
1294           BY FUNCTION,PROD_TERMINATION(F1,L,M1);
1295           SOME D FIXED.(D>=0 & MONUS(M2+1,L)<D)
1295           BY FUNCTION,PROD_TERMINATION(F2,L,M2);
1296         N = PROD(F1,L,M1) = PROD(F2,L,M2);
1297         L<=M1; L<=M2;
1299         PROD(F1,L,M1) = F1(L)*PROD(F1,L+1,M1) BY FUNCTION,PROD(F1,L,M1);
1300         PROD(F2,L,M2) = F2(L)*PROD(F2,L+1,M2) BY FUNCTION,PROD(F2,L,M2);
1301         DEFINE D0 = PROD(F1,L+1,M1); DEFINE P0 = F1(L);
1303         DEFINE D1 = PROD(F2,L+1,M2); DEFINE P1 = F2(L);
1305         N = P0*D0; N = P1*D1;
1307         DEFINE P = P0;
```

```
1270                  DOM(A,UU) & UU-LL = U-L.(DIV(P,PROD(A,LL,UU))  &
1270                  ALL I FIXED WHERE LL<=I<=UU.A(I)>0  =>
1270                  DIVIDES_A_FACTOR(A,LL,UU,P)) BY ALLEL,STMT2(U-L),P;
1271              DIVIDES_A_FACTOR(F,L,U,P) BY ALLEL,LA,F,L,U;
1272              SOME J FIXED WHERE L<=J<=U. DIV(P,F(J));
1273              CHOOSE K FIXED WHERE L<=K<=U & DIV(P,F(K));
1274              PRIME(F(K)) BY ALLEL,PRIME_FACTORS(N,F,L,U),K;
1275              P=F(K) BY ALLEL,ALL D FIXED WHERE D>1 & DIV(D,F(K)).D=F(K),P;
1276              L1: P=F(K);
1277              L2: P<F(K) BY ALLEL,LESS,K;
1278              FALSE BY ARITH,L1,L2;
1279              */
1279              RETURN('1'B);
1280              /* A SUBTLE POINT: THE VALUE RETURNED IS IRRELEVANT          */
1280              /* SINCE IT DOES NOT ENTER THE PROOF EXCEPT IN THE           */
1280              /* FORM VALUE=VALUE.  IT IS NOT POSSIBLE TO INTRODUCE        */
1280              /* FALSE INTO A PROOF THIS WAY UNLESS A CONTRADICTION        */
1280              /* IS ACTUALLY PROVED.                                       */
1280          END FTA_LEMMA;
*PROCESS
1281          FTA_UNIQUENESS:   PROCEDURE(N,F1,L1,M1,F2,L2,M2) RETURNS(BIT(1));
1282          DECLARE (N,F1(*),L1,M1,F2(*),L2,M2) FIXED ;
1282            /* PRIME FACTORIZATION IS UNIQUE                              */
1283          · /*/ DEFINE TRUE = '1'B; DEFINE FALSE = '0'B;                 */
1285          /* ********** INPUT CONDITIONS **********                     */
1285          /*/ ASSUME N > 1, FACTORIZATION(N,F1,L1,M1), FACTORIZATION(N,F2,L2,M2),
1285                  DOM(F1,L1),DOM(F1,M1),DOM(F2,L2),DOM(F2,M2),
1285                  L1 = L2;                                              */
1286          /*/ FOR (F(*),G(*)) FIXED DEFINE EQ(F,G) =
1286              ALL I FIXED WHERE L1<=I<=M1. F(I) = G(I);                 */
1287          /*/ ATTAIN OUT: M1 = M2 & EQ(F1,F2);                          */
1288          /*/ ARBITRARY D FIXED WHERE N<=D;  /#D IS THE TERMINATION PARAMETER#/ */
1289          /* ********* BODY OF THE PROOF ***********                    */
1289          /*/
1289          ^(N<=0) BY ARITH,N>1;
1290            DEFINE L = L1; L =L2 = L1;
1292              /# TERMINATION FOR VARIOUS USES OF PROD                      #/
1292              SOME D FIXED.(D>=0 & MONUS(M1+1,L+1)<D)
1292              BY FUNCTION,PROD_TERMINATION(F1,L+1,M1);
1293              SOME D FIXED.(D>=0 & MONUS(M2+1,L+1)<D)
1293              BY FUNCTION,PROD_TERMINATION(F2,L+1,M2);
1294              SOME D FIXED.(D>=0 & MONUS(M1+1,L)<D)
1294              BY FUNCTION,PROD_TERMINATION(F1,L,M1);
1295              SOME D FIXED.(D>=0 & MONUS(M2+1,L)<D)
1295              BY FUNCTION,PROD_TERMINATION(F2,L,M2);
1296          N = PROD(F1,L,M1) = PROD(F2,L,M2);
1297          L<=M1; L<=M2;
1299          PROD(F1,L,M1) = F1(L)*PROD(F1,L+1,M1) BY FUNCTION,PROD(F1,L,M1);
1300          PROD(F2,L,M2) = F2(L)*PROD(F2,L+1,M2) BY FUNCTION,PROD(F2,L,M2);
1301          DEFINE D0 = PROD(F1,L+1,M1); DEFINE P0 = F1(L);
1303          DEFINE D1 = PROD(F2,L+1,M2); DEFINE P1 = F2(L);
1305          N = P0*D0; N = P1*D1;
1307          DEFINE P = P0;
```

```
1308            PRIME(P) & DIV(P,N) BY ALLEL,PRIME_FACTORS(N,F1,L,M1),L1;
1309             PRIME(P1) & DIV(P1,N) BY ALLEL,PRIME_FACTORS(N,F2,L,M2),L2;
1310            P^=0 BY ARITH,P>1; P>=0; N>0;
1313            P<= N BY ALLEL,DIVISOR_SIZE,P,N;
1314            0<P<=N;
1315            N/P > 0 BY FUNCTION,DIVISION(N,P);
1316            N = P*(N/P) + MOD(N,P) BY FUNCTION,DIVISION(N,P);
1317            MOD(N,P) = 0 BY ALLEL,DIV_MOD_EQUIVALENCE,N,P;
1318            DOM(F1,L); DOM(F2,L);
1320            SD1: P0 = P1 | P0 < P1 | P1 < P0 BY ARITH;
1321    /# SHOW THAT THE CONCLUSION FOLLOWS IN EACH CASE                    #/
1321      M1 = M2 & EQ(F1,F2) BY CASES, SD1,
1321      PROOF;
1322        CASE P0 = P1;
1323        DEFINE P = P0; P = P1;
1325        /# IN THIS CASE WE CAN DIVIDE OUT P FROM N AND CONCLUDE BY      #/
1325        /# INDUCTION THAT N/P HAS A UNIQUE FACTORIZATION, SAY F.  THEN  #/
1325        /# P*F IS THE UNIQUE FACTORIZATION OF N.  THIS CASE DECOMPOSES  #/
1325        /# INTO TWO SUBCASES DEPENDING ON WHETHER P = N.                #/
1325        SD2: N/P = 1 | N/P > 1 BY ARITH,N/P>0;
1326        M1 = M2 & EQ(F1,F2) BY CASES,SD2,
1326        PROOF;
1327        CASE N/P = 1;
1328        /# IN THIS CASE THE RESULT IS TRIVIAL SINCE N IS THE PRIME P    #/
1328        /# AND BOTH M1 AND M2 ARE L.  SO F1 AND F2 ARE ONE ELEMENT      #/
1328        /# SEQUENCES CONSISTING OF P ALONE.                            #/
1328        /# WE NEED A LEMMA TO DEDUCE THAT M1 = M2.  IT COULD BE A       #/
1328        /# GENERAL LEMMA ABOUT INCREASING FUNCTIONS LIKE PROD(...)      #/
1328        /# BUT WE ONLY PROVED A VERY SPECIAL CASE CALLED               #/
1328        /# PROD_INCREASING, STORED IN PRODTHY.                         #/
1328        ALL I FIXED WHERE L<=I<=M1. F1(I)>1 BY INTRO,
1328        PROOF;
1329          PRIME(F1(I)) BY ALLEL,ALL I FIXED WHERE L<=I<=M1.
1329                      (PRIME(F1(I)) & DIV(F1(I),N)),I;
1330          F1(I) > 1; /# PRIMES ARE GREATER THAN ONE                    #/
1331        QED;
1332        ALL I FIXED WHERE L<=I<=M2. F2(I)>1 BY INTRO,
1332        PROOF;
1333          PRIME(F2(I)) BY ALLEL,ALL I FIXED WHERE L<=I<=M2.
1333                      (PRIME(F2(I)) & DIV(F2(I),N)),I;
1334          F2(I) > 1;
1335        QED;
1336        N = P*1 + 0; N = P;
1338    /# NEED PROD INCREASING                                            #/
1338        0<(M1-L)+1 BY ARITH,L<=M1,-,L=L;
1339        0<(M2-L)+1 BY ARITH,L<=M2,-,L=L;
1340        SOME D FIXED .(D>=0 & M1-L<D) BY INTRO,(M1-L)+1;
1341        SOME D FIXED .(D>=0 & M2-L<D) BY INTRO,(M2-L)+1;
1342        PROD(F1,L,M1) = PROD(F1,L,L)  =>  M1 = L
1342        BY FUNCTION,PROD_INCREASING(F1,L,M1);
1343        PROD(F2,L,M2) = PROD(F2,L,L)  =>  M2 = L
1343        BY FUNCTION,PROD_INCREASING(F2,L,M2);
1344        PROD(F1,L,M1) = N; N = P;
```

```
1346              PROD(F2,L,M2) = N;
1347              /# TERMINATION OF PROD                                            #/
1347              SOME D FIXED.(D>=0 & MONUS(L+1,L)<D)
1347              BY FUNCTION,PROD_TERMINATION(F1,L,L);
1348              DOM(F1,L); DOM(F2,L);
1350
1350              PROD(F1,L,L) = F1(L) BY FUNCTION,PROD(F1,L,L);
1351              PROD(F2,L,L) = F2(L) BY FUNCTION,PROD(F2,L,L);
1352              PROD(F2,L,M2) = N;
1353              F1(L) = N = P; F2(L) = N = P;
1355              M1 = L; M2 = L; M1 = M2;
1358              EQ(F1,F2) BY INTRO,
1358              PROOF; I=L BY ARITH,L<=I<=L; P = F1(L) = F2(L); QED;
1362              CASE N/P > 1;
1363              /# IN THIS CASE WE CAN CALL THE THEOREM RECURSIVELY TO             #/
1363              /# CONCLUDE THAT N/P HAS A UNIQUE FACTORIZATION.                   #/
1363              /# FOR TERMINATION WE NEED N/P <= D-1.                            #/
1363              MOD(N,P) = 0 BY ALLEL,DIV_MOD_EQUIVALENCE,N,P;
1364              N = (N/P)*P + MOD(N,P);
1365              N = (N/P)*P + 0;
1366              N = (N/P)*P;
1367              DD: N/P >=N | N/P < N BY ARITH;
1368              N/P < N BY CASES,DD,
1368              PROOF;
1369               CASE N/P >= N;
1370               (N/P)*P >= N*P BY ARITH,N/P>=N,*,P>0,P>1;
1371               N >= N*P;
1372               N < N*P BY ARITH,P>1,*,N>0,N>1;
1373               '0'B BY ARITH,N>=N*P,N<N*P;
1374              QED;
1375               N/P <= D-1 BY ARITH,N<=D,-,1=1,N/P<N;
1376              /# END OF TERMINATION PART                                        #/
1376              /# ESTABLISH HYPOTHESES FOR RECURSIVE CALL                        #/
1376              L1: (N/P)*P = P*PROD(F1,L+1,M1);
1377              L2: (N/P)*P = P*PROD(F2,L+1,M2);
1378              N/P = PROD(F1,L+1,M1) BY ARITH,L1,/,P>0;
1379              N/P = PROD(F2,L+1,M2) BY ARITH,L2,/,P>0;
1380              /# NOW ESTABLISH THAT THE BOUNDS ARE PROPER.  THESE PROOFS         #/
1380              /# ILLUSTRATE THE NEED FOR PROOF MACROS TO ALLOW DUPLICATION       #/
1380              /# OF NEARLY IDENTICAL PROOFS WHICH WE DO NOT WANT TO SPLIT OFF     #/
1380              /# AS LEMMAS.  WE PROVIDE A POSSIBLE SYNTAX FOR SUCH MACROS         #/
1380              /# BEGIN LOWERBOUND(M1)                                            #/
1380              DD1: L+1 > M1 | L+1 <= M1 BY ARITH;
1381              L+1 <= M1 BY CASES,DD1,
1381              PROOF;
1382               CASE L+1 > M1;
1383               ^(L+1<=M1) BY ARITH,L+1>M1;
1384               PROD(F1,L+1,M1) = 1 BY FUNCTION,PROD(F1,L+1,M1);
1385               N/P = PROD(F1,L+1,M1);
1386               N/P = 1;
1387               FALSE BY ARITH,N/P = 1, N/P > 1;
1388              QED;
1389              /# END OF LOWERBOUND(M1);                                          #/
```

```
1389          /# NOW PROVE L+1 <= M2 BY THE SAME METHOD, JUST USE THE        #/
1389          /# PROOF MACRO, LOWERBOUND(M2)                                 #/
1389          DD2: L+1 > M2 | L+1 <= M2 BY ARITH;
1390          L+1 <= M2 BY CASES,DD2,
1390          PROOF;
1391             CASE L+1 > M2;
1392             ^(L+1<=M2) BY ARITH,L+1>M2;
1393             PROD(F2,L+1,M2) = 1 BY FUNCTION,PROD(F2,L+1,M2);
1394             N/P = PROD(F2,L+1,M2);
1395             N/P = 1;
1396             FALSE BY ARITH,N/P=1,N/P>1;
1397          QED;
1398             L+1<=HBOUND(F1,1) BY ARITH,L+1<=M1,DOM(F1,M1);
1399             LBOUND(F1,1)<=L+1 BY ARITH,L<L+1,DOM(F1,L);
1400             DOM(F1,L+1);
1401             L+1<=HBOUND(F2,1) BY ARITH,L+1<=M2,DOM(F2,M2);
1402             LBOUND(F2,1)<=L+1 BY ARITH,L<L+1,DOM(F2,L);
1403             DOM(F2,L+1);
1404          /# NOW ESTABLISH THE PROPERTIES WHICH ARE TEDIOUS TO PROVE     #/
1404          /# BECAUSE THE SYSTEM DOES NOT RECOGNIZE THAT POINTWISE        #/
1404          /# PROPERTIES OF FUNCTIONS ARE INHERITED BY SUBFUNCTIONS       #/
1404          PRIME_FACTORS(N/P,F1,L+1,M1) BY INTRO,
1404          PROOF;
1405           L<=I BY ARITH,L<=L+1,L+1<=I;
1406           L<=I<=M1; L+1<=M1;
1408           PRIME(F1(I)) & DIV(F1(I),N) BY ALLEL,PRIME_FACTORS(N,F1,L,M1),I;
1409           PROD(F1,L+1,M1) = PROD(F1,L+1,I)*PROD(F1,I+1,M1)
1409           BY ALLEL,PROD_SPLIT,F1,L+1,I,M1;
1410           LBOUND(F1,1)<=I BY ARITH,L<=I,DOM(F1,L);
1411           I<=HBOUND(F1,1) BY ARITH,I<=M1,DOM(F1,M1);
1412           DOM(F1,I);
1413           SOME D FIXED.(D>=0 & MONUS(I+1,L+1)<D)
1413           BY FUNCTION,PROD_TERMINATION(F1,L+1,I);
1414           PROD(F1,L+1,I) = PROD(F1,L+1,I-1)*F1(I)
1414           BY FUNCTION,PROD(F1,L+1,I);
1415           N/P = PROD(F1,L+1,I-1)*F1(I)*PROD(F1,I+1,M1);
1416           N/P = PROD(F1,L+1,I-1)*PROD(F1,I+1,M1)*F1(I);
1417           DIV(F1(I),N/P) BY INTRO,PROD(F1,L+1,I-1)*PROD(F1,I+1,M1);
1418          QED;
1419          PRIME_FACTORS(N/P,F2,L+1,M2) BY INTRO,
1419          PROOF;
1420           L<=I BY ARITH,L<=L+1,L+1<=I;
1421           L<=I<=M2; L+1<=M2;
1423           PRIME(F2(I)) & DIV(F2(I),N) BY ALLEL,PRIME_FACTORS(N,F2,L,M2),I;
1424             I<=HBOUND(F2,1) BY ARITH,I<=M2,DOM(F2,M2);
1425             LBOUND(F2,1)<=I BY ARITH,L<=I,DOM(F2,L);
1426             DOM(F2,I);
1427           PROD(F2,L+1,M2) = PROD(F2,L+1,I)*PROD(F2,I+1,M2)
1427           BY ALLEL,PROD_SPLIT,F2,L+1,I,M2;
1428             SOME D FIXED.(D>=0 & MONUS(I+1,L+1)<D)
1428             BY FUNCTION,PROD_TERMINATION(F2,L+1,I);
1429           PROD(F2,L+1,I) = PROD(F2,L+1,I-1)*F2(I)
1429           BY FUNCTION,PROD(F2,L+1,I);
```

```
1430        N/P = PROD(F2,L+1,I-1)*F2(I)*PROD(F2,I+1,M2);
1431        DIV(F2(I),N/P) BY INTRO,PROD(F2,L+1,I-1)*PROD(F2,I+1,M2);
1432        QED;
1433        ORDERED(F1,L+1,M1) BY INTRO,
1433        PROOF;
1434         L<=I BY ARITH,L<=L+1,L+1<=I;
1435         L<=I<=J<=M1;
1436         F1(I)<=F1(J) BY ALLEL,ORDERED(F1,L,M1),I,J;
1437        QED;
1438        ORDERED(F2,L+1,M2) BY INTRO,
1438          PROOF;
1439           L<=I BY ARITH,L<=L+1,L+1<=I;
1440           L<=I<=J<=M2;
1441           F2(I)<=F2(J) BY ALLEL,ORDERED(F2,L,M2),I,J;
1442         QED;
1443        /# NOW WE HAVE THE INPUT ASSUMPTIONS FOR A RECURSIVE CALL          #/
1443        FACTORIZATION(N/P,F1,L+1,M1);
1444        FACTORIZATION(N/P,F2,L+1,M2);
1445         LBOUND(F2,1)<=L+1 BY ARITH,L<L+1,DOM(F2,L);
1446         L+1<=HBOUND(F2,1) BY ARITH,L+1<=M2,DOM(F2,M2);
1447         DOM(F2,L+1); DOM(F2,M2); DOM(F1,L+1); DOM(F1,M1);   L+1 = L+1;
1452         C1: M1 = M2 & ALL I FIXED WHERE L+1<=I<=M1.F1(I) = F2(I)
1452         BY FUNCTION,FTA_UNIQUENESS(N/P,F1,L+1,M1,F2,L+1,M2);
1453        /# NOW THE ATTAIN CONDITION, OUT, IS PROVED BY A ROUTINE          #/
1453        /# DOMAIN EXTENSION                                               #/
1453        EQ(F1,F2) BY INTRO,
1453        PROOF;
1454         D1: L=I | L+1<=I BY ARITH,L<=I;
1455         F1(I) = F2(I) BY CASES,D1,
1455          PROOF;
1456         CASE L=I; /# IMMEDIATE FROM P0=P1 CASE ASSUMPTION                 #/
1457         CASE L+1<=I ;
1458         F1(I) = F2(I) BY ALLEL,ALL I FIXED WHERE L+1<=I<=M1.F1(I)=F2(I),I;
1459         QED;
1460         QED;  /# END OF CASE N/P<1                                       #/
1461        QED;
1462       /# END OF THE CASE P0=P1                                           #/
1462       CASE P0 < P1;
1463       /# DERIVE THE CONTRADICTION THAT P0 EQUALS ONE OF THE FACTORS      #/
1463       /# IN PROD(F2,L,M2) WHICH ARE ALL ASSUMED TO BE LARGER THAN P0     #/
1463       /# USE THE LEMMA THAT IF P0, A PRIME, DIVIDES A LONG PRODUCT,      #/
1463       /# THEN IT DIVIDES ONE OF THE FACTORS.  SINCE THESE FACTORS ARE    #/
1463       /# ALL PRIME, IT MUST EQUAL THE FACTOR IT DIVIDES.                 #/
1463       ALL I FIXED WHERE L<=I<=M2. P0 < F2(I) BY INTRO,
1463       PROOF;
1464        F2(L)<=F2(I) BY ALLEL,ORDERED(F2,L,M2),L,I;
1465        P0 < F2(I) BY ARITH,P0<P1=F2(L)<=F2(I);
1466       QED;
1467        '0'B BY FUNCTION,FTA_LEMMA(N,P,F2,L,M2);
1468        /# THE LEMMA ESTABLISHES THE CONTRADICTION                        #/
1468       /# END OF P0 < P1 CASE                                             #/
1468       CASE P1 < P0;
1469       /# THIS CASE IS EXACTLY LIKE THE PREVIOUS CASE WITH P0,P1          #/
```

```
1469        /# INTERCHANGED.                                              #/
1469        ALL I FIXED WHERE L<=I<=M1. P1 < F1(I) BY INTRO,
1469        PROOF;
1470            F1(L)<=F1(I) BY ALLEL,ORDERED(F1,L,M1),L,I;
1471            P1 < F1(I) BY ARITH,P1<P0=F1(L)<=F1(I);
1472        QED;
1473            '0'B BY FUNCTION,FTA_LEMMA(N,P1,F1,L,M1);
1474        /# END OF P1 < P0 CASE                                        #/
1474     QED; /# END OF PROOF BY CASES #/                                 */
1475     RETURN('1'B);
1476     /* ************* END OF FTA UNIQUENESS PROOF **********          */
1476   END FTA_UNIQUENESS;
1477  /*  CHECKED TO THIS POINT ON FEBRUARY 17 1980                       */
```

Appendix D

An Algorithm for Checking PL/CV Arithmetic Inferences[*]

1. Introduction

Arithmetic operations constitute an indispensible component of alge-braic computing languages. Consequently, arithmetic reasoning plays a vital role in verification schemes for programs written in these languages. The most indispensible type of arithmetic reasoning involves only the integers.

The PL/CV 2 verification system, Constable and O'Donnell [3], and Constable and Johnson [4], provides a theory of integer arithmetic which is a fragment of a constructive quantifier-free theory of discrete ordered integral domain.[+] A verification rule, called the <u>arithmetic rule</u>, allows the conclusion of a disjunction of arithmetic relations from a conjunction of arithmetic relations provided the disjunction can be deduced from the conjunction in the underlying quantifier-free theory of arithmetic (in a restricted manner to be described later). This appendix describes the operation and implementation of the arithmetic rule.

The organization is as follows. Section 2 summarizes the underlying arithmetic axioms and formulates the arithmetic rule in terms of quantifier-free proofs using these axioms. Section 3 considers the imple-mentation of the rule, i.e. the question of how to verify its applicabil-ity. This is essentially a proof existence problem, which will be shown to be equivalent to the satisfiability problem for a set of arithmetic rela-tions over constants and monic linear univariate polynomials. In proving this equivalence, we shall introduce the closely related problem of the satisfiability of directed graphs with edges weighted by the integers, and make use of the lemma that such a graph is satisfiable if and only if it contains no cycle of positive weight. Besides being a useful tool in the

[*] This work was supported in part by NSF grants MCS76-14293 and MCS75-09433.

[+] Although the PL/CV 2 arithmetic theory is constructive (even Intuitionis-tic), since we are dealing only with quantifier-free proofs involving com-putable relations, all the relevant results from classical logic remain ap-plicable (see Kleene [6]).

theoretical discussion, this graph-theoretic result will play an important role in the actual implementation. In Section 4, we establish the NP-completeness of the arithmetic satisfiability problem of Section 3. The problem is then represented as a tree of directed, weighted graphs, and an algorithm for its solution by searching for a satisfiable leaf is developed. Section 5 contains an account of the actual implementation of the arithmetic rule and some examples of its use. We conclude with some remarks on possible extensions in Section 6.

This appendix is essentially [2] revised for the improved treatment of factoring in the arithmetic rule.

2. The Arithmetic Rule

The arithmetic rule will be concerned only with arithmetic propositions, which are quantifier-free propositions whose atoms are arithmetic relations. Arithmetic relations in PL/CV 2 are of the form $t_1 \rho t_2$, where t_1, t_2 are polynomial expressions involving the integers, program variables (possibly subscripted), logic variables, and function designators, and ρ is one of the six relational operators $<, \leq, =, \neq, \geq$ and $>$. For simplicity, this appendix considers only expressions involving simple variables. A discussion of subscripted variables and function designators can be found in [4].

PL/CV2 admits four groups of arithmetic axioms. These are

(I)   the ring axioms,

(II)   the discrete linear order axioms,

(III)   the relation definition axioms, and

(IV)   the monotonicity axioms.

Group I axiomatizes the properties of the integers as a commutative ring $(\mathbf{Z}, +, \cdot, 0, 1)$. Group II axiomatizes the properties of the discrete linear order "less than" $(<)$, while Group III defines $>$, $\leq$ and $\geq$ in terms of $<$ and the logic connectives. Finally, Group IV axioms allow the combination of two arithmetic relations by the binary arithmetic operations; they are all instances of the following four basic schemes and their variants:

(addition) $\qquad t_1 \geq t_2 \ \& \ t_3 \geq t_4 \ \Rightarrow \ t_1 + t_3 \geq t_2 + t_4$

(subtraction) $\qquad t_1 \geq t_2 \ \& \ t_3 \leq t_4 \ \Rightarrow \ t_1 - t_3 \geq t_2 - t_4$

(multiplication) $\qquad t_1 \geq 0 \ \& \ t_2 \geq t_3 \ \Rightarrow \ t_1 * t_2 \geq t_1 * t_3$

(factoring) $\qquad t_1 > 0 \ \& \ t_2 \geq t_3 \ \Rightarrow \ \dfrac{t_2}{t_1} \geq \dfrac{t_3}{t_1}$ (only when divisions are exact)

A complete list of all the schemes of arithmetic axioms can be found section 7.

A **proof** of an arithmetic proposition Q from an arithmetic proposition P in quantifier-free arithmetic is a sequence of arithmetic propositions $P_1, P_2, \ldots, P_k$, such that (1) each P_i is either P or an arithmetic axiom, or is obtained by a rule of inference from zero or more P_j's, $j < i$, and (2) P_k is Q. P is the **hypothesis** and Q is the **conclusion** of the proof. The rules of inference are the rule of propositional calculus and the following rules of equality:

(reflexivity) $\qquad \dfrac{\rule{2em}{0.4pt}}{t = t}$

(symmetry) $\qquad \dfrac{t_1 = t_2}{t_2 = t_1}$

(transitivity) $\qquad \dfrac{t_1 = t_2, t_2 = t_3}{t_1 = t_3}$

(comparand substitution) $\qquad \dfrac{t_1 = t_2, t_1 \rho t_3}{t_2 \rho t_3} \qquad\qquad \dfrac{t_1 = t_2, t_3 \rho t_1}{t_3 \rho t_2}$

Note that comparand substitution is general substitution restricted to disallow the substitution of only part of a comparand. For example, from $x \neq x * y$ and $x = z$ it can be used to justify $z \neq x * y$ but not $z \neq z * y$. As usual, while it is a matter of routine to check whether a **given** sequence of arithmetic propositions (with justifications) constitutes a proof, determining whether there is a proof of an **arbitrary** conclusion C from an **arbitrary** hypothesis H is more challenging and more interesting.

By repeated applications of the ring axioms, any polynomial expression t can be proved equal to some polynomial of the form c+p (c≠0), p, or c, where c is an integer constant and p is a constant-free polynomial in some chosen canonical form. For appropriately chosen canonical forms, the expression c+p, p or c will also be the canonical form of t. In the remainder of this section, we shall consider two comparands to be the same if they have the same canonical form, since comparand substitution allows the replacement of each by the other.

Obviously, "useful" applications of the axioms of Groups I, II and III can only produce conclusions involving the same constant-free polynomials as occurs in the hypothesis. Applications of the monotonicity axioms introduce new constant-free polynomials in some, but not all, cases. Prominent among those which do not are the additions in which one relation has constant comparands, e.g.

$$x^2 \geq y \ \& \ -2 > -3 \Rightarrow x^2 - 2 > y - 3$$

In the remainder of this appendix, we refer to such additions as <u>trivial monotonicity</u>, and all other applications of the monotonicity axioms as <u>nontrivial monotonicity</u>.

Thus, a quantifier-free proof using only propositional calculus, the equality rules, the arithmetic axioms of the first three groups and trivial monotonicity essentially involves only those constant-free polynomials that occur in the hypothesis, and is therefore of limited complexity. We call such a proof a <u>restricted arithmetic proof</u>. If we further restrict the hypothesis and the conclusion to be, respectively, a conjunction and a disjunction of arithmetic relations, then the decision problem for the existence of a restricted arithmetic proof is reducible to an integer satisfiability problem, solvable by graph algorithms. This reduction, which will be formulated and proved rigorously in the next section, is exploited in the design of the arithmetic verification rule, which is intended to embody as many applications of the arithmetic axioms as possible without rendering the validity checking (i.e., proof existence) problem impossible. Specifically, the arithmetic rule can be used to justify the deduction of a conclusion C from a hypothesis H if and only if

(1) H is a conjunction of arithmetic relations,

(2) C is a disjunction of arithmetic relations, and

(3) there exists a restricted arithmetic proof of C from M, where M is either H, or H enhanced by one application of nontrivial monotonicity to be specified by the user.

Note that the set of constant-free polynomials involved becomes fixed after the single application of nontrivial monotonicity (if specified).

Example 2.1 The argument

$$x+y>z \ \& \ 2x \geq z \Rightarrow 3x+y \geq 2z-1$$

can be justified by one invocation of the arithmetic rule, whereas the argument

$$x>y \ \& \ y>0 \ \& \ z>w \ \& \ w>0 \Rightarrow xz>yw$$

requires three invocations:

$z>w \ \& \ w>0 \Rightarrow z>0$ (transivity)

$x>y \ \& \ z>0 \Rightarrow xz>yz$ (multiplication by z)

$z>w \ \& \ y>0 \ \& \ xz>yz \Rightarrow xz>yw$ (multiplication by y followed by transitivity).

3. Reduction of the Validity Checking Problem

The module of PL/CV 2 which checks the applicability of the arithmetic rule to a verification step is called the arithmetic checker. Nontrivial monotonicity aside, its function is to decide whether there exists a restricted arithmetic proof for a disjunction of arithmetic relations C from a conjunction of arithmetic relations H. For convenience, we shall abbreviate the term restricted arithmetic proof to A-proof. Extending this terminology, we say that a proposition Q is A-provable from a proposition P, denoted $P \vdash_A Q$, if there exists an A-proof of Q from P, and that P is A-contradictory if a contradiction (i.e. a proposition of the form Q & ~Q) is A-provable from P. We now reduce the A-proof existence problem to an integer satisfiability problem.

Theorem 3.1: Let P, Q be arithmetic propositions. Then $P \vdash_A Q \Leftrightarrow$ P & ~Q is A-contradictory.

Proof: Standard result in logic. □
Thus it suffices for the arithmetic checker to decide whether the conjunction of relations H & ~C is A-contradictory.

Theorem 3.2: Let P be a conjunction of arithmetic relations, and let P_C be the conjunction of the same relations with all comparands converted to canonical form. Then P is A-contradictory $\Leftrightarrow P_C$ is A-contradictory.

Proof: Follows from the fact that $P \vdash_A P_C$ and $P_C \vdash_A P$ by propositional calculus, the equality rules and the ring axioms. □

The next theorem allows us to simplify the problem by considering the distinct constant-free polynomials in P_C as "atomic". Intuitively, this abstraction, whereby we ignore relations that may exist among the constant-free polynomials by virtue of their internal structures, is allowable because A-proofs, being deprived of the use of nontrivial monotonicity, are not powerful enough to exploit these structures anyway. Note that, as mentioned in the previous section, it is precisely this limitation of the power of A-proofs which makes their existence problem easier (yet still NP-complete, as we shall see later).

Thus, let P_C be a conjunction of arithmetic relations with canonical form comparands, and let P_A be P_C with all distinct non-zero constant-free parts of the comparands replaced by new, distinct variables. For example, if P_C is

$$1+2x = z+xy \ \& \ -3-2x > -4+z+xy$$

then P_A is

1+u = v & -3+w > -4+v.

Then we have

Theorem 3.3: P_C is A-contradictory $\Leftrightarrow$ P_A is A-contradictory.

Proof: "$\Leftarrow$" Take an A-proof of contradiction from P_A. Replace all occurrences in the proof of those whose variables that are in P_A by their corresponding constant-free polynomials, and leave occurrences of variables that are not in P_A unchanged. The result is a proof in which justification by the arithmetic axioms and by the various rules of inference remain valid, since the relevant structures of the comparands and the propositional structures are left intact by the replacements. The only change is that an appeal to P_A becomes an appeal to P_C. Since a contradiction in the old proof is transformed to a contradiction in the new proof, we have shown that P_C is A-contradictory.

"$\Rightarrow$" Again we proceed by "proof-massaging".

Take an A-proof of contradiction from P_C, and compute the canonical form of each comparand. There are several possibilities for the canonical form, and we transform the comparands according to the following rules:

(T1) The canonical form is c or for some integer c: the original comparand is left unchanged.

(T2) The canonical form is p or c+p where c is an integer $\neq$ 0, and p is the non-zero constant-free part of some comparand in P_C: replace the comparand by x_p or $c+x_p$ where x_p is the variable corresponding to p.

(T3) The canonical form is p or c+p as in (T2) except that p is not the constant-free part of any comparand in P_C: Replace each occurrence of any variable in the comparand by some fixed variable y not in P_A. Note that both (T1) and (T3) leave the tree structure of the comparand intact.

We next manipulate the intermediate text resulting from comparand transformation into a valid A-proof from P_A. This is achieved by a tedious case analysis of the justification of each step in the old A-proof. In the following analysis, t' denotes the transformation of comparand t.

(1) Rules of inference. The justification remains valid because if comparands t_1, t_2 are identical, then so are t_1', t_2', so that the structures of the arithmetic propositions are preserved.

(2) Appeal to P_C. Transformed to an appeal to P_A.

(3) Arithmetic axioms. (These axioms are listed in section 7.)

(i) Ring axioms. The proposition is an equality, the two sides of which necessarily have the same canonical form. Hence either they both transform under (T2) to the same new comparand, in which case the equality becomes an identify justified by reflexivity of equality, or they are left unchanged except for possible replacement of variables under (T1) or (T3), so that the new proposition is still an axiom of the same scheme.

(ii) Irreflexivity, trichotomy, transitivity, and relation definitions The original justification remains valid for the same reason as in (1).

(iii) Discreteness $\sim(t_1 < t_2 < t_1 + 1)$. Clearly the same transformation applies to both comparands t_1 and $t_1 + 1$. If this transformation is (T1) or (T3), then discreteness remains a valid justification. It remains to consider transformation by (T2). If t_1 and $t_1 + 1$ transform to x_p and $1 + x_p$ for some constant-free polynomial p in P_C, insert in front of the transformed proposition the steps

$$\sim(x_p < t_2' < x_p + 1) \quad \text{discreteness}$$
$$x_p + 1 = 1 + x_p \quad \text{commutativity}$$

If x and $x+1$ transform to $-1 + x_p$ and x_p, insert steps

$\sim(-1+x_p < t_2' < (-1+x_p)+1)$ discreteness

.
.
.

proof that $(-1+x_p)+1=x_p$ (by ring axioms)

.
.
.

Finally let x and x+1 transform to $c+x_p$ and $\overline{c+1}+x_p$, $c\neq0$ or -1. Insert steps

$\sim(c+x_p < t_2' < (c+x_p)+1)$ discreteness

.
.
.

proof that $(c+x_p)+1=\overline{c+1}+x_p$ (by ring axioms)

Then, in all three cases, also insert a proof of the transformed step using comparand substitution.

(iv) Trivial monotonicity. The proposition is in one of two formats:

$$t_1 \; \rho \; t_2 \; \& \; c_1 \; \sigma \; c_2 \; \Rightarrow \; t_1+c_1 \; \theta \; t_2+c_2 \text{ or}$$
$$t_1 \; \rho \; t_2 \; \& \; c_1 \; \sigma \; c_2 \; \Rightarrow \; t_1+c_1 \; \theta \; t_2+c_2 \; | \; t_1+c_2 \; \omega \; t_2+c_1$$

where c_1, c_2 are integer constants, and ρ, σ, θ, ω are relational operators. Thus we know that c_1 and c_2 are left unchanged (T1), while t_1, t_1+c_1 and t_1+c_2 have the same constant-free part and so undergo similar transformations, and similarly for t_2, t_2+c_1 and t_2+c_2. If neither t_1 nor t_2 is transformed by (T2), then we know that the original justification remains valid. Now suppose at least one of t_1, t_2 is transformed by (T2). Then replace the transformed step by the sequence:

$$t_1' \rho t_2' \ \& \ c_1 \sigma c_2 \ \Rightarrow \ t_1' + c_1 \ \theta \ t_2' + c_2 \quad \text{trivial monotonicity}$$

.
.
.

$$\text{proof that } t_1' + c_1 = (t_1 + c_1)' \quad \text{(if } t_1 \text{ transformed by (T2))}$$

.
.
.

$$\text{proof that } t_2' + c_2 = (t_2 + c_2)' \quad \text{(if } t_2 \text{ transformed by (T2))}$$

.
.
.

$$t_1' \rho t_2' \ \& \ c_1 \sigma c_2 \ \Rightarrow \ (t_1 + c_1)' \ \theta \ (t_2 + c_2)' \quad \text{(comparand substitution)}$$

Note that if t_1 (respectively t_2) is not transformed by (T2), then $t_1' + c_1 = (t_1 + c_1)'$ (resp. $t_2' + c_2 = (t_2 + c_2)'$) already.

Similarly for the second format.

Since contradictory propositions are transformed to contradictory propositions, P_A is A-contradictory. $\square$

So far, we have simplified the problem to deciding whether a conjunction of arithmetic relations $R_1 \& \cdots \& R_m$ is A-contradictory, where each R_i has comparands of the form 0, c, x or c+x for some nonzero constant c and some variable x. From the distributive laws for & and |, trivial monotonicity, and the A-provable equivalences:

$$x > y \quad \vdash_A \quad x \geq y+1,$$
$$x < y \quad \vdash_A \quad y \geq x+1,$$
$$x = y \quad \vdash_A \quad x \geq y \ \& \ y \geq x,$$
$$x \neq y \quad \vdash_A \quad x \geq y+1 \mid y \geq x+1, \text{ and}$$
$$x \leq y \quad \vdash_A \quad y \geq x,$$

it follows that $R_1 \& \ldots \& R_m \vdash_A S_1 \mid S_2 \mid \ldots \mid S_n$ where each S_i is a conjunction of m' ($m' \geq m$) relations of the form

$$\{^0_x\} \geq \{^c_{y[+d]}\}$$

for variables x,y and constants c,d, d≠0. Here, $n=2^k$ where k is the number of disequalities (i.e. ≠ relations) among the R_i's. From this equivalence we immediately obtain, by classical logic, the following lemma:

Lemma 3.1: $R_1 \& \ldots \& R_m$ is A-contradictory ⇔ $S_1 \mid \ldots \mid S_n$ is A-contradictory.

It should be obvious what is meant when we say a proposition P is **satisfied** by an assignment of integers to its variables, or that P is **satisfiable**. Clearly:

Lemma 3.2: $R_1 \& \cdots \& R_m$ is unsatisfiable ⇔ $S_1 \mid \ldots \mid S_n$ is unsatisfiable. □

The following are equally obvious

Lemma 3.3: $S_1 \mid \ldots \mid S_n$ is A-contradictory ⇔ each S_i is A-contradictory. □

Lemma 3.4: $S_1 \mid \ldots \mid S_n$ is unsatisfiable ⇔ each S_i is unsatisfiable. □

Thus, provided we can establish

Lemma 3.5: S_i is A-contradictory ⇔ S_i is unsatisfiable

we have achieved the last step in our reduction:

Theorem 3.4: $R_1 \& \cdots \& R_m$ is A-contradictory ⇔ $R_1 \& \cdots \& R_m$ is unsatisfiable. □

Proof of Lemma 3.5: We prove this lemma by introducing a directed, weighted graph associated with S_i. This graph will play an important role in the satisfiability algorithm actually implemented. Thus let G be a graph whose vertices are the variables in S_i plus an extra vertex for 0 if there is any constant comparand. For each relation

$$\{^x_0\} \quad \geq \quad \{^c_{y[+d]}\}$$

in S_i, there is an edge from x or 0 to 0 or y with weight c or 0 or d as the case may be. Paths and cycles in this graph are directed. The weight of a path is the algebraic sum of the weights of the edges in the path. A positive cycle is a cycle with positive weight. A graph G is satisfiable if there exists an assignment of integers $\bar{u}$ to the vertices u of G, such that for each edge u→v of weight m in G, we have $\bar{u} \geq \bar{v} + m$.

We now show that the following statements are equivalent:

(1) S_i is A-contradictory,

(2) S_i is unsatisfiable,

(3) The graph associated with S_i is unsatisfiable,

(4) The graph associated with S_i has a positive cycle.

(1) ⟹ (2). Obvious.

(2) ⟹ (3). By a contrapositive proof. Suppose the associated graph is satisfiable. If there is no constant comparand in S_i, the same assignments to the variables as to their corresponding vertices satisfy S_i. Otherwise there is a 0 vertex in the graph. Assigning $\bar{x}$ - $\bar{0}$ to the variable x satisfies S_i.

(3) ⟹ (4). We use induction to prove the contrapositive assertion. It is clear that a graph with one vertex and no positive cycles (equivalently, no positive edges) can be satisfied by any integer whatsoever. For the inductive step, we employ the "elimination of variables" technique of Kuhn [7] and King [5]. Thus take a graph G with no positive cycles. Let G have k>1 vertices, and choose a vertex w. Let G' be the graph obtained from G by

1)   removing w and all edges incident on w,

2)   adding, for each pair of edges in G of the form u→w of weight j
and w→v of weight k, where u≠w, v≠w, a new edge u→v of weight
j+k. (The number of edges added = in-degree of w × out-degree of
w, assuming there is no loop on w in G.)

Obviously, since G does not have a positive cycle, neither does G'. By the
inductive hypothesis, we can assign integers to G' satisfying the inequalities associated with its edges, including those edges of G not incident on
w. It remains to extend this by assigning a value to w so that all edges
of G incident on w are satisfied also. If G has no edge of the type u→w
for u≠w, or of the type w→v for v≠w, we need only assign $\bar{w}$ sufficiently
large, or small, respectively. If G has edges of both types, then the
edges added in step 2) in the construction of G' will guarantee that the
upper and lower bounds on w defined by the edges incident on w and by the
assignment to G' will leave a nonempty interval from which to make an
assignment for w. Formally, let

$$m=\max\{\bar{v} +k\,|\,w{\rightarrow}v \text{ is an edge of weight k in G, } v{\neq}w\}$$
$$M=\min\{\bar{u} -j\,|\,u{\rightarrow}w \text{ is an edge of weight j in G, } u{\neq}w\}.$$

Then M≥m. For otherwise m>M, and there exist edges in G

u→w of weight j, u≠w,

w→v of weight k, v≠w,

such that $m=\bar{v} +k$, $M=\bar{u} -j$. By construction, we know that G' has an edge u→v
of weight j+k, so $\bar{u}{\geq}\bar{v}+(j+k)$. But $m>M \Rightarrow \bar{v}+k>\bar{u}-j\Rightarrow \bar{v}+(j+k)>\bar{u}$, which is a
contradiction. Thus let $\bar{w}$ be any integer in the nonempty interval [m,M].
Then for each edge u→w of weight j, $\bar{u} -j{\geq}M{\geq}\bar{w}{\Rightarrow}\bar{u}{\geq}\bar{w}+j$. Similarly for edges
w→v. Hence all edges of G are satisfied, since any loop on w must have the
nonpositive weight and is trivially satisfied.

(4) ⇒ (1). The positive cycle obviously mirrors an A-proof of an assertion of the form x≥x+c or 0≥c, where c>0, using trivial monotonocity,
the ring axioms, and transitivity. Since c>0, x>x or 0>0 follows by
transitivity (after applying trivial monotonocity in the first case).

But we have $\sim x>x$, $\sim 0>0$ by irreflexivity, and hence an A-proof of contradiction. $\square$

Remark The equivalence of (2) and (4) was observed by Pratt [8]; he gave the name separation theory to arithmetic propositions of the same form as S_i.

4. The Satisfiability Problem

By the reduction of the last section, we have simplified the task of the arithmetic checker to one of deciding the satisfiability of a set of arithmetic relations whose comparands are either constants or monic linear univariate polynomials (x or x+c). Without loss of generality we can further restrict the problem to one in which all the comparands are monic linear univariate polynomials.

As shown in the previous section, we can replace a conjunction of relations other than disequalities by an equivalent conjunction of relations of the form $x \geq y[+c]$. Clearly each disequality can also be put into the form $x \neq y[+c]$. Once again, we formulate the problem in terms of the satisfiability of a weighted directed graph, but in a slightly different manner than in the previous section. As before, the variables are the vertices, and the $\geq$-relations provide the weighted, directed edges. However, we now leave the disequalities as additional constraints on the integer assignments. In comparison with the previous approach, we see that a graph satisfiability problem with k disequalities is in fact equivalent to 2^k problems without such constraints. This exponential proliferation of unconstrained problems leads us to suspect that the constrained problem would be much harder than the unconstrained problem. Theorems 4.1 and 4.2 below reinforce this suspicion.

Consider a weighted, directed graph G whose vertices are numbered from 1 to say, n. The edge weights are (finite) integers, which are augmented by $\{-\infty, +\infty\}$ so that we can talk about general maximum path weights. The resulting algebraic structure is the closed semiring

$$(\mathbf{Z}^*, -\infty, 0, \max, +)$$

where $\mathbf{Z}^* = \mathbf{Z} \cup \{-\infty, +\infty\}$,

> max is the semiring addition, corresponding to weight maximization over a set of paths, with identity $-\infty$ for the maximum over an empty set, and

> $+$ is the semiring multiplication, corresponding to path concatenation, with identity 0 for the null (or 0-edge) path.

Formally, we require $-\infty + x = -\infty$ for all x, consistent with out interpretation of concatenation for $+$ and disconnection for $-\infty$. We also extend the "$<$" relation to $\mathbf{Z}^*$ by requiring

$$-\infty < x \qquad \text{for all } x \neq -\infty$$

$$x < +\infty \qquad \text{for } x \neq +\infty.$$

Also $x^* = \begin{cases} 0 & \text{if } x \leq 0 \\ +\infty & \text{if } x > 0 \end{cases}$.

As in Algorithm 5.5 of Aho et al [1], let c_{ij}^k denote the maximum weight of paths from i to j without passing through (ie. entering and leaving) vertices numbered higher than k. If there is no such path, $c_{ij}^k = -\infty$; if the weights of such paths are unbounded from the above, $c_{ij}^k = +\infty$; in all other cases c_{ij}^k is finite. Clearly $c_{ij}^0 \neq +\infty$ for all i, j. We shall show that [1, Algorithm 5.5] can be modified to discover a positive cycle if there is one, and to compute the c_{ij}^n values (which are necessarily $< +\infty$) otherwise. It will be seen that $+\infty$ need never enter into the computation. The use of this algorithm was also observed by Pratt [8].

Theorem 4.1

(1) G has a positive cycle $\Leftrightarrow c_{ii}^k > 0$ for some i, k.

(2) Suppose $c_{ii}^k \leq 0$ for all i, for all $k < k_0$ for some k_0. Then $c_{ij}^k < +\infty$ for all i, j and all $k \leq k_0$.

Proof:

(1) is obvious.

(2) We know $\forall i,j(C_{ij}^0 < +\infty)$. So using $C_{ij}^k = \max(C_{ij}^{k-1}, C_{ik}^{k-1} + C_{kk}^{k-1*} = C_{kj}^{k-1})$ and the fact that $C_{kk}^{k-1*} = 0$ for all $k \leq k_0$, we can show by induction that $C_{ij}^k < +\infty$ for all k, $0 < k \leq k_0$. $\square$

Corollary: The unconstrained satisfiability problem is solvable in $O(e+n^3)$ time, where n is the number of vertices and e is the number of edges.

Proof: The existence of positive cycles can be detected by the following modified version of [1, Algorithm 5.5], which also computes the maximum path weights C_{ij}^n if no positive cycle is found.

> Initialize A_{ij} to C_{ij}^0 ;
>
> poscycle := false;
>
> for k := 1 to n while ¬poscycle do
>
> > for i:=1 to n while ¬poscycle do
> >
> > > for j:=1 to n do
> > >
> > > > $A_{ij} := \max(A_{ij}, A_{ik} + A_{kj})$ od;
> > >
> > > poscycle := $(A_{ii} > 0)$
> > >
> > > od
>
> od;

To justify the assignment

$$A_{ij} := \max(A_{ij}, A_{ik} + A_{kj})$$

notice that by the proof of (2), since $C_{kk}^{k-1} \leq 0$,

$$C_{ij}^k = \max(C_{ij}^{k-1}, C_{ik}^{k-1} + C_{kj}^{k-1}).$$

Under the same condition, it is easy to see that

$$C_{ik}^{k-1} = C_{ik}^k \text{ and } C_{kj}^{k-1} = C_{kj}^k.$$

Hence in fact

$$C_{ij}^k = \max(C_{ij}^{k-1}, C_{ik}^k + C_{kj}^{k-1}) \quad = \max(C_{ij}^{k-1}, C_{ik}^{k-1} + C_{kj}^k) \quad = \max(C_{ij}^{k-1}, C_{ik}^k + C_{kj}^k)$$

so that we can update the matrix A_{ij} from C_{ij}^{k-1} to C_{ij}^k *in situ*. □

Theorem 4.2 The constrained graph satisfiability problem is NP-hard.

Proof: By a reduction of the k-colorability problem. Given a connected, undirected graph G and an integer k, we construct a weighted, directed graph G' whose vertices are those of G plus a new vertex v_0. For each vertex v of G, introduce edges $v \rightarrow v_0$, $v_0 \rightarrow v$ of weights 1 and -k respectively for G'. For each edge (u,v) of G, introduce a constraint $u \neq v$. The resulting constrained problem is satisfiable if and only if G is k-colorable. For connected graphs G, the reduction can be done in polynomial time. Since the k-colorability problem for connected graphs is NP-hard so is the constrained satisfiability problem. □

Corollary: The constrained satisfiability problem for strongly connected graphs is NP-hard.

Proof: The proof of the theorem also proves this corollary. □

The next observation allows us to break the problem into sub-problems defined by the strongly connected components (SCC's) of the graph, and to ignore inter-SCC edges and constraints. The constraints retained, i.e. those which relate pairs of (not necessarily distinct) vertices both inside the same SCC, are called the *internal constraints* of their respective SCC's.

Theorem 4.3 A directed weighted graph G with constraints is satisfiable ⇔ each SCC, together with its internal constraints, is satisfiable.

Proof: "⇒" is obvious.

"⇐" First make satisfying assignments to each SCC separately. Then consider the quotient graph H = G modulo SCC's, i.e. the vertices of H are the SCC's of G, and for every pair of SCC's U, V of G, there is a edge U→V in H if and only if there exist vertices u, v of G such that u∈U, v∈V, and there is an edge u→v in G. H is also known as the condensation of G. Clearly H is a dag, so we can do a topological sort on it. Now visit the SCC's in the reverse of the topological order. For each SCC, add an appropriate constant to the assignments of all its vertices so as to satisfy all the inter-SCC edges and constraints involving it and some previously visited SCC.□

Theorem 4.4 The constrained graph satisfiability problem is NP, and hence is NP-complete.

Proof: For each constraint x≠y, guess x>y or x<y and add edge to graph accordingly. After making guesses for all constraints (in nondeterministic linear time), run the algorithm of the corollary to Theorem 4.1 on the unconstrained augmented graph to determine its satisfiability. The original constrained graph is satisfiable if and only if the augmented graph for some set of guesses for the constraints is satisfiable. Hence the problem is solvable in nondeterministic polynomial time. In conjunction with Theorem 4.2 this proves NP-completeness. □

Corollary: The constrained problem for strongly connected graphs is NP-complete.

Proof: By Theorem 4.4, and the corollary to Theorem 4.2. □

Thus the constrained satisfiability problem for strongly connected graphs is a member of a class of problems which are solvable in exponential time, but for which no polynomial time algorithm has yet been devised. The exponential time algorithm in this case can be derived from the equivalence of the constrained problem to an exponential number of unconstrained problems each solvable in polynomial time. As shown in Section 3, this equivalence is obtained by replacing each constraint x≠y+c with x>y+c | x<y+c, the exponential explosion arising from the binary choice of each disjunction. However, notice that if more than one constraints relate the

same pair of variables, say $x \neq y+c_1$,..., $x \neq y+c_r$, for $r>1$, and $c_1 < c_2 < ... < c_r$, then many of the resulting unconstrained problems are trivially unsatisfiable, namely, those for which the choices for the disjunctions result in $x<y+c_i$ and $x>y+c_j$ for some $i<j$. A more efficient approach makes use of the following equivalence instead:

$$(*) \quad x \neq y+c_1 \ \&...\& \ x \neq y+c_r$$
$$\equiv x<y+c_1 \ | \ (x>y+c_1 \ \& \ x<y+c_2) \ | \ ... \ | \ x>y+c_r$$

For a problem with $r_1, r_2, ..., r_k$ constraints relating k different pairs of vertices, this alternative approach give rise to $(1+r_1)(1+r_2)...(1+r_k)$ unconstrained problems. It is easy to show that for all positive integers $r_1, ..., r_k$, we have

$$(1+r_1)(1+r_2)...(1+r_k) \leq 2^{r_1+ \cdot \cdot \cdot +r_k}$$

with equality holding if and only if $r_1=r_2= \cdot \cdot \cdot =r_k=1$. Thus there is a uniform, but not necessarily positive, economy which roughly increases with the difference $(r_1+ \cdot \cdot \cdot +r_k)-k$.

The problem now becomes one of searching a tree of weighted, directed graphs for a satisfiable leaf graph. At the root of this tree is the original graph. The other levels of the tree are defined by the distinct (unordered) pairs of vertices that are constrained by one or more disequalities. Suppose there are k levels, represented by the constraints:

$$\bigwedge_{1 \leq i \leq k} \ \bigwedge_{1 \leq j \leq r_i} \quad (x_i \neq y_i+c_{i,j})$$

where $r_i>0$ for all i, and $c_{i,j}<c_{i,j+1}$ for all i,j such that $1 \leq j<r_i$. By equation $(*)$, these k levels of constraints are equivalent to a conjunction of k disjunctions,

$$\bigwedge_{1 \leq i \leq k} \ \bigvee_{0 \leq j \leq r_i} \quad P_{i,j}$$

where $P_{i,0}$ denotes $x_i < y_i + c_{i,1}$

$\quad$ $P_{i,j}$ denotes $x_i > y_i + c_{i,j}$ & $x_i < y_i + c_{i,j+1}$

$\qquad$ for $0 < j < r_i$

and $\quad$ P_{i,r_i} denotes $x_i > y_i + c_{i,r_i}$.

In terms of satisfiability, we have the equivalences

$$P_{i,0} \equiv y_i \geq x_i + (-c_{i,1} + 1)$$

$$\text{for } 0 < j < r_i$$

$$\text{and} \quad P_{i,r_i} \equiv x_i \geq y_i + (c_{i,r_i} + 1).$$

This shows that each $P_{i,j}$ represents one or two edges. For each $d=1, 2, \ldots$ or k, we can rewrite the above conjunction as an equivalent discunctive normal form

$$\bigvee_{0 \leq j_1 \leq r_1, \ldots, 0 \leq j_d \leq r_d} (P_{1,j_1} \& P_{2,j_2} \& \ldots \& P_{d,j_d}).$$

Each disjunct $P_{1,j_1} \& \ldots \& P_{d,j_d}$ defines a node at depth d of the tree. The graph of this node is obtained by adding the edges represented by the disjunct to the root graph. Its father is the node defined by the disjunct $P_{1,j_1} \& \ldots \& P_{d-1,j_{d-1}}$ in the disjunctive normal form for the first d-1 levels. Thus the graph of every node other than the root is obtained by adding one or two levels to the graph of its father.

To search this tree for a satisfiable leaf graph, we employ a recursive depth-first trasversal algorithm. Since the descendants of a node with an unsatisfiable graph all have unsatisfiable graphs, there is no need to search the subtree rooted at such a node. However, in order to exploit this fact, we need to be able to decide which of the sons of a node with a satisfiable graph also have satisfiable graphs. Suppose the node is is at depth d-1 with graph G_{d-1}. The constraints corresponding to depth d relate vertices x_d and y_d. Let the maximum path weights in G_{d-1} from x_d to y_d and from y_d to x_d be a,b respectively. Since G_{d-1} is satisfiable, by Theorem 3.4, $a+b\leq0$, or $a\leq-b$, and these weights define lower and upper bounds for the difference x_d-y_d, i.e. $x_d-y_d \in [a,-b]$. Similarly, $P_{d,j}$ defines bounds for x_d-y_d:

$$P_{d,0} \equiv x_d-y_d \in (-\infty,c_{d,1})$$

$$P_{d,j} \equiv x_d-y_d \in (c_{d,j},c_{d,j+1}) \quad 0<j<r_d$$

$$P_{d,r_d} \equiv x_d-y_d \in (c_{d,r_d},+\infty).$$

The sons of the node have graphs obtained by adding the edges representing these intervals to G_{d-1}. Obviously, if the interval defined by $P_{d,j}$ is disjoint from $[a,-b]$, then the graph of the corresponding son is unsatisfiable. This happens if either the inteval is itself empty, i.e. $0<j<r_d$ and $c_{d,j}=c_{d,j+1}-1$, or if it is entirely to the left or right of $[a,-b]$. On the other hand, we shall prove that if this interval is not disjoint from $[a,-b]$, then the graph of the corresponding son is satisfiable, and hence a candidate for recursive search. Along with the proof, we shall exhibit an ($O(n^2)$) algorithm to update the maximum path weight matrix of a graph to reflect the addition of a new edge. First we present some notation.

We shall be concerned with a strongly connected, directed graph G whose edges are weighted by the inegers. A **simple** path in G is a path which enters and leaves any vertex at most once, so that a cycle is a closed simple path. For a path p in G, we denote its weight by w_p. Let us also let m_{xy} denote the maximum path weight from vertex x to vertex y, i.e. $m_{xy}=c_{wy}^n$ where n is the number of vertices in G.

Lemma 4.1: Suppose G has no positive cycle. Then for any path p from vertex x to vertex y, there exists a simple path q from x to y such that $w_p\leq w_q$.

Proof: By induction on the length of path p, using the fact that removal of any cycle from a path does not decrease the weight. □

Lemma 4.2: $m_{xy} < +\infty$ for all vertices x,y in G $\Leftrightarrow$ G has no positive cycle.

Proof: "$\Leftarrow$" By Lemma 4.1, all paths from x to y have weights dominated by the weights of the finitey may simple paths aont them.

"$\Rightarrow$" Assume G has a positive cycle p through vetex x. Then $m_{xx}=+\infty$ by concatenating p to itself arbitrarily many times. $\Box$

Lemma 4.3: If G has no positive cycle, then for any pair of vetices x,y, there is a simple path from x to y such that $w_p=m_{xy}$.

Proof: By Lemma 4.2, $m_{xy} < +\infty$, so there exists a path q from x to y such that $w_q=m_{xy}$. By Lemma 4.1, there is a simple path p from x to y such that $w_p \geq w_q=m_{xy}$. But by definition, $w_p \leq m_{xy}$ also. $\Box$

Lemma 4.4: Suppose G has no positive cycle. Let x,y be vertices in G, let edge e from x to y of weight w_e be an edge not in G, let G' be the graph obtained by adding e to G. Then

$$\text{G' has a positive cycle} \Leftrightarrow w_e+m_{yx}>0.$$

where m_{uv} denotes the maximum path weights in G.

Proof: "$\Leftarrow$" is obvious.

"$\Rightarrow$" Assume G' has a positive cycle p. If p does not contain e at all, then G has a positive cycle, contrary to assumption. Hence p contains e, but only once since p is simple. Thus p can be decomposed into a path q from y to x that lies completely in G, and the edge e, with

$$w_p = w_e+w_q > 0.$$

But q is a path in G $\Rightarrow w_q \leq m_{yx}$

$\therefore w_e+m_{yx} \geq w_e+w_q >0.$ $\Box$

Theorem 4.5 Let G, e, G', m_{uv} be as in Lemma 4.4. Let m'_{uv} denote maximum path weights in G'. Suppose G' has no positive cycle. Then for all vertices u,v,

$$m'_{uv} = \max(m_{ux}+w_e+m_{yv}, m_{uv}).$$

Proof: Since m_{uv}, $m_{ux}+w_e+m_{yv}$ are both weights of paths from u to v in G', they are both dominated by m'_{uv}. Hence $m'_{uv} \geq \max(m_{ux}+w_e+m_{yv}, m_{uv})$. On the other hand, since G' has no positive cycle, by Lemma 4.3 there is a simple path p from u to v such that $m'_{uv}=w_p$. If p does not contain e then p is in G $\Rightarrow w_p \leq m_{uv}$. If p contains e, it contains e exactly once because it is simple. So p can be decomposed into a path q from u to x, the edge e from x to y, and a path r from y to v, where all edges of q, r are in G. Hence

$$w_p = w_q + w_e + w_r$$

where $w_q \leq m_{ux}, w_r \leq m_{yv}$.

$\therefore w_p \leq m_{ux}+w_e+m_{yv}$.

In either case, $m'_{uv}=w_p \leq \max(m_{ux}+w_e+m_{yv}, m_{uv})$. □

Corollary: (Maximum path weight update). Assumptions as in Theorem 4.5. Then

$$m'_{uv} = \max(m'_{ux}+w_e+m_{yv}, m_{uv}) \qquad (1)$$
$$= \max(m_{ux}+w_e+m'_{yv}, m_{uv}) \qquad (2)$$
$$= \max(m'_{ux}+w_e+m'_{yv}, m_{uv}) \qquad (3)$$

Proof: We only prove (3); (1) and (2) are proved similarly. By Theorem 4.5, $m'_{uv}=\max(m_{ux}+w_e+m_{yv}, m_{uv})$. Also by Theorem 4.5, $m_{xy} \leq m'_{xy}$ for all x,y, so

$$m_{ux} \leq m'_{ux} \text{ and } m_{vy} \leq m'_{vy}$$

$$\therefore m'_{uv} \leq \max(m'_{ux} + w_e + m'_{vy}, m_{uv}).$$

However, $m_{uv}, m'_{ux} + w_e + m'_{vy}$ are both weights of paths from u to v in G', so by definition

$$m'_{uv} \geq \max(m'_{ux} + w_e + m'_{vy}, m_{uv}) \text{ also.}$$

Note the similarlity to the proof of the corollary to Theorem 4.1. □

Theorem 4.5 gives us an $O(n^2)$ algorithm for updating a maximum path weight matrix; its corollary allows us to perform the update _in situ_. However, we only need to do the update when the new graph has no positive cycle. The next results allows us to decide when this condition holds.

<u>Theorem 4.6</u> Suppose G has no positive cycle. Let x,y be distinct vertices such that $m_{xy}=a$, $m_{yx}=b$. We know that $a+b \leq 0$, or $a \leq -b$, and that G is satisfiable by (Theorem 3.4). Then for any c such that $a \leq c \leq -b$, there is an assignment which satisfies G and the additional relation x=y+c.

<u>Proof:</u> It suffices to show that the graph G″, obtained by adding edges p from x to y of weight c and q from y to x of weight -c to G, has no positive cycle. First add p to G to obtain G'. Let m_{uv}, m'_{uv}, m''_{uv} denote the maximum path weights in G, G', G″ respectively. Now G has no positive cycle, and $c+m_{yx}=c+b \leq 0$ since $c \leq -b$, so we know that G' has no positive cycle by Lemma 4.4. Then Theorem 4.5 is applicable, and

$$m'_{xy} = \max(m_{xx} + c + m_{yy}, m_{xy})$$
$$= \max(0 + c + 0, a) = c.$$

Next add q to G' to obtain G″. Again, G' has no positive cycle, and

$(-c)+m'_{xy} = -c+c = 0 \Rightarrow G''$ has no positive cycle.

$\therefore$ By Theorem 3.4, G'' is satisfiable. $\square$

Theorem 4.6 completes the justification of our criterion for deciding the satisfiability of the graph of a son from the maximum path weights of the father's graph and the edges added for the son. We now state the recursive traversal algorithm in pidgin Algol:

```
boolean procedure nodesat (maxwt,d);
integer array maxwt (n,n); integer d;
comment maxwt is max path weight matrix of father,
        d is depth of sons,
        n = no. of vertices in graph, a global 8parameter,
        lc = no. of levels of constraints;
begin integer array newmaxwt (n,n); integer a,b;
        nodesat := false;
        let x,y be vertices related by level d constraints;
        let level d constraints be x≠y+c_1,....,x≠y+c_r,c_1<...<c_r;
        a := maxwt(x,y); b := maxwt(y,x);
        for each of the intervals (-∞,c_1), (c_1,c_2),....,(c_r,+∞)
            while ¬nodesat do
             if interval not disjoint from [a,-b] then do
                   if d=lc-1 then nodesat := true
                   else do compute newmaxwt from maxwt and from edges
                               defining the interval, using Theorem 4.5
                               and its corollary;

                         nodesat := nodesat(newmaxwt, d+1)
                         od
             od
        od
end nodesat;
```

In connection with the computation of newmaxwt, note that for the first edge defining an interval, Theorem 4.5 suffices since we do not disturb the original maximum path weights in maxwt, but for the second edge (if interval is finite) we have to use the corollary to Theorem 4.5 so that we can justify updating newmaxwt in situ.

The main program is:

Run the algorithm in the corollary to Theorem 4.1 to compute max path weights of original graph in array A (setting poscycle);

```
if ¬poscycle then do
    sort the disequalities into k levels;
    poscycle := nodesat(A,1)
od;
```

5. Implementation

An arithmetic checker for PL/CV 2 has been implemented in PL/I (Optimizing Compiler) using the procedures described above. This checker functions as an independent module of the verifier, which invokes it to decide the validity of arithmetic arguments embedded in correctness proofs. The assertions in these arguments are passed to the checker as strings of encoded operators and operands in prefix form.

The checker converts the operands, recursively, into their canonical form representations. We adopt a linked list of terms as our canonical form for a polynomial. Each term consists of a product of variables, represented as an order "degree string" of the encoded variables, and an associated integer coefficient. For example, assuming the variable x_1 precedes the variable x_2, the term $3x_1^3x_2^3$ is represented by the degree string $x_1x_1x_1x_2x_2$ and the coefficient 3. The linked list is sorted in the lexicographic order of the degree strings of variables of the terms. This implies that the terms are ordered in increasing total degrees; in particular, any nonzero constant term always occurs at the head of the list, so that a canonical form polynomial can be easily separated into the canonical forms of its constant and constant-free parts. As usual, the degree of a polynomial is the degree of its highest term. In the computer program, these polynomials are constructed from the PL/I based structures and pointers.

Additions, subtractions and multiplications of polynomials are implemented with the standard merge-add technique. The algorithm for polynomial division, required for factoring, is a straightforward generalization of the familiar long division method for univariate polynomials:

```
comment P = dividend, D = divisor,
        d = quotient, R = remainder;
Q := 0;
R:= P;
while (R≠0 and degree(R)≤_L degree(P) and 1(D)|1(R)) do
      S := 1(R)/1(D);
      Q := Q+S;
      R := R-S*D
      od;
comment if R=0 then D divides P with quotient in Q, otherwise D
        does not divide P;
```

This algorithm generates the terms of the quotient in increasing lexicographic order of degrees. P,Q,R,D and S are really pointers to polynomials. $\leq_L$ represents lexicographic string comparison. 1(D) is the leading
term of the polynomial D, i.e. the term with the lowest degree. |
represents divisibility of terms, which is easily implemented, as is the
operation / which is the actual division of terms. +,- and * in the algorithm represent the respective polynomial operations. the algorithm terminates because there are only finitely many degree strings lexicographi-
cally less than a given degree string.

After all hypotheses (including those obtained by applications of nontrivial monotonicity) and conclusions have been set up in canonical form,
we negate the conclusions, and substitute new distinct variables for distinct constant-free polynomials as justified by Theorem 3.3. the procedures of Section 4 are then applied to decide the satisfiability of the
system. We summarize the steps involved:

(1) Construct directed, weighted graph from the relations other than dise-
     qualities. The graph is represented as a matrix in which each entry
     contains the weight of the edges directed from the vertex of the row
     to the vertex of the column. An entry corresponding to an actual edge
     of the graph is significant; all other entries are insignificant and
     set to -∞. The significant entries of each row, equivalently the
     edges emanating from the corresponding vertex, are linked into a list
     to facilitate graph manipulations.

(2) The graph is separated into is SCC's by a depth first search.

(3) For each SCC, we compute the maximum path weight matrix, and then apply the nodesat algorithm of the last section to this matrix and the sorted internal disequalities. As soon as an SCC is found to be unsatisfiable, we terminate with an affirmative answer; otherwise the system is satisfiable, and the original argument is not justifiable by the arithmetic rule.

We conclude this description with the following remarks. first of all, a relation involving the same variable on both sides is equivalent to a relation with constant comparands, and hence either always true or always false. In the former case, the relation is redundant; in the latter case, the system is trivially contradictory.

Secondly, the complexity of the decision problem clearly increases with the dimension, i.e. the number of distinct variables, of the system of inequalities. It is therefore to our advantage to reduce the dimension whenever possible. Such an opportunity arises when an equality relating two different variables is detected. Obviously, one variable can be expressed in terms of the other throughout the system, thereby decreasing the dimension by 1. Since such a substitution might give rise to more equalities, in fact we group variables related by equalities into equivalence classes using the union-find algorithm [1, Algorithm 4.3] with weighted edges. When all equalities have been processed, we pick a representative from each equivalence class, and substitute it for each non-representative of the same class with an appropriate constant displacement. Note that an equality can be implied by a pair of inequalities (e.g. $x \geq y + c$ and $y \geq x - c$). The checker looks for both explicit and implicit equalities.

Following are some examples of the use of the arithmetic rule.

Example 5.1

$$H: \begin{cases} x-y \leq y \ \& \ y \leq x+1 \\ \& \ x-1 \leq z \ \& \ z \leq x+1 \\ \& \ y-1 \leq z \ \& \ z \leq y+1 \end{cases}$$
$$C: \quad x=y \mid y=z \mid z=x$$

Intuitively, if three integers, x,y,z differ from each other by at most 1, then they cannot be all distinct. This inference is justifiable by the arithmetic rule, and we sketch an outline of an A-proof of contradiction from H & $\sim$C:

(1) $x-1 \leq y$ & $y \leq x+1$ H

(2) $y=x-1 \mid y=x \mid y=x+1$ A-provable from (1) using the lemma
                                       $x<y \Leftrightarrow x+1 \leq y$

(3) $y \neq x$ $\sim$C

(4) $y=x-1 \mid y=x+1$ (2) & (3)

(5) $z=x-1 \mid z=x+1$ similar proof as for (4)

(6) $y=z-1 \mid y=z+1$ similar proof as for (4)

(7) $[y=x-1 \mid y=x+1]$ (4) & (5)
     & $[z=x-1 \mid z=x+1]$

(8) $[y=x-1 \ \& \ z=x-1]$ distributive law, (7)
    $\mid [y=x-1 \ \& \ z=x+1]$
    $\mid [y=x+1 \ \& \ z=x-1]$
    $\mid [y=x+1 \ \& \ z=x+1]$

(9) $(y=z) \mid (z=y+2)$ A-provable from (8), using
    $\mid (y=z+2) \mid (y=z)$ trivial monotonicity and the equality
                                     rules

(10) $(y=z) \mid (z=y+2) \mid (y=z+2)$ (9)

(11) $y \neq z$ $\sim$C

(12) $z=y+2 \mid y=z+2$ (10) & (11)

(13) $[z=y+2 \mid y=z+2]$ (6) & (12)
     & $[y=z-1 \mid y=z+1]$

(14) $[z=y+2 \ \& \ y=z-1]$ distributive law, (13)
    $\mid [z=y+2 \ \& \ y=z+1]$
    $\mid [y=z+2 \ \& \ y=z-1]$
    $\mid [y=z+2 \ \& \ y=z+1]$

(15) $(z=z+1) \mid (z=z+3)$ A-provable from (14), using trivial
    $\mid (z+2=z-1) \mid (z+2=z+1)$ monotonicity and the equality rules

Contradiction

Example 5.2

$$H: \begin{cases} x_1 \geq x_2 - 1 & x_5 \geq x_6 & x_8 \geq x_9 - 1 \\ x_2 \geq x_3 & x_6 \geq x_7 & x_9 \geq x_{10} \\ x_3 > -x_4 - 1 & x_7 \geq x_5 - 1 & x_{10} \geq x_8 - 1 \\ x_4 \geq x_1 \\ x_5 \leq x_2 + 10 & x_7 \leq x_3 + 700 & x_8 \leq x_6 + 52 \\ x_9 \leq x_4 + 33 & x_{10} \leq x_1 + 58 & x_{10} \leq x_7 - 580 \end{cases}$$

$$C: \begin{cases} x_1 = x_2 & | & x_3 = x_4 - 1 & | & x_6 = x_5 \\ | & x_8 + 1 = x_9 & | & x_{10} = x_9 - 1 \end{cases}$$

This inference is invalid. To see this, notice that the SCC's are $\{x_1, x_2, x_3, x_4\}$, $\{x_5, x_6, x_7\}$ and $\{x_8, x_9, x_{10}\}$, so that the last 6 hypothesis relations can be ignored. The negated conclusion ~C gives 6 internal constraints. Clearly, the SCC's and their respective internal constraints can be individually satisfied by

$$x_1 = 0, \ x_2 = 1, \ x_3 = 0, \ x_4 = 0,$$
$$x_5 = 0, \ x_6 = 0, \ x_7 = 0,$$
$$x_8 = 0, \ x_9 = 0, x_{10} = 0.$$

Hence, H & ~C is satisfied by, for instance,

$$x_1 = 2000, \ x_2 = 2001, x_3 = 2000, x_4 = 2000,$$
$$x_5 = 1001, \ x_6 = 1000, x_7 = 1000,$$
$$x_8 = 0, \ x_9 = 0, \ x_{10} = 0.$$

$\therefore$ H $\nvdash_A$ C.

Example 5.3

$$H: \begin{cases} x<x^2 \\ x\neq 0 \end{cases}$$
$$\overline{\;C: \quad 2\leq x \mid x<0}$$

This is valid and is justifiable by the arithmetic rule because it involves only one application of nontrivial monotonicity - factoring:

(1) $x<x^2$ & $x\neq 0$

(2) $1<x \mid 1>x$ factoring, (1)

(3) $1<x \mid 0\geq x$ (2)

(4) $x\neq 0$ (1)

(5) $(1<x \mid 0\geq x)$ & $x\neq 0$ (3) & (4)

(6) $(1<x$ & $x\neq 0) \mid (0\geq x$ & $x\neq 0)$ distributive law, (5)

(7) $1<x \mid 0>x$

(8) $2\leq x \mid 0>x$

Notice that actually $x<x^2 \Rightarrow x\neq 0$, but this fact is not A-provable.

6. Conclusion

We have taken an arithmetic proof system designed for PL/CV 2 and have shown that it is at least possible to verify proofs in this system by implementing a proof-checker for it. The fact that the algorithm used has exponential worst-case time-complexity need not bother us unduly, as arithmetic arguments that occur in program verifications can be expected to remain within reasonable size limits. It is more important to have a useful and easily applicable rule; this remains to be seen until PL/CV 2 becomes more widely used. We mention two possible extensions.

First, the checker can only verify the inference of a given conclusion from given hypotheses. Since the truth of these hypotheses must have been established by preceding arguments or by assumption, and since PL/CV2 maintains a table of all such established assertions, it is theoretically possible to omit the specification of the hypotheses. However, unless we are willing to try all possible established quantifier-free assertions, we must be able to select, on the basis of the structure of the conclusion and of any nontrivial monotonicity operator, those assertions that could possibly participate in the argument as hypotheses. Unfortunately, the transitivity of the order relation and the combinations and cancellations of terms that occur in polynomial arithmetic render such a backward selection extremely difficult.

Second, it is possible, and probably desirable, to strengthen the arithmetic rule by adding new axioms to the underlying proof system. For example, A-proofs cannot make use of the fact that two polynomials are negatives of each other, so that the proof

$$\frac{-x \geq y, \ x \geq z}{-y \geq z}$$

requires the use of nontrivial monotonicity. It is possible to allow axioms of the form

$$-t_1 \geq t_2 \ \& \ t_1 \geq t_3 \ \Rightarrow \ -t_2 \geq t_3$$

in A-proofs, so that the above example becomes A-provable. Such an enhancement would entail the following additional tasks for the checker: (1) checking every pair of constant-free canonical-form polynomials to see if they are negatives of each other, and (2) deciding satisfiability of systems of inequalities of the forms

$$\pm x \pm y \leq c, \ \pm x \pm y \neq c, \ \pm x \leq c, \ x \neq c.$$

(1) can be readily implemented. For (2), we note that there is a polynomial time algorithm for separation theory extended to include inequalities of the form $\pm x \pm y \leq c$. The algorithm proceeds by elimination of variables as in the proof of Lemma 3.5. If the variable to be eliminated is x, then all

inequalities involving x are converted to the forms

$$(I) \quad x \geq \pm y + c \text{ or } x \geq c$$

$$\text{or } (II) \quad \pm z + c' \geq x \text{ or } c' \geq x$$

If only type (I) or only type (II) inequalities occur, they can all be discarded. Otherwise every inequality of type (I) is combined with every inequality of type (II) using transitivity of $\geq$, to produce an inequality of one of the forms

$$(i) \quad \pm y \pm z \leq c$$

$$(ii) \quad \pm zy \leq c, \text{ or } \pm y \leq \lfloor c/2 \rfloor$$

$$(iii) \quad 0 \leq c$$

An inequality of type (iii) either is redundant (if $c \geq 0$) or proves unsatisfiability of the original system (if $c < 0$). Inequalities of types (i) and (ii) are of the same forms as those of the original system and take part in the elimination of the next variable together with the inequalities that did not involve x. The algorithm runs in polynomial time provided we eliminate redundancies at every step. For example, if there are inequalities

$$y + z \leq c_i \quad \text{for } i=1, 2 \quad c_1 \neq c_2$$

then we only retain

$$y + z \leq \min(c_1, c_2).$$

This algorithm may be used instead of the "positive-cycle" algorithm as the basis of a tree search. The details of implementation remain to be worked out.

For another example of possible enhancement by addition of axioms, consider the proof

$$\frac{x \neq 0}{x^2 > 0}.$$

With the current system, this proof requires two invocations of the arithmetic rule, because the multiplications of x by itself for the cases x<0 and x>0 use different nontrivial monotonicity axioms:

$$\begin{array}{ll} & x>0 \ \& \ x>0 \implies x^2>0 \\ \text{and} & x<0 \ \& \ x<0 \implies x^2>0. \end{array}$$

(Note that in general, $x \neq 0$ and $y \neq 0$ only allow us to conclude $xy \neq 0$). Adding a "squaring axiom" will remove the awkwardness in this case, and other extensions may suggest themselves as we gain experience in the use of PL/CV 2.

7. Arithmetic Axioms for PL/CV 2

(1) Ring axioms and the definition of minus, -.
    For all polynomial expressions t, t_1, t_2, t_3 and variable x:

(i)	$t(x/t_1+t_2)=t(x/t_2+t_1)$	commutativity
	$t(x/t_1*t_2)=t(x/t_2*t_1)$	
(ii)	$t(x/(t_1+t_2)+t_3)=t(x/t_1+(t_2+t_3))$	associativity
	$t(x/(t_1*t_2)*t_3)=t(x/t_1*(t_2*t_3))$	
(iii)	$t(x/t_1*(t_2+t_3))=t(x/t_1*t_2+t_1*t_3)$	distributivity
(iv)	$t(x/t_1+0)=t(x/t_1)$	additive identity
(v)	$t(x/t_1*1)=t(x/t_1)$	multiplicative identity
(vi)	$t(x/t_1+(-t_1))=t(x/0)$	additive inverse
(vii)	$t(x/t_1-t_2)=t(x/t_1+(-t_2))$	subtraction

$t(x/t_1+t_2)$ is the result of substituting the expression t_1+t_2 for the variable x in the expression t, etc.

(2) Discrete linear order.

For all polynomial expressions t_1,t_2,t_3

(i)	$\sim(t_1<t_1)$	irreflexivity
(ii)	$t_1<t_2 \mid t_2<t_1 \mid t_1=t_2$	trichotomy
(iii)	$t_1<t_2 \; \& \; t_2<t_3 \Rightarrow t_1<t_3$	transitivity
(iv)	$\sim(t_1<t_2<t_1+1)$	discreteness

(3) Definitions of order relations and inequality.

For all polynomial expressions t_1,t_2,t_3

(i) $t_1 \leq t_2 \Leftrightarrow t_1<t_2 \mid t_1=t_2$

(ii) $t_1>t_2 \Leftrightarrow t_2<t_1$

(iii) $t_1 \geq t_2 \Leftrightarrow t_1>t_2 \mid t_1=t_2$

(4) Monotonicity of + and *.

For all polynomial expressions t_1,t_2,t_3,t_4

(i) $t_1 \geq t_2 \; \& \; t_3 \geq t_4 \Rightarrow t_1+t_3 \geq t_2+t_4$ monotonicity of +

If t_3,t_4 are constants, this is called an instance of <u>trivial monotonicity</u>.

(ii) $t_1 \geq t_2 \; \& \; t_3 \leq t_4 \Rightarrow t_1-t_3 \geq t_2-t_4$ monotonicity of −

If t_3 and t_4 are constants, this is called an instance of <u>trivial monotonicity</u>.

(iii) $t_1 \geq 0 \; \& \; t_2 \geq t_3 \Rightarrow t_1*t_2 \geq t_1*t_3$ monotonicity of *

(iv) $t_1>0 \; \& \; t_2 \geq t_3 \Rightarrow \dfrac{t_2}{t_1} \geq \dfrac{t_3}{t_1}$ cancellation (factoring) - applies only when t_2,t_3 are divisible by t_1.

To make the proof system more powerful, many variants of the above axioms are incorporated into the arithmetic proof rule. These variants are given in the following tables, in which each entry contains the conclusion from the hypotheses corresponding to its row and column.

Addition	$t_3 > t_4$	$t_3 \geq t_4$	$t_3 = t_4$	$t_3 \neq t_4$
$t_1 > t_2$	$t_1+t_3 \geq t_2+t_4+2$	$t_1+t_3 \geq t_2+t_4+1$	$t_1+t_3 \geq t_2+t_4+1$ & $t_1+t_4 \geq t_2+t_3+1$	X
$t_1 \geq t_2$	$t_1+t_3 \geq t_2+t_4+1$	$t_1+t_3 \geq t_2+t_4$	$t_1+t_3 \geq t_2+t_4$ & $t_1+t_4 \geq t_2+t_3$	X
$t_1 = t_2$	$t_1+t_3 \geq t_2+t_4+1$ & $t_2+t_3 \geq t_1+t_4+1$	$t_1+t_3 \geq t_2+t_4$ & $t_2+t_3 \geq t_1+t_4$	$t_1+t_3 = t_2+t_4$ & $t_1+t_4 = t_2+t_3$	$t_1+t_3 \neq t_2+t_4$ & $t_1+t_4 \neq t_2+t_3$
$t_1 \neq t_2$	X	X	$t_1+t_3 \neq t_2+t_4$ & $t_1+t_4 \neq t_2+t_3$	X

Subtraction	$t_3 > t_4$	$t_3 \geq t_4$	$t_3 = t_4$	$t_3 \neq t_4$
$t_1 > t_2$	$t_1-t_4 \geq t_2-t_3+2$	$t_1-t_4 \geq t_2-t_3+1$	$t_1-t_4 \geq t_2-t_3+1$ & $t_1-t_3 \geq t_2-t_4+1$	X
$t_1 \geq t_2$	$t_1-t_4 \geq t_2-t_3+1$	$t_1-t_4 \geq t_2-t_3$	$t_1-t_4 \geq t_2-t_3$ & $t_1-t_3 \geq t_2-t_4$	X
$t_1 = t_2$	$t_1-t_4 \geq t_2-t_3+1$ & $t_2-t_4 \geq t_1-t_3+1$	$t_1-t_4 \geq t_2-t_3$ & $t_2-t_4 \geq t_1-t_3$	$t_1-t_4 = t_2-t_3$ & $t_2-t_4 = t_1-t_3$	$t_1-t_4 \neq t_2-t_3$ & $t_1-t_3 \neq t_2-t_4$
$t_1 \neq t_2$	X	X	$t_1-t_4 \neq t_2-t_3$ & $t_1-t_3 \neq t_2-t_4$	X

Multiplication	$t_2 \geq t_3$	$t_2 > t_3$	$t_2 = t_3$	$t_2 \neq t_3$
$t_1 > 0$	$t_1*t_2 \geq t_1*t_3$	$t_1*t_2 > t_1*t_3$	$t_1*t_2 = t_1*t_3$	$t_1*t_2 \neq t_1*t_3$
$t_1 \geq 0$	$t_1*t_2 \geq t_1*t_3$	$t_1*t_2 \geq t_1*t_3$	$t_1*t_2 = t_1*t_3$	X
$t_1 = 0$	$t_1*t_2 = t_1*t_3$ & $t_1*t_3 = 0$	$t_1*t_2 = t_1*t_3$ & $t_1*t_2 = 0$	$t_1*t_2 = t_1*t_3$ & $t_1*t_2 = 0$	$t_1*t_2 = t_1*t_3$ & $t_1*t_2 = 0$
$t_1 \leq 0$	$t_1*t_2 \leq t_1*t_3$	$t_1*t_2 \leq t_1*t_3$	$t_1*t_2 = t_1*t_3$	X
$t_1 < 0$	$t_1*t_2 \leq t_1*t_3$	$t_1*t_2 < t_1*t_3$	$t_1*t_2 = t_1*t_3$	$t_1*t_2 \neq t_1*t_3$
$t_1 \neq 0$	X	$t_1*t_2 \neq t_1*t_3$	$t_1*t_2 = t_1*t_3$	$t_1*t_2 \neq t_1*t_3$

Cancellation (factoring)	$t_2 > t_3$	$t_2 \geq t_3$	$t_2 = t_3$	$t_2 \neq t_3$
$t_1 > 0$	$\dfrac{t_2}{t_1} > \dfrac{t_3}{t_1}$	$\dfrac{t_2}{t_1} \geq \dfrac{t_3}{t_1}$	$\dfrac{t_2}{t_1} = \dfrac{t_3}{t_1}$	$\dfrac{t_2}{t_1} \neq \dfrac{t_3}{t_1}$
$t_1 < 0$	$\dfrac{t_2}{t_1} < \dfrac{t_3}{t_1}$	$\dfrac{t_2}{t_1} \leq \dfrac{t_3}{t_1}$	$\dfrac{t_2}{t_1} = \dfrac{t_3}{t_1}$	$\dfrac{t_2}{t_1} \neq \dfrac{t_3}{t_1}$
$t_1 \neq 0$	$\dfrac{t_2}{t_1} \neq \dfrac{t_3}{t_1}$	X	$\dfrac{t_2}{t_1} = \dfrac{t_3}{t_1}$	$\dfrac{t_2}{t_1} \neq \dfrac{t_3}{t_1}$

The cancellation axioms apply only when t_2 and t_3 are exactly divisible by t_1 in the ring of multivariate integral polynomials. Alternatively, we can state these axioms in more explicit forms such as

$$t_1 > 0 \ \& \ t_1*t_2 > t_1*t_3 \Rightarrow t_2 > t_3.$$

Then the deduction of $\dfrac{t_2}{t_1} > \dfrac{t_3}{t_1}$ from $t_1 > 0$ and $t_2 > t_3$ when t_1 divides both t_2 and

t_3 may be achieved by converting t_2 and t_3 to the forms $t_1 * \frac{t_2}{t_1}$ and $t_1 * \frac{t_3}{t_1}$ by ring axioms and then applying factoring.

8. References

1. A.V. Aho, J.E. Hopcroft and J.D. Ullman, The Design and Analysis of Computer Algorithms, Addison-Wesley, Reading, Massachusetts, 1974.

2. T. Chan, An algorithm for checking PL/CV arithmetic inferences, TR77-326, Cornell University, Department of Computer Science, Ithaca, New York, 1977.

3. R.L. Constable and M.J. O'Donnell, A Programming Logic, Winthrop, Cambridge, Massachusetts, 1978.

4. R.L. Constable and S.D. Johnson, Program Verification Reference Manual with User's Guide to PL/CV 2, Cornell University, Department of Computer Science, Ithaca, New York, 1978.

5. J.C. King, A program verifier, Ph.D. Thesis, Carnegie-Mellon University, Department of Computer Science, Pittsburgh, Pennsylvania, 1969.

6. S.C. Kleene, Introduction to Metamathematics, D. Van Nostrand Company, Inc., Princeton, New Jersey, 1952.

7. H.W. Kuhn, Solvability and consistency for linear equations and inequalities, Amer. Math. Monthly 63 (1956), 217-232.

8. V. Pratt, Two easy theories whose combination is hard, unpublished manuscript, MIT, Cambridge, Massachusetts, 1977.

Appendix E

The AVID System

A new interactive implementation of PL/CV2 is now available. The system, known as AVID, allows the programmer to develop PL/CV2 proofs and programs in the style of the Cornell Program Synthesizer [3]. In this approach, the programmer uses simple commands to select templates for program and proof constructs. These templates contain the purely syntactic elements of the constructs together with nonterminal placeholders. For example, the template for an implication introduction has the following form:

```
<implication-assertion> BY IMPIN,
   PROOF;
      ASSUME <*implication hypothesis>;
      {argument}
      <*implication conclusion>;
   QED;
```

The "<implication-assertion>" is a nonterminal. It can be refined by the direct entry of an implication assertion. The "BY IMPIN," is a purely syntactic element that allows the programmer to identify the template.

In general, nonterminals can be refined by either the direct entry of assertions or expressions (known as phrases), or by the selection of another template. For example, the "{argument}" nonterminal in the figure above can be refined by an assertion or by another template (even another implication introduction). In fact, this is an iterated nonterminal, and so it can be refined by zero or more of these elements. The program is developed by the continued stepwise refinement of nonterminals, from the initial starting point to the final complete program.

Unlike the batch implementation of PL/CV2, AVID provides a friendly user-interface to the programming logic. Templates for complex program/proof constructs (such as the DO WHILE loop with its invariant and termination proof) can be selected with a single command. Redundant specification of assertions, often required in PL/CV2, is eliminated in AVID. Whenever an assertion in the proof can be determined automatically from assertions already entered, this work is done by the system rather than the programmer. For example, in the display of the implication introduction above, the hypothesis and conclusion of the implication were shown as "<*implication hypothesis>" and "<*implication conclusion>". When the "<implication-assertion>" is refined, these two fields will be automatically filled in by the system.

The interactive nature of the AVID implementation also made it possible to provide several new facilities. AVID allows the verification of partially developed programs and proofs. To this end, it introduces a new program construct, the ATTAIN block, which formalizes the notion of a stepwise refinement level. The system checks the refinement of an ATTAIN block against its specification, and it simultaneously checks the rest of the proof while assuming that the ATTAIN block is correctly refined. In a top-down development, this allows the user to verify his program at every level of refinement.

AVID also allows the display of logical dependency within a proof, a facility unavailable in the batch system. The automatic deduction facilities of PL/CV2 frequently make the question of dependency among proof assertions less than transparent. The display of dependency information can be particularly useful when the programmer wishes to modify an existing proof, perhaps to weaken a hypothesis, and needs to determine the effect of a potential change.

The AVID system has been implemented on a DEC VAX 11/780 running Berkeley VAX/UNIX. The system runs in about 250K of virtual memory. The specific user interface is very similar to that of the Berkeley screen editor _vi_. The system appears to be reasonably efficient. Editing changes take place in real time on the user's screen, and the system can verify a proof of several pages in just a few seconds.

To give a better idea of how the AVID system is used in practice, we will sketch out a short sample development session. The development shown was actually performed on the VAX implementation of AVID. The figures were created by editing files produced by the AVID **:print** command.

A few comments on the general format of the figures. They basically show the screen as it would appear to a user of the AVID system. Messages and commands appear at the top of the screen. The edit buffer for phrases is at the bottom of the screen. When the edit buffer is shown in a figure, it is separated from the main screen display by a line containing three dots (...). The bold box (▉) is used throughout these examples to indicate the current position of the cursor on the screen.

In the sample session, we are developing a proof of the PL/CV2 assertion

ALL (p, q, r) PROP . ((p => q) & (q => r) => (p => r))

We will describe the development process step by step.

When the AVID system begins execution, the single nonterminal "<object>" is displayed. To begin a proof, the user must enter the command **:proof** to create the proof template (which just consists of the iterated nonterminal "{argument}"). In Figure 1 we show the screen as it would appear after the user had entered the **:proof** command.

:allin▉

{argument}

Figure 1: Just prior to selecting an all introduction template

In this figure, the user has also entered the text of the **:allin** command, used to select an all introduction template, but has not yet typed the return key, which will execute the command. The next figure

```
█<all-assertion> BY ALLIN,
   PROOF;
      <*arbitrary statement>
      {argument}
      <*all conclusion>;
   QED;
```

Figure 2: An empty all introduction template

shows the user display immediately after execution of the :allin command.
The cursor is positioned at the start of the all introduction template. To
enter the all assertion itself, the user types the return key to move the
cursor to the "<all-assertion>" nonterminal and types i (insert) to begin
the insert. This command moves the cursor to the edit buffer area of the
screen, and allows the user to type in the all assertion in the normal
fashion.

```
   <all-assertion> BY ALLIN,
      PROOF;
         <*arbitrary statement>
         {argument}
         <*all conclusion>;
      QED;
```

...

```
all (p,q,r) prop.((p=>q)&(q=>r)=>(p=>z))█
```

Figure 3: Completing entry of an incorrect all assertion

     In Figure 3 we show the screen as it would appear after the user has
typed the all assertion, but before he indicates it should be inserted into
the template. In order to demonstrate AVID's response to errors, there is
an error in the typed input (the variable "z" has not been declared and
should actually be a "q").

```
   Undeclared variable in expression

#█11 (p,q,r) prop.((p=>q)&(q=>r)=>(p=>z)) BY ALLIN,
      PROOF;
         <*arbitrary statement>
         {argument}
         <*all conclusion>;
      QED;
```

Figure 4: Error message resulting from incorrect all assertion

     To enter the all assertion into the template, the user types the
return key (this is one of several possible actions to indicate that the
entry of this phrase has been completed). Figure 4 shows the screen
immediately after this action. An error message has been displayed at the
head of the program, and the line in error has been flagged at the left

margin with "**##**". To correct the error, the user enters the _vi_ command string **f&rr**. The _vi_ command **f** searches in the phrase for the first occurrence of the next character typed (**&**) (also moving the phrase back into the edit buffer). The **r** command replaces the character under the cursor with the next typed character (**r**). Figure 5 shows the screen immediately after this change.

        Undeclared variable in expression

        ##all (p,q,r) prop.((p=>q)&(q=>r)=>(p=>z)) BY ALLIN,
            PROOF;
                <*arbitrary statement>
                {argument}
                <*all conclusion>;
            QED;

        all (p,q,r) prop.((p=>q)&(q=>r)=>(p=>◪))

                    Figure 5: Correcting the error

At this point, the user again types the return key to indicate that the line is complete and that the cursor should be moved to the next legal position. The display resulting from this action is shown in Figure 6.

        ALL (p, q, r) PROP . ((p => q) & (q => r) => (p => r)) BY ALLIN,
            PROOF;
                ◪ARB (p, q, r) PROP
                {argument}
                ((p => q) & (q => r) => (p => r));
            QED;

        Figure 6: All introduction with all assertion correctly entered

        The user now types the return key three times. This moves the cursor to an optional "justification" template. This nonterminal element is only displayed when the cursor is moved to the appropriate loaction, as in Figure 7.

        ALL (p, q, r) PROP . ((p => q) & (q => r) => (p => r)) BY ALLIN,
            PROOF;
                ARB (p, q, r) PROP
                ((p => q) & (q => r) => (p => r))◪<justification>;
            QED;

        Figure 7: Preparing to enter justification for all conclusion

This suppression of optional nonterminals helps reduce the amount of unnecessary information displayed on the screen.

        Returning to the development, to reach the state shown in Figure 7, the user typed the return key three times. This had the effect of moving the cursor through the program, suppressing the "{argument}" nonterminal (since no refinement was entered), and causing the display of the "<justif-ication>" optional nonterminal.

The next figure

```
ALL (p, q, r) PROP . ((p => q) & (q => r) => (p => r)) BY ALLIN,
    PROOF;
        ARB (p, q, r) PROP
        ((p => q) & (q => r) => (p => r))☐ BY IMPIN,
            PROOF;
                ASSUME (p => q) & (q => r);
                {argument}
                (p => r);
            QED;;
    QED;
```

Figure 8: After justifying all conclusion

shows the display immediately after executing an **:impin** command to select an implication introduction template to justify the conclusion of the all introduction. Observe that the hypothesis and conclusion of the implication have been automatically broken out and displayed.

At this point the user might wish to try to verify the proof. In Figure 9 we show the effect of a verify command.

```
:verify
Verification error: Cannot deduce implication conclusion

    ALL (p, q, r) PROP . ((p => q) & (q => r) => (p => r)) BY ALLIN,
        PROOF;
            ARB (p, q, r) PROP;
            ((p => q) & (q => r) => (p => r))  BY IMPIN,
                PROOF;
                    ASSUME (p => q) & (q => r);
    ??          ☐(p => r);
                QED;
        QED;
```

Figure 9: Attempting to verify proof

The system is not able to verify the proof, and the error message and "??" flag serve to identify the problem. In this case, the automatic deduction facilities of PL/CV2 are not sufficiently powerful to allow it to directly deduce "p => r" from "(p => q) & (q => r)". The user must provide a more detailed proof.

```
:verify
Verification complete: no errors

    ALL (p, q, r) PROP . ((p => q) & (q => r) => (p => r)) BY ALLIN,
        PROOF;
            ARB (p, q, r) PROP;
            ((p => q) & (q => r) => (p => r))  BY IMPIN,
                PROOF;
                    ASSUME (p => q) & (q => r);
                    (p => r)▯ BY IMPIN,
                        PROOF;
                            ASSUME p;
                            r;
                        QED;
                QED;
        QED;
QED;
```

Figure 10: Successful verification of completed proof

In our example development, the user now justifies the conclusion of the first implication with a second **:impin** command. After this, the user again enters a **:verify** command. This time, the automatic facilities of PL/CV2 are sufficient. From "p" and "(p => q) & (q => r)", the system can deduce "r". The final state of the screen, with the proof and verification status displayed, is shown in Figure 10.

We hope that this short example has given the reader some understanding of the process of developing and verifying AVID proofs. We have demonstrated only a very few of the many AVID commands and facilities.

To learn more about the implementation and design of AVID, the reader is referred to [2]. For information on actually using the AVID system, the reader should consult the AVID User's Manual [1].

References

1. Dean B. Krafft, AVID User's Manual, in preparation Nov. 1981.

2. Dean B. Krafft, Avid: A system for the Interactive Developement of Verifiably Correct Programs, PhD. Thesis, Dept. of Computer Science, Cornell University, August 1981.

3. Tim Teitelbaum and Thomas Reps, The Cornell Program Synthesizer: A Syntax-Directed Programming Environment, Computer Science Technical Report 80-421, Cornell University, May 1980.

The Type Theory of PL/CV3

1.0. Overview

Since July 1978 when the PL/CV2 verifier became operational, we have done dozens of examples. Those proofs whose intuitive form maps directly into the logical and arithmetical facilities of the logic were fairly easily translated. The formalization of algorithmic number theory carried out by Constable (see Appendix C) is a straightforward translation of the usual textbook proofs, although somewhat longer because of the formal rigour.

When the concepts from an informal proof cannot be directly expressed in the theory, then one concept translates into many special cases which must be repeated every time the concept is needed. In PL/CV2, a glaring example of this occurs when a proof involves extensive modification of an array. It occurs also when we attempt to reason about transformations of programs or propositions.

From our experience with PL/CV2 we felt that the most pressing theoretical issue was expressiveness of the underlying logic. The type theory described in this appendix is an attempt to provide adequate expressiveness within the scope of a useable constructive logic. Our theory is based on [Martin-Löf 75], but differs from it by treating functions and types intensionally and by using a quotient type constructor. It also provides an explicit coding of recursive data types and a concept of induction over the type structure.

A type can be thought of as the intensional version of a set, i. e. it is more than a collection of objects, it is a method of constructing elements of the type. Proofs are among the objects of the theory, as well as the integers, booleans, sets, and other standard types. Types are themselves objects of a higher type, forming an open hierarchy of universes.

The logic of the underlying theory is constructive. As a consequence of the constructivity, all objects claimed to exist can be exhibited; in particular all functions are computable and every statement has computational meaning. It makes sense to execute the proofs of theorems of the form "for all x of type A there is a y of type B". By providing an object "a" of type A, the user can ask the proof to compute an object of type B.

The primitive operations introduced in this appendix can be used as the basis for an applicative programming language. Giving specifications for functions as types, the proof that a constructed function satisfies those specifications is a matter of checking that the type of the function is the specified type.

1.1. Primitive Concepts

To understand the concept of a small type and the type of all small types, one must understand the concept of an inductive definition, the notion of an algorithm, and the notion that the range type of an algorithm can depend on its argument.

First one defines a finite number of primitive types which are familiar from informal mathematical experience. From these examples, one understands a more abstract concept of type and the notion of what it means to specify a new primitive type. To specify a type, one tells how to construct the canonical objects of the type, and one gives a condition (in the form of an equivalence relation) telling when two such constructions are to be considered equal. The canonical objects are specified linguistically in terms of collections of signs, but the signs are understood to name mental objects in such a way that the properties of the object can be determined from the arrangement of the signs. The possibility of adding new primitive types is left open, but a fixed finite number (three, to be exact) are specified in advance.

Second, the concept of an operation which assigns to the elements of a type, say A, objects of another type, say B, is assumed. In particular, it is possible to assign to elements of a previously specified type small types which have already been built. At the intuitive level, these algorithms or operations will be presented by a typed λ-notation, e.g. $\lambda x \underline{in} A.x$ is the identity operation on type A.

Third, one of the important notions used to describe operations in the theory is the intuitive function space operation, $\rightarrow$. The notation $x \underline{in} A \rightarrow B(x)$ denotes the type of all functions which, on input of an element of A, say x, return an element of the type given by evaluating the function B on x. This is the informal idea of what it means for an algorithm to have a range that depends on its argument.

1.2. The Type Hierarchy

With these preliminary concepts understood, we are ready to specify precisely the type of small types. This is done by defining first the primitive types, then individuals of these types, then the basic type constructors, finally a method of building individuals (canonical objects) of each constructed type. Thus the type of small types has an inductive character, and the definition of the type of small types (denoted V) is to be understood as an open-ended inductive definition. It is summarized in figure 1.

In this core theory, the primitive types are chosen to be the types with, respectively, zero, one and two elements. The type with zero elements, is denoted VOID. It is a contradiction to construct any object whose type is VOID. The type with one element is denoted UNIT, and has as its only element uu. The type with two elements is denoted BOOL, and has as its elements True and False.

Product Creation

Product types are built with the ALL operation, which takes as arguments a type T from V, and an operation F which maps elements of T to elements of V. Elements of a product type are operations which map elements x of T to elements of F(x).

Union Creation

Union types are created by the SOME operator, which takes arguments with the same type specifications as the ALL operator. Union types, however, are a generalization of binary disjoint union in that the union can be indexed by any arbitrary type, including one with an infinite number of elements.

Well-ordering Creation

The ORD operator creates a well-ordering type upon application to a type A in V and a function B from A to types in V. An element of a well-ordering can be thought of as a tree formed so that each branch has finite length, but the number of descendants from any node in the tree may be infinite. The nodes of one of these trees have values associated with them, taken from the type A. The fan-out from a node labelled with a value a in A can be put in one to one correspondence with the elements of B(a). More formally, an element of a well-ordering type is represented by an element a of A, and a function, which on application to an element b of B(a) gives the element of the well-ordering type at the end of the edge labelled with b that comes out of the node labelled with a. This function is a generalized predecessor function, as an element of a well-ordering has as many predecessors as there are elements in the type specified by applying B to the label on the root node.

Quotient Creation

A quotient type is created from a type A in V and an operation E of type $A \rightarrow A \rightarrow V$, and is denoted $A // E$. The elements of a quotient type are equivalence classes of elements of A, under the equivalence relation formed by taking the reflexive, symmetric, transitive closure of E treated as a relation.

The process of defining types continues at a higher level by taking the entire collection of small types as an object, called a large type, and by defining various operations which analyze the structure of small types and then closing under the type forming operations. This process can be repeated indefinitely to produce an open hierarchy of universes, V1 (small types), V2 (large types), V3 (very large types), etc. We will use V and V1 synonomously.

Equality Creation

Now that we have the hierarchy to use, we can define generalized equality types. For elements x and y of a type T which is itself of type Vi (note that T may be Vi-1, and x and y may thus be types), the equality operation on type T produces a type that is empty if and only if x is the same object as y. The type expressed by $= (T)(x)(y)$ is an element of Vi.

1.3. Introduction and Elimination

Having described the primitive types and their elements, and how to construct new types from pre-existing types, it remains to show how to build elements of composite types. This will be done separately for each type constructor. For each type formation method, there are operations for building elements of the type, and operations which, given an element of the type, produce different elements, possibly of other types. We refer to these two types of operations as "introduction" and "elimination" operations.

For every type T, we will specify the equality operation $= (T)$, with the intuitive type $= (T)$: $x \underline{in} T \rightarrow (y \underline{in} T \rightarrow V)$. For each method of defining

---

Primitive small types:
```
    VOID      the empty type                            VOID in V
    UNIT      the type with exactly one element         UNIT in V
    BOOL      the Boolean type with exactly two elements  BOOL in V
```

Individuals:
```
    uu in UNIT
    True in BOOL
    False in BOOL
```

Type constructors:
```
    ALL : A in V → (A → V) → V      the product constructor
    SOME : A in V → (A → V) → V     the union constructor
    ORD:  A in V → (A → V) → V      the well-ordering constructor
    // : A in V → (A → A → V) → V   the quotient constructor
```

Figure 1

---

new types, we will give conditions under which elements of that type are equal. (Note that on quotient types, equality is not always decidable.)

Most of the functions introduced here are parameterized with respect to the types they will take as arguments when finally applied. Thus the equality operation described above actually has the type $=: T$ in $V → (T → (T → V))$. Operations will be described without the extra parameters and will be used in examples without explicitly giving these parameters, but their full proper typing will be given in the table that follows.

Primitive Type Introduction

There are no functions which introduce elements of our primitive types. The elements of the primitive types are assumed to exist.

Primitive Type Elimination

We need functions which operate on (eliminate) elements of our primitive types. For any choice of type T, there is a function contra which maps elements of VOID into an element of T. (Since there are no elements of VOID, this corresponds to being able to construct an element of any type from the contradiction that an element of the empty type was supplied.) For any choice of a function T: BOOL → V, there is a function if which given elements t1 and t2 of type T(False) and T(True), repectively, maps an element b of BOOL to t1 if b=False and to t2 if b=True. (Note that UNIT elimination falls under the K combinator discussed below.) This gives us the intuitive types

```
    contra: VOID → T
    if: x in T(False) → (T(True) → (x in BOOL → T(x)))
```

Product Introduction

To construct objects of types built with the "product constructor" ALL , we must have operations which construct functions and manipulate functions. The most primitive set of such functions, borrowed from the (untyped) combinatory calculus, are the S and K functions. Intuitively, we have the relations

$$K(x)(y) = x \qquad \text{or} \qquad K = \lambda x.\lambda y.x$$
$$S(f)(g)(x) = f(x)(g(x)) \qquad S = \lambda f.\lambda g.\lambda x.f(x)(g(x))$$

A strict composition rule for typed combinators would require that the domain of the first operation be exactly that of the range of the second operation. In a system with operations whose range type can depend on the argument to the function, such a strict rule impedes the building of generalized operations. For specific terms of the argument type we would be able to compose the operations, but it would be impossible to build the general composition. Therefore, we allow a more liberal form of composition by modifying the S combinator. It can compose two functions provided that a proof is supplied demonstrating that the composition is type correct on all elements of the intended range.

The type of the S and K operations is, for some choice of types A, B(x) and C(x) and D(x,y):

$$K: \ x \underline{\text{in}} A \rightarrow (B(x) \rightarrow A)$$
$$S: \ (x \underline{\text{in}} A \rightarrow (y \underline{\text{in}} B(x) \rightarrow D(x,y))) \rightarrow g \underline{\text{in}} (x \underline{\text{in}} A \rightarrow C(x))$$
$$\rightarrow (x \underline{\text{in}} A \rightarrow (B(x) = C(x))) \rightarrow x \underline{\text{in}} A \rightarrow D(x,g(x))$$

Many of the properties of untyped combinators carry over to these typed combinators, although the types do introduce more complexity. In untyped combinators, the identity combinator can be defined in terms of S and K by I=SKK. Using these typed combinators, we can construct an identity function for any type T by: replacing A by T and B(x) by ALL (A)($\lambda x \underline{\text{in}} A$.T) in the type of the first K; replacing A by T and B(x) by A in the type of the second K; and replacing A by T, B(x) and C(x) by ALL (A)($\lambda x \underline{\text{in}} A$.T), and D(w,z) by T in the type of S. For untyped combinators, given an expression involving a variable x, we can abstract with respect to x to obtain a combinatory term containing no instances of x, but which when applied to a value v evaluates to the same value as the original expression would if v were substituted for all occurrences of x. Similar transformations are possible with typed combinators, given that we know the type of the variable being abstracted. Thus our intuitive notion of functions denoted by means of λ's can be brought into the theory.

Product elimination

The elimination of elements of ALL types is carried out by the operation of application. Given an element f of the type ALL (A)(B), and an element a in A, then f(a) is an element of the type B(a).

Two operations are equal (under $= (BPI(A)(B))$) if and only if they have identical normal forms. This aspect of function equality will be discussed later.

Union Introduction

The introduction of elements of a type formed by the SOME operation is done by the "pair" function. It maps an element t of a type T and an element s of a type S(t) into the type SOME (T)(S).

Union Elimination

The elimination of such types corresponds to taking a pair'ed element apart into the pieces it was formed from. Two projection functions, "left" (the "first" element) and "right" (the "second" element) exist to perform that action.

    pair: t $\underline{in}$ T $\rightarrow$ (S(t) $\rightarrow$ SOME (T)(S))
    left: SOME (T)(S) $\rightarrow$ T
    right: x $\underline{in}$ SOME (T)(S) $\rightarrow$ S(left(x))

Two elements of a union type are equal if the first elements are equal according to their type, and the second elements are equal according to the type that they belong to. In terms of the operations introduced above, we have, for a and b of type SOME (A)(B),

$$a = b \equiv (\text{left}(a) = \text{left}(b) \ \& \ \text{right}(a) =_{B(\text{left}(a))} \text{right}(b))$$

Well-ordering Introduction

Creating elements of ORD types closely corresponds to definition by induction. Given an element x of a type A, and a function from B(x) to the ORD type in question, the function sup creates an element of the ORD type.

Well-ordering Elimination

One form of elimination from a well-ordering type is similar to using the left and right operations on elements of a union type. That is, given an element sup(a,f), we can operate on it to obtain the a and f objects. lb(x) gives as its value the label associated with a node in the tree; pd gives the predecessor function for that node. The other form of elimination of ORD types corresponds to the definition of recursive functions on the ORD type. The operation rec takes as its argument a function, which on an element x of the ORD type and a function to create elements of the type C(y) for all predecessors y of x produces an element of C(x). rec produces as its result a function, which given an element x of the ORD type produces an element of C(x).

    sup: x $\underline{in}$ A $\rightarrow$ (B(x) $\rightarrow$ ORD(A)(B)) $\rightarrow$ ORD(A)(B)
    lb: x $\underline{in}$ ORD(A)(B) $\rightarrow$ A
    pd: x $\underline{in}$ ORD(A)(B) $\rightarrow$ (B(lb(x)) $\rightarrow$ ORD(A)(B))
    rec: x $\underline{in}$ ORD(A)(B) $\rightarrow$ (v $\underline{in}$ B(lb(x)) $\rightarrow$ C(pd(x)(v))) $\rightarrow$ C(x)
                                        $\rightarrow$ ALL (ORD(A)(B))(C)

Two elements of a ORD type are equal if they have the same label at their root, and the same predecessor function. For the label, "the same" means equal by the equality defined for the type of the label.

    x = y $\equiv$ (lb(x) = lb(y) & pd(x) = pd(y))

Quotient Introduction

Elements of $/\!/$ types are formed by a "one way" operation; it is one of the few in the theory that is not in some sense "reversible". Consider a quotient type A $/\!/$ E. Let the equivalence relation induced by E be F. F(x)(y) is a type which is non-empty if x = y or if there is a chain $x_1, \ldots, x_n$ where $x_1 = x$ and $x_n = y$ and for each x_i, x_{i+1} pair, either E(x_i)(x_{i+1}) or E(x_{i+1})(x_i) is non-empty. For a particular function E and element x of a type A, the value quot(x) is an element of the type A $/\!/$ E such that if F(x)(y) is non-empty, then quot(x) = quot(y).

Quotient Elimination

Elimination of quotient types can only be carried out by functions formed in a special way. We say that a function f respects the equivalence relation when F(x)(y) non-empty implies f(x) = f(y). A function f of type x in A→B(x) can be converted into one that maps from elements of the quotient type into the same range as specified by B, if both B and f respect the equivalence relation.

    quot: A → (A // E)
    qfunc: f in ALL (A)(B) → ALL (A // E)(qfunc(B))
        where f and B both respect F (the equivalence relation induced
        by E), such that (qfunc(f))(quot(a)) = f(a)

Note that in this formulation it appears at first glance that the type requirements for qfunc are circular, or at least recursive. But since any B to which qfunc will be applied the second time will have a type such as ALL (A)(KV), the "recursion" stops there, since the constant function KV can easily be rewritten to be a function of type ALL (A // E)(V), by changing the type of the K combinator used.

Two elements quot(a) and quot(b) of a quotient type are equal if and only if F(a)(b) is a non-empty type. Note that this definition of equality is in general undecidable, as it depends on the type F(a)(b) being empty or non-empty.

    quot(a) = quot(b) $\equiv$ F(a)(b),
        where F is the induced equivalence relation

Equality Introduction

Elements are assumed to exist for all equality types of the form = (T)(x)(x). The elements are written Ax(T,x,x) and can be thought of as primitive proofs or axioms stating that objects are equal to themselves.

Equality Elimination

In order to make an equivalence relation out of equality, we assume operations that modify elements of equality types to give us the properties of symmetry and transitivity.

    sym: = (T)(x)(y) → = (T)(y)(x)
    tran: = (T)(x)(y) → = (T)(y)(z) → = (T)(x)(z)

So to add to our summary of the theory in figure 1, we can list the functions mentioned above with their types, as in figure 2.

1.4. Typings Within the Theory

The type constructor ALL is intended to represent the intuitive arrow, →, so that for B of type A→V, ALL (A)(B) represents x in A→B(x). Sometimes to show the correspondence to the intuitive concept we will write ALL (A)(B) as ALL x in A.B(x)

Using the correspondences noted above and in the previous section, we can convert the above type specifications to expressions called typings which are written in the notation of the V types themselves. For example, I in A→A can be written I in ALL (A)(λx in A.A). This says that

```
=:  T in V → (T → (T → V))
sym:  T in V → x in T → y in T → = (T)(x)(y) → = (T)(y)(x)
tran: T in V → x in T → y in T → z in T → = (T)(x)(y) → = (T)(y)(z) → = (T)(x)(z)

contra: T in V → (VOID → T)
if: T in (BOOL → V) → x in T(False) → (T(True) → (x in BOOL → T(x)))

K: A in V → B in (A → V) → x in A → (y in B(x) → A)
S: A in V → B in (A → V) → C in (A → V) → D in (x in A → B(x) → V) →
        (x in A → (y in B(x) → D(x,y))) → g in (x in A → y in C(x))
        → (x in A → (B(x) = C(x))) → x in A → D(x,g(x))

pair: A in V → B in (A → V) → t in A → (s in B(t) → BBIG(A)(B))
left: A in V → B in (A → V) → BBIG(A)(B) → A
right: A in V → B in (A → V) → x in BBIG(A)(B) → B(left(x))

sup: A in V → B in (A → V) → x in A → (B(x) → ORD(A)(B)) → ORD(A)(B)
lb: A in V → B in (A → V) → x in ORD(A)(B) → A
pd: A in V - B in (A - V) → x in ORD(A)(B) → (B(lb(x)) → ORD(A)(B))
rec: A in V → B in (A → V) → C in (ORD(A)(B) → V)
        x in WW(A)(B) → (v in B(lb(x)) → C(pd(x)(v))) → C(x)
        → ALL (ORD(A)(B))(C)

quot: A in V → E in (A → A → V) → A → (A // E)
qfunc: f in A in V → B in (A → V) → E in (A → A → V) → ALL (A)(B)
        → ALL (A // E)(qfuncB)
     where f and B both respect the equivalence relation induced by E
```

Figure 2

ALL (A)(λx in A.A) represents the intuitive type A→A. Since A in V and λx in A.A is a constant operation A→V, the application of ALL to A and λx in A.A is type correct.

Once we realize the correspondence between ALL and →; K, S and λ-terms, and hence combinators, it is tempting to express the intuitive concepts in the formal system itself. But when doing this, one must be careful about levels. We need the concept of → and λ to define ALL and K. This will be clear from an attempt to define the type ALL (A)(λx in A.A) entirely within the system. We would expect this to be ALL (A)(KA), but the K used here is λy in V.λx in y.y, which has type v in V → (v → V), which if written as a typing, K in ALL (V)(λx in V.(x→V)), would be misleading because this ALL is a more abstract operation mapping from the large type containing V. We would have to distinguish it from the first ALL by writing the first as ALL 1 and the second as ALL 2. Then we could say K in ALL 2(V)(λx in V.(x→V)).

1.5. Large Types

What we have said up to this point effectively describes the collection of small types. But also we can see that the collection itself is a type. We can imagine other objects like it, formed from different base types and closed under different operations. We can grasp the meaning of mappings $V \rightarrow V$ and unions SOME $(V)(\lambda x \underline{in} V.V)$. If there were another large type U, say the type of sets, we could imagine operations between them: $V \rightarrow U$, $U \rightarrow V$.

The particular concept of a large type that we have in mind consists of V as a new primitive, and permits all of the types of V to be "lifted" to large types (but it is not possible to create small types by mapping V2 into V1). It is also closed under large versions of ALL , SOME , ORD, and $/\!/$. For example, ALL 2 has the type $x \underline{in} V2 \rightarrow (x \rightarrow V2) \rightarrow V2$.

1.6. Intensionality

In the theory it is possible to analyse the structure of all objects. The first step in the analysis is to be able to recognize the building blocks out of which they are constructed. In order to build as strong a decidable equality as possible in the face of an open-ended universe, we must ensure that equality on the basic constants of the theory is decidable. We assume that basic constants (the ones mentioned in this paper) are recognizable by the use of the atom operation, and that equality of such atoms is decidable by the eq operation.

atom: $T \underline{in} V \rightarrow x \underline{in} T \rightarrow BOOL$
eq: $T \underline{in} V \rightarrow SOME \ x \underline{in} T.atom(x) \rightarrow SOME \ y \underline{in} T.atom(y) \rightarrow BOOL$

Using these operations, we can construct the operations isVOID, isUNIT and isBOOL which will recognize the basic types from V, and the decidable equality on boolean types comes from eq.

We also have a discriminator

isap: $T \underline{in} V \rightarrow x \underline{in} T \rightarrow BOOL$

which will decide if an object is of the form f(a). Objects of this form arise whenever a primitive function (such as S or K, for instance) is applied to fewer arguments than is necessary to be able to reduce the application to a simpler form. They also arise in cases where the form of an object is given by the application of one function to some arguments, for example with functions formed by rec or qfunc.

isap and atom are related by the fact that isap(T)(t) $\Rightarrow \neg$ atom(T)(t), and atom(T)(t) $\Rightarrow \neg$ isap(T)(t). But the open-ended universe allows the possibility that an object is neither an atom nor formed by application, but is rather imported into the system by some new method of constructing objects.

Given that an object is an application, we want to be able to analyze out the function being applied and the object to which it is being applied. The operation split performs this function, returning an element of a union type which contains all the relevant information.

```
split: T in V → x in T → isap(x) →
          SOME S in V.SOME B in S → V.SOME f in ALL (S)(B).SOME s in S.
          SOME p in S(s) = (V)T.f(s) = (T)x
```

Using these operations, we can build operations which analyze the intensional structure of Vl objects. Each such operation maps Vl into BOOL.

```
isSOME : V → BOOL                    isORD: V → BOOL
is // : V → BOOL                     isALL : V → BOOL
```

We can construct decomposition operations that allow us to analyze an element of a function type that is not a single primitive combinator, and in particular to obtain information about its domain and range.

```
optype: SOME y in ALL (T)(F).isap(y) → V
argtype: SOME y in ALL (T)(F).isap(y) → V
op: x in SOME y in ALL (T)(F).isap(y) → optype(x)
arg: x in SOME y in ALL (T)(F).isap(y) → argtype(x)
```

We can also construct combinators to decompose the types. For ALL , SOME , and ORD combinators, one can obtain the type over which the quantification is being performed, and the function mapping the type to V. For quotient types, one can obtain the base type and the equivalence relation being used.

```
index: SOME y in V.(isALL (y) ∨ isSOME (y) ∨ isORD(y)) → V
family: x in SOME y in V.(isALL (y) ∨ isSOME (y) ∨ isORD(y)) → (index(x) → V)
base: SOME y in V.is // (y) → V
rel: x in SOME y in V.is // (y) → (base(x) → base(x) → V)
```

```
where
index(ALL (A)(F)) = A
family(ALL (A)(F)) = F
base(A // E) = A
rel(A // E) = E
```

The strength of allowing intensionality lies in the ability to completely break down an object and build a new one from its components. This is accomplished in informal reasoning by a form of structural induction on the expression representing the object. To mirror that in the theory, we must have as a primitive a combinator allowing recursion on the form of an object, with appropriate typing to ensure the recursion terminates.

```
RecV: C(VOID) → C(UNIT) → C(BOOL) →
          (x in SOME y in V.isALL (y) → C(index(x)) →
              f in ALL (index(x))(C(family(x))) → C(x)) →
          (x in SOME y in V.isSOME (y) → C(index(x)) →
              f in ALL (index(x))(C(family(x))) → C(x)) →
          (x in SOME y in V.isORD(y) → C(index(x)) →
              f in ALL (index(x))(C(family(x))) → C(x)) →
          (x in SOME y in V.is // (y) → C(base(x)) →
              f in ALL (base(x))(ALL (base(x))(C(rel(x)(y)))) → C(x)) →
          (x in V → C(x)) → (x in V → C(x))
```

The eight operands are functions which return a result under the assumption that the argument is the type VOID, the type UNIT, the type BOOL, formed from a ALL operation, etc. It reduces in the "obvious" manner:

$RecV(f_1, \ldots, f_8)(x) =$
    if x = VOID then f_1
  else if x = UNIT then f_2
  else if x = BOOL then f_3
  else if x = ALL (T)(F) then $f_4(x, RecV(f_1, \ldots, f_8)(index(x)),$
                               $\lambda x \underline{in} T.(RecV(f_1, \ldots, f_8)(family(x))))$
  else if x = SOME (T)(F) then $f_5(x, RecV(f_1, \ldots, f_8)(index(x)),$
                                $\lambda x \underline{in} T.(RecV(f_1, \ldots, f_8)(family(x))))$
  else if x = ORD(T)(F) then $f_6(x, RecV(f_1, \ldots, f_8)(index(x)),$
                               $\lambda x \underline{in} T.(RecV(f_1, \ldots, f_8)(family(x))))$
  else if x = T // E then $f_7(x, RecV(f_1, \ldots, f_8)(base(x)),$
                         $\lambda x \underline{in} T.\lambda y \underline{in} T.RecV(f_1, \ldots, f_8)(E(x)(y)))$
  else $f_8(x)$

In a similar manner, we want to break apart operations into their components. There is a structural recursion combinator on the ALL (T)(F) types similar to RecV that makes this possible.

$Recf: T \underline{in} V \rightarrow x \underline{in} T \rightarrow (T \rightarrow C(op(x)) \rightarrow C(arg(x)) \rightarrow C(x))$
       $\rightarrow (T \rightarrow C(x)) \rightarrow (T \rightarrow C(x)) \rightarrow C(x)$

The combinator acts as

$Recf(T)(f_1, f_2, f_3)(x) =$
    if T = ALL (T)(F)
    then if $isap(x)$
        then $f_1(x, Recf(optype(x))(f_1, f_2, f_3)(op(x)),$
                     $Recf(argtype(x))(f_1, f_2, f_3)(arg(x)))$
        else $f_2(x)$
    else $f_3(x)$

We can summarize these intensionality functions as is done in figure 3.

Using V2 concepts and functions, we can formalize the informal notions used to define V1. For example, ALL 1 has the type

ALL 1 $\underline{in}$ ALL 2(V1)($\lambda x \underline{in} V1.(x \rightarrow V1) \rightarrow V1$).

But this concept requires the informal concept of a dependent operation. By leaving the level structure open-ended, we create the illusion that the entire system can be formalized within itself.

The theory, although complex and powerful, has been reduced to a simple core of combinators and primitive types. The summarized form in figures 1 through 3 presents all the information necessary to describe level 1 of the theory.

1.7. Definitional Equality

In practice, one wants to introduce various definitions. For example, one might want to define the binary disjoint union, say, as

S+T = SOME (BOOL)(if(S)(T))

This form of definition and the notion of equality used in it is a

```
atom:  T in V → x in T → BOOL
eq:  T in V → SOME x in T.atom(x) → SOME y in T.BATOM(y) → BOOL
isap:  T in V → x in T → BOOL
split:  T in V → x in T → isap(x) →
          SOME S in V.SOME B in S → V.SOME f in ALL (S)(B).
             SOME s in S.SOME p in S(s) = (V)T.f(s) = (T)x


isVOID:  V → BOOL            isSOME :  V → BOOL
isUNIT:  V → BOOL            isORD:  V → BOOL
isBOOL:  V → BOOL            is // :  V → BOOL
isALL :  V → BOOL


index:  SOME y in V.(isALL (y) ∨ isSOME (y) ∨ isORD(y)) → V
family:  x in SOME y in V.(isALL (y) ∨ isSOME (y) ∨ isORD(y)) → (index(x) → V)
base:  SOME y in V.is // (y) → V
rel:  x in SOME y in V.is // (y) → (base(x) → base(x) → V)


RecV:  C(VOID) → C(UNIT) → C(BOOL) →
      (x in SOME y in V.isALL (y) → C(index(x)) →
          f in ALL (index(x))(C(family(x))) → C(x)) →
      (x in SOME y in V.isSOME (y) → C(index(x)) →
          f in ALL (index(x))(C(family(x))) → C(x)) →
      (x in SOME y in V.isORD(y) → C(index(x)) →
          f in ALL (index(x))(C(family(x))) → C(x)) →
      (x in SOME y in V.is // (y) → C(base(x)) →
          f in ALL (base(x))(ALL (base(x))(C(rel(x)(y)))) → C(x)) →
      (x in V → C(x)) → (x in V → C(x))


optype:  SOME y in ALL (T)(F).isap(y) → V
argtype:  SOME y in ALL (T)(F).isap(y) → V
op:  x in SOME y in ALL (T)(F).isap(y) → (Bopdom(x) → Boprng(x))
arg:  x in SOME y in ALL (T)(F).isap(y) → T


Recf:  T in V → x in T → (T → C(op(x)) → C(arg(x)) → C(x))
         → (T → C(x)) → (T → C(x)) → C(x)
```

Figure 3

linguistic matter. That is, S+T is not a new canonical form of the theory, it is merely an abbreviation of existing forms. The equality S+T = SOME (BOOL)(if(S)(T)) is not a new mathematical identity over V, it simply relates expressions.

We adopt the approach to definitional equality taken in [Martin-Löf 75]. The form of definitions is

$$\underline{for}\ x_1\ \underline{in}\ A_1,\ldots,x_n\ \underline{in}\ A_n(x_1,\ldots,x_{n-1})$$
$$\underline{define}\ f(x_1)\cdots(x_n) = exp$$

where exp cannot refer to f.

The rules of definitional equality are standard and the relation is decidable in time n·log(n).

1.8. Equality and Normal Forms

The normal form of an expression is obtained by performing all substitutions for definitional equalities, and then performing all the reductions given by the equalities in Figure 4 below. The resulting expression will have no occurrences of applications which could be simplified by substituting arguments for parameters, or by applying the "obvious" simplification rules.

We can now discuss function and type equality in more detail. Two types or functions are equal if their normal forms are the same. With the intensionality functions described in an earlier section, we can almost write a function of level V2 which would decide equality for types (or functions) of level V1. Such a decision procedure does not handle types and functions allowed into the universe by the open-ended nature of the constructive theory. We can agree that a type which is from outside the theory and one constructed with SOME, for example, are different types; but there is no obvious answer in the case of two un-analyzable objects.

1.9. Working at Higher Levels

One simplifying restriction made on functions is that one is not able to build a function which maps from a V2 type to create new V1 types. In

---

if(x)(y)(False) = x
if(x)(y)(True) = y

K(x)(y) = x
S(f)(g)(x) = f(x)(g(x))

pair(left(x))(right(x)) = x
left(pair(x)(y)) = x
right(pair(x)(y)) = y

sup(lb(x))(pd(x)) = x
lb(sup(x)(f)) = x
pd(sup(x)(f)) = f

qfunc(f)(quot(x)) = f(x)

isALL (ALL (A)(B)) = True
isALL (T) = False otherwise
isSOME (SOME (A)(B)) = True
isSOME (T) = False otherwise

isORD(ORD(A)(B)) = True
isORD(T) = False otherwise
is // (A // E) = True
is // (T) = False otherwise

ALL (index(T))(family(T)) = T
index(ALL (A)(B)) = A
family(ALL (A)(B)) = B

ORD(index(T))(family(T)) = T
index(ORD(A)(B)) = A
family(ORD(A)(B)) = B

SOME (index(T))(family(T)) = T
index(SOME (A)(B)) = A
family(SOME (A)(B)) = B

base(T) // rel(T) = T
base(A // E) = A
rel(A // E) = E

Figure 4

---

order to be able to work at higher levels using concepts from lower levels, we include the up combinator. This combinator raises elements of V1 to be elements of V2, and similarly transforms elements of those types to be elements of the newly created type.

This final combinator, given in figure 5, allows us to "renumber" the levels at which we have constructed objects. All that is necessary to describe any level of the hierarchy are the descriptions in figures 1 to 5.

1.10. Theories

In PL/CV3, a specific theory is an element of a dependent product type, and theories can be parameterized. In this core version, we simply take a theory to be a sequence of typings, definitions and definitional equalities. This is a linguistic notion of theory which we do not attempt to identify with a mathematical object. Typings of the form x in T for x a variable are assumptions, other typings must follow from previous typings and equations by one of the rules listed in the previous sections.

2. Examples

2.1. Building the Integers

We have not assumed the existence of the type of non-negative integers in the core theory because they can be built as a well-ordered type. Thinking of elements of an ORD type as trees, the integer 0 will be represented as a tree of one node labelled with False, the successor of n will be represented as a tree with a root labelled by True and a single outward edge to the tree which represents n. So labels for the nodes come from the type BOOL, and there are either no edges out of a node if the label is False, or one edge if the label is True, i.e. the number of outward edges corresponds to the number of elements of VOID and UNIT, respectively. In order to build such an ORD type, we need a function f of type BOOL → V such that f(False) = VOID, and f(True) = UNIT. Such a function is λx in BOOL.if(VOID)(UNIT)(x), or, using combinators, if(VOID)(UNIT). So the type

Int = ORD(BOOL)(if(VOID)(UNIT))

describes the type of non-negative integers.

---

up: $V_1 \rightarrow V_2$
up_T: $T \rightarrow up(T)$ for every type T

Figure 5

2.2. Cantor's Theorem

We can easily prove the corollary to Cantor's theorem that $N \rightarrow N$ is not enumerable. The notation used here is closely related to the syntax of PL/CV2, the way we would use the type theory. This proof assumes that the theory of integers embodied in the PL/CV2 ARITH rule has been translated into the type theory; in an implemented system the above definition of Int and the corresponding ARITH rule would be part of the user's environment.

```
¬ SOME E in Int → (Int → Int). ALL f in Int → Int. SOME n in Int. E(n)=f
BY INTRO, PROOF;
    /* suppose such an E exists and derive a contradiction */
    CHOOSE E in Int → (Int → Int) WHERE
            ALL f in Int → Int. SOME n in Int. E(n)=f;
    DEFINE D(x) = (ARB x in Int; E(x)(x)+1);
    /* D is the diagonal function */
    SOME d in Int . E(d) = D
            BY ALLEL, ALL f in Int → Int . SOME n in Int . (E(n)=f), D;
    CHOOSE d IN Int WHERE E(d) = D;
  L1: D(d) = E(d)(d)+1;   /* by definition of D */
  L2: E(d)(d) = D(d);     /* by definition of E */
    false BY ARITH,L1,L2;
QED;
```

3. References

Aczel, Peter. The Type Theoretic Interpretation of Constructive Set Theory. *Logic Colloquium '77*. A. Macintyre, L. Pacholaki, J. Paris (Eds.). North-Holland Publishing Co., Amsterdam, 1978, pp. 55-66.

Cartwright, R. A Constructive Alternative to Axiomatic Data Type Definitions. Technical Report TR 80-427, Computer Science Department, Cornell University, 1980.

Constable, R.L. Programs and Types. *Proceedings of the 21st Annual Symposium on Foundations of Computer Science*. Syracuse, N. Y., 1980.

Constable, R.L. and Zlatin, D. Report on the Type Theory (V3) of the Programming Logic PL/CV3. Technical Report TR 81-454, Computer Science Department, Cornell University.

de Bruijn, N.G. A Survey of the Project AUTOMATH. *Essays on Combinatory Logic, Lambda Calculus and Formalism*. Academic Press, 1980, 579-606.

Feferman, S. Constructive Theories of Functions and Classes. *Logic Colloquium 78*. North-Holland, Amsterdam, 1979, pp. 159-224.

Gordon, M., Milner, R., and Wadsworth, C.. Edinburgh LCF, A Mechanized Logic of Computation. *Lecture Notes in Computer Science*, Springer-Verlag, 1979.

Hoare, C.A.R. Recursive Data Structures. *International Journal of Computer and Information Sciences* Vol. 4 No. 2. (June, 1975) 105-132.

Johnson, S.D. *A Computer System for Checking Proofs*. Ph.D. thesis, Department of Computer Science, Cornell University, Ithaca, New York, November 1980.

Martin-Löf, P. An Intuitionistic Theory of Types: Predicative Part. <u>Logic Colloquium</u> '<u>73</u>. H.E. Rose, J.C. Shepherdson (Eds.). North-Holland, Amsterdam, 1975, pp. 73-118.

Martin-Löf, P. Constructive Mathematics and Computer Programming. <u>6th International Congress for Logic, Method. and Phil. of Science</u>. Hannover, August, 1979.

Prawitz, D. <u>Natural Deduction</u>. Almqvist and Wiksell, Stokholm, 1965.

Scott, D. Data Types as Lattices. <u>SIAM Journal on Computing</u> Vol. 5 No. 3. (September, 1976)

Stenlund, S. <u>Combinators, Lambda-terms, and Proof-Theory</u>. D. Reidel, Dordrecht, 1972, 183 pp.

REFERENCES

1. Bates, J.L. A Logic for Correct Program Development, Ph.D. thesis, Cornell University, Department of Computer Science, 1979.

2. Bell, J. and M. Machover. A Course in Mathematical Logic, North-Holland, New York, 1977

3. Boyer, R.S. and J.S. Moore. A Computational Logic, Academic Press, New York, 1979, 397 pp.

4. Chan, T.H. An Algorithm for Checking PL/CV Arithmetic Inferences, Cornell University, Department of Computer Science, Technical Report TR79-326,1979.

5. Constable, R.L. On the Theory of Programming Logics, Proceediings of the Ninth Annual ACM Symposium on Theory of Computing, ACM, New York, 1977. 269-285.

6. Constable, R.L. and M.J. O'Donnell. A Programming Logic, Winthrop, Cambrdge, Massachusetts, 1978.

7. Constable, R.L. and S.D. Johnson. A PL/CV Precis, Conf. Record of the ACM Symposium on Principles of Programming Languages, ACM, New York, 1979, 7-20.

8. Constable, R.L. and D. Zlatin. Report on the PL/CV3 Programming Logic, Cornell University, Department of Computer Science Technical Report, June 1980.

9. Conway, R.W. A Primer on Disciplined Programming (using PL/I, PL/CS, PL/CT), Winthrop, Cambridge Massachusetts, 1978.

10. Conway R.W. and R.L. Constable. PL/CS: A Disciplined Subset of PL/C, Cornell University, Department Of Computer Science, TR76-273, 1976.

11. Conway R.W. and D. Gries. An Introduction to Programming, A Structured Approach Using PL/I and PL/C, Third Edition, Winthrop, Camridge, Massachusetts, 1979.

12. Dijkstra, E.W. A Discipline of Programming, Prentice-Hall, Englewood Cliffs, New Jersey, 1976.

13. Goldberg, A. and P. Suppes. Computer-Assisted Instruction in Elementary Logic at the University Level, Stanford University, Psychology and Education Series Technical Report 239.

14. Johnson, S.D. A Computer System for Checking Proofs, Ph.D. Thesis, Cornell University, Department of Computer Science, January, 1981.

15. Kleene, S.C. *Introduction to Metamathematics*, D. Van Nostrand, Princeton, Ney Jersey, 1952.

16. Manna, Z. *Mathematical Theory of Computation*, McGraw Hill, New York, 1974.

17. Moor, J. and J. Nelson. *Computer-Assisted Instruction in Logic*, BERTIE, *Teaching Philosophy* 2:1, Spring 1977, 1-6.

18 Prawitz, D. *Natural Deduction*, Almqvist & Wiskell, Stockholm, Sweden, 1965.

19. Teitelbaum, R. and T. Reps. The Cornell Program Synthesizer: A Syntax-directed Programming Environment, (to appear CACM, 1981).

Index